INTERDISCIPLINARY FRAMEWORKS FOR SCHOOLS

INTERDISCIPLINARY FRAMEWORKS FOR SCHOOLS

BEST PROFESSIONAL PRACTICES FOR SERVING THE NEEDS OF ALL STUDENTS

VIRGINIA WISE BERNINGER

WITH CONTRIBUTIONS BY Sharan Brown, G. Andrew H. Benjamin, Kristen Bishop, Thomas Power, and Deborah Wabe

American Psychological Association • Washington, DC

Published by
American Psychological Association
750 First Street, NE
Washington, DC 20002
www.apa.org

To order
APA Order Department
P.O. Box 92984
Washington, DC 20090-2984
Tel: (800) 374-2721; Direct: (202) 336-5510
Fax: (202) 336-5502; TDD/TTY: (202) 336-6123
Online: www.apa.org/pubs/books
E-mail: order@apa.org

In the U.K., Europe, Africa, and the Middle East, copies may be ordered from
American Psychological Association
3 Henrietta Street
Covent Garden, London
WC2E 8LU England

Typeset in Meridien by Circle Graphics, Inc., Columbia, MD

Printer: Edwards Brothers, Inc., Lillington, NC
Cover Designer: Mercury Publishing, Rockville, MD
The opinions and statements published are the responsibility of the authors, and such opinions and statements do not necessarily represent the policies of the American Psychological Association.

Library of Congress Cataloging-in-Publication Data

Berninger, Virginia Wise.
  Interdisciplinary frameworks for schools : best professional practices for serving the needs of all students / Virginia Wise Berninger.
     pages cm.
  Including bibliographical references and index.
   ISBN 978-1-4338-1808-0—ISBN 1-4338-1808-6 1. Children with disabilities—Education.
2. Children with disabilities—Psychological testing. 3. Interdisciplinary approach in education.
4. Education—Evaluation. 5. Needs assessment. 6. Learning, Psychology of. 7. Learning—Physiological aspects. 8. Brain. I. Title.

  LC4019.B42 2014
  371.9—dc23
                                    2014009105

British Library Cataloguing-in-Publication Data

A CIP record is available from the British Library.

Printed in the United States of America
First Edition

http://dx.doi.org/10.1037/14437-000

Contents

PREFACE   *vii*

I

Basic Principles of Interdisciplinary Teamwork   1

1. Introduction to the Interdisciplinary Frameworks   *3*
2. Using the Interdisciplinary Frameworks in Practice   *17*

II

Developmental Stepping Stones in Assessment and Instruction   49

3. Evidence-Based Use of Tests and Assessments in 21st-Century Education   *51*
4. Linking Instruction and Assessment in Early Childhood   *69*
5. Linking Instruction and Assessment in Middle Childhood   *111*
6. Linking Instruction and Assessment in Adolescence   *137*

III

Interdisciplinary Frameworks for Understanding the Biological Bases of Development and Learning   169

7. A Genetics Primer and Brain Primer for Interdisciplinary Frameworks   *171*
8. Diagnosing Pervasive and Specific Developmental Disabilities and Talent   *197*
9. Diagnosing Specific Learning Disabilities and Twice Exceptionality   *221*
10. Neurogenetic Disorders   *249*
11. Brain-Related Disorders and Other Health Conditions   *271*

IV

Interdisciplinary Frameworks for Understanding Environmental Bases of Development and Learning 287

12. Racial, Cultural, Family, Linguistic, and Socioeconomic Diversity and the Story of Rose *289*

V

Interdisciplinary Frameworks for Understanding Legal, Ethical, and Institutional Issues 309

13. Perspectives of a Neuropsychologist Working in an Interdisciplinary Setting With Students With Learning Disabilities and Their Parents and Teachers *311*

14. Opportunities for Educators to Advocate for Students *319*

15. Child Custody Litigation and School Personnel Fostering Positive School–Family Relationships *341*

APPENDIX A: BECOMING A CRITICAL CONSUMER OF INTERDISCIPLINARY RESEARCH FOR TRANSLATING RESEARCH INTO PRACTICE *359*

APPENDIX B: HONOR ROLE MODEL LIST REPRESENTING EXEMPLARY PRACTICES BY MEMBERS OF DIFFERENT PROFESSIONS ON INTERDISCIPLINARY TEAMS IN SCHOOLS *365*

INDEX *367*

ABOUT THE AUTHOR *383*

Preface

The idea for this book originated in a workshop on treatment-relevant, differential diagnosis of specific learning disabilities. I presented this workshop at the 2010 Annual Convention of the American Psychological Association (APA), and APA subsequently translated the workshop into an online continuing education course. Although course materials were available online, both APA and I received requests for related hard-copy materials that educational professionals could use. Recognizing the potential of such a resource that could be used by interdisciplinary teams in schools and in the community, APA invited me to prepare such a book and to put related materials on a companion website, and I agreed to do so with input and feedback from an interdisciplinary advisory panel. The full list of advisory panel members appears at the end of this preface. Of this panel, three members also contributed chapters, which appear in Part V. These chapters illustrate the following key ideas:

- Diversity among students poses challenges for teachers and parents but can be served well by interdisciplinary teams involving community–school partnerships focusing on the whole student (see Chapter 13).

Preparation of the book was supported, in part, by HD P50HD071764 Interdisciplinary Research Center Grant on Learning Disabilities ("Defining and Treating Specific Learning Disabilities," Principal Investigator, Virginia Berninger) from the Eunice Kennedy Shriver National Institute of Child Health and Human Development (NICHD) at the National Institutes of Health (NIH) to the University of Washington. This grant support does not indicate endorsement by NICHD or NIH for the book.

- Educators are empowered to advocate proactively for the educational needs of all students, whether or not they qualify for pull-out services (see Chapter 14).
- Educators can create more positive school–family relationships and serve the students who struggle with challenging family issues that may affect their ability to learn and behave at school (see Chapter 15).

In addition, other panel members provided contributions that are either featured in a chapter (see Rose's story in Chapter 12) or are posted on the companion website (e.g., the use of technology, studies of the incidence of specific learning disabilities and attention-deficit/hyperactivity disorder, assessment of language skills, and concussions in student athletes).

All royalties from this book will be donated to APA's Division 16 (School Psychology), which will manage and periodically update the website associated with this book. Educational scientist–practitioners are encouraged to submit to APA Division 16 additional readings and resources to post on the website. The division will also manage the nominations submitted for additions to the honor role model list in this book to honor exemplary educational practitioners from varied disciplines who are role models for best professional practices. Nominations are also encouraged for the Rose Awards on the website honoring exemplary practitioners serving students living in poverty. Although the current focus is on K–12, future web postings and revisions may also cover birth to prekindergarten and postsecondary.

I would like to thank all members of the interdisciplinary advisory panel for their important, valuable contributions to this effort, which required a team now and will also in the future, and Linda Malnasi McCarter of APA Books for support in developing the book. In addition, I thank Wendy H. Raskind, MD, PhD, a geneticist, for her helpful suggestions for the genetics primer in Chapter 7.

This book is dedicated to the memory of Thomas Lovitt (1930–2013), who, during his distinguished teaching and research career at the University of Washington as a professor of special education, founded the innovative Coach House, an after-school program for low-income children living in small apartments. After he retired, he volunteered for 9 years at the Coach House and 1 day a week in local classrooms to help the students with their writing, math, and reading. Throughout his career, he modeled how educational professionals can support the learning of all students whether or not they qualify for special education and whether or not they live in low-income families.

Advisory Panel Members[1]

SCHOOL PSYCHOLOGY SCIENTIST–PRACTITIONERS (TRAINERS, RESEARCHERS, CLINICIANS)

Vincent Alfonso, PhD, Gonzaga University, Spokane, WA (cross-battery assessment; Dean of College of Education; teacher and school psychology training)

Dawn Flanagan, PhD, St. John's University, Queens, NY (cross-battery assessment; specific learning disability identification and intervention)

Laurie Ford, PhD, University of British Columbia, Vancouver, Canada (early childhood)

Daniel Miller, PhD, Texas Women's University, Denton (school neuropsychology)

Stephen Peverly, PhD, Columbia University, New York, NY (assessment; instruction; diversity)

Thomas Power, PhD, Children's Hospital of Philadelphia, Philadelphia, PA (school–hospital collaboration; interdisciplinary training)

Linda Reddy, PhD, Rutgers University, New Brunswick, NJ (attention deficit)

David Wodrich, PhD, University of Arizona, Tucson (health issues)

SCHOOL PSYCHOLOGY PRACTITIONERS

Ted Alper, PhD, private practice, Palo Alto, CA (diagnosis; consultation; counseling; former trainer; cogiphobia)

Zenia Lemos Britton, PhD, Windsor Unified School District, Windsor, CA (middle and high school psychologist; bilingual; director special education)

Alnita Dunn, PhD, retired from Los Angeles Unified School District, Los Angeles, CA (university–school partnerships; director school psychology)

Sharon Missiasen, PhD, Bellingham Public Schools, Bellingham, WA (comprehensive services K–12)

Pamala Trivedi, PhD, United States Department of Health and Human Services, Washington, DC (Society for Research in Child Development Fellow, early and middle childhood)

Jim Van Velzer, MEd, Scotts Valley Unified School District, Scotts Valley, CA (three-tier model of behavioral consultation)

---

[1]Panel members are listed in alphabetical order within each disciplinary specialization. See the book's companion website at http://www.apadivisions.org/division-16/publications/interdisciplinary-frameworks-supplement/index.aspx for their biographies.

GENERAL EDUCATION TEACHERS, SCIENTIST–PRACTITIONERS, AND LEADERS

Whitney Griffin, PhD, University of Washington, Seattle (student athletes; concussions; African Americans)

Young-Suk Kim, PhD, Florida State University, Tallahassee (former teacher; literacy research; Koreans)

Yen-Ling Lee, PhD, University of Washington, Seattle (science education and technology; Chinese)

Jasmin Niedo, PhD, University of Washington, Seattle (teacher; administrator; researcher; Pacific Islanders)

Sylvia Valdes Fernandez, MEd, doctoral candidate, University of Washington, Seattle (classroom teacher; math tutor; Latinos)

Jennie Warmouth, PhD, Edmonds School District, Lynnwood, WA (classroom teacher; emotional support; diversity)

SPECIAL EDUCATION AND GIFTED EDUCATION

Linda Brody, PhD, Johns Hopkins University, Baltimore, MD (gifted and twice exceptional)

Brian Bryant, PhD, University of Texas, Austin (learning disabilities; math; assistive technology)

Rob Horner, PhD, University of Oregon, Eugene (single-subject design and evidence-based practice)

Charles MacArthur, PhD, University of Delaware, Newark (teaching writing across the life span)

H. Lee Swanson, PhD, University of California, Riverside (learning disabilities in reading, math, writing)

SPEECH AND LANGUAGE

Jane Coolidge, MS, private practice (child and adolescents; Native Americans)

Nickola Nelson, PhD, Western Michigan University, Kalamazoo (assessment-instruction for specific language impairment [SLI])

Cheryl Scott, PhD, Rush University Medical Center, Chicago, IL (written language disorders in children with SLI)

Elaine Silliman, PhD, University of Southern Florida, Tampa (SLI; reading and writing problems in SLI and other disorders)

Julie Washington, PhD, Georgia State University, Atlanta (language; literacy; dialect variation; code switching)

OCCUPATIONAL AND PHYSICAL THERAPY

Jane Case-Smith, PhD, Ohio State University, Columbus (sensory and motor disorders affecting writing)

Deborah Kartin, PhD, University of Washington, Seattle (educational issues of children with physical disabilities)

CLINICAL NEUROPSYCHOLOGY (SCIENTIST–PRACTITIONERS IN MEDICAL SETTINGS)

Robert Colligan, PhD, Mayo Medical School and Mayo Graduate School of Medicine, Rochester, MN (diagnosis and incidence of disorders)

Deborah Waber, PhD, Harvard University, Boston, MA (learning disabilities; neuropsychology)

MEDICINE

Tina L. Cheng, MD, MPH, Johns Hopkins University, Baltimore, MD (general pediatrics; public health; community outreach)

Barry Solomon, MD, MPH, Johns Hopkins University, Baltimore, MD (general pediatrics; public health; community outreach)

Eric Tridas, MD, Medical Director of the Tridas Center for Child Development, Tampa, FL (developmental pediatrics; community outreach)

FOUNDATIONS IN DEVELOPMENTAL, COGNITIVE, AND EDUCATIONAL PSYCHOLOGY

David Geary, PhD, University of Missouri, Columbia (math)

Richard Mayer, PhD, University of California, Santa Barbara (basic and translation research on instruction across the curriculum)

Margaret G. McKeown, PhD, University of Pittsburgh, Pittsburgh, PA (reading)

LEGAL AND ETHICAL ISSUES FOR SCHOOL-BASED PRACTICE

G. Andrew H. Benjamin, PhD, JD, University of Washington, Seattle (psychology and law)

Sharan Brown, PhD, JD, University of Washington, Seattle (special education law; advocate for children's rights)

BASIC PRINCIPLES OF INTERDISCIPLINARY TEAMWORK

Introduction to the Interdisciplinary Frameworks

1

Maximizing the educational success of children requires an interdisciplinary approach. If a student appears to be struggling in school, professionals with diverse expertise must work together to determine the cause of this struggle and to plan the supports necessary to meet the student's learning needs. Take, for example, a student who frequently fails to follow oral instructions. This failure can have multiple possible causes, for example, hearing or neurological deficits, English as a second language, attention deficits, distraction resulting from hunger or social problems, "acting out" behavioral problems, and so forth. No single professional has the expertise to assess all possible causes and design the appropriate instruction and intervention. A team of diverse professionals is needed to address the needs of diverse students who exhibit many biologically based developmental and individual differences as well as racial, family, cultural, linguistic, and socioeconomic differences. In recognition of this need, the law mandates that for children with disabilities, interdisciplinary teams conduct the assessments

http://dx.doi.org/10.1037/14437-001
Interdisciplinary Frameworks for Schools: Best Professional Practices for Serving the Needs of All Students, by V. W. Berninger

and plan the educational interventions. Only a team with multi-disciplinary expertise has the skill set necessary to optimize the development and learning of all students.

But professionals who are legally mandated to work together often have disparate training and disciplinary expertise. The use of a framework offers a starting point for effective communication and collaboration. This book provides such frameworks. It emphasizes five domains of development: (a) cognitive and memory, (b) understanding and producing language, (c) sensory and motor, (d) social and emotional, and (e) attention and executive functions. These developmental domains are linked to several functional systems—including oral language, aural language, reading, writing, and math—which children's brains construct as the children interact with their physical and social learning environment.

This book provides an evidence-based approach to assessment and instruction that takes into account children's "developmental stepping-stones" in learning specific skills in school curricula. Both common core standards for all students and individualized education plans (IEPs) for students who qualify for special education services specify educational goals, but neither typically provides a road map for achieving these goals. In contrast, the developmental stepping-stones approach that this book takes identifies specific skills to be assessed and taught in early childhood, middle childhood, and adolescence. Although these skills should be assessed and taught for all students, guidelines are provided for tailoring assessment and intervention for individuals. Thus, interdisciplinary educational professionals can apply the framework in this book to the specific needs of a student by

- using multiple assessment tools for a variety of educational purposes (see Chapter 2);
- teaching domain-specific skills from a developmental stepping-stone perspective that takes into account where a child is developmentally and instructionally (see Chapters 3, 4, and 5 for stepping-stones in early childhood, middle childhood, and adolescence, respectively);
- assessing response to instruction on a regular basis and modifying instruction as needed for the individual student (see Chapters 2, 3, 4, and 5); and
- using interdisciplinary assessment to determine why some students enter school already behind age peers or fail to respond to developmentally appropriate instruction (see Chapters 6, 7, 8, 9, 10, and 11), and designing specialized instruction for these students to be implemented in the least restrictive environment (often the general education classroom) with collaboration and support from the interdisciplinary team.

This book is written at a time when there has been an explosion of interdisciplinary research knowledge about normal development and learning, disabilities in development and learning, and evidence-based instructional practices. There is an urgent need to disseminate this knowledge for implementation in educational practice. At the same time, this book is grounded in past contributions of interdisciplinary training, research, and practice. In the 1970s and 1980s, the interdisciplinary clinical training in 48 university-affiliated programs (UAPs) throughout the United States provided preservice and in-service interdisciplinary training. At one such UAP in the late 1970s and early 1980s at Boston Children's Hospital, where I received predoctoral and postdoctoral interdisciplinary training, 23 different professions participated. Now only 12 of the former UAPs remain, and these tend to focus on research, not on cross-disciplinary practitioner training. This volume is designed to stimulate interest once again in preservice preparation for, and in-service participation in, interdisciplinary teams.

The volume can be used by interdisciplinary teams in school settings and community organizations, including medical institutions that work with educational professionals in school settings to serve school-age children and youth. Unlike mental health professionals, who can consult the American Psychiatric Association's recently revised *Diagnostic and Statistical Manual of Mental Disorders* (fifth ed.; *DSM–5*) and the World Health Organization's *International Statistical Classification of Diseases and Related Health Problems* (10th rev.; *ICD–10*), school professionals do not have a dedicated guide that can inform their decisions on the daily assessment and instruction of children in grades K–12. This book aims to fill that gap. The volume is not intended as a substitute for the *DSM–5* or *ICD–10*. Rather, it is a supplementary approach tailored to the timely challenges schools face, and it can be used by educational professionals who work with medical professionals on interdisciplinary teams but nevertheless do their work in schools, not medical settings. Classroom teachers are expected to provide evidence-based, individually tailored instruction for groups of diverse students and monitor responses to that instruction. They are held accountable for all students meeting high-stakes, common core standards. Not only does it take a village to raise a child but it also takes an interdisciplinary team to support classroom teachers in achieving optimal student learning outcomes, and it takes interdisciplinary frameworks to support these teams in doing so.

The remainder of this introduction explains the interdisciplinary team approach used to develop this book, introduces the book's companion websites, presents five key themes to consider while applying the book's frameworks, and briefly reviews educational challenges—both of the past (for historical perspective) and of the present and future. An overview of the book's five major sections appears at the end of the chapter.

Companion Website and Team Approach for This Volume

This book has a companion website at http://www.apadivisions.org/division-16/publications/interdisciplinary-frameworks-supplement/index.aspx which is maintained by the American Psychological Association (APA) Division 16 (School Psychology). The website complements the book by providing a wealth of resources and recommended readings for scientists, practitioners, and scientist–practitioners who work in school settings. One part of the website features a list of research-based readings that support the frameworks provided in this book. Another part features a list of practical resources. The resource list also includes four papers authored by members of the advisory panel.[1]

APA Division 16 has well-established working relationships with many other specializations within psychology, with schools (through collaborations with the National Association of School Psychologists), and with other disciplines (e.g., various medical specializations; special education; speech, hearing, and language; and occupational and physical therapy). Thus, Division 16 is especially well positioned to host a website devoted to interdisciplinary frameworks for developmentally appropriate and individually tailored assessment and instruction for diverse school-age children and youth.

To further model interdisciplinary team work that guides best practices in schools, this book has benefited from considerable input from an advisory panel of representative professionals with diverse, relevant disciplinary expertise. These individuals are listed at the front of the book, and their biographies are posted on the companion website for resources. In addition to providing input on the book, each member of the advisory panel was invited to share entries for the companion website.

Together, the book and website offer easy-to-access guidance and additional resources and readings. The addition of a website allows the sharing of more readings and resources, organized by topic, than is possible in book form only, and postings are expected to grow as APA Division 16 manages postpublication additions. This approach also supports a format that many practitioners prefer: separating content relevant to daily professional practice from academic citations, yet making those citations accessible to interdisciplinary professionals.

---

[1]These papers, and the chapters most relevant to them in this book, are as follows: *Annotated Summary of the Epidemiological Studies of the Incidence of Learning Disabilities* by Robert Colligan and Slavica Katusic (Chapter 8), *Assistive and Instructional Technology* by Brian Bryant (Chapters 3 and 8), *Test of Integrated Language and Literacy Skills (TILLS)* by Nickola Nelson (Chapters 2 and 8), and *Concussions Related to Sports* by Whitney Griffin (Chapter 10).

However, citations within the text and a list of recommended readings are included in each chapter.

Differences in perspectives within and across professional specializations are inevitable. At times, interdisciplinary teams may have to revisit the original meaning of *politics*, a word of Greek origin, derived from *politic*, meaning wisdom. Such wisdom may require learning to listen to each other to costrategize how to help students by applying interdisciplinary research to practice. Thus, this book has attempted to represent multiple perspectives among researchers and practitioners. Despite the professional differences that will inevitably arise, I hope and believe that using the interdisciplinary frameworks presented in this book will result in more effective teamwork for optimizing learning outcomes for more students.

Five Key Themes of the Interdisciplinary Frameworks

Five key ideas should guide readers as they use the interdisciplinary frameworks in this book.

First, each member of the team brings specialized disciplinary and practitioner expertise to the cases at hand and works collaboratively with the other team members who play different but important roles.

Second, the interdisciplinary team at the local level is as crucial as the policymakers at the national or state level, many of whom have never worked in schools or engaged in scientific research. The policymakers translate research based on group findings into national or state policy, but it takes school professionals at the local level, with interdisciplinary expertise, to implement such policy for students who exhibit developmental, individual, cultural, linguistic, racial, and socioeconomic differences.

Third, because diversity is sizable, based on both biological and environmental sources, holding educators accountable for optimizing the educational outcomes of all students requires granting them professional autonomy. This autonomy is necessary so that they can work flexibly with students, parents and other family members, and the community to implement the guidelines discussed throughout this book.

Fourth, multiple players contribute to learning outcomes: (a) classroom teachers, who plan and provide instruction and other learning activities, monitor progress, and evaluate student learning; (b) students, who learn from the teacher, each other, and their own self-generated strategies and cognitions; (c) administrators and other educational professionals and support staff, who work in the local school building and the school district;

(d) parents or others at home with whom many students, in the course of a day, spend more time than they do with professionals at school; and (e) the larger community, where many learning and relevant services may be available from professionals who consult with or partner with parents and local schools.

Fifth, it is easy for educational professionals working in contemporary school settings to become discouraged because of increasing expectations and dwindling resources. To deal with these issues, we emphasize grounding today's challenges in the history of education (Beadie, 2010; Cohen, 1974; Parkerson & Parkerson, 2001; Spring, 2008; Tyack, 2003). Just as educators in the past met daunting challenges, we too can meet the challenges in the present, with hope for the future. To that end, the following section presents a brief history of challenges in U.S. education.

Challenges in Education— Past, Present, and Future

FREE PUBLIC EDUCATION

Educating all children and youth is a relatively new endeavor in the history of human civilization. In the United States, free public education was introduced for the first time in the mid-19th century, when the predominant economy was agriculture. Typically, the one-room schoolhouse (such as the one in Figure 1.1) was in session during seasons when children were not needed to help on the farm.

The curriculum focused on the basic skills known as the three Rs: reading, 'riting, and 'rithmetic. Reading often focused on reading religious writings. Writing focused on handwriting and spelling. Arithmetic focused on computation. Citizens who could read a newspaper and sign their names in cursive were considered literate. Teachers were typically students who had completed 3 to 6 years of such primary grade schooling. Rarely did teachers have formal training in teaching, and teaching was typically not a lifelong career path. When contemporary teachers are having a difficult day, they sometimes are consoled by being reminded education has come a long way since the one-room school for all grades taught by one teacher without preparation.

As the economy transitioned from agriculture to industry in the 20th century and many families moved from farms to the cities, teacher training programs were created, which some, but not all, teachers completed. Also, secondary schools were introduced, but only a small percentage of the population graduated from high school. Rates of high

FIGURE 1.1

One-room schoolhouse early in the 20th century. The teacher (fifth from left in the top row) had completed six grades but had no formal training as a teacher. Shown here with her 45 students.

school graduation increased after World War II, and so did the number of college-level teacher training programs. Still, a large percentage of the population did not graduate from high school.

During the industrial age, teaching remained largely a female profession. Teaching was one of three occupations open to women, who could also become nurses or secretaries. Earlier in the 20th century, often only unmarried women could be teachers, but by the mid-20th century, women often married at time of college graduation and taught for 1 to 5 years after completing college and then left the teaching ranks to raise their own children; they sometimes returned to teaching after their children left home. Principals were typically master teachers who became instructional leaders in the schools. Many current issues in the professionalization of education are often attributed to the earlier feminization of teaching as a profession. Accordingly, conscious or unconscious stereotypes about women and their abilities and roles may contribute to current criticisms of schools and teachers.

With the emergence of the information age economy at the end of the 20th century and the beginning of the 21st, expectations for access to education and educational achievement levels have skyrocketed. However, a large percentage of the population still does not graduate from high school. Despite the rhetoric calling for college access for all, many adolescents and adults need help to complete a high school education, learn marketable skills to support their families economically, and acquire the skills to support their children educationally. But parents vary greatly in how well they can offer this support to their children at the K–12 levels. Thus, educators have the challenging task of not only educating children and youth who attend schools but also of helping their parents, who have various levels of resources, to support their children's education.

On the bright side, more men are entering the educational ranks, and the ratio between men and women in the teaching ranks is becoming more balanced. Despite the current role of many principals as chief operating officer, on the basis of the business model, many schools are rediscovering the need for administration team members to serve as instructional leaders to mentor new teachers, consult with all teachers regarding struggling students, and develop building-level plans for assessment and curriculum in local schools.

FREE AND APPROPRIATE PUBLIC EDUCATION (FAPE)

Children with developmental disabilities did not attend public schools during the first 100 years of public education in the United States. For example, one mother reported to an interdisciplinary team that she was told by the school in the 1940s to put her son with severe disabilities in a residential placement rather than keep him at home and send him to school. She chose instead to educate him at home. At age 40, he was functioning on a 2- to 3-year age level cognitively, but he was a source of joy to his mother and the interdisciplinary team that evaluated him to assess his needs when his mother was no longer able to care for him. A father in the 1960s reported being told to keep his daughter, who had Down syndrome, at home because the school did not know how to educate her. Other children and youth had learning disabilities despite otherwise normal development. They started school but tended to drop out because they struggled to learn to read, write, and/or do arithmetic.

In the 1960s and 1970s, parents of children and youth with severe developmental disabilities and milder specific learning disabilities joined forces to work for the passage of a federal law that ensured a free and appropriate education for students with educationally handicapping conditions. Now students with developmental disabilities are typically educated in public schools rather than sent to residential treatment centers or educated at home. Also, the school dropout rate for those with specific learning disabilities has been reduced and educational services for them increased.

However, three major problems persist. First, the legislation does not use evidence-based, instructionally relevant diagnoses to define and differentiate students' specific learning and developmental disabilities nor identify evidence-based instruction for them. Instead, the law directs states to develop eligibility categories for qualifying for services. Moreover, how the students are identified and qualify for services varies from state to state.

Second, this approach on the basis of eligibility criteria sends a message that any students with developmental or learning disabilities or other educationally handicapping condition should be referred for special education services. Many general education teachers now assume that it is not their responsibility to provide specialized, differentiated instruction for these students, and boundaries have been carved between general and special education.

Third, the federal special education law and the state codes have been written in such a way that many parents think that they have to seek independent evaluations and take legal action against schools if their children are not succeeding at school. As a result, parental advocacy often results in adversarial relationships between parents and schools, and many schools use their limited economic resources for defending against lawsuits, rather than for best professional practices to plan, implement, and evaluate specialized instruction proactively. Educational administrators often do not understand that the law does not prevent educators from proactively using best educational practices, which are typically more cost-effective. Much work remains to create more positive, trusting home–school relationships.

THREE-TIER MODELS

Three-tier models have been developed for early identification and intervention for reading problems (Tier 1), supplementary instruction in general education (Tier 2), and special education pull-out services (Tier 3). Although Tier 1 and Tier 2 interventions have been more effective than having students fail for years before they qualify for help, there is no evidence that Tier 3 pull-out services are more effective than differentiated instruction in the general education classroom for students with persisting learning disabilities, especially when the classroom teacher receives support from supervised paraprofessionals and other professionals on the interdisciplinary team. According to the epidemiological studies at the Mayo Clinic (see Chapter 9, this volume), at least one in five students has a specific learning disability or attention-deficit/hyperactivity disorder. Pull-out services are, therefore, also not cost-effective.

PREPARING STUDENTS FOR THE WORLD OF WORK

One source of the current anxiety over whether students can meet high-stakes common core standards is related to preparing them for future participation in the economy after they graduate from high school. Two alternatives that might be more constructive than a focus solely on high-stakes tests are (a) a curriculum already developed for preparing students for future participation in the world of work and financial responsibility by creating a classroom economy with jobs and paychecks (see Day & Ballard, 2006; resources website; Chapter 2, this volume) and (b) co-op programs in which the business community partners with schools to provide on-the-job supervised experiences for high school students to supplement their classroom studies and facilitate the transition to the world of work (see Chapter 6).

ALTERNATIVES TO TEACHING THE HIGH-STAKES TEST

According to Sahlberg (2011), a former junior high math and science teacher, test scores rose dramatically in Finland when (a) cooperation among teachers replaced competition, (b) trust in teachers and principals replaced judging them solely on basis of test scores, (c) national tests were given only once—at end of high school, and (d) equity of student opportunity was emphasized. Moreover, in Finland, teaching is a highly respected profession. As Dr. Seuss showed in his last book, *Hooray for Diffendoofer Day*, teaching students to think and enjoy learning is more effective than teaching the test.

PRESERVICE PROFESSIONAL DEVELOPMENT FOR JOINT PROFESSIONAL AUTONOMY AND ACCOUNTABILITY

Before the early 20th century, medicine was not a respected profession. Then, in 1910, Flexner wrote a report commissioned by the Carnegie Foundation for the Advancement of Teaching. Flexner recommended that physicians should receive more course work in the basic research foundations in biology and chemistry. Once such course work was introduced, great strides were made in the control of infectious diseases and outcome of surgery. As a result, the status of medicine was greatly enhanced. For the most part, preservice training in the basic science foundations in relevant disciplines, such as developmental science, cognitive science, instructional science, social science, psycholinguistics, and neuroscience and genetics, which could help teachers optimize students' learning and behavioral outcomes, has not been incorporated in preservice teacher education programs. However, see this book's companion website readings related to Chapter 2 for representative textbooks that could be used for this purpose. Such professional preparation in the scientific foundations of learning and teaching is necessary but not sufficient for preparing teachers to be accountable for helping all students achieve reasonable and optimal learning outcomes for their own unique profile. Professional autonomy is also needed for teachers and other members of the interdisciplinary team to work collaboratively to problem solve educational solutions for all students, given the enormous biological and environmental diversity among students.

How This Book Is Organized

This book consists of five major parts. Part I provides the basic principles of interdisciplinary teamwork (Chapter 1) and guidelines for using this book (Chapter 2) so that the achievement of all students can be optimized, including, but not restricted to, those with diagnosable developmental or learning disabilities or other conditions.

Part II provides an overview of multiple assessment tools for assessing current learning outcomes, areas of relative strength and weakness, and response to instruction, as well as an overview of evidence-based developmental steppingstones for each of the content domains of the school curriculum, organized by three well-established stages of development. First, it provides background discussion of the difference between testing and assessment and the appropriate uses of test and assessment data for educational decision making about schools and curriculum versus individual students (Chapter 3). While acknowledging that individual students may follow alternative developmental paths at different rates in their educational journey, the chapters then present the typical skills that should be taught and assessed in early childhood (Chapter 4), middle childhood (Chapter 5), and adolescence (Chapter 6). The importance of frequent monitoring and modifying as necessary both within and across grades is emphasized.

Part III considers how biological factors influence learning. It begins with a basic primer on genetics and a primer on brain systems (Chapter 7). Next, it gives guidelines for using developmental profiles in diagnosing developmental disabilities (Chapter 8) and using learning profiles and associated phenotype profiles (biological markers of genetic bases) to diagnose specific learning disabilities (Chapter 9). It provides an overview of specific neurogenetic disorders (Chapter 10) and describes medical and health issues that can affect learning and may occur in students with or without developmental or learning disabilities or neurogenetic disorders (Chapter 11).

Part IV highlights environmental factors that can affect learning (Chapter 12). Cultural, family, linguistic, and socioeconomic differences should be considered when assessing children's learning needs and planning appropriate instruction and intervention.

Part V provides additional guidance for interdisciplinary teams. Chapter 13 serves as a reminder of the importance of taking the whole child into account and models how professionals situated in community medical settings can consult and collaborate with school teams on behalf of children. Although a theme in this book is to rely on best professional practices for proactively individualizing instruction to prevent learning and behavioral problems rather than to rely only on legal regulations for qualifying students for special education, the book ends by illustrating how participation of the legal profession on interdisciplinary teams can make many important contributions to students' education through public advocacy (Chapter 14) and family work (Chapter 15).

Most educators are not trained as researchers, yet a basic knowledge of research concepts is necessary to evaluate how research might be appropriately implemented in their schools for their students. That is, a basic knowledge of research concepts is necessary to translate science into educational practice. Thus, Appendix A reviews basic concepts and research designs that are commonly accepted as meeting standards for evidence-based practices for federal funding agencies and should inform policy as well as translation of research into practice.

In several chapters, exemplary educational professionals are honored in a feature called the Honor Role Model List. Those honored serve as role models of how the various disciplines on interdisciplinary teams can make important contributions. The full list of names appears in Appendix B, but each person is described and their contributions to education are summarized throughout the book. All advisory panel members qualify for the Honor Role Model List, but selected members, along with others not on the advisory panel, are featured to illustrate key themes in the book and represent the various disciplines on interdisciplinary teams. The stories of those on the full list in Appendix B provide inspiration for others as to what can be done even in challenging times. Educational practitioners who observe other inspiring examples of outstanding professional practice are encouraged to submit their stories to APA Division 16 for consideration for posting on the companion website. Let us spread the word that teachers and educators are the solution, not the problem. The hope is that practitioners on multidisciplinary teams will be key characters in the next chapter in the history of the evolution of education (see Geary, 2008, 2011).

A Final Note About References

In response to practitioners' desire for a user-friendly text with minimal interruptions, and because of space limitations, the research literature is cited only occasionally in the chapter text. Thus, although the frameworks presented in this book are supported by a vast breadth and depth of interdisciplinary research, most of the chapters have minimal in-text citations. Instead, each chapter ends with a sample of supportive research-based readings, as well as practical resources. Much more extensive lists of recommended readings and resources appear in the book's companion website. Moreover, by listing the references on the website, we can update them from time to time. Readers are encouraged to visit the companion website and use the readings and resources there in their own professional work.

Readings and Resources[2]

American Psychiatric Association. (2013). *Diagnostic and statistical manual of mental disorders* (5th ed.). Washington, DC: Author.

Beadie, N. (2010). *Education and the creation of capital in the early American republic.* New York, NY: Cambridge University Press.

Cohen, S. (Ed.). (1974). *Education in the United States: A documentary history.* New York, NY: Random House.

Day, H. R., & Ballard, D. (2006). *The classroom mini-economy: Integrating economics into the elementary and middle school curriculum* (3rd ed.). Indianapolis: Indiana Department of Education.

Dr. Seuss, Prelutsky, J., & Smith, L. (Illustrator). (1998). *Hooray for Diffendoofer Day!* New York, NY: Alfred A. Knopf.

Flexner, A. (1910). *Medical education in the United States and Canada. A report to the Carnegie Foundation for the Advancement of Teaching.* New York, NY: Carnegie Foundation for the Advancement of Thinking.

Geary, D. C. (2007). Educating the evolved mind: Conceptual foundations for an evolutionary educational psychology. In J. S. Carlson & J. R. Levin (Eds.), *Educating the evolved mind* (Vol. 2, pp. 1–99). Greenwich, CT: Information Age.

---

[2]Additional research readings and practitioner resources for this chapter can be found at http://www.apadivisions.org/division-16/publications/interdisciplinary-frameworks-supplement/index.aspx

Geary, D. C. (2008). An evolutionarily informed education science. *Educational Psychologist, 43*, 279–295.

Geary, D. C. (2011). The evolved mind in the modern classroom. *Scientific American Mind, 22*, 44–49.

Goodheart, C. (2014). *A primer for ICD–10–CM users: Psychological and behavioral conditions.* Washington, DC: American Psychological Association.

Parkerson, D., & Parkerson, J. (2001). *Transitions in American education: A social history of teaching.* New York, NY: Routledge.

Sahlberg, P. (2011). *Finnish lessons. What can the world learn from educational change in Finland?* New York, NY: Teachers' College Press.

Spring, J. (2008). *The American school: From the Puritans to No Child Left Behind* (7th ed.). New York, NY: McGraw-Hill.

Tyack, D. (2003). *Seeking common ground: Public schools in a diverse society.* Cambridge, MA: Harvard University Press.

Using the Interdisciplinary Frameworks in Practice 2

T his chapter begins by identifying the various disciplines that may be represented on the interdisciplinary team. It then covers proactive best practices for each profession and for the interdisciplinary team. Guidelines are provided for best professional practices for effective collaboration within schools, between schools and parents, and between schools and community professionals. Examples of educational practitioners from diverse disciplines implementing best professional practices are provided as inspirational role models for members of other interdisciplinary teams. General principles are provided for becoming critical consumers of scientific research (see Appendix A, this volume, for more detail) and translating scientific research into educational practice. The chapter ends with proposals for how interdisciplinary teams might use the book to provide solutions for contemporary educational challenges.

http://dx.doi.org/10.1037/14437-002
Interdisciplinary Frameworks for Schools: Best Professional Practices for Serving the Needs of All Students, by V. W. Berninger

Disciplines Represented on an Interdisciplinary Team in School Settings

Some team members have a clear professional identity with education—teachers, principals, and district administrators—even though their pre-service and in-service professional preparation may be very different. Others specialize in the following:

- psychology—for example, school psychology, clinical psychology, counseling psychology, educational or clinical neuropsychology, educational psychology, and developmental psychology;
- communication sciences—for example, audiology and speech and language pathology;
- occupational and physical therapy for sensory and motor systems in daily functioning in home, school, or work settings (occupational therapy) and in treating developmental or acquired motor disorders in infants, children, and youth through early intervention programs, natural environments, schools, and clinical settings, including hospitals (physical therapy);
- medicine—for example, nurse practitioners (in school or community) and physicians in the community with specialized training in pediatric neurology, developmental pediatrics, or child and adolescent psychiatry; and
- law—specializing in education or other areas relevant to advocating for students and their families.

Note that many members of an interdisciplinary team are located within the same school building or within the same school setting. Other members are located in a nonschool setting but may collaborate with schools on a case-by-case basis for a student of concern.

Best Professional Practices Within and Across Professions

DIFFERENTIATING BEST PROFESSIONAL PRACTICES AND LEGAL ISSUES

Professionals on interdisciplinary teams should take into account four issues: best professional practices of their respective disciplines, the policies of their employers, ethics, and law relevant to schools and school-age children and youth. One of the unfortunate consequences of the federal laws related to free and appropriate public education and accommodations for educationally handicapping conditions and the related state legal code for implementation is that the legal code only, rather than best professional practices, is often used to guide daily operations. Thus, one theme in this book is that each professional discipline should consider how best professional practices in one's own discipline can be used proactively to support the development, learning, and/or behavior of all students. The legal code for special education becomes relevant when schools are not providing free and appropriate public education but does not prohibit professionals from doing so proactively. It follows that each professional working on an interdisciplinary team should participate in ongoing professional development activities for best practices in her or his profession. However, although professionals bring detailed knowledge of best practices from their own disciplinary specialization, they also need common guidelines for working collaboratively to meet the educational needs of students.

GUIDELINES FOR BEST PROFESSIONAL PRACTICES IN INTERDISCIPLINARY TEAMWORK

Guideline 1

Identify which disciplines may be relevant to a student's difficulty. For example, if there are sensory or motor issues, relevant disciplines on the team may be audiology, speech and language, occupational or physical therapy, pediatric neurology, and clinical or school neuropsychology. All those with expertise in these areas receive some training in some aspects of sensory and motor processes. If there are speech or language issues, relevant disciplines may be audiology, speech and language, pediatric neurology, developmental pediatrics, school psychology, and clinical or school neuropsychology, each of which focuses on different aspects of speech and language. If there are social–emotional and/or cognitive issues, relevant disciplines may be school psychology, speech and language, and child and adolescent psychiatry, all of which have expertise in social and/or emotional issues. Medicine should be included anytime there are medical or health issues or disorders that affect the central (brain and spinal cord), peripheral, or autonomic nervous system; that are chronic (persistent) or acute (presenting currently); or that require medication that may affect school learning and behavior.

Guideline 2

All professionals with expertise relevant to the concerns of an individual student should assess that student (e.g., both the speech and language specialist and psychologist for assessing oral and written language skills). The team can then compare results to evaluate the reliability of findings across assessment tools, assessors, and clinical settings. For example, speech and language specialists are increasingly also assessing and treating written language disorders in reading and writing, and school psychologists are assessing and treating oral language (listening and speaking) in addition to written language (reading comprehension and written expression). Teachers bring yet other relevant tools to assessing both oral and written language skills such as oral and silent reading and handwriting, spelling, and composing in daily work in the classroom.

Guideline 3

Include parents as active members of the team. Professionals should listen to the developmental, family, and educational history, as well as current concerns about the student provided by the parent, and consider all of these factors in assessing current educational needs, planning and implementing intervention plans, and evaluating response to intervention. Such team conferencing with parents is desirable whether or not the student is being considered for special education services. Moreover, it can be helpful to include the child, as appropriate, in team meetings.

Guideline 4

Each professional on the interdisciplinary team provides an evaluation or consultation report. One team member serves as the case leader to prepare an integrative summary report, which is then used to provide interdisciplinary feedback to parents and plan differentiated instruction in the least restrictive classroom (general education, unless educational handicapping conditions are so severe that a self-contained program is warranted).

Role Models for Exemplary Interdisciplinary Teamwork

BEST PRACTICES IN MULTIMODAL ASSESSMENT

Cross-disciplinary assessment and problem-solving consultation require a willingness go beyond a bureaucratic approach that prescribes procedures that cannot be adapted flexibly to the individual student at home and engage in creative thinking. Ted Alper, PhD (Honor Role Model 1), is an excellent exemplar of the creative thinking approach. He has been a special educator, school psychology trainer, and psychology practitioner, and has adopted a thinking-and-caring approach tailored to each student or client for assessment and planning, implementing, and evaluating intervention. Using branching diagnosis, Alper only assessed the academic skills relevant to those that the teacher reported were a source of difficulty for the student, and used measures of processes that research has shown may explain reasons for specific kinds of struggles and provide clues to what effective intervention might be. That is, he did not give a standard battery to everyone referred to him. A sign, "I Treat Cogiphobia," was posted on his office when he was a university professor. *Cogiphobia* is a word of Greek origin—the first base word is *cognition* (thinking) and the second base word means "fear of." An unfortunate consequence of the federal and state special education laws has been to relegate, all too often, school psychologists to the bureaucratic role of giving tests, entering scores into state-designed tables by nonpsychologists, and determining whether the scores meet arbitrary criteria for various categories of special education service delivery. These laws have also had the effect of generally discouraging professionals from exerting autonomous professional judgment—that is, thinking based on best practices.

Alper pioneered an alternative best practice that requires one to overcome the fear of exercising professional judgment and to think using a branching diagnosis approach with students of diverse backgrounds. Alper's process involves three steps: (a) assess specific reading, writing, and math skills to determine which ones might be underdeveloped for age or grade; (b) assess the processes shown by research to be related to learning those skills that are underdeveloped; and (c) observe the student and interview the parents and teachers, and take into account these observational and interview data, along with test results, in multimodal diagnosis and treatment planning.

SCHOOL PSYCHOLOGISTS REACHING OUT TO CLASSROOM TEACHERS

As coordinator of psychological services in the second largest school district in the country, Los Angeles Unified School District (LAUSD), Alnita Dunn, PhD (Honor Role Model 2), provided the leadership for developing, implementing, and evaluating an innovative, evidence-based model for bridging the gap between general education and special education in the lowest achieving schools in LAUSD. This new model was developed because school psychologists serving the neediest students were increasingly frustrated with performing comprehensive assessment to document what was already obvious to all professionals: The referred child was failing to learn to read. They reasoned that best professional practices would be to partner with the teachers and support their efforts to transform the failing students into succeeding students. Dunn also turned to researchers to design and evaluate an innovative, evidence-based pilot intervention in six of the schools serving the lowest achieving students in the large, diverse urban school system. However, the intervention was carried out solely by LAUSD school psychologists working with classroom teachers. Tier 1 interventions, already in place, provided a core curriculum emphasizing phonological awareness, phonics, and oral reading and repeated oral reading. School psychologists administered a screening battery to identify those children whose real word reading (without context clues) and pseudoword reading fell in the lowest quartile. These children were randomly assigned within the same school to either a contact control (more time with the Tier 1 intervention) or one of two Tier 2 supplementary treatments (sequential reading followed by writing or integrated reading–writing in same lesson) using lessons organized by levels of language (subword, word, and text).

Measures of processes related to real word and pseudoword reading were given at pretest and posttest, and probes for reading and spelling taught and transfer words were collected throughout the lessons. Results were analyzed for (a) response to intervention (RTI) for individual students in each group, (b) group comparisons of the most average scores of treatment and contact control groups, and (c) group comparisons that used the school rather than the individual as the unit of analysis. Regardless of method used, results showed that adding the supplementary Tier 2 integrated reading–writing treatment was more effective than the Tier 1 reading treatment only. Tier 1 treatment appeared necessary but not sufficient for these lowest achieving students. Consistent with other research, children who received the integrated writing–reading lessons showed the most improvement in decoding. Improvement on measures of processes related to reading and writing was also observed.

Following the initial pilot, Dunn led the interdisciplinary team of school psychologists and classroom teachers in extending the program to more schools. This involved training more cross-disciplinary staff and soliciting input from them and district administrators. The story of this collaboration, completed when Dunn had become director of psychological services for LAUSD, is testimony to the effectiveness of an interdisciplinary team in bridging general and special education with evidence-based practices for the most at-risk students.

SCHOOL PSYCHOLOGISTS REACHING OUT TO TEACHERS THROUGH PROBLEM-SOLVING CONSULTATION

Another school psychologist set aside time each morning during teacher planning time, before students arrived, for problem-solving consultation. Teachers could stop by without an appointment to discuss concerns about any student's learning or behavior. In addition, the school psychologist, a former teacher, volunteered to visit the classroom and teach the students in a small group or large group to get deeper insight into what the problems might be. She also chaired the weekly prereferral team meetings at which any teacher could discuss concerns with the interdisciplinary team and principal to deal with modifications to a student's general education program.

REACHING OUT TO PARENTS

One way to reach out to parents is through questionnaires sent to parents of all kindergarten and first-grade students to find out which students may currently have, or had during the preschool years, developmental, medical, family, or educational concerns. The team then makes contact with the parents to make sure these earlier concerns are taken into account in planning current educational programs. Another approach is to create a parent room in a local elementary school where parents can visit, with or without their infants, toddlers, and preschoolers, to (a) share with other parents issues related to parenting their children, including home literacy and numeracy activities, and (b) obtain parenting tips from school professionals for preparing their children for transition to schooling or for parenting older school-age children. Another approach is to sponsor parent support groups for parents of students who have developmental disabilities or who had received preschool special education services and are in transition to kindergarten or first grade or who are in transition from schooling at ages 18 to 21.

Yet another approach targets special populations in the community for services unique to their needs—for example, children living in military families who may experience sadness due to one or both parents being away from home for extended periods of time, death of a parent or extended family member in a war zone, or a parent returning home with war-related injuries. Or schools create home–school partnerships for parents who homeschool their children, or homework clubs to help students with their homework after school and help parents support homework in the home. Finally, parent–teacher conferences during the school year may be used to foster parent–school partnerships and improve home–school communication and collaboration through classroom portfolios that identify their child's strengths as well as weaknesses to work on (see Chapter 3).

THREE-TIER MODEL OF BEHAVIORAL INTERVENTIONS INVOLVING CHILD, FAMILY, AND TEACHER

For 37 years, Jim Van Velzer, MEd (Honor Role Model 3), has applied his unique interdisciplinary background to his work as a school psychologist specializing in a three-tier model for behavioral interventions. His experience includes education in psychology and biology at the undergraduate level and applied behavioral science and educational leadership (principal, director special education, and superintendent credentials) at the graduate level. The model, which he has implemented in different schools in the same school system and school systems in five states, has been shown over and over not only to improve current behavior but also to substantially reduce the number of referrals, special education assessments, and number of special education placements for behavioral problems. According to Van Velzer, this approach to preventing and treating behavior problems does require some extra hours of work but is professionally rewarding because it results in students' improved behavior in following school rules, interacting appropriately socially, and completing academic assignments at school and home.

This approach, which begins at school entry in kindergarten and first grade, involves communicating closely with students, teachers, counselors, and administrators in the school, and with parents and extended family members (grandparents, aunts, uncles, and cousins), family physicians, mental health counselors, other professionals, and pastors or other religious leaders outside of school. *Behavior problems* are defined to include one or more of the following difficulties:

- following school rules and routines and complying with teacher requests;
- interacting appropriately socially with others—not pushing, hitting, fighting verbally or physically, name calling, or bullying; and
- engaging in and completing assignments at school and home.

At Tier 1, Van Velzer frequently observes in kindergarten and first-grade classrooms and encourages teachers to discuss with him any children whose behavior is of concern because it interferes with the child's learning or that of others in the class. He explains to the teacher the difference between externalizing behaviors in which the "acting out" is visible to all and internalizing behaviors, such as sadness, which may be invisible to others unless adults note when students are unusually withdrawn or may be sad because they are dealing with losses or other adverse life events. When a teacher identifies a child whose behavior is of concern, his first step is not to administer a comprehensive assessment to determine whether the child qualifies for special education under the category of behavioral disabilities. Rather, his first step is to work with the student to teach the student appropriate behaviors and to work with the teacher on strategies for teaching and reinforcing the student appropriate behavior.

Van Velzer has noted over the years that many children come from homes in which parents have not taught them appropriate behaviors for school (and often for home) for a variety of reasons, including lack of time because of work or personal problems, or significant stressors in the home due to a variety of family problems preoccupy the child. In many cases, parents did not complete much formal education and do not know how to prepare their child to behave at school. Therefore, the Tier 1 approach often involves listening to the student, the teacher, and the parent and relevant others to identify behavioral goals to work on, rewards for meeting goals, and a plan for frequently monitoring whether goals are being met and sustained and modifying the plan if goals are not. Over the years, he has learned that when most of the time and attention is focused on Tier 1 in kindergarten and first grade, and sometimes into second grade, few students qualify for or need special education services for behavior problems.

Tier 2 is necessary if Tier 1 was not implemented in kindergarten or first grade, or if problems emerge for the first time in later grades. For example, some students move to a school after kindergarten and first grade and exhibit behavioral problems. Van Velzer's first step then is to carefully review the students' school records, followed by classroom observations and interviews with the student, teacher, and parent. He has been struck over the years by the fact that the behavioral problems of these newcomers were invariably first evident in the kindergarten and first grade but were not addressed when initially observed and thus have persisted. Some behavior problems may be the result of developmental or learning disabilities that interfere with academic success, but in many cases children do not have learning problems, but for a variety of reasons are not engaged in learning. Often relationships with parents or other family members interfere with learning and behavior at school and have to be addressed. Alternatively, other social, emotional, motivational, and self-efficacy issues may be related to the behavioral problems at school. For example, a child or adolescent may not think it is worth investing in learning because the cost–benefit ratio is too low. Listening, observing, and identifying problems are crucial to setting goals and identifying potential rewards if goals are met. Interestingly, many of these students referred for behavioral problems have passed the high-stakes tests, but are not behaving acceptably at school. Passing a test does not guarantee success at school or in life.

The key at Tier 1 or Tier 2 is to write a four-step behavioral plan for bringing about change. The first step is to identify clear goals to work on that are appropriate and achievable. If the goal behavior is not currently within the child's repertoire, the behavior may have to be taught. The second step is to identify a reward that the child will receive when a goal is met. Parents, who should provide the rewards, should not be asked to provide rewards they cannot afford to provide or object to providing. Both Steps 1 and 2 will require brainstorming with the student, teacher, parent, and psychologist. Some students may also need individual or group counseling to provide emotional supports in addition to the behavioral rewards. The third step is to implement the plan and develop a communication system between school and home—for example, a slip the teacher sends home daily to the parent, who gives the award when the goal is met and signs the slip to be returned to the teacher. The fourth step is to monitor frequently whether goals are being met by operationally defining how behavior will change if the goal is met and the behavioral frequency required to meet the goal (e.g., 95% of the time).

If the goal or goals are not met, then goals and/or rewards need to be readjusted. For example, sometimes the number of goals has to be reduced. Other times the nature of the goal may need to be modified. If goals are being met, then the rewards need to be withdrawn in degrees— for example, from every day to every other day or from weekly to every other week. However, it is important to continue monitoring behavior even after the goals are reached and rewards are no longer provided. If appropriate behavior is not maintained, the former plan may need to be reinstituted or a new one crafted.

Tier 3 is needed for some behaviors that do not respond to the Tier 1 approach at transition to schooling or the Tier 2 approach in later elementary and secondary grades or for behaviors that require a different approach. For example, drug and alcohol problems require referral to professionals who specialize in substance abuse treatment. If students are hearing voices or seeing visions or killing animals or setting fires, they should be referred to child and adolescent psychiatrists. If they are losing consciousness, they should be referred to a pediatric neurologist. For example, Van Velzer recently saw a child who had previously been diagnosed as having attention-deficit/hyperactivity disorder and characteristics of autism, but when the child showed signs of momentary loss of consciousness, he referred the boy to a neurologist who diagnosed absence seizure disorder (see Chapters 10 & 11).

Van Velzer emphasizes that this approach to the practice of school psychology requires more professional judgment than comprehensive assessment and legally mandated criteria for deciding that a child does or does not qualify for special education services for behavioral disability. This approach also requires that Van Velzer spend extra time beyond the union-negotiated workday, but the professional rewards of seeing behaviors improve more than make up for working harder and longer.

FAMILY APPROACH TO TIER 1
EARLY INTERVENTION

The following example illustrates a multimodal, family-oriented Tier 1 intervention. A school psychology intern reported to her internship supervisor that a first-grade teacher wanted a boy who could not read sent back to kindergarten. The school psychologist remembered learning that grade retention is not effective in increasing achievement and may result in mental health problems later in development. She also recalled that the National Association of School Psychologists's review of research on grade retention supported an alternative, two-step approach beginning with assessment to find out why the student is struggling and then intervention designed to address that.

First-step screening measures showed that the boy was having trouble analyzing sounds in spoken words, segmenting written words into single letters or letter groups, and integrating sounds and letters to decode written words. Second-step reading instruction addressing each of these skills was instituted in the first-grade classroom by a paraprofessional supervised by the classroom teacher. The intern frequently used brief measures of single word reading to monitor the boy's response to this instruction. The intern also invited the boy to share with her why he had trouble behaving at school. She learned that he was sad because he never got to see his father, who had left his mother. The school psychologist and intern invited the mother to meet with them to develop a plan to help her son. Because the mother did not have a car, the supervising psychologist and intern went to the boy's home and learned that the mother was going through a bitter divorce and was struggling with a prescription drug addiction. The school team convinced the mother that her son might benefit from visiting with his father, even if the mother did not want to see the father. They also informed the mother of several community agencies that provide low-cost counseling and addiction treatment, but made it clear it was her right to decide whether she wanted to use any of these services.

By the end of the school year, the boy was reading above grade level, and his behavior improved markedly once he learned to read and was visiting with his father again on a regular basis. His mother was in recovery after successful treatment for addiction. The first-grade teacher could see the value of early intervention, supplemental instruction, and progress monitoring as an alternative to grade retention. The time invested by the school psychology supervisor and intern was no more than if they had spent a day administering a full battery of tests, another day writing a report, and the equivalent of another day participating in a team meeting and preparing a written individualized education plan.

TIER 2 SCHOOL–PARENT–COMMUNITY PARTNERSHIPS

Another interdisciplinary team member built school–community partnerships by creating a list of mental health resources in the community with a range of funding possibilities: free (funded by a charity for those who meet low-income criteria), sliding scale (fees according to ability to pay), or prepaid health insurance plans. As he worked with students, he also held parent conferences and listened to learn about possible family issues or stressors that might affect school learning or behavior. When he thought they were relevant, he would share with the parent the "Yellow Pages of community mental health services" he had created. However, he made it clear that his job was to work with the child at school on educational issues, and it was the parent's choice whether to pursue support services in the community for issues outside of school that might be affecting learning and behavior at school. His goal was simply to make the parents aware of such issues and of existing community resources for dealing with them. Many parents used the resources and expressed gratitude for the information. Sometimes community providers also then participated in multidisciplinary team meetings at school.

LARGE-SCALE TIER 3 INTERVENTIONS

A state legislative act in California for implementing federal legal mandates requires that local school districts work toward successful reentry and transition to school for any student who is returning to school after being suspended or expelled from school, whether or not the student qualified for special education because of an educationally handicapping condition and whether or not the student was sent to a juvenile camp or prison for an infraction of the law. This legal mandate is based on increasing recognition that (a) the United States is spending more money on prisons than public education and (b) it is in the students' and society's best interests to help these returning students become successful in the educational system and acquire marketable skills. As Johnny Cash expressed in the song "San Quentin," prison is not the solution in the long run. Rather, successful reentry-to-school programs are more cost-effective. At the same time, there is increasing recognition that African American male students are at greater risk of not completing school and for being incarcerated.

Some schools have responded by developing successful transition programs and alternative school placements. For example, LAUSD has introduced policy requiring comprehensive assessment of students with severe behavioral and emotional problems, alternative school placements, and programs for supporting transitions back to school if students are expelled or incarcerated. In the 2011–2012 school year, the LAUSD established the innovative Successful Transition Program (STP), also known as Successful Transition and Re-Integration Into a Viable Education (STRIVE). Both STP/STRIVE psychologists and STP/STRIVE teachers participate in this program that supports continuation of education for students who have been incarcerated.

The following job responsibilities of psychologists and teachers illustrate what can be done to ensure that more students become successful in school and life and fewer are doomed to a life in prison or inability to earn a living. Job responsibilities of the STP/STRIVE psychologists include (a) designing, coordinating, and implementing programs in STRIVE centers; (b) supporting students with disabilities transitioning from juvenile justice facilities; (c) participating in multidisciplinary teams and collaborating with school sites and the central office in providing support services and increasing attendance; (d) developing a viable positive behavioral management system for returning students; (e) providing or facilitating the provision of social skills training and counseling services; (f) conducting psychoeducational assessments; (g) connecting the student and family with community organizations and social services; and (h) gathering data to monitor student progress and meet state and federal mandates. Job responsibilities of STP/STRIVE teachers, who are supervised by an STP/STRIVE psychologist, include (a) designing, coordinating, and implementing the program in the STRIVE center; (b) teaching an intensive instructional program designed for the transitioning student; (c) using technology to engage the student and support learning; (d) designing a strong positive behavior management system; (e) participating in multidisciplinary teams working with the transitioning student; (f) collaborating with the local school site and central office to increase attendance and school performance of each student; and (g) evaluating on a regular basis the effectiveness of the differentiated instruction and behavioral supports.

WITH OTHER INTERDISCIPLINARY PROFESSIONALS IN THE COMMUNITY

Since 2012, the Johns Hopkins Medical School's Harriet Lane Clinic has offered a model program that delivers comprehensive medical and other services to a low-income, predominantly African American inner city neighborhood in East Baltimore in which the medical school is located. The pioneers in this *translational science*—translating basic science to the bedside and clinical practice to make a difference in the real world—are Tina L. Cheng, MD, MPH (Honor Role Model 4), and Barry Solomon, MD, MPH (Honor Role Model 5). They are developmental pediatricians who are active in the Academic Pediatric Association (see http://www.ambpeds.org) and who have translated their vision for community-based services into reality to meet all the needs of underprivileged students through comprehensive medical and interdisciplinary services in an urban community.

As shown in Figure 2.1, this medical center that reaches out to the community and schools provides a circle of preventive care, acute care, chronic care, developmental assessment and intervention services, and education. Parents of children birth to 21, more than 90% of whom are on medical assistance because of low income, can access in one neighborhood clinic (a) medical, dental, family-centered mental health, social work, nutrition, and other health services; (b) parent support services from infancy to adolescence; (c) developmental assessments and early intervention; (d) educational services for tutoring, support, and outreach across schooling from early childhood to adolescence; (e) legal advocacy services; (f) a safety center for preventing injury; and (g) a fitness program to treat a variety of nutritional issues, including obesity and lactation support, as well as a special program for patients affected by HIV.

JHU Harriet Lane Clinic:
A Community Clinic Model

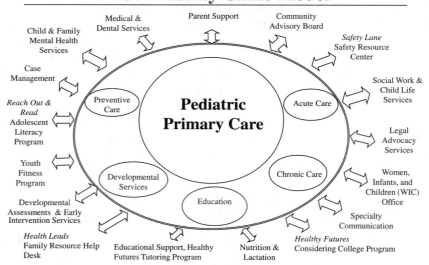

Comprehensive, cross-disciplinary service model for school age children and youth. Copyright by Harriet Lane Clinic, Johns Hopkins Children's Center. All rights reserved. Reprinted with permission.

The clinic specializes in adolescent medicine, adolescent education, and adolescent addictions and pregnancy and provides on-line programs created by the Harriet Lane Clinic for serving adolescents, which are now available for other programs to use. Multiple disciplines work collaboratively to provide these comprehensive primary care services in a center that also serves as a training facility for preservice and in-service professionals. Pediatricians and pediatric residents provide basic medical services. Psychologists and social workers provide mental health and social services. Family support service workers screen mothers for postpartum substance abuse. Educational services range from tutoring services by undergraduate volunteers at the Johns Hopkins main campus, who also give tests to monitor progress and work with parents, to educational outreach to a high school for teenage mothers, to career counseling for patients 14 years and older. Volunteer lawyers from Project Heal (Health, Education, and Advocacy Law), a medical–legal partnership in Maryland (Baltimore) and Massachusetts (Boston), provide legal advocacy—for example, for landlords who refuse to make housing accommodations for children with special needs.

A community Health Leads desk (http://healthleadsusa.org), which is staffed by undergraduate volunteers, connects patients to basic resources (e.g., food, utility assistance, job training, benefits, education) to improve their health and well-being (for more information, contact Chuck Gordon at cgordon@healthleadsusa.org). Safety Lanes shares safety tips and tools for keeping children and parents safe in and outside the home. The Harriet Lane Clinic Needs Survey completed by parents identifies their and their children's needs for assistance: (a) finding GED programs, (b) finding job resources or training, (c) finding child care or day care programs, (d) paying utility bills, (e) finding health care insurance or health care, (f) finding food resources, (g) finding emergency housing or shelters, and (h) finding bicycle helmets for the child.

Thus, this one-stop community center, funded by grants and philanthropy, provides comprehensive, interdisciplinary services and offers a model that is developmental—for tots to teens—and cross-generational—from children to parents to extended family in parents' and grandparents' generation—and designed for children whose parents have low levels of income and education. Cheng's research, clinical skills, and teaching contribute to translational science: (a) teen pregnancy and parenting guidance, (b) community-based violence prevention, (c) interventions for adolescents seen in emergency departments, and (d) child health disparity amelioration. Solomon's team provides comprehensive services, taking into account the whole child and the child's family and the nonmedical issues that may affect and be affected by health for (a) health issues prevalent in low income communities, such as lead poisoning, obesity, diabetes, asthma, sickle cell anemia, developmental disabilities, behavior and mental health problems, child abuse, and youth violence; (b) general health care checkups, immunizations, acute illness care, gynecological services including family planning, intensive treatment for those affected by HIV infection and other sexually transmitted infections, substance abuse counseling, and treatment and prevention of personal injuries; and (c) an on-site integrated mental health program for children, adolescents, and adult caregivers in pediatric primary care.

Role Models for Systems-Level Change to Support Best Professional Practices

At times, systems-level change is needed to support best professional practices of interdisciplinary teams. Currently, the belief is widespread that one reason the United States is losing competitive ground in the world economy is that schools are responsible and teachers must be held accountable. As folk singer Pete Seeger conveyed in the song "Trouble at the Bottom?", trouble can come from multiple levels in a system—not only curriculum and teaching at the bottom, but also high-level administration or school board at the top. A theme of this book is that not only the problems but also the educational solutions can come from both the bottom and the top, especially if both levels coordinate their efforts. To support this position, two examples of the administrators working with teachers and other professionals across levels in the system are showcased to inspire other interdisciplinary teams about what could be.

MIDDLE SCHOOL PRINCIPAL MONITORING PROGRESS OF EVERY STUDENT

Devin McLane (Honor Role Model 6), principal of Olympic View Middle School in Mukilteo, WA, is an instructional leader who cares deeply whether each student in the middle school is continuing to make reasonable progress in literacy, and he works closely with his teachers to accomplish this goal. In his office is a large chart on which he keeps the RTI data for each middle school student in this school, which serves a diverse student body. He regularly monitors these data and consults with his literacy team about the instructional programs. When he deems it appropriate, he makes modifications in the programs and then monitors students for improvement. He has also designed and implemented an innovative after-school homework club to help students with homework whose parents cannot—for example, because they are working and not at home or because they speak limited English.

McLane's system-level leadership is paying off for the state's annual assessments of student progress. This school is among the few public middle schools in Washington to receive a distinguished Great Schools Rating of 8 out of 10. Olympic View Middle School has 37% of students eligible for free or reduced-price meals under the National School Lunch Program. Under McLane's leadership and the progress monitoring by the whole instructional team, Olympic View sixth, seventh, and eighth graders have exceeded the district or state performance on the Washington State Yearly Student Progress for Reading.

DISTRICT SUPERINTENDENT REACHING OUT TO THE WHOLE INSTRUCTIONAL SUPPORT TEAM AT THE BUILDING LEVEL

Drawing on his broad, interdisciplinary experience in secondary education, teaching and coaching, district-level administration, planning and social policy, Greg Baker, EdD (Honor Role Model 7), superintendent of Bellingham Public Schools, has implemented a system-wide leadership role, with a focus on teacher assistance teams. Every morning, Baker visits local schools and staff in his district. On a typical morning he "walks about" two local buildings and interacts with every teacher, the principal, and staff, including janitor and secretaries. As superintendent he encourages each school to put into place teacher assistance teams that serve as prereferral alternatives to the refer–test–place model that has created the barriers between general and special education. Baker models his philosophy that the strength of a school and district lies in the interdisciplinary team meeting all the educational needs of students. He is remarkable in that although he is responsible for the administration of all the schools in his district under applicable state and federal laws and policies of the school board, leadership for the whole school district—staff, facilities, budgets, public relationships with parents and the community, and opportunities and outcomes for student learning—he finds time to be a leader throughout the system from top to bottom. With this kind of top-down support from the superintendent, it is no wonder the Washington State Teacher of the Year in 2013 was from Bellingham.

The Bellingham multilevel-system model also works because of participation not only at the top and bottom but also at the middle level by interdisciplinary professionals on the teacher assistant teams. For example, Sharon Missiasen, PhD (Honor Role Model 8), serves in two schools on the teacher assistance teams introduced by Baker. In this teamwork, Missiasen draws on her rich, interdisciplinary background and expertise that includes not only school psychology but also classroom teaching, university teaching, experience as director of special education, psychotherapy and family counseling, and clinical psychology, and participation on teams with psychiatrists, social workers, nurses, teachers, and occupational therapists, and even consultants from the United Nations to advise on assessing immigrants with bilingual backgrounds.

Bellingham School District draws about two thirds of its student population from affluent families in which parents are in business and professions such as medicine and college teaching and one third from low-income families in which a language other than English is spoken at home. The school psychologist is not viewed as having just one responsibility, evaluating whether students qualify for special education services. Rather, under the leadership of the new superintendent, who wants to narrow the gap between research and practice, the goal is more targeted, focused interventions. It is not unusual for professionals to work 12 hours a day, both at school and after school, to achieve these goals, but the school psychologist finds the interdisciplinary teamwork professionally rewarding. She gives, as an example of the value of the team approach, the recent suicide prevention training provided for all staff following a suicide in the district. Subsequently, a janitor observed a crying child who dropped a note while departing the bus; the attendance officer recognized the handwriting on the note, which was full of suicidal ideation and a plan. Thanks to teamwork, the child was identified and a team intervention prevented the suicide.

This experienced school psychologist emphasizes the importance of reaching out to teachers and linking assessment with instruction. She spends considerable time observing in classes, listening to teacher concerns, and finding solutions in meetings of the instructional assistance team, also known as the instructional support team. When psychological assessment is needed, she focuses on the whole child, including developmental history, socioeconomic functioning, and strengths and weaknesses—both what the child can do and what the child cannot do or finds difficult to do. She addresses self-esteem problems, which she finds common in children with learning problems across socioeconomic backgrounds. She has observed that now that medical interventions are saving more children before and after birth, the cases are often complex, with co-occurring conditions, all of which need to be identified and taken into account in planning interventions.

This dedicated school psychologist also emphasizes the importance of reaching out to parents and families. She has observed that, compared with the past, she is dealing with more parents who themselves were in special education and are still coping with negative educational experiences. Also, parents in general know more about disabilities, ask good questions, and want to be involved in their children's education. She strongly recommends that parents be at the decision-making table. She is encouraged by the number of parent volunteers—both mothers and fathers—who lend their time to helping not only their own child but also other children. In a presentation in the fall of 2013 to the Washington State school psychologists, she summarized the challenges of being a psychologist on an interdisciplinary team as having to go through so many layers of emotional complexity to build trust. She explains that a psychologist can be an outstanding diagnostician, but without the ability to get the parents, teachers, and others on the school team to work together on behalf of the student, the psychologist will not be able to effect any change to make a meaningful difference.

STATE–LOCAL SCHOOL PARTNERSHIPS

Some systems-level collaborations involve the state department of education partnering with local school districts. For example, the Office of the Superintendent of Public Instruction in Washington State encouraged university–school district partnerships for implementing the most recent reauthorization of the Individuals With Disabilities Education Improvement Act and provided small grants for the partnerships called Connecting Ideas. The Northshore School District, in partnership with a faculty member at the University of Washington, individually tailored a three-tier model to the different needs and goals of each participating local school within the school district. For example, one school focused on first grade. A team of four regular education first-grade teachers, one special education teacher, one reading specialist, and one paraprofessional implemented a 1-hour reading block 4 days a week and met once a week to plan and monitor student progress. Students were tested at the beginning of the year and grouped according to instructional level, but adjustments in reading groups were made during the year if needed. The team worked with the lowest achieving readers and the regular education teachers worked with the other first graders.

Outcomes showed that at the team collaboration site 77% of first graders increased in standard scores on normed reading measures; of these, 86% improved more than a 0.5 standard deviation. A school psychologist at two sites found that at the site participating in the Connecting Ideas project half as many students were referred to special education as at the site not participating. Participating teams reported that they were beginning to use diagnostic testing to differentiate instruction for students who were not responding to instruction. Schools reported overall more satisfaction with team collaboration and fewer referrals to special education.

Becoming Critical Consumers and Translators of Interdisciplinary Research

EVALUATING RESEARCH

In an era emphasizing evidence-based educational practice, educational professionals have to become critical consumers of interdisciplinary research. Not all research published in peer-reviewed journals is of equal quality or is replicated by other researchers, and not all commercial products touted to be evidence based are. Guidelines for practitioners becoming critical consumers of educationally relevant research are provided in Appendix A.

ORGANIZING RESEARCH FINDINGS

One of the challenges of the information age is dealing with too much information. One way to deal effectively with the explosion of research studies and findings is to organize them into conceptual frameworks that capture general principles for translating research to educational practice. Conceptual frameworks based on multiple research studies with converging findings provide the kind of evidence-based foundation that is needed for educational practice. As an example of translating research into practice, advisory panel member Richard Mayer, a leading researcher, bridged psychology and education and conducted top-notch scientific research on learning and instruction. His translational science is grounded in the distinction between learning and instruction.

Learning is what students do, whereas instruction is what teachers do. Learning is a lasting cognitive change reflected in behavioral change that depends on both learner characteristics and teacher behaviors. Teachers cannot bring about learning independent of learners, whose minds mediate response to instruction. Three kinds of learning have been identified by researchers in different research traditions within psychology. First, learning can create or strengthen associations between incoming or internally existing stimuli and outgoing or internal responses. Second, learning can add factual information or other kinds of knowledge to what is already represented in the mind, or learning can result because learners construct new knowledge or new relationships among existing knowledge. Third, learning can lead to conceptual understanding or change in conceptual understanding. Five kinds of knowledge have been identified: (a) facts, (b) concepts (categories and schemas), (c) procedures (step-by-step activities), (d) strategies (controlled, self-regulated process for performing task or problem solving), and (e) beliefs (thoughts linked to emotions).

Instruction refers to the teacher's total repertoire of behaviors in the learning environment. Examples of instruction include the following: (a) priming motivation to learn; (b) providing verbal or nonverbal feedback to the student about verbal or nonverbal behavior; (c) providing hands-on, concrete problem-solving activities; (d) modeling rule application (deductive thinking); (e) explaining with examples or cases to illustrate principles; (f) providing teacher-guided questions, signals (prompts), and advanced organizers; (g) providing teacher-taught strategies for self-regulation of memory (mnemonics), organization (creating structure), integration of knowledge (summarizing and generating questions for synthesis), problem solving and thinking, and linking school learning with learning outside school; (h) supporting self-discovery from teacher-designed activities (inductive thinking); and (i) providing abstract simulations in which concepts are modeled rather than studied empirically.

Currently in the United States there is emphasis on science, technology, engineering, and math (STEM) subjects. Such emphasis is related to the belief that increasing achievement levels in these content areas of the curriculum will bode well for the success of Americans in the global economy. An overview of research-supported principles for science, technology, and math from Mayer's programmatic research follows.

Evidence-Based Conceptual Model for Science

Science learning involves more than learning new facts (declarative knowledge). Also important is conceptual understanding and often a three-step conceptual change process that proceeds from (a) recognizing an anomaly in preexisting assumptions, (b) constructing a new model, and (c) using the new model to go beyond description only to explanations. The model can then be used to generate new predictions based on the model (hypotheses) to test by collecting new data. If hypotheses are confirmed, new knowledge is generated, which is then evaluated for whether it can be replicated in new studies.

Evidence-Based Conceptual Model for Technology-Learning

Cognitive representations and operations exist independent of language and may be translated into verbal or nonverbal codes. Technology has changed the way verbal and nonverbal materials and methods can be used in learning and instruction. Twelve general principles have emerged from Mayer's longstanding programmatic research on use of verbal and nonverbal media in instruction, which shows students learn better from combining words and nonverbal tools than from words alone.

Five instructional design principles reduce extraneous processing and facilitate learning: (a) excluding extraneous words, pictures, and sounds; (b) using cues to highlight organization; (c) using graphics and narration rather than graphics, narration, and on-line text; (d) presenting corresponding words and pictures close together; and (e) presenting corresponding words and pictures simultaneously rather than sequentially. Three instructional design principles facilitate the management of essential processing and, thus, learning: (a) user-pacing is better than continuous presentation; (b) pretraining in names and main concepts facilitates learning; and (c) combining graphics and narration is more effective than graphics and on-screen text. Four instructional design principles foster generative processing and thus learning: (a) using words and pictures rather than words alone, (b) using conversational rather than formal language (academic register), (c) using a friendly human voice rather than a machine voice, and (d) not adding the speaker's static image to screen, which has no benefit.

Evidence-Based Conceptual Model for Math

Math problem solving requires four processes, which instruction can support in a variety of ways: (a) problem translation, (b) problem integration, (c) solution planning and monitoring, and (d) solution execution. Two processes contribute to problem translation: (a) restating the given problem and (b) restating the problem goal. Two processes contribute to problem integration: (a) recognizing problem types and (b) recognizing relevant and irrelevant information. Two processes contribute to solution planning and monitoring: (a) establishing subgoals and (b) drawing conclusions. Two processes contribute to solution execution: (a) carrying out single calculations and (b) carrying out chains of calculations. Relevant to the goals set by the National Math Panel for students meeting standards in algebra are the 18 problem types identified by Hinsley, Hayes, and Simon, which are needed to go from words to equations to solve algebra problems: (a) triangle—three-step walk, (b) distance, rate, and time, (c) averages, (d) scale conversion, (e) ratio, (f) interest, (g) area, (h) maximum–minimum, (i) mixture, (j) river current, (k) probability, (l) number, (m) work–time management, (n) navigation, (o) progressions to common meeting place, (p) progressions in number line, (q) physics, and (r) exponentials. Another review by Mayer identified problems in algebra books related to classification of items (families) for amount per time, cost per unit, amount per amount, number story, and geometry.

TRANSLATING RESEARCH INTO PRACTICE

In addition to designing and implementing evidence-based educational practices, educational practitioners should evaluate whether their applications of research to practice are effective with students in their school. According to Dean Fixsen and colleagues at the National Implementation Research Network at the University of North Carolina, Chapel Hill, implementation is an emerging science in its own right that deserves more attention to bridge national policy and resources available to teachers in local schools and their classrooms. Robert Horner, a member of this book's advisory panel, noted that good science and good practice have in common a need for both creative confidence and humility. Indeed, translation involves art as well as science. Some even advocate for adding art to transform STEM into STEAM, because of evidence of mutually facilitatory efforts across these domains of knowledge. See the links for Common Core Standards for the Arts as well as for Language and STEM subjects at the end of this chapter.

Grounding educational practices in evidence-based conceptual frameworks is necessary but not sufficient. Interdisciplinary teams should also evaluate whether the educational practices in place are working—both for individuals and for students in general in local buildings and the district. This evaluation requires multiple kinds of evidence, ranging from how individual students are responding to instruction or behavioral intervention on a daily, weekly, monthly, and yearly basis to how students in general within a school or school district are performing on group-administered tests. The evidence gathered is used to address what works for whom in which setting and for what purpose. See Chapter 3 for guidance in the various kinds of assessments that can be conducted for different purposes.

To gather evidence related to the implementation of evidence-based practices, begin by defining the practice operationally (that is, the elements that can be observed and measured or counted), and specify the kind(s) of data that will be collected. In addition, describe the conceptual framework on which the practice is based. Also, define the setting in which the practice is implemented (e.g., grade level of the student or students) and context in which the instructional or behavioral component is embedded within the context of the larger intervention or behavioral intervention program. In addition, the characteristics of the students should be defined—are they typically developing learners or students with developmental or learning disabilities or other kind of disorder? Also, the qualifications of the professionals or paraprofessionals who implement the intervention should be defined. The same intervention is more effective when a teacher, for example, has deep knowledge of the relevant learning as well as instructional processes beyond the teaching procedures per se. Finally, specify the expected, measurable outcomes both immediately and long term. If possible, specify benchmark criteria for achieving learning or behavioral goals to inform evaluation of outcomes.

Programs have been developed to help teams of educational professionals learn to gather evidence about the effectiveness of their translation of science into practice. For example, Team-Initiated Problem Solving (TIPS) is a program for teaching school teams to improve their identification of problems, use data to arrive at solutions, and develop and implement action plans. Research evidence to date shows that using TIPS improves both student outcomes and the effectiveness of the team functioning. The National Evaluation and Technical Assistance Center for Education of Children and Youth Who Are Neglected, Delinquent, or At-Risk has also developed a program that can be used in both schools and juvenile facilities: Positive Behavioral Interventions and Support.

Creative Interdisciplinary Solutions for Contemporary Educational Challenges

RETHINKING ACCOUNTABILITY

In response to beliefs that the United States is losing its competitive edge in the world economy, members of the business community and policymakers have promoted the idea that teachers should be held accountable for all student learning outcomes. Just as businesses rely on accountants to figure out how much money is being spent and how much profit is being earned, they argue that teachers are responsible for the bottom line. In place of money, as an indicator of accountability, they use test scores as a major indicator of whether schools are doing their jobs and building-based evaluations of teachers as an indicator of teacher competence. Moreover, they hold the students accountable if they do not perform at criterion levels on these tests of educational standards set by policymakers, not education professionals.

There are three reasons why holding teachers alone accountable and placing too much focus on students passing a single test are not viable educational solutions. First, this approach has created an epidemic of anxiety throughout the country. Living in an era of high expectations and often low economic resources is a significant source of anxiety for teachers and other educational professionals, for students and their families, and for school administrators. Thus, strategies for reducing anxiety and helping students gain pleasure from learning are sorely needed. Second, given research showing that student learning depends not only on teaching but also on (a) biologically based individual differences (see Part III, this volume) and (b) environmentally based individual differences (see Part IV, this volume) in learners, conceptual frameworks are needed that take all the relevant factors into account—not just the teacher, who is but one variable in the educational equation or the curriculum (e.g., common core).

Third, accountability without professional autonomy is not fair or likely to have the desired outcomes. Physicians, lawyers, and psychologists are held accountable but are granted professional autonomy for exercising independent professional judgment when they are licensed after successfully participating in supervised practicum experiences and internships and passing state credentialing exams. In contrast, teachers are typically not given this privilege of professional autonomy, which is thinking through the issues for individual students and groups of students and exercising best professional judgment for meeting those educational needs. Rather, teachers are expected to follow state department of education procedures for assessment, such as high-stakes tests and common core standards, or special education assessment and services without necessary flexibility. If teachers are held accountable, they also need permission to take into account their professional judgments about how to provide appropriate, differentiated instruction and obtain consultation and collaboration from other professionals in doing so. Also, professionals who have professional autonomy as well as professional accountability outside schools—for example, psychologists or speech and language specialists—are often not permitted to exercise this professional judgment when working in schools. Student rights for free and appropriate public education do not eliminate the need for best professional practices defined by professionals and not the law or government alone.

Teachers who are flagged for not being effective or who desire to become more effective might contact their preservice training programs and recommend that more training in basic science foundations of education be included in the future to better prepare graduates for their work in the real world of schools. This training in basic science foundations will enable them to better communicate with the various members of the interdisciplinary team and to engage in translation science.

ALTERNATIVE FUNDING APPROACHES

Interdisciplinary teams in schools might explore alternative approaches to funding their work so that they can implement best professional practices using a lesson from brain science. The brain separates the mechanisms that provide energy sources (e.g., oxygen that burns the glucose to provide the energy to fuel its work) from the mechanisms underlying its work. Likewise, instead of tying funding to an individual student who meets eligibility criteria, funding might be tied to interdisciplinary teams in local schools developing a viable plan for meeting the educational needs of all students, including those with diagnosed disabilities for whom general education is the least restrictive environment. For example, one special educator and one school psychologist might be assigned to a school to provide ongoing collaboration with classroom teachers in providing instructional-assessment leadership in each school under an inclusion model. Speech–language pathologists (SLPs) and occupational or physical therapists (OT/PTs) might be shared across two or more schools for collaboration in such inclusion models and also consortia for serving students with pervasive developmental disorders and other severe disorders that preclude mainstreaming and require daily SLP and OT/PT services (see Part III, this volume).

The special educator might teach the lowest achieving students during a language arts block and/or a math block in which children "walk about" to instructional groups in reading and writing at their instructional levels (see Chapter 4). In addition, the special educator might at other times before, during, and after school engage in problem-solving consultation with all teachers in the school regarding supplementing, modifying, and differentiating instruction for any students in the school in any area of the curriculum. The school psychologist, in collaboration with the SLPs and OT/PTs, could take the lead in designing, administering, and interpreting (a) the screening assessment at each of the critical transition points, (b) progress monitoring (RTI; see Part II, this volume), and (c) differential diagnosis and treatment planning (see Part III, this volume), as well as in participating in problem-solving consultation. In the long run, the educational needs of more students, including those who are English language learners or who have developmental or learning disabilities, might be met in a more cost-effective way by linking funding to professionals on the team rather than to eligibility categories for services for students. The school is still held accountable under special education law for documenting that they have met those needs.

IMPLEMENTING INTERDISCIPLINARY, COMPREHENSIVE K–12 MODELS

K–12 Model

Although Tier 1 interventions are usually applied only in the early grades, they are also applicable at other critical transition points in schooling. For example, many problems surface for the first time in the transition to fourth grade when (a) most reading is silent rather than oral, (b) reading comprehension may be taxed by increasing complexity of texts read and volume of reading expected, (c) amount and complexity of writing assignments increases, and (d) written assignments increasingly require the integration of reading and writing or integration of reading and math problem solving. Also, many problems surface in middle school when children transition from spending the full day with one teacher to having to move from teacher to teacher in blocks of time during the school day. Interdisciplinary teams might meet on a weekly basis to plan Tier 1 and Tier 2 screening and intervention for students flagged as needing assistance during these later transition times in schooling. Funding might be contingent on developing, implementing, and evaluating such plans.

Behavioral and Social–Emotional Services

Interdisciplinary teams should provide ongoing problem-solving consultation for not only learning but also behavior and social–emotional functioning. Some schools may opt to have separate teams for instructional support and for positive behavioral support. Others may opt for one team to deal with both instructional and behavioral issues. Some teams meet before school, some during the school day, and some after school. Some deliver services by pulling students out of the classroom, but others provide services during recess or lunchtime or after school. Decisions have to be made for how best to do the team's work and when and how to evaluate the effectiveness of the team's work.

Self-Guided Professional Development

In addition to the required clock hours for professional development, some interdisciplinary teams find it helpful to develop their own self-guided professional development in their own professional communities to address issues of concern in their own buildings. It is worth exploring whether there may be district-level assistance and recognition of these other professional development activities, which are more likely to realize positive educational outcomes in a local building.

Caring for One Student at a Time

At times, the team, collectively and individually, may feel overwhelmed with the enormity of students' needs. At such times, they should try to imagine what it must have been like for the single teacher, often without teacher training, in the one-room school house (see Chapter 1), and remind themselves that best practices are to do what they realistically can—even if it is just to make educational outcomes better for one student who otherwise would have continued to struggle, which is better than doing nothing. As Mother Teresa put it, when it is not possible to feed a hundred people, one can just feed one. As cited in the voices of Honor Role Models earlier in this chapter, the extra time it takes is professionally rewarding.

Alternative No-Fault Approach

Instead of blaming the teachers, the parents and families, or the students themselves for the problems children and youth exhibit at school, a solution-oriented, no-fault approach is emphasized in which the teacher and team of multiple professionals work together to optimize learning and behavior of all students, including those who may struggle at times. To aid practitioners in applying a flexible, thinking approach to best practices, "thinking points" are offered as a flexible alternative to the assumption that "one size fits all" for assessment, instruction, or assessment–instruction links. Part of the solution is for compassionate educators to remain in thinking mode, not fearing to ask why, like Woody Guthrie in "Why Oh Why" and going beyond the bureaucratic rules for implementing special education services that often do not provide an effective educational solution. Teacher bashing (or other forms of scapegoating) is not the solution. Rather, we need to give teachers and educational professionals permission to think and seek those solutions.

Thinking Outside the Box

Replacing an accountability model that places the responsibility for high achievement solely on teachers does not mean that expectations for high achievement are necessarily wrong and should not be encouraged. Past research has shown the beneficial effects of expectations on student learning, such as the classic 1968 study by Rosenthal and Jacobson,

Pygmalion in the Classroom. The problem with the current accountability model is that it does not allow educators to exercise professional judgment in (a) setting reasonable levels of achievement for each student's strengths and weaknesses in their developmental and learning profiles, (b) designing learning environments and goals for doing so taking into account developmental stepping stones (small sequential and simultaneous steps needed to reach goals) and the individual students' relative strengths and weaknesses, and (c) evaluating whether each student has reached those individually tailored levels. Each tier of Jim Van Velzer's (Honor Role Model 3) three-tier model requires professional judgment, which is thinking outside the box—that is, finding creative solutions for the case at hand. Such thinking benefits from common sense as well as uncommon sense and compassion for others.

Thinking With the Moving Box

Across disciplines, professionals working with school-age children and youth also work within the context of a moving box—a constantly changing set of characters (individual students, their teacher[s], their parent[s], their families) and of settings (school, home, community, and educational goals and standards), as well as a constantly changing school system responding to an ever-changing society. Educational professionals across disciplines should also be given permission to think with a moving box so that they can be flexibly responsive to changing educational needs of an ever-changing society. In the 1960s Bob Dylan sang a song about a changing society titled "The Times They Are a-Changin'." In the second decade of the 21st century a new song needs to be written about contemporary educational challenges: "The Times They Still Need to Change."

Conceptual Frameworks for Interdisciplinary Communication and Collaboration

On the one hand, professionals bring detailed knowledge of their own disciplinary specialization. On the other hand, they need a common framework for working collaboratively to meet the educational needs of students. One such interdisciplinary model draws on existing knowledge of cognitive development (e.g., Piaget's sensorimotor, preoperational, concrete operational, and formal operational stages), social development (e.g., Vygotsky's zone of proximal development), functional brain systems (e.g., Luria's model of arousal, information processing), and self-regulation systems (e.g., Minsky's model of society of mind), which together support learning through interaction with the physical and social environments and in turn are changed by the environmental experiences. This wealth of knowledge informs the conceptual frameworks provided in this book.

Readings and Resources[1]

COMMON CORE STANDARDS FOR THE ARTS

http://www.aep-arts.org/resources-2/common-core-and-the-arts/

COMMON CORE STANDARDS

http://www.corestandards.org

INTERDISCIPLINARY FRAMEWORK MODEL

Luria, A. R. (1973). *The working brain.* New York, NY: Basic Books.

Minsky, M. (1986). *Society of mind.* New York, NY: Simon & Schuster.

Piaget, J. (1970). Piaget's theory. In P. Mussen (Ed.), *Carmichael's manual of child psychology* (3rd ed., pp. 703–732). New York, NY: Wiley.

Vygotsky, L., Steinver, V., Cole, M., & Schribner, S. (Eds). (1980). *Mind in society: Development of higher psychological processes.* Boston, MA: Harvard University Press.

BASIC SCIENCE FOUNDATIONS FOR EDUCATION (SELECTED)

Bargmann, C. I., & Gilliam, T. C. (2012). Genes and behavior. In E. Kandel, J. Schwartz, & T. Jessell (Eds.) *Principles of neural science* (5th ed., pp. 39–68). New York, NY: McGraw-Hill.

Berko Gleason, J., & Bernstein Ratner, N. (2008). Development of language (7th ed.). New York, NY: Allyn & Bacon.

Berninger, V., & Richards, T. (2002). *Brain literacy for educators and psychologists.* New York, NY: Academic Press/Elsevier.

Blakemore, S.-J., & Frith, U. (2005). *The learning brain: Lessons for education.* New York, NY: Blackwell.

Bornstein, M., & Lamb, M. (2010). *Developmental science: An advanced textbook* (6th ed.). New York, NY: Psychology Press.

Cassiday, L. (2009, September 14). *Mapping the epigenome.* Retrieved from http://cen.acs.org/articles/87/i37/Mapping-Epigenome.html

Clark, R., & Mayer, R. E. (2008). *E-learning and the science of instruction* (2nd ed.). San Francisco, CA: Jossey-Bass.

---

[1]Additional research readings and practitioner resources for this chapter can be found at http://www.apadivisions.org/division-16/publications/interdisciplinary-frameworks-supplement/index.aspx

Collins, F. (2010). *The language of life: DNA and the revolution in personalized medicine.* New York, NY: HarperCollins.

Hinsley, D., Hayes, J., & Simon, H. (1977). From words to equations: Meaning and representation in algebra word problems. In M. Just & P. Carpenter (Eds.), *Cognitive processes in comprehension* (pp. 89–106). Hillsdale, NJ: Erlbaum.

Hirsh-Pasek, K., & Golinkoff, R. (2003). *Einstein never used flash cards: How our children really learn—And why they need to play more and memorize less.* Emmaus, PA: Rodale.

Kolb, B., & Whishaw, I. (2009). *Fundamentals of neuropsychology* (6th ed.). New York, NY: Worth.

Mayer, R. E. (2008). *Learning and instruction* (2nd ed.). Boston, MA: Pearson.

Mayer, R. E. (2009). *Multimedia learning* (2nd ed.). New York, NY: Cambridge University Press.

Moats, L. C. (2000). *Speech to print: Language essentials for teachers.* Baltimore, MD: Brookes.

Posner, M., & Rothbart, M. (2007). *Educating the human brain.* Washington, DC: American Psychological Association.

Ridley, M. (1999). *Genome: The autobiography of a species in 23 chapters.* New York, NY: Perennial/HarperCollins.

Stahl, S., & Nagy, W. (2005). *Teaching word meaning.* Mahwah, NJ: Erlbaum.

Venezky, R. L. (1999). *The American way of spelling: The structure of origins of American English orthography.* New York, NY: Guilford Press.

TRANSLATION SCIENCE

Forman, S. G., Shapiro, E. S., Codding, R. S., Gonzales, J. E., Reddy, L. A., Rosenfield, S. A., . . . Stoiber, K. C. (2013). Implementation science and school psychology. *School Psychology Quarterly, 28,* 77–100. doi:10.1037/spq0000019

Mayer, R. E. (2011). *Applying the science of learning.* Boston, MA: Pearson.

Worrell, F. C., Casad, B. J., Daniel, D. B., McDaniel, M., Messer, W. S., Miller, H. L., Jr., . . . Zlokovich, M. S. (2010). Promising principles for translating psychological science into teaching and learning. In D. F. Halpern (Ed.), *Undergraduate education in psychology: A blueprint for the future of the discipline* (pp. 129–144). Washington, DC: American Psychological Association.

HONOR ROLE MODELS

Berninger, V., Dunn, A., & Alper, T. (2004). Integrated models for branching assessment, instructional assessment, and profile assessment. In

A. Prifitera, D. Saklofske, L. Weiss, & E. Rolfhus (Eds.), *WISC–IV Clinical use and interpretation* (pp. 151–185). San Diego, CA: Academic Press.

Berninger, V., Dunn, A., Lin, S., & Shimada, S. (2004). School evolution: Scientist–practitioner educators creating optimal learning environments for ALL students. *Journal of Learning Disabilities, 37,* 500–508.

Cheng, T. L. (2010). Academic Pediatric Association presidential address: The wisdom, the will, and the wallet: Leadership on behalf of kids and families. *Academic Pediatrics, 10,* 81–86.

McFarlane, E., Dodge, R. A. B., Burrel, L., Crowne, S., Cheng, T. L., & Duggan, A. K. (2010). The importance of early parenting in at-risk families and children's social–emotional adaptation to school. *Academic Pediatrics, 10,* 330–337. doi:10.1016/j.acap.2010.06.011

Solomon, B. S., Bradshaw, C. P., Wright, J., & Cheng, T. L. (2008). Youth and parental attitudes toward fighting. *Journal of Interpersonal Violence, 23,* 544–560. doi:10.1177/0886260507312947

SCHOOL–COMMUNITY PARTNERSHIPS

Power, T., & Bradley-Klug, K. (2013). *Pediatric school psychology: Conceptualization, applications, and strategies for leadership development.* New York, NY: Routledge.

Power, T., DuPaul, G., Shapiro E., & Kazak A. (2003). *Promoting children's health: Integrating school, family, and community.* New York, NY: Guilford Press.

SRIVE/STP. For information on this successful program for transition of incarcerated youth to complete their education, contact Ruben Carranza, ruben.carranza@lausd.net

Wright, J. L., Cheng, T. L. (1998). Successful approaches to community violence intervention and prevention. *Pediatric Clinics of North America, 45,* 459–467.

MUSICAL RECORDINGS

Cash, J. (2000). San Quentin. On *At San Quentin* [CD]. New York, NY: Columbia Records.

Dylan, B. (1964). The times they are a-changin'. On *The times they are a-changin'* [Record]. New York, NY: Columbia Records.

Guthrie, W. (1997). Why, oh why. On *The Asch recordings, volume 1* [CD]. Washington, DC: Smithsonian Folkways.

Seeger, P. (2000). Trouble on the bottom. On *Pete Seeger live* [CD]. Washington, DC: American Psychological Association.

DEVELOPMENTAL STEPPING STONES IN ASSESSMENT AND INSTRUCTION

II

Evidence-Based Use of Tests and Assessments in 21st-Century Education

3

This chapter begins by discussing the distinction between testing and assessment. It then addresses the appropriate uses of test and assessment data for educational decision making about schools and curricula rather than individual students. Multiple examples are provided of the kinds of assessment that can inform instruction and evaluate its effectiveness for students in general as well as individual students. Two examples from educational practitioners are shared to illustrate innovative approaches to assessment that go beyond the narrow focus of a single, high-stakes test given annually or periodically. This chapter provides an interdisciplinary framework for assessment to use in connection with the other chapters in Part II for linking assessment with instruction in early childhood (Chapter 4), middle childhood (Chapter 5), and adolescence (Chapter 6).

http://dx.doi.org/10.1037/14437-003
Interdisciplinary Frameworks for Schools: Best Professional Practices for Serving the Needs of All Students, by V. W. Berninger

Differences Between Testing and Assessment

Testing and assessment are not synonyms. *Tests* are measures that undergo a series of development procedures, which include construction of test items to differentiate among test takers at comparable ages or grades, followed by national norming of the tests and studies evaluating their validity and reliability. National norming should be conducted on samples that are representative of the entire population or the population for which the tests will be used. The norming yields a distribution of quantitative scores for comparing with others of the same age or grade. *Validity studies* evaluate whether the test measures the constructs, skills, or processes as claimed. *Reliability studies* evaluate the degree to which readministration of the test yields the same results.

Assessment, on the other hand, refers to using a variety of data sources, including, but not restricted to, test scores. For example, psychologists and speech–language specialists often use parent and child interviews; medical, developmental, family, and educational histories; and behavioral observations during testing and in the classroom, along with test scores, in reaching a case formulation and generating recommendations. Educational tests are used for formative (for instructional decision making by teachers) or summative (for evaluating student learning) assessment, but assessments based on multiple data sources about the whole child, the classroom and school, and the child's family, culture, and language(s) are more likely to identify all educational needs and potential solutions than are test scores in isolation.

Appropriate Use of Test and Assessment Results for Educational Decision Making

In choosing appropriate tests or assessment tools and interpreting results, a number of issues should be considered, including their measurement properties and educational purpose. For example, measurement properties to consider include reliability and validity. The educational purposes should also be considered because specific tests or assessment approaches may be appropriate for one educational purpose but not another. Examples of questions to ask regarding educational purposes of tests or assessment include the following:

- Is the child, school, school system, or the teacher being evaluated?
- How will the assessment results be used?
  - (a) To summarize (describe domain-specific, summative achievement levels)?
  - (b) To formulate solutions (identify skills to target in classroom instructional program)?
  - (c) To give feedback to parents about their child's educational achievement or progress?
  - (d) To give feedback to teachers for instructional decision making?
  - (e) To give feedback to administrators for evaluating teacher effectiveness?
  - (f) To give feedback to the public about the school district or local school performance?
  - (g) To identify at-risk students for early intervention to prevent more serious learning problems?
  - (h) To support problem-solving consultation with the classroom teacher or team for students who are struggling in some area(s) of the curriculum at any grade level?
  - (i) To diagnose specific developmental or learning disabilities or other condition?
  - (j) To assess a student's response to medication for a variety of conditions, including attention-deficit/hyperactivity disorder, seizures or other medical conditions, and/or psychiatric disorders?

Evaluating Schools, School Districts, and Curricula

Results of tests administered to groups of students to assess high-stakes, common core standards can be appropriately used to evaluate (a) overall school performance at a specific grade level and (b) effectiveness of the curriculum in place in a local school or district in a given year. Results can be compared across years to identify trends related to the school or the curriculum: improving, staying steady, or declining. Results can also be compared across schools, which may be serving different kinds of student populations. Meaningful cross-school comparisons within a school district or cross-district comparisons within a state should take student characteristics (e.g., number of students on free and reduced lunch, number of students whose parents are college graduates) into account in evaluating student learning outcomes.

The *curriculum* is the sum total of instructional activities, materials, and learning goals at specific grade levels (scope) and times within a school year and across the grades (sequence). At one time in the

United States, all school districts developed a curriculum that was implemented across all schools in the district to ensure continuity from grade to grade. Now many schools rely on state standards or national common core standards for curriculum goals. Schools vary greatly in whether they develop a district-wide curriculum for each grade level and provide for all teachers guidance on grade-specific instructional activities and materials for implementing those instructional activities to meet state or common core standards or district goals.

School districts that do have curriculum committees may develop such a road map, with scope and sequence defined at each grade level. School districts that do not have one should consider creating a curriculum committee to develop a curriculum with scope and sequence for specific grade levels, and implement the following kinds of formative assessments:

- evaluation of the fidelity of the district's curriculum implementation;
- observation of teachers during instruction, and review of lesson plans linked to implementation of district curriculum with sequence and scope for each grade level;
- teacher questionnaire or interview for practitioner input regarding the range of developmental and individual differences in individual classrooms at each grade level; and
- comparison of schools within a district at a given time or over time, or school district performance over time to evaluate whether teacher differences and/or student population differences play a significant role in overall school performance, and if they do, develop metrics that take such differences into account in assessing school, teacher, and student performance.

School districts that rely primarily on state or national standards to inform the curriculum may want to take a closer look at the measurement properties and educational purposes of high-stakes tests for assessing those standards. Currently, little attention has focused on the measurement properties of high-stakes tests mandated by state departments of education. Interdisciplinary teams at the local level might inquire about the norming, validity, and reliability of the measures used in their state. In contrast to psychometric tests, high-stakes tests do not typically generate quantitative scores along a distribution that can be interpreted in reference to age or grade norms yoked to a normal, bell-shaped curve. Thus, these high-stakes tests cannot be used to assess normal variation in the population at a given age or grade that is relevant to planning and implementing differentiated instruction. Normal variation is relevant in assessing student-learning outcomes because human abilities have been shown in over a century of behavioral research to fall along a normal curve.

In contrast, high-stakes tests generally use arbitrary cutoffs: Those above the cutoff pass, and those below the cutoff fail. This approach does not take into account measurement error to set confidence bands around an observed score for obtaining the same result if the test is repeated. This test–retest reliability issue is of special concern if the state tests are used to make decisions about whether a student can graduate from high school.

Local interdisciplinary teams and school districts might request both reliability and validity studies of the high-stakes tests to use in interpreting test results for varied educational purposes. Specifically, validity studies are needed to evaluate (a) whether state or common core standards are representative and valid indicators of developmentally and grade-appropriate educational goals, (b) whether the tests are valid measures of those standards, and (c) whether the tests have predictive validity for how students later perform in the world of work or higher education. Much work remains to demonstrate the validity of what is measured and how it is measured on tests based on state and common core standards.

The important guideline for school practitioners is that group-administered high-stakes tests are most appropriately used for evaluating performance of schools and curriculum and should be used cautiously to draw conclusions about individual students. At the very least, such tests should be supplemented with a variety of other kinds of tests, including individually administered tests and other multimodal assessment approaches. The learning of individual students, who vary considerably in their developmental levels, individual abilities, and learning patterns in response to instruction, is more appropriately assessed with the kinds of measures discussed in the next section and on multiple measures.

However, assessment at the school and district levels can make an important contribution to improving the design and delivery of the curriculum. Although most states now have educational standards, and most states are adopting the common core standard (top-down educational goals), best practices for school districts are also to design, implement, and evaluate the curriculum to be used district-wide that is informed by developmental stepping-stones and individual differences, as outlined in Part II of this volume (bottom-up translation science). The standards define desired goals but not the road map for reaching them. A district-wide curriculum is likely to result in greater continuity across grade levels within schools and for mobile students across schools within a district. A curriculum committee should specify both (a) skills to be taught at each grade level in each content area of the curriculum and across content areas and (b) instructional tools to be made available to teachers for accomplishing these goals, given that there will be developmental and individual differences within each grade level.

The curriculum committee should also perform an annual review on the basis of data across the student population to evaluate the effectiveness of the curriculum in place and decide whether modifications are warranted and, if so, determine what they might be. Such data should include not only high-stakes test scores but also the following kinds of data: (a) number of students who, on the basis of multiple kinds of evidence, were achieving at a higher level at the end of the school year than at the beginning of the school year; (b) number of students referred to, and served effectively by, problem-solving consultation teams; (c) number of students referred by parents or teachers for special education evaluations; (d) number of lawsuits; (e) number of students who meet evidence-based criteria for developmental or learning disabilities or other diagnostic categories; (f) number of students retained at each grade level; (g) number of students who dropped out of school at each grade level; (h) number of students who got in trouble with the law; and (i) number of students who graduated from high school. All of these outcomes are sensitive to whether the whole team—educational professionals, parents, students, and community partners—functions cohesively on behalf of students.

Although such data collection may at first seem like an overwhelming task, schools that have initiated these proactive, preventive approaches have reported that their workload decreases in the long run as more students are served early on and fewer severe problems remain in the upper grades. At the district level, cost savings should be evaluated for introducing and evaluating new approaches, such as programs for reaching out to parents and building trust in home–school relationships or introducing screening and intervention at critical transitions beyond the early grades. Cost savings associated with specific outcomes (decrease or increase numbers as relevant) should be noted—for example, a reduction in lawsuits.

Evaluating Individual Students

Results of tests administered to individuals may be appropriately used to evaluate individual differences in how well individual students are learning the curriculum at a specific grade level. The reason is that during individual assessment an examiner may more adequately monitor the individual's attention and engagement in the test-taking process, render professional judgment of whether the test administration is valid, and try to focus the student's attention and engagement when necessary. Computer-administered assessment may be problematic because, as emerging research has shown, some students may not attend to computerized tasks involving language or write as well with computer tools as pen and paper.

Simply administering individual computerized tests to students does not eliminate the need to monitor their attention and engagement during the testing and exercise professional judgment about the validity of the results that are then used to make educational decisions about whether individuals are making adequate progress and modifying instruction if they are not. However, results of group-administered or computer-administered tests of state or common core standards are often used to evaluate the learning of individual students or their teacher's teaching ability rather than to evaluate the curriculum in place—that is, whether it is sufficiently tailored to the developmental and individual differences among students at any given grade level.

Moreover, the current focus of high-stakes testing is on identifying students who meet state standards (*summative assessment*). Not enough attention is devoted to identifying instructional approaches for helping individual students who do not meet these standards (*formative assessment*). Such formative assessment should be based on the student's current learning profile for specific reading, writing, and math skills and behavioral markers of specific learning disabilities and, if the developmental, medical, or educational history suggests that development is not completely within the normal range, then the developmental profile (see Chapters 8, 9, and 10). Patterns in developmental profiles may be relevant to individually tailoring instruction to struggling learners with pervasive or specific developmental disabilities to teach them at their developmental level. Moreover, diagnosed neurogenetic disorders, brain injuries, conditions related to environmental toxins or substance-abuse, or medical conditions affecting health may also be relevant to designing individually tailored instruction and educational learning environments. Each of these kinds of profiles and diagnoses, which are currently not taken into account in designing, administering, or interpreting results of state-mandated tests, is discussed briefly now and in greater detail in chapters in Parts III and IV.

DEVELOPMENTAL PROFILES AND LINKS TO INSTRUCTION

Just as the platforms for technology are constantly changing, brains and minds of learners change across development (see Chapter 7). The changes are not always discrete, sequential stages and may be better described as qualitative, cascading change with periodic plateaus followed by bursts of developmental change. Of relevance to linking assessment to instruction is that what children should be taught and how they learn most effectively are affected by their current developmental levels across the five domains of development: (a) sensory and motor, (b) social and emotional, (c) language, (d) cognitive and memory, and (e) attention and executive functions (see Chapters 8 and 9). Also, curriculum components may need to be adjusted for students whose development is either above or below the normal range in one or more of the five developmental domains.

LEARNING PROFILES AND LINKS TO INSTRUCTION

Considerable research has now identified the important skills in learning to read, write, and do math at different stages of schooling: early grades, middle grades, and upper grades, corresponding in general to early childhood, middle childhood, and adolescence, respectively. Developmentally appropriate, individually tailored instruction should be based on learning profiles for these reading, writing, and math skills for two reasons. First, as Lewis Carroll pointed out in *Alice's Adventures in Wonderland*, the grin without the cat is not the same as the cat with the grin. Context and patterns matter and should be considered instead of focusing on a single skill in isolation from other skills. Second, brain research has shown that functional systems drawing on multiple component processes underlie learning to read, write, and do math. Depending on the task at hand, different brain areas and processes are activated, just like different musicians play at different times during an orchestra performance.

Consequently, in assessing educational needs and planning and implementing instructional and learning activities, educators should consider a current profile of related skills rather than an isolated skill that is related to current instructional levels but not necessarily patterns of all relevant skills in current learning profiles. Moreover, the scope and sequence of academic curriculum should be grounded in what is known about the typical developmental stepping-stones in the various academic skills within and across specific domains of curriculum.

DEVELOPMENTAL AND LEARNING PROFILES FOR DIFFERENTIATED INSTRUCTION

Formative assessment draws on a variety of tests and other assessment tools to design instruction that is individually tailored to individuals. Some of these are normed for age or grade, and others are based on criterion levels of performance linked to instructional or developmental levels or evidence-based clinical ranges. Some may use measures given to large or small groups for screening purposes, but these should always be supplemented with ongoing individual observations of the students in the classroom.

In the following, we use the terms *response to instruction*, which all students receive and *response to intervention*, which only students targeted for learning differences receive. Examples of individually administered assessments for individually tailored instructional planning, implementing, and evaluating include

- teacher-designed classroom assessments for planning teacher-designed instructional activities and evaluating (grading) student learning outcomes;
- probes during lessons that are graphed for a visible record of response to instruction and that may be analyzed using single-subject design methods and used to make instructional decisions, including planning future instructional goals;
- publisher-designed assessments to be used with commercially available instructional materials (sometimes after each lesson but more often after completing a unit test following multiple lessons) for placement (instructional level), instructional decision making, and/or evaluation (response to instruction or grading);
- authored, criterion-referenced, informal inventories that generate instructional levels for specific skills in the curriculum to use in delivering and evaluating response to instruction and modifying instruction as appropriate and organizing or reorganizing instructional groups for differentiated instruction;
- teacher- and student-created portfolios (work samples collected across the year and used in conferences with teachers, students, and parents to evaluate progress and set future goals);
- team screening for at-risk students for early intervention and prevention programs;
- team screening for pull-out or accelerated programs for the highly capable (gifted);
- team differential diagnosis (identifying a condition regardless of whether a student meets eligibility criteria for special education): pervasive developmental disability (PDD) in all five domains of development; specific developmental disability or disabilities (SDDs) in one or more but not all domains of development; or specific learning disabilities (SLDs) in students with characteristic patterns of impairment in reading, writing, and/or math, but no PDD or SDDs (see Part III, this volume);
- rating scales completed by teachers and/or parents and interpreted by team professionals for assessing attention, executive functions, social–emotional issues, language, and behavior;
- parent questionnaires and/or interviews to obtain information about developmental history from conception, gestation, birth, post-birth development (infant, toddler, preschool), and school years, and medical history, family history, and school history; and

- team monitoring of the child at developmentally sensitive periods in schooling:
  - at school entrance (preschool to kindergarten transition and kindergarten to first grade transition);
  - at transition to middle childhood (third- to fourth-grade transition) or middle school (fifth- to sixth-grade or sixth- to seventh-grade transition);
  - at any time when a child is not succeeding and/or passing a high-stakes test, problem-solving consultation that includes some assessment is warranted;
  - at times when grade promotion or high school graduation is in question; at transition from schooling, for assessment of students with PDDs or SDDs, for independent living, and/or viable vocational opportunities; and
  - transition from high school for students regarding career planning and access to post-secondary education.

GUIDELINES FOR CURRICULUM-BASED MEASURES AND CURRICULUM-BASED ASSESSMENTS

A widespread belief is that measures of how fast a student can read orally or write are curriculum-based measures. Real curriculum-based assessment carefully assesses all instructional components at specific grade levels of a well-articulated curriculum. So measuring reading speed only would be an incomplete measure. Carefully designed research has shown that some children are both inaccurate and slow in their reading, whereas others are accurate but slow. Thus, repeated administration of a timed task (a curriculum-based measure), typically with a brief 1-minute time limit, will not be sensitive to the differential instructional needs of a student who is accurate but slow versus both inaccurate and slow. Assessment is also needed to identify the instructional needs for teaching related skills for accurate reading or writing skills (the underlying problem) rather than to treat only the symptom (slow reading or writing). Likewise, assessment is needed to identify the instructional needs of a student who is accurate but slow.

Finally, basic research has documented important differences among rate, automaticity, and fluency, but educational practitioners and researchers often use these terms interchangeably and inappropriately. *Rate* refers to time per response unit for task held constant; *speed* refers to total time. *Automaticity* refers to accessing information in memory or producing a response without conscious, controlled, strategic thinking. Automatic processes and responses may be quicker than those that require controlled, strategic processing, but speed alone is not what differentiates strategic and automatic processing and production. In fact, different regions of the brain are involved in controlled, strategic processing (frontal cortex) and automatic processing (subcortical striatum and basal ganglia; see Chapter 7). *Fluency* refers to coordinating multiple processes smoothly as well as quickly. For example, during fluent oral reading, words are chunked into word groups according to the stress patterns and rhythm of oral language, and a sentence reflects the melody of spoken language, for example, with rising intonation at the end of a question and falling intonation at the end of a statement. Again, although fluent processing and production may be quicker, speed alone is not what differentiates fluent and nonfluent processing and production. Fluent reading requires more than decoding—it also depends on comprehending sentences and understanding the melody of spoken language.

RESPONSE-TO-INTERVENTION MEASURES

Although RTI typically refers to intervention of any kind, in many cases the intervention is an instructional one, and thus RTI can also refer to response to instruction, as discussed in Part II of this volume. On the one hand, educators should know the basic research foundations that inform educational practice. On the other hand, educators should know whether the educational programs they implement on the basis of developmental stepping-stones and individual differences are working for each of the individual students in their classrooms. That is, they need to evaluate what works for whom for what purpose.

A variety of approaches are needed to address this important practical issue. One important approach for monitoring an individual's RTI is with single-subject design methods recommended by the National Panel on Single-Subject Design in 2009. First, the teacher selects a probe measure that is relevant to the goals of sequential lessons in a unit of instruction or independent work in which a student practices skills taught. Second, probe measures are collected and inspected over time to evaluate whether performance shows a trend of improving over time. The probes can also be inspected for periods of time when a specific kind of instruction is withdrawn or an alternative approach is introduced. Teachers can also collect measures at target times of the year—such as beginning, middle, and end—that are yoked to the curriculum or instructional materials they are using. These, too, can be inspected for trends of increasing scores. In addition, teachers can define *probes*, that is, target skills, which they, in collaboration with individual students, examine in the student's portfolio for indicators of improvement.

At the building level, teams can choose commercially available or building-designed progress-monitoring measures to administer at the beginning, middle, and end of the school year. These can be analyzed in reference to trends for improvement or change in category from at-risk to making expected progress. Some schools, in response to parents who are concerned that their children are making expected progress in reference to grade or age peers, compare each student's performance on normed measures at the beginning, middle, and end of the school year.

One limitation of current normed measures is that they are constructed to assess individual differences (variation) at a single point in time defined on the basis of age or grade rather than change over time. Norms for typical growth—the change over time for a 9-month school year—are also needed to combine the contributions of single-subject design for evaluating change over time and normed measures for documenting individual differences at the same point compared with peers. Such measures would allow schools to assess how a student is achieving compared with peers, on the basis of both level and rate of learning, and compared with oneself—that is, whether skills have improved from the beginning to the middle to the end of the school year. The goal is for each student to know more and perform at a higher level at the end of the school year than at the beginning.

Interdisciplinary Team Assessment–Intervention Links

As shown in Chapter 9, all of the four language systems—language by ear (listening), language by mouth (oral expression), language by eye (reading), and language by hand (writing)—are multileveled. That is, each language system has *subword* (smaller than a word), *word*, and *multiword* (syntax that orders words and text that orders syntax) levels. Each language system teams with a sensory or motor system and interacts with cognitive systems via executive functions that self-regulate attention, working memory, learning, and behavior. Also, each motor system gets sensory feedback (e.g., tactile and visual for hands). Given the complexity of these functional systems, the collective expertise of multiple disciplines may be needed to assess and pinpoint bottlenecks that interfere with RTI in some students: school psychology or other specialization in psychology, speech and language sciences, audiology, occupational therapy, physical therapy, pediatric neurology, and developmental pediatrics. Pinpointing the nature of the problem(s) contributes to design of appropriate, individually tailored instruction in content areas of the curriculum. The key principle to keep in mind, however, is that although some instructional components should be directed at overcoming the bottleneck, instruction should also include all the components required to create functional reading, writing, and math systems (see Chapters 4–6).

Communicating Assessment Results With Parents and Other Professionals

Parents should be included in the interdisciplinary process from the beginning. Early in schooling, at least one member of the interdisciplinary team at school should reach out by sending parent questionnaires to all parents of kindergartners and first graders and students new to the school. These questionnaires should ask if the parents have any concern about their child's overall development, motor development, language development, or social and emotional development. They should also ask about any possible medical problems, family issues, or other issues that may help the school understand and teach the child. On the basis of the returned questionnaires, parents of kindergartners and first graders or new students for whom current and/or past concerns are reported should be contacted and invited to the school to talk with appropriate team members. When warranted, the appropriate team members(s) should conduct an assessment related to the concern(s) at hand.

It is important that interdisciplinary team professionals who conduct these assessments are honest in communicating results and focus on current functioning. Words such as *delay* should not be used if the child appears to have a pervasive or specific developmental disability; although the child will likely grow in each developmental domain, there is no guarantee the child will eventually function within the normal range (see Chapter 8). For parents of students with significant developmental problems in the preschool years that continue during the school years, parent support groups might be formed. Connecting with other parents may help parents deal with the emotional impact of raising a child with developmental, learning, and/or behavioral concerns and may also help them learn constructive ways to work with the school to facilitate their child's development, learning, and behavior.

Moreover, when a diagnosis of an SLD is warranted, it should be made whether or not a child meets state criteria for eligibility for special education services. Diagnosis is different than special education eligibility. Students who struggle with reading, writing, oral language, and/or math should receive differential instruction whether or not they meet state criteria for special education eligibility. Evidence-based diagnosis can be made for dysgraphia, dyslexia, oral and written language learning disability or specific language impairment, and dyscalculia (see Chapter 9). If diagnoses are not made, when warranted, parents may become frustrated, self-diagnose, and/or seek services outside the school, and adversarial home–school relationships may develop. Appropriate assessment and honest communication of diagnostic assessment results can often reduce or eliminate frustration and adversarial relationships on the part of both parents and schools. Also, an ongoing record of assessment, differentiated instruction, and RTI should be kept. On the one hand, that may serve as documentation that appropriate education was provided even if a student does not receive pull-out special education services. On the other hand, an initial diagnosis may change over time if the student responds to instruction tailored to his or her profile. In general, it is advisable to make current diagnoses and not make promises for the future.

A Viable Alternative: Cost- and Time-Effective Evidence-Based Assessment–Instruction

Key to achieving the goal of appropriate, differentiated instruction for all students is an interdisciplinary team approach to implementing evidence-based best professional practices. The interdisciplinary team should not restrict its contributions to assessments of students referred for special education as mandated by federal and state law. Rather, the team can collaborate and address needs proactively, for example, in weekly, before-school, building-wide meetings of school instructional support teams, in problem-solving consultation, as needed, and in evaluating RTI for instruction and other interventions implemented proactively throughout the school year and across grade levels. Although this approach may, at first glance, seem to require too much work given the resources at hand, many professionals (see Honor Role Models 3, 8, and 10) report that, once implemented, it becomes a more efficient way to help more students and is both feasible and professionally more rewarding.

Achieving the goal will require working with parents to build positive, constructive home–school relationships to facilitate student learning and development. In addition, achieving the goal will require replacing a misguided accountability approach that assumes all students can reach the same learning outcome using the same evidence-supported methods with acknowledgement of the diversity among school-age children and youth. It is also misguided to believe that a single high-stakes test by itself can measure validly or completely all of what is needed for the success of current students during the school years or their preparation to be in an ever-changing economy.

Learning From Educational Professionals in Schools

Two examples illustrate how schools can draw effectively on a multi-modal approach to assessment as described in this chapter. On the basis of a long-standing career in education as a teacher and reading specialist, a principal at two suburban schools—the lab school at Stanford University and then the lower school at the American School in London—Julie Ryan (Honor Role Model 9) developed and implemented a model in which portfolios were used school-wide for multiple purposes. Each student, from kindergarten and through graduation from elementary school, keeps a portfolio of daily written work across the curriculum, which even includes audio recordings, for example, of oral reading. Weekly and monthly, the classroom teacher and the student collaboratively evaluate how the student's performance in daily work is changing across the year. The goals are to identify—and celebrate—strengths and to identify weaknesses and set realistic goals for improvement. Students show visible pleasure in noting how their work has improved over the year. Also, they are better able to accept the weaknesses they have to work on because attention is also drawn to their strengths. The teacher and student discuss the student's strengths not only in classwork, homework, and tests but also in behavior, social skills, leadership, performing arts (music, art, drama), and sports.

When parent–school conferences are scheduled during the year, these portfolios are shared with parents along with written evaluations of their child's strengths (areas to celebrate) and weaknesses (areas to work on) that have been cowritten by the teacher and the child. Parent feedback has indicated that parents appreciate seeing work samples and not just letter grades; they appreciate hearing good news as well as about problems. Also, the portfolios enable a conversation about how the parents can participate in helping the student meet goals for improvement as well as nurture their child's strengths, which are relevant throughout schooling and to planning their career paths in the world of work after school.

Jeanne Patton (Honor Role Model 10) serves as an inspiring example of how one special education teacher transcended the divide between general and special education by demonstrating how a team can implement evidence-based reading instruction in a cost-effective way in a school serving economically and culturally diverse students. In the spirit of cross-disciplinary collaboration, she invited school psychology interns from a local university to help her evaluate the effectiveness of this cross-classroom collaboration. Adopting a multimodal approach, school psychology interns helped the teachers give informal reading inventories to identify instructional levels and normed, standardized reading tests to determine achievement levels at the beginning of the school year. All second and third graders were then grouped by instructional and achievement levels (zone of proximal development) and taught in a "walk-about model" during a common language arts block when all second- and third-grade teachers taught reading. Two or three groups comparable in achievement and instructional levels were assigned to each teacher so that it was manageable to deliver differentiated instruction. All the lowest achieving readers were assigned to the special education teacher's class. Children were not aware of which groups were high or low, only that they might have an opportunity to work with a teacher other than their homeroom teacher during language arts. America Reads tutors provided supplementary assistance in listening to children read orally, much as paraprofessionals or community volunteers do in some schools.

The reassessment at the end of the school year showed that the initially lowest achievers, for whom Patton provided evidence-based instruction in phonological awareness, phonics, oral reading and rereading, listening comprehension, reading comprehension, integrated listening–reading–writing, handwriting, spelling, and composing, did not differ significantly from the other students at the end of the year on the normed referenced reading measures that were readministered. They were at or above grade level. Of greatest satisfaction to Patton were the numerous students who asked to visit her class because they heard how much fun it was. Also satisfying to Patton was that because of this team approach more students were taught to read well than could have been using a pull-out model.

Readings and Resources[1]

RELIABILITY AND VALIDITY OF TESTS

Buros Center for Testing. *Mental measurements yearbook*. Lincoln: University of Nebraska Press.

Reynolds, C., & Livingstone, R. (2012). *Mastering modern psychological testing: Theory and methods*. Boston, MA: Pearson Education.

---

[1]Additional research readings and practitioner resources for this chapter can be found at http://www.apadivisions.org/division-16/publications/interdisciplinary-frameworks-supplement/index.aspx

HIGH-STAKES TESTS

Waber, D. P., Gerber, E. B., Turcios, V. Y., Wagner, E. R., & Forbes, P. W. (2006). Executive functions and performance on high-stakes testing in children from urban schools. *Developmental Neuropsychology, 29*, 459–477. doi:10.1207/s15326942dn2903_5

CURRICULUM-BASED MEASUREMENT

Peverly, S. (2009). Beyond the monitoring of students' progress in classrooms: The assessments of students, curricula, and teachers. In S. Rosenfield & V. Berninger (Eds.), *Implementing evidence-based academic interventions in school settings* (pp. 575–600). New York, NY: Oxford University Press.

INFORMAL INVENTORY

Leslie, L., & Caldwell, J. S. (2011). *Qualitative Reading Inventory–5*. Boston, MA: Pearson.

Woods, M. L., & Moe, A. (2003). *Analytical reading inventory* (7th ed.). Upper Saddle River, NJ: Merrill/Prentice Hall.

CROSS-BATTERY ASSESSMENT

Flanagan, D. P., Ortiz, S., & Alfonso, V. C. (2007). *Essentials of cross-battery assessment* (2nd ed.). New York, NY: Wiley.

ACCURACY AND RATE DISABLED VERSUS RATE DISABLED

Lovett, M. (1987). A developmental approach to reading disability: Accuracy and speed criteria of normal and deficient reading skill. *Child Development, 58*, 234–260. doi:10.2307/1130305

SINGLE-SUBJECT DESIGN AND RTI: WHAT WORKS FOR WHOM

Horner, R., & Anderson, C. M. (in press). Applied behavior analysis. In E. Anderman (Ed.), *Psychology of classroom learning: An encyclopedia.* Detroit, MI: Macmillan.

Horner, R., & Spaulding, S. (in press). Rewards. In E. Anderman (Ed.), *Psychology of classroom learning: An encyclopedia.* London, England: Thomson.

Kratochwill, T. R., Hitchcock, J., Horner, R. H., Levin, J. R., Odom, S. L., Rindskopf, D. M., & Shadish, W. R. (2010). *Single case design technical documentation.* Retrieved from: http://ies.ed.gov/ncee/wwc/pdf/wwc_scd.pdf

White, O. (2009). A focus on the individual: Single-subject evaluations of response to instruction. In S. Rosenfield & V. Berninger (Eds.), *Implementing evidence-based academic interventions in school settings* (pp. 531–558). New York, NY: Oxford University Press.

WALK-ABOUT MODEL

Berninger, V. (2002). Best practices in reading, writing, and math assessment-intervention links: A systems approach for schools, classrooms, and individuals. In A. Thomas & J. Grimes (Eds.), *Best practices in school psychology IV* (Vol. 1, pp. 851–865). Bethesda, MD: National Association of School Psychologists.

Slavin, R. (1987). Ability grouping and student achievement in elementary schools: A best-evidence synthesis. *Review of Educational Research,* 293–336. doi:10.3102/00346543057003293

Linking Instruction and Assessment in Early Childhood

4

For two reasons, devoting time and resources to these assessment-instruction links during early childhood results in more students having optimal learning outcomes and ultimately is more cost-effective. First, little changes early in the process can result in major differences in outcomes later in the process. Second, school performance by the second or third grade is predictive of who will drop out of school or continue to fail.

This chapter describes an evidence-based approach that teaches and assesses both low- and high-level skills to create functional reading, writing, and math systems. This approach (see Exhibits 4.1, 4.2, and 4.3) differs from a narrow focus on only low-level skills (e.g., sounding out words, learning math facts) or only high-level skills (e.g., comprehending or expressing ideas in written language, math problem solving). The approach draws on Posner's metaphor of "orchestra of mind" in which multiple component processes are coordinated in time to create music rather than noise. Just as musicians produce music using

http://dx.doi.org/10.1037/14437-004
Interdisciplinary Frameworks for Schools: Best Professional Practices for Serving the Needs of All Students, by V. W. Berninger

many different end organs—mouths vocalizing song or blowing air, fingers moving sequentially on strings or wooden or metal parts, arms sliding metal parts, or hands tapping drums with or without a stick of metal or ivory—students learn to orchestrate internal mental processes with different sensory and motor end organs for different academic tasks. Interdisciplinary team members are encouraged to draw on the extensive readings and resources listed on this book's companion website and at the end of each chapter in Part II to creatively and flexibly modify, differentiate, or supplement instruction; plan, screen, and intervene at critical transition points during schooling; participate in instructional support teams, positive behavioral support teams, and school-wide curriculum committees; and interpret comprehensive assessment. Teams are encouraged to use Provided Thinking Points and develop their own guidelines for helping individual students.

EXHIBIT 4.1

Early Childhood Developmental Stepping-Stones by Levels of Language

Aural Language
- Understanding word meaning (vocabulary with semantic correspondence or idioms)
- Attending to, understanding, and following directions
- Transition from conversation only to teacher talk

Oral Language
- Finding, choosing, and using vocabulary words
- Constructing syntax units
- Discourse—discussion across the curriculum

Mapping Aural/Oral and Read/Written Language

Subword Mapping (One- and Two-Syllable Words of Anglo-Saxon Origin)
- Alphabet principle—correspondences between one- and two-letter spelling units and phonemes
- Word families—correspondences between written *rimes* (i.e., what remains after onset phoneme[s] of syllable omitted) and their pronunciation
- Morphemes—inflectional suffixes for tense, number agreement, comparison, high frequency derivational suffixes in primary-grade reading material (e.g., *-ing*) and prefixes
- Syllables—spelling patterns related to syllable types: *open* (ending in a vowel), *closed* (ending in a consonant), *vowel teams* (*digraph*s such as *ie*, in which one of the sounds corresponds to one of the two letters [as in *pie*], and *diphthongs* such as *oi* [as in *join*] in which together the two letters stand for a sound different from either alone [as in *hot* or *hit*]), *r-* and *l*-controlled vowels (*r* or *l* modifies the vowel, for example, *ar* [as in *car*] or *il* [as in *pill*] sounds different than *a* [as in *ran*] or *i* [as in *tip*]), and *le* (order of sounds reversed)

Reading

Word Identification (Words of Anglo-Saxon Origin)
- Orally decoding unfamiliar single words—vertical subword mapping across written and spoken word subunits within horizontal whole written word units, synthesizing into whole spoken words without any vocabulary meaning (semantic) or context clues

EXHIBIT 4.1 *(Continued)*

- Oral reading of familiar single words—same as oral decoding except that vocabulary (semantic) cues may be used

Oral Reading of Text (Accuracy and Fluency)

- Reading comprehension organized by word-, sentence-, and text-levels of language for text read orally or silently
- Vocabulary meaning—semantic concepts activated by word-specific spelling
- Sentences—meaning constructed from syntax (word order, content and function words, parts of speech, and independent and independent plus dependent clauses)
- Text—meaning constructed from a series of sentences and higher-order discourse schema

Writing

Subword Letter Production

- Handwriting—print (taught in Grades 1 and 2, reviewed in Grade 3) and cursive (taught in Grade 3)
- Computer keyboard or forming with finger or stylus on a tablet or screen (teach if possible)

Spelling

- Dictated spelling real words with word-specific spellings or pseudowords
- Spelling during composing

Written Expression

- Word choice (vocabulary meaning and spelling)
- Sentences
- Text

Math

Number Concepts

- More or less and other estimated judgments
- Rote counting versus one-to-one correspondence in counting
- Cardinal values versus ordinal relations among numbers
- Place value
- Fractions (part–whole relationships)
- Linear and circular number lines

Computations and Calculations

- Number facts
- Four operations (each with unique spatial and temporal processing)

Problem Solving

- Word problems
- Everyday math

Geometry

- Recognizing, naming basic shapes
- Drawing shapes

Reading–Writing–Math Connections

EXHIBIT 4.2

Assessing Response to Instruction Across Early Childhood From an Interdisciplinary Model and Developmental Stepping-Stones Conceptual Framework

Aural and Oral Language

Listening

- analyzing subword sound patterns (syllables, phonemes—identity, positions, sequences, and onsets or rimes)
- understanding word meaning
- understanding syntax
- understanding text structures

Expressing

- word retrieval (finding words in memory)
- explaining word meaning
- constructing syntax
- creating oral text structures

Reading

- analyzing subword letter patterns (letter identities, positions, and sequences)
- oral reading of real words out of context—accuracy and rate
- oral reading of real words in passage context—accuracy, rate, fluency (fast and smooth)
- oral reading of pseudowords out of context—accuracy and rate
- silent word reading rate
- silent sentence-level comprehension—accuracy and rate
- silent text-level comprehension—accuracy

Writing

Letter Knowledge

- naming letters
- writing letters by hand (by pen—printing or cursive; finger or stylus; keyboard)
- legibility on handwriting tasks (copied from a model)
- automatic, legible letter retrieval and production of letters from memory
- sustained, legible letter retrieval and production of letters from memory
- legibility of letters in timed or untimed copying or composing tasks
- total speed or rate

Spelling

- accuracy of spelling pseudowords and real words
- recognizing correctly spelled word among choices; accuracy and rate
- accuracy of spelling during composing

Composing

- sentence syntax—constructing sentences from provided words
- sentence combining—expressing all the ideas from two sentences in one sentence
- writing in different genres such as narrative or expository—or summaries

EXHIBIT 4.2 (*Continued*)

Math

- counting (one-to-one correspondence) with manipulatives and a mental number line
- math fact accuracy and retrieval rate—addition and subtraction (Grades 1–2), multiplication and division (Grade 3)
- standard computational algorithms for basic operations—addition and subtraction
- math reasoning and problem solving—arithmetic word problems

Cross-Academic Skill Domain Integration

- Reading and writing—answering questions and writing summaries about read texts
- Writing and math—writing numerals legibly and automatically, writing number facts, writing numbers using place value correctly in basic operations in computation
- Reading and math—reading word problems to identify and solve the problem

EXHIBIT 4.3

Teaching to Create Multilevel, Multicomponent Functional Reading, Writing, and Math Systems

Reading: Teach to All Levels of Language Close in Time

Subword Level

- Play sound games to develop phonological awareness (first for syllables and then phonemes as a heard word is held in the "mind's ear").
- Play looking games to develop orthographic awareness (first for all the letters in order in a written word and then for a designated letter or letters while the word is held in the "mind's eye").
- Look at, touch, and name a letter or letter group, name the picture that goes with it, and say the target sound in the named word that goes with the letter or letter group (procedural knowledge based on engaging attention and multiple sensory and motor systems).

Word Level

- Apply previously practiced skills to sounding out target words (high frequency for grade level).
- Graph the number correct for visible record of progress in oral word reading without context clues.

Text Level

Read orally a short text at the instructional level following these steps:
1. Listen to the teacher read while touching each word she says. When she stops, children predict and say the next word.
2. Children independently read the text orally, first in unison, and then taking turns. Feedback is given for correct pronunciation of any mispronounced words.
3. Children take turns summarizing what was read orally.
4. Children answer questions posed by the teacher to talk about the text.

(continued)

EXHIBIT 4.3 (*Continued*)

Writing: Teach to All Levels of Language Close in Time

Subword Level

- Writers warm up (just like pushups before a sports event): Once for each of 26 alphabet letters, study numbered arrow cues, use them to form sequential strokes of each letter, close eyes, and write the letter from memory.
- Write the letter that goes with each dictated letter name. Graph the number of legible letters.
- Say the sound in the pictured word, and then look at, touch, and name letter or letter group that goes with that sound (procedural knowledge).

Word Level

- Say, sound out by letter or letter group, and write each letter or letter group to spell each of the high frequency spelling words at the instructional level for a lesson.
- Spell each word in a dictated sentence that contains some of the words previously spelled alone.
- Graph the number of correctly spelled words in the previous two steps for a visible record of progress.

Text Level

- Write for 5 minutes about a provided topic using the "what I think I can say, what I say I can write" strategy.
- Read what was written to another child ("writing buddy").
- Illustrate what was written and place it in the writing portfolio.

Math: Teach Counting (Number Line), Calculation, and Problem Solving Close in Time Using Manipulatives as Appropriate

Counting, Naming, and Writing Numbers (the same procedures as for the handwriting warm-up are used to teach children how to write each numeral from 0 to 9)

- Count by naming and touching numerals on a masking tape or paper number line for 5 addition facts. Then write the number facts.
- Do the same for subtraction facts.

Calculating (performing operations on numbers)

- Write addition problems with two numbers in one's place to be added or write subtraction problems in which a one-place number has to be subtracted from a one- or two-place number.
- Orally state the steps in regrouping and when it is necessary.
- Add or subtract the numbers and write the answer, using regrouping if needed.

Problem Solving With Numbers

- The teacher presents orally a problem to solve. Children discuss what the question is, what information is relevant to answering it, and whether it requires addition or subtraction to solve it. They then use paper and pencil to solve it, compare their answers, and discuss any differences among themselves.
- Children create their own math problems to solve with addition or subtraction.

Note. Examples are provided for first grade but can be extended to other grades.

Developmental Stepping-Stones in Early Childhood Curriculum and Instruction

TRANSITION TO SCHOOL: LEARNING TO LEARN AND BEHAVE

Proactive Best Professional Practices

Increasingly, attention is given to the "criterion for the next environment" to plan for the transition from early childhood to primary school and beyond. The following approaches help educational professionals deal effectively with these developmental and individual differences among students at transition to kindergarten: (a) screen to identify developmental and instructional levels of beginning kindergartners; (b) teach developmentally appropriate skills for kindergartners, with necessary individual tailoring of instruction; (c) evaluate response to instruction; and (d) reach out to parents through questionnaires sent home to identify any current or prior concerns or problems. The team can review responses to the parent questionnaires and determine whether parents should be contacted to discuss these concerns; parents who did not return the questionnaire should be asked the questions over the phone or in person. If the parent does not read or speak English, an interpreter should participate in the face-to-face interview. The time devoted to this initial reaching out to parents can go a long way toward optimizing the child's transition to kindergarten and preventing future problems, as Honor Role Model 3 has shown (see Chapter 2). Many parents do not trust schools because of the bad experiences they had during their school years. Listening to parents' concerns about their child and showing interest and empathy contribute to building positive relationships with the school that are in the child's best interest.

Special emphasis should be placed on language development prior to school and during the transition to schooling for two reasons. First, any aural or oral language problems prior to transition to schooling can be predictive of language learning problems during the school years. Second, instruction and learning activities during early childhood depend greatly on processing and producing a variety of kinds of language, as explained next.

Aural Language—Listening

Many think that children learn aural language (through the ears) and oral language (through the mouth) during the preschool years and that the purpose of kindergarten is to help them begin to learn academic skills such as reading, writing, and math. Despite this widespread belief, listening and speaking are important language systems for learning all academic skills throughout schooling and functioning outside school.

The first lesson about language by ear (listening) that kindergartners need to learn is that teachers' instructional talk heard at school is different from conversation in or outside school. In conversations, turns are frequent and relatively short, but the teacher's turn at talk in school goes on for longer stretches of time. Students also learn to listen to turns at talk by other students. It is important, beginning in kindergarten, to learn when to be quiet and listen and when it is OK to talk. Teachers often use a nonverbal signal—touching their ears with their hand or turning lights on or off—to signal nonverbally when children should be quiet and listen.

Kindergartners also need to learn that teachers use talk for many different purposes, each of which requires a different kind of listening: Sometimes the teacher gives information. Sometimes the teacher talks while demonstrating procedures for students to use. Sometimes the teacher gives directions for students to follow. When children have trouble with listening skills, teachers should confer with the interdisciplinary team to pinpoint why: (a) middle ear or sensorimotor hearing loss, (b) attending to aural input through the ears, (c) processing heard language, or (d) some combination of these. Attention difficulties can interfere with processing heard language, and difficulties processing heard language can interfere with attending to the teacher talking. The team can then determine how best to help the child with whatever appears to be causing the problem.

Oral Language—Speaking

Kindergartners also have to learn that talking at school during learning activities may be different from talking in conversations. Not only do they not get as many turns to talk but they also have to wait while many others take their turn. This skill of knowing when one can and cannot talk requires considerable self-regulation of internal language processing and overt language behaviors. Teachers can use nonverbal signals, such as pointing to their mouth when talking is appropriate for everyone and pointing to the one child chosen at a particular time for a turn to talk. Children who have difficulty controlling when and how well they talk should be discussed with the interdisciplinary team to determine whether the problem is with the child's oral language, speech, self-regulation skills, or a combination.

It is also important to have times when children are encouraged to talk with each other. Some children come from homes that do not encourage and sometimes discourage verbal communication. Children may be socialized in the home to use language differently than how language is used at school. In some cases, parents have little formal education and knowledge of how verbal interactions with adults at home can stimulate language development. They may believe that "children are to be seen and not heard." One way to encourage productive talk at school is to encourage children to think aloud (talk) while writing and orally sharing their writing with their writing buddies, a visible audience, as in conversation. Silence is not always golden.

Integrating Listening and Speaking With Reading to Create Functional Reading Systems

Learning to read requires *mapping*, that is, creating connections among different societies of mind (systems that specialize in specific functions)—in this case, different language systems: aural language (through the ears), oral language (through the mouth), and written language (input through the eyes or output through the hands). By listening to language, kindergartners become aware of all the levels of aural language and their relationships to levels of written and oral language. Not only does each of the levels of language in these different language systems make separate contributions but there may also be accumulating contributions from the lower levels of language to higher levels of language across different language systems (see Exhibit 4.1).

At the *subword level*, children need to learn the interrelationships among the subword and word levels for (a) sounds in heard words, (b) single letters or letter groups in written words, and (c) subword sound–letter correspondences in the alphabetic principle and specific whole words.

At the *word level*, they need to learn abstract patterns in spoken words (identity, word position, and sequencing of individual sounds in heard words) and in written words (identity, word positions, and sequencing of single letters or letter groups) and subword units (single and multiple syllables and parts of syllables—initial sound or blend and the remaining part of the syllable), and the stress patterns (musical melody) for words with more than one syllable. They also need to learn single word meanings and the interrelationships among word and syntax levels: (a) vocabulary meanings in heard, viewed, spoken, and written words that may depend on both bases (word parts without any affixes) and suffixes that mark parts of speech and (b) vocabulary meanings for words sharing common pronunciations but different word-specific spelling depending on sentence context (e.g., *too* and *two)* or that share common spellings but different meanings (e.g., *ball* as a round object or *ball* as a formal dance).

At the *syntax level*, children need to learn about how words, which have different functions—to signal content (nouns, verbs, adjectives, adverbs) or function (prepositions, conjunctions, pronouns, articles)—are combined using different word orders and packaging units (phrases and clauses) in sentences.

At the *discourse level*, children need to learn (a) how sentences are combined sequentially and in larger text structures and (b) how words and phrases are used as cohesive ties, such as repeating a prior word or using words such as *first* and *second* or pronouns to link sentences and create coherent text that ties ideas together.

By listening and looking as adults read books, kindergartners begin to learn how the sounds in spoken words might map onto written words, word meaning might map onto written words, small groups of ordered words might map onto sentences, and how longer stretches of talk might map onto written text. However, this mapping process is more likely to succeed if the kindergartners can also talk—convert written words into sounds (predict and say orally the next word in the sentence when the teacher stops), talk about the meaning of specific written words in the book, talk about the meaning of a sentence in the book, and talk about the unfolding text.

As programmatic research at the University of Pittsburgh by Isabelle Beck and advisory panel member Margaret McKeown has shown, this talk is most likely to achieve the desired results if teachers *scaffold* it—that is, guide it with instructional cues—and the child's attention to language is engaged by the act of talking. For example, when reading a book to kindergartners, the teacher can ask questions when important events in the story unfold. Another helpful approach is for the teacher to introduce key ideas before reading and then ask the children to talk about the ideas as the story moves along. When the book is completed, different children might orally share what they learned from the book as a whole. For example, the teacher could invite one child to share "What happened first?" Then another child could be invited to add "What happened next?" Yet another child could be invited to explain "Why was that important?" This collaborative sharing facilitates children attending to peers' ideas and creating connections among the ideas and, thus, comprehension.

Another way to foster comprehension is to provide children the opportunity to interact with language that is more sophisticated than what they can read on their own in books. During early childhood, children's thinking and oral language skills are typically advanced well beyond their written word identification levels. Reading aloud to young children from books that match their thinking and oral language levels rather than their reading levels gives them content to think about and discuss. In the process they learn that the purpose of reading is to comprehend text—learn from it, think about it, and discuss it. Giving children opportunities to talk engages their minds through their mouths more than does only passive listening through the ears. Again, children are learning that they cannot all talk at the same time, but at the same time taking turns at talk contributes to their learning.

Learning to Identify Written Words

Kindergartners benefit from *sound games*—for example, listening to a word the teacher pronounces and then saying it again without a designated part such as a syllable or phoneme—and *looking games*—for example, carefully naming each letter in a word, closing their eyes and seeing the word in the mind's eye, and then answering, without opening their eyes, questions the teacher poses about all the letters in the word, a single letter, or letter group in various word positions. The sound games help children develop phonological awareness of syllable and phoneme units in words that will help them map subword units in heard language onto subword units in written language. The looking games help them develop orthographic awareness of subword units in written words onto which they can map the spoken word units. Oral reading activities are necessary to learn to map the spoken word units onto the written word units and synthesize those mappings to pronounce a whole written word—that is, transform it into a spoken word with appropriate stress patterns and intonation.

Informal reading inventories can be used to identify instructional levels for oral reading, which in many kindergartens at the beginning of the year range from nonreader to second- or third-grade level. These instructional levels can be used to group children so that teachers can adapt instruction to groups of children with comparable zones of proximal development for optimal learning in response to instruction. In addition, all oral reading should be followed by talking about the meaning of what was just read—for example, retelling or summarizing or predicting what will happen next.

Learning to Understand and Use Word Meaning

Vocabulary instruction is also important during early childhood and goes well beyond learning to identify words by reading them aloud. Instruction should cover both familiar word meanings and new word meanings. Like other skills, learning vocabulary word meaning benefits from drawing on language by ear, mouth, eye, and hand. On the one hand, word meanings used in everyday conversations can be taught and reviewed as classmates listen and share orally and also during written activities in which children read and write about the same words. On the other hand, beginning in early childhood, children benefit from teacher-guided instructional activities to introduce meanings that are specific to academic language used at school across the curriculum in various content areas (academic register).

Children are unlikely to learn academic word meanings on their own without guidance from the teacher. Vocabulary meanings taught should be based on those most essential to understanding the words in the content areas of the curriculum during early childhood—for example, math, science, and social studies, as well as reading. Vocabulary instruction might include definitions but should go well beyond looking definitions up in a dictionary to include *bountiful language interactions*. Beck and McKeown, who introduced the term, also introduced the concept of three tiers of vocabulary instruction: basic words, words useful across multiple contexts, and subject specific words. Young children's language comprehension benefits from talking about basic word meanings (Tier 1), finding and using them in multiple texts (Tier 2), and applying them in their own writing, reading, and speaking activities in the classroom for different content areas of the curriculum (Tier 3). Not only single word meaning (Tier 1) but also word meaning in passages should be taught. For example, for a Tier 2 vocabulary activity, the teacher could explain what a word means in student-friendly language: "If you are *eager* to do something, you can hardly wait to do it." The teacher would then ask students to apply the word to their own lives ("What is something you are *eager* to do?") in oral or written sentences. In addition, beginning in the primary grades, teaching math-specific vocabulary (Tier 3) is critical for learning math. In addition, as first shown by Mann and colleagues, play with language—for example, reading and talking about riddles and jokes—can also develop word meanings for academic register.

Integrating Oral Language and Written Language to Create Functional Writing Systems

Alphabet letters are the building blocks of written expression. Kindergartners should learn to name letters and write letters—names serve as retrieval cues in accessing letters in memory. They should learn both lower case letters (most frequent in written language) and upper case letters (easier to differentiate and mark sentence beginnings). In the United States, manuscript (printed) letters are typically taught before cursive. Children who have difficulty in learning to write letters can be discussed with the interdisciplinary team, especially the occupational therapist, to find approaches to helping them with any sensory and motor processes that are interfering with their ability to form letters. Input from the classroom teacher, who has expertise in teaching handwriting, can also be valuable. The important general principle to keep in mind, from the perspective of an interdisciplinary framework, is that both internal mental processes in the mind's eye (referred to as orthographic coding and processing) as well as motor output (planning, control, and production) processes are involved in producing letters.

Kindergartners can also express ideas in writing and should be given an opportunity to do so. Their invented spellings will reflect their emerging knowledge of how written words reflect the sounds they hear in spoken words. Their texts are typically a T-unit (independent plus dependent clauses) in length, as is also typical of turns at talk in conversation.

Jennifer Katahira (Honor Role Model 11), a kindergarten teacher in a low-income, culturally diverse urban school, developed a novel program for integrating language by mouth, eyes, hands, and ears and was given a small grant by a local philanthropic organization to evaluate its effectiveness. The components of this innovative approach, engaging all the language systems, included the following:

- Daily modeling by the teacher of the "what I think, I can say; what I say, I can write" strategy for composing a sentence based on a topic of the day, with students in the class offering suggestions for spelling the words the teacher thought aloud and then wrote on the board.
- Daily writing by each student on a self-selected topic and then thinking aloud about the topic while translating the thoughts into spoken words and each spoken word into spelling using small plastic "Sunshine" cards published by the Wright Company that depict pictures of common objects with the letter that stands for the first sound in each picture. Children were also encouraged to illustrate their writing.
- Daily oral sharing by the author reading orally what was written to a small group of "writing buddies" who first listened and then discussed what they liked about the writing and what they might change in the next draft for the classroom book that is published to share their writing with the whole school.

This master teacher discovered four cognitive processes in writing that writing researchers have identified: (a) planning and translating (by thinking aloud to capture flow of ideas into language), (b) transcription (using the first sound in a picture to identify the letter that goes with the sound and then using the viewed letter as model for writing it), (c) reviewing what is written while sharing it with writing buddies, and (d) revising future drafts to communicate effectively with an audience. Research conducted by the university partnering with the school showed that Katahira's approach was effective. Measures of reading and related skills were administered at the beginning and end of the year. Daily writing samples were collected and analyzed. All children were able to express ideas in writing and read their writing to writing buddies. By end of the year all children but one were reading at the 90th percentile or better on a standardized test of reading; the one who was not was at the 70th percentile.

Math

Kindergartners learn to go beyond rote counting (naming numbers by mouth) to counting quantity with one-to-one correspondence (each counted item is tagged with only one count word) by coordinating hand (touching to keep track of the count) and mouth (naming). They should be given frequent opportunities to count objects at school and at home by touching them with their hand as they increase in quantity one by one while they name the numbers in counting order. This sensory–motor experience engages not only the mind and the internal representation of quantity along a linear number line in the mind but also the hand and mouth. The most important counting concepts children need to come to understand are *cardinality* (i.e., the last number word in the count represents the number of counted items) and *ordinality* (i.e., number words and quantities can be ordered from smaller to larger).

Kindergartners also need to link this internal representation of number (cognitive concept of quantity) with writing by hand the numerals (visual symbols of specific quantities). They also need to learn to link this internal representation of number with the eye by reading numeral names they see, write, and say (overtly or covertly). Then they need to learn to link this internal representation of number with the aural and oral vocabulary of early math words such as *add* (count objects forward) and *subtract* (count objects backward). It is of critical importance that children understand that numerals represent specific quantities that can be ordered (e.g., on a number line) and that they are related to one another. For example, 5 can be broken into 4 and 1 or 3 and 2. These relations are related to addition ($3 + 2 = 5$) and subtraction ($5 - 3 = 2$).

Kindergartners also need to learn to draw by hand and name by mouth basic shapes such as horizontal and vertical lines, circles, triangles, and squares, the building blocks of future geometry learning. They can also learn about shapes by building objects from component shapes and solving puzzles that require putting shapes together to construct larger wholes. And they should start to think about the features of these shapes—for instance, that a square has four points, a triangle three points, and a circle none. From the beginning, kindergartners should be engaged in thinking about quantity in the everyday world and using all their sensory and motor modalities in solving everyday math problems.

Assessing Response to Instruction

As shown in Exhibit 4.2, the key skills to assess during kindergarten are (a) accuracy in naming lower and upper case manuscript letters and in naming numerals; (b) accuracy in writing letters and numerals when copying from a model or writing a letter or numeral from its dictated name; (c) accuracy of syllable and phoneme awareness in heard words in the "mind's ear"; (d) accuracy of analysis of letter identity and order in written words in the mind's eye; (e) accuracy of one-to-one correspondence in counting to 20; (f) aural language vocabulary, syntax, and oral comprehension; (g) identification of the cardinal value of number words and numerals; and (h) self-regulation of behavior.

For the most part, teacher-made materials can be used for this assessment given at the beginning, middle, and near end of the school year, which is curriculum-based assessment instruction. The assessment can be done, for example, by writing each lower case and each upper case letter on a 3 × 5 card. Shuffle the cards and ask each child to name each letter; keep a running record of which ones the child can accurately name. Then show the cards again and ask the child to copy the letter; note which ones are accurate and legible. Next, say the name of each letter and ask the child to write it from dictation in either lower case or upper case form. Again, keep a running record of accuracy. Finally, ask the child to write the whole alphabet in order from memory in lower case letters; score this for accuracy.

Repeat this procedure for naming and writing numerals 1 to 20. In addition, ask the child to count a set of 20 objects, and note whether a different object is touched as the numbers are named for increasing order in correct counting order. To assess phonological awareness and orthographic awareness, create a set of items on the basis of the sound games and looking games used for instruction. To assess knowledge of cardinal value, present the child with a pile of objects (e.g., small toys) and ask them to hand you 3, 5, 6 toys, and so on. Children who understand cardinal value will count the correct number and hand the toys to the teacher; those who do not will grab a handful toys and hand them to the teacher.

Results at the beginning and middle of the year inform instructional goals and activities that follow. Results at the end of school year are shared with the next year's teacher to inform instructional goals and activities at beginning of next grade. Because of the importance of early identification and treatment of oral and written language learning disability, standardized tests should be used to assess aural and oral vocabulary, aural and oral syntax, and aural comprehension and oral expression of all kindergartners at midyear (see Chapters 8 and 9, this volume). Ratings for self-regulation of attention and behavior should also be obtained from both teachers and parents across settings because of the importance of these skills for self-regulation of learning and behavior.

GRADE 1

Aural Language—Listening

First graders continue to learn to process teachers' instructional talk, especially language used in decontextualized ways without the nonverbal and situational cues typically used in informal conversation. First graders also continue to learn that they must wait to take their turn to ask or answer questions during instruction and to listen when other students take their turn to ask or answer questions. They also continue to learn that teachers use instructional talk for many different purposes, ranging from giving information (*declarative knowledge*) to explaining and modeling steps of an action or operation (*procedural knowledge*), to giving directions for students to listen to and then follow (listening comprehension), to setting rules and expectations for behavior at school.

As with younger children, difficulty with attention might interfere with processing heard language, and processing heard language might result in inattention. Children with difficulty in one or more of these skills should be referred to the instructional or behavioral support team for problem-solving consultation and, if warranted, branching diagnostic assessment for aural language. For example, if the underlying problem causing inattention is difficulty in processing heard language, instruction should focus on learning to pay attention to aural language; medication for attention-deficit/hyperactivity disorder (ADHD) may not be warranted. Only if the underlying problem is found to be ADHD would medication be warranted. Other children may have *speech perception* problems (difficulty processing the sounds in the speech they hear) or *speech production* problems (articulation or stuttering) and should be referred to the speech–language pathologist (SLP) on the interdisciplinary team.

Oral Language—Speaking

First graders continue to learn that there are appropriate and inappropriate times for them to talk and also that there are appropriate and inappropriate kinds of language that can be used at school. Language can be inappropriate because certain words are considered in bad taste or because they hurt the feelings of others. Teachers can also provide helpful verbal feedback about how children express themselves in oral language when it is appropriate to talk. For example, they can offer verbal praise and ask questions so that children elaborate what they are saying or clarify when it is not clear. Teaching children self-talk strategies to self-regulate and manage their behavior at school can be helpful to all first graders and those with self-regulation difficulties in particular. Children who have difficulty controlling when they talk should be discussed with the interdisciplinary team to determine whether the problem is with their oral language or speech skills and/or with their self-regulation skills. Other children have difficulty producing speech that is intelligible to others. They should be referred to the SLP on the interdisciplinary team to identify the underlying problem and recommend individually tailored instruction for that problem as well as for developing oral expression in general.

Reciprocal teaching in which children take turns playing the role of teacher during reading activities helps them develop their oral and written language skills. Likewise, asking children to explain math concepts to their peers helps them develop both language and math skills. Finally, using oral language when the whole class problem solves how to handle violations of classroom rules provides a way to develop *pragmatics*, the social use of language.

Reading

Research has shown that beginning readers benefit from (a) sound games to develop *phonological awareness* of syllables and phonemes within syllables in the heard words children reproduce without designated syllables or phonemes; (b) looking games that help them develop *orthographic awareness* of single letters or letter groups in words children first spell, then see in their mind's eye while they answer questions about the identity of letter(s) in targeted positions; (c) abstracting *phonotactic patterns* (deciding whether a made-up word without meaning could be a real English word because the sound elements, positions, and sequences occur in English); (d) abstracting *orthotactic patterns* (deciding whether a made-up word without meaning could be a real English word because the letter identities, positions, and sequences occur in English); and (e) learning and applying the alphabetic principle (correspondences between one- and two-letter graphemes and phonemes) to decode written words—that is, convert them into spoken words.

Often referred to as *phonics*, the alphabetic principle is learned readily if applied to the most frequent words in the spoken and written language, which were identified by Edward Fry and his students at Rutgers University for Grades 1 through 6. Decoding is learned through both orally stating rules of grapheme–phoneme correspondence (declarative knowledge) and applying the correspondences in sequential order to decode written words (procedural knowledge). *Graphemes* are one- or two-level units that correspond to phonemes. *Phonemes* are abstract categories for sounds in heard words (the smallest difference in sound that makes a difference in meaning), rather than the larger phonetic units for producing syllables in spoken words (coarticulated continuous vowels and segmental consonants). Nevertheless, the abstract phoneme categories provide helpful clues in applying sequential grapheme–phoneme correspondences at the subword level to pronounce all the syllables at the word level which vary in the relative stress (emphasis) given to them.

Informal reading inventories are used to identify instructional levels for first-grade oral reading activities for real words without and with passage context and reading comprehension (answering factual and inferential questions and retelling passages from memory). Answers to factual questions are stated in a written passage, whereas answers to inferential questions are not stated but can be inferred from what is stated. The instructional levels are used to group children at comparable instructional levels, that is, zones of proximal development (see Vygotsky et al., 1980).

Two widely used approaches to teaching oral reading skills for connected text include the following. For the first approach, a different strategy is used each day of the week. On Monday, the teacher reads the passage orally while the children listen and point with a finger to each word as the teacher pronounces it. On Tuesday, both the teacher and the children read in unison the same passage that the teacher had read during finger-point reading on Monday. On Wednesday, during "buddy reading," the children read the same text to a partner that had been read collectively in choral reading on Tuesday. On Thursday, the children practice the same text alone and then take it home to read to their parents. On Friday, the teacher listens to each child read the same text a final time while the teacher or aid keeps a running record of which words are not pronounced correctly. These words can be used for future instruction on word decoding with the group or individuals; the percentage of correctly read words can be recorded each week and kept in the child's portfolio for progress monitoring. For the second approach, the teacher listens to the child read orally and records the rate at which the child can read the text independently with a designated level of accuracy (e.g., 90%). Then repeated readings of the same text continue until a criterion level of mastery on the basis of rate and accuracy is reached. After that, a new goal for reading fluency is set. Reading rates for specific levels of accuracy are recorded on a graph kept in the child's portfolio, which can be inspected for growth over time.

Writing

Research supports teaching two *transcription skills*—handwriting and spelling—as well as *translation skills* (transforming ideas into written language) so that children develop functional writing systems across the subword (letter), word (spelling), and text (composing) levels. At the beginning of the year, first-grade teachers should consult with the kindergarten teachers to find out whether each child had met kindergarten benchmarks for copying letters (from visual retrieval cues), writing letters from dictated names (verbal retrieval cues), and writing the alphabet legibly from memory. For those children who did not meet the kindergarten benchmarks, these skills should continue to be targeted for instruction and progress monitoring during first grade along with the target first-grade handwriting goals for automaticity and sustainability of handwriting. This collaborative approach fosters developmental continuity across grade levels.

First-grade handwriting instruction should teach writing the alphabet from memory in alphabetic order, with a focus on both legibility and automaticity. When letters are written legibly, others can recognize them whether there is or is not word context. When letters are written automatically, they are formed the same way each time and require fewer mental resources to produce them quickly, freeing up limited mental resources for other writing processes, such as spelling and composing. In contrast to kindergarten children, who often draw their letters—starting at the bottom rather than top or forming strokes in variable orders each time a letter is written—first-grade children should learn to write letters the same way each time—starting at the top and with consistent order of strokes. Automatic legible letter writing can be assessed by the number of legible letters that can be written in correct alphabetic order within the first 15 seconds when writing the alphabet from memory in order. Research has shown that initial automatic access and retrieval gives way after 15 seconds to more controlled, strategic processes. An evidence-based approach to teaching automatic legible letter writing combines two components for practicing each letter of the alphabet once in a lesson: (a) studying numbered arrow cues for forming each stroke in order for the named letter followed by (b) holding the named letter in the mind's eye and then opening the eyes and writing the named letter from memory. Research also shows that another developmentally appropriate goal is to develop sustained letter writing over time—for example, copying all the words in a paragraph legibly over time without sacrificing accuracy.

First-grade spelling instruction, like word reading instruction, should be based on the alphabetic principle, but in this case in the spelling direction, which is not always the same as the reading direction. For example, in the reading direction the letter *a* is typically pronounced like the phoneme for the vowel in the first syllable of *table* or the first syllable of *candle* or the schwa (unstressed sound) in *about;* but in the spelling direction the phoneme sound that corresponds to the vowel in the first syllable of *table* can be spelled as *a, ai, ay, ey,* or *eigh* in different word contexts. As with decoding for oral reading, the most frequent correspondences between phonemes and graphemes for spelling should be taught for the most frequent words in the language or words that children use most frequently in their spelling. In addition, children should learn to spell single words from dictation as well as words in the context of dictated sentences, which provides the semantic context for choosing among word spellings for words pronounced the same.

First graders write longer text on average than kindergartners and begin to write texts that reflect different genres—for example, narrative or storytelling, and expository–informational. Prompts in the form of single-word topics may help some beginning writers generate text if they cannot self-generate text on their own. Many beginning writers benefit from "thinking aloud" as they compose, perhaps because talking engages the phonological loop of working memory which supports the translation of cognitions into written language.

Math

First graders may benefit from continuing to count objects or pictured objects, but they are also developing the ability to count along an internal number line in their working memory. Two instructional approaches help first graders develop this internal number line, which contributes to their continued learning about counting and its relationship to basic math operations.

The first approach engages their sensory, motor, and oral language systems to link an external number line with their internal number line. Each child has on his or her desk a masking tape or paper number line on which numerals are written in increasing counting order from left to right. To grasp that the number line is linear and the distance between each successive whole number is identical no matter where you are on the line, teachers can point out the start (0), end point (100), and the middle (50). Learning math facts is linked to the number line by naming orally each numeral the children touch, one number at a time, as they move forward for addition or backward for subtraction from a starting point.

For addition, the child counts forward from 0 by touching the number line for each number from left to right in the addition fact, and the final number at the destination point is the sum. Each time the child touches a numeral, the child names that numeral. After the journey by hand and mouth along the number line, the child writes the basic number fact by hand using numerals and the addition operation sign. For subtraction, touching the number line starts at the largest number and proceeds backward in a right-to-left direction along the number line for the number of steps in counting order for the number to be subtracted. The final number touched is the difference between the two numbers. Again the number fact can be written for the subtraction using the numerals and the appropriate sign for subtraction. In this way, the student has engaged cognitive (internal number lines and quantitative concepts related to counting order and basic operations in math operations), oral language (naming numerals), motor (finger movement and touching, naming by mouth, finger planning, control, and production of written numerals), and sensory (somatosensory from touch, and auditory from speech) systems to support math learning. Thus, multiple functional systems contribute to learning math.

The second approach facilitates the internalization of the number line in working memory. Children are given simple addition and subtraction problems to solve as mental arithmetic. For example, the teacher says the following "if you start at (a number), add (a second number) and then add (a third number), what is the ending number?" Or, "if you start at (a number), subtract (a second number), and then add (a third number), what is the ending number?"

First graders also should be engaged in problem solving—not only with word problems that the teacher poses but also child-generated math problems (see Exhibit 4.3 for integrating problem solving with the other component math skills). Some early everyday math problem solving can be linked to a classroom economy in which children learn quantitative skills related to money while learning to perform classroom jobs for which they earn "money." Board and card games and building games (e.g., blocks, Tinker Toys, Lego) during free choice time can also contribute to learning beginning math skills and geometric relationships. Exploration through play can be an important contributor to early math learning, but it is also important to keep in mind the need for explicit, teacher-guided learning activities in learning math. Children do not learn math solely by discovering it through play or solely by being explicitly told about it without having opportunities to explore how math relates to their daily life.

Reading-Writing

Research has shown a clear link between reading and writing. For example, instruction designed to improve handwriting automaticity also resulted in improvements in word reading. Instruction in spelling also resulted in improved word reading. Many instructional resources teach word reading and spelling in an integrated way. Many first-grade classroom assignments require children to write about what they read and, for example, answer questions. Also, first graders should have opportunities to read what they write to others.

Math-Writing

Writing skills for math are necessary in first grade for writing single numerals, writing numbers in the context of place value, and writing addition and subtraction facts and operations. Some first graders can do mental arithmetic at a higher level than they can do written arithmetic because of problems with writing the numerals or understanding place value, especially when regrouping from the one's place to the 10's place is needed in addition or from the 10's place to the one's place in subtraction.

Math-Reading-Writing-Oral Language

Some first graders have difficulty with math because they do not understand the math vocabulary—for example, the meaning of the word *sum* or the meaning of the word *difference* used in instruction. They may not understand how to interpret the phrases used in math word problems, such as, "How many more does this person have than that person?" First graders benefit from instruction in math-specific oral and written vocabulary and written phrases used in oral and written word problems.

Science

First graders learn the ideas and the practice of science from hands-on experiments—for example, building models of neurons talking to each other in the brain from pipe cleaners and balls made from Play-Doh. They also learn from illustrated books that explain science facts and concepts in simple text. Also, they learn from talking about facts and concepts in science and listening to the teacher and classmates talk about those ideas. They begin to learn to record their observations in writing.

Social Studies

First graders learn about people, the communities in which they live and work, and history through (a) activities that illustrate concepts about people, (b) books with simple text and nonverbal illustrations, (c) group discussions, and (d) listening to discussions and multimedia presentations on videos or films.

Assessing Response to Instruction and Branching Diagnosis

The key skills to assess for all first graders are (a) accuracy of real-word reading on lists without context clues and/or passages without context clues; (b) accuracy of pseudoword reading (decoding); (c) vocabulary understanding; (d) sentence comprehension; (e) text comprehension; (f) automatic letter naming; (g) automatic, legible letter writing on an alphabet writing task from memory (lower-case manuscript letters); (h) sustained handwriting on sentence and paragraph copy tasks; (i) spelling dictated real and pseudoword (j) composition fluency for both sentences and text; (k) automatic, legible numeral writing from 1 to 20; and (l) accuracy of math facts for addition to sums of 20 and related subtraction facts. Only accuracy of real-word and pseudoword reading is assessed in first grade because, just as children have to walk before they run, the first developmental milestone is to become accurate in oral decoding that is grade-appropriate (see Chapter 3 for the important distinction between accuracy and rate in word reading). Children who lag behind in any of the target first-grade skills should be referred to the problem-solving consultation team to discuss supplementary interventions and assessments with branching diagnosis to identify possible reasons why a child is not making progress in specific developmental milestones. If these are still not met by end of first grade, the second-grade teacher should be alerted to keep working on them.

GRADE 2

Aural Language—Listening

Play with language has been shown to be an excellent way to develop metalinguistic awareness. Second graders are learning to enjoy riddles and jokes, which rely on similarly pronounced words having different meanings. Teachers can start the day or a lesson with an orally presented riddle or joke with the class and have children discuss why it does or does not make them laugh. Laughter also helps children develop a sense of humor, which can facilitate resiliency and create a positive affect in both language and life in general. Second graders continue to benefit from listening to teachers read high-quality children's literature to them and from teacher-guided classroom discussions of what was read.

Oral Language—Speaking

Second graders enjoy reading short plays as a class or in a small group. Play scripts have several advantages for developing oral language skills. First, the turns at talk are relatively short. Second, reading play scripts is an enjoyable way to practice oral reading skills with expression. Third, while reading a play script, a child can stand up, move, make facial expressions and gestures, as used in both real-life oral language expression and in plays that are being acted out. In the process of reading play scripts, some children may discover a passion and talent for drama (another way ideas can be expressed and a way in which some earn their living as adults).

Reading

Riddles and jokes can also be presented in written form for children to see as they discuss. Children enjoy keeping these riddles or jokes of the day in a folder they can reread when they need a laugh. Second-grade reading instruction should continue to refine linguistic awareness, oral decoding, oral reading fluency, vocabulary meaning, and comprehension skills for both sentences and text as outlined for first grade. What changes is the goal to become not only accurate but also automatic in recognizing familiar written words, fast in oral decoding of unfamiliar words, and fluent in oral reading of sentences and text. Oral reading fluency has a bidirectional relationship with reading comprehension. On the one hand, the more fluent the child is in coordinating word identification through automatic recognition or fast, controlled decoding and the word meaning and syntactic structures, the better the comprehension of the unfolding text will be. On the other hand, linguistic awareness, vocabulary knowledge, and syntactic and discourse comprehension all contribute to oral reading fluency.

Reading choice time is as important as instruction because emerging skills are mastered only by practicing them. Students are more likely to engage in sustained practice of their reading skills if they derive pleasure from reading, and the opportunity to choose which books to read (e.g., from a classroom library) contributes to this pleasure. In second grade, the selections should include chapter books. Second graders typically consider reading chapter books rather than shorter books without chapters as a concrete symbol of their success as a reader. Subscriptions to magazines on science, nature, technology, cars, and other topics of personal interest also offer important choices for free reading. Many parents evaluate whether their children are learning to read well by whether their children choose to read on their own and seem to derive pleasure from it.

Writing

Second graders continue to need explicit instruction in transcription skills (handwriting and spelling) and translation (strategies for expressing their ideas in multiple genres of writing). Given the many demands on classroom time, the good news is that effective handwriting instruction does not require a lot of time. Just like the orchestra tunes up their instruments before practice or a public concert, second-grade writers continue to benefit from a brief "writer's warm-up" in which they practice writing each letter of the alphabet once from dictation before beginning the more challenging translation work. The teacher can review these to determine which letters individual students have not mastered, and invite them to practice them using the combined strategies outlined for first graders (studying numbered arrow cues for letter formation, writing named letters from memory, and comparing them with a model). The advantage of devoting 5 to 10 minutes a day to automatic legible letter writing is that achieving this developmental milestone in writing frees up the limited space in working memory for the more demanding tasks of translating ideas into writing—choosing words, spelling them, and organizing words into sentences and sentences into text.

Second graders continue to require instruction in spelling so that they can communicate their ideas using correctly spelled real words that others can identify and understand. The goal of spelling instruction continues to be for students to learn how the sounds of spoken words are interrelated with the letters in written words, but by second grade the morphology of written words is increasingly relevant in learning to spell. Both spoken and written words have a *morphology* (base words with optional prefixes and/or suffixes), which bridges words by ear or mouth and words by eye or hand (see Chapter 9). At the second grade level, *inflectional suffixes*, which mark tense (present vs. past), number (singular— just one—or plural—more than one), and comparison (of two things or of more than two things), are grade-appropriate instructional tools. In addition, the derivational suffix *ing* appears in many word forms in second-grade reading and writing (e.g., *singing*, which converts a verb with the rime *ing* in the base to a noun with the derivational suffix *ing*, which has the same spelling but now marks grammar function). Second graders benefit from (a) spelling single words from dictation, receiving immediate feedback as to whether they wrote the correctly spelled word or not and if not, why, and (b) how to spell correctly from dictation, again with immediate feedback. Research has shown that mastery of word-specific spelling takes many multiple experiences in spelling the same word from memory with and without sentence context, which helps select the correct spelling for a particular meaning and pronunciation. Devoting 10 to 15 minutes a day of class time to spelling can benefit both the composing and reading second graders do.

Second graders also benefit from a variety of experiences in expressing their ideas in writing: (a) personal writing—for example, during free writing in journals; (b) social writing to share ideas with classmates and receive feedback from them and the teacher during the author's turn; and (c) writing different kinds of text, referred to as *genres*, such as narratives and informative essays. Teachers can support this learning of genre-specific written expression by (a) providing prompts, often in form of a phrase or sentence, that generate different kinds of genre-specific writing and (b) teaching strategies for generating text that are genre-specific.

Strategies for generating stories might include a series of *W* questions: Think about the characters in the story (*who*), the setting (*where*), and the plot or series of events (*what* and *when*). Strategies for generating information essays might be to add information in steps about the topic: Make a comment about the topic and then add another comment and so on until you cannot think of any more comments about the topic.

Math

In second grade, the target math skills include place value, calculation procedures involved in column addition and subtraction, and continuing to automatize basic addition and subtraction math facts (easy recall). Once children can write the numerals 1 to 0 legibly and automatically, they need to learn to use the small set of 10 numerals (digits) to represent an unlimited number of numbers by arranging them in places. As children move to numbers more than 10 it is important that they understand that these numbers can be broken into sets of 10s and sets of ones—that is, 12 is one 10 and two ones, which provides the basis for coming to understand place value. To teach place value, teachers need to point out that, unlike reading, which in English proceeds from left to right, in math the places in which numerals occur proceed in a right to left direction to signal what a total quantity is. For example, the same numeral signals a different quantity in the one's place, the ten's place to the left of the one's place, and hundred's place to the left of the 10's place. Understanding this place value concept, which is the syntax of math, much as the sentence is the syntax of written language, is critical to learning how to perform math calculations for addition or subtraction (as well as multiplication and division in later grades) of more than one multiplace number.

All the relevant systems in the interdisciplinary framework should be engaged in learning place value and its application to multiplace, multicolumn numbers. Sensory and motor systems can be used to manipulate beads on wires that represent multiplace numbers, which are named using language by mouth and then symbolized in written symbols using language by hand. For example, the child first uses beads on wires representing places to symbolize a quantity in the one's place (e.g., 7) to which another number (e.g., 3) is added. To show the sum of the two numbers, all beads are removed from the one's place and one bead is added to the 10's place. This regrouping process can then be represented with a written two-place number using two sequenced numerals, 10.

The beads on wires can also be used to learn the steps in the addition operation in a place value framework (e.g., $17 + 3 = 20$): First the child places seven beads on the wire for the one's place and one bead on the wire for the 10's place. Then the child adds three beads to the one's place, and because the sum equals 10 or more, regroups the sum by removing all beads from the one's place and adding one bead to the 10's place. Throughout the process the child names the quantity of beads on each wire and explains the regrouping process. Then the child writes the addition operation in numerals with place value while naming the steps in the operation: "Seventeen plus 3 equals 20, which is written with a zero as place holder for no quantity in the first place on right and 2 in the 10's place to stand for the original 10 plus added group of 10."

This process of applying place value to writing multiplace numbers, regrouping across places, and performing computations on multiplace numbers can also be applied to subtraction. For subtraction, a multiplace number is first represented with the correct number of beads on each wire, followed by taking away a designated single or multiplace number, with regrouping if necessary. Again, each step of the operation can be named and explained and then expressed in writing. This process can also be learned and practiced with other kinds of concrete aids that can be manipulated by hand to learn the concept of place value. For example, small blocks are often used where blocks for each place have a different color and 10 small blocks of one color are equal in length to one block of another color that symbolizes 10 times the first color.

In learning the application of place value to calculation, second graders also learn that computation is a journey through space (across adjacent places and rows) and time (sequenced steps). In contrast to the number line where that journey is along one-dimensional linear space, for subtraction where the numbers are arranged vertically, the journey is along two-dimensional space (right-left and top-down axes). Although basic number facts are often practiced in a horizontal arrangement, as in algebra equations, the vertical arrangement for subtraction and addition involving multiplace numbers makes it clearer to second-grade math learners the horizontal as well as vertical relationships in space among the numbers to be subtracted or added. Children who can accurately and quickly recall sums and differences in math facts will have an easier time calculating with multiplace numbers. For those who do not have automatic recall, rather than flash cards which drill only look–say, practicing the sums and differences with a variety of sensory-input and motor-output combinations can be beneficial: look–say, look–write, listen–say, and listen–write.

As in first grade, second graders should be given many opportunities to apply this knowledge of calculation, computation, and basic operations to solve math problems, both designed by the teacher and created by the students. Perhaps such problems are referred to as word problems, even though they are expressed in sentences, because understanding math-specific vocabulary is critical to solving them correctly as is understanding that phrases signal what the problem or question is and clues to solving it. For example, "How many more does Joe have than Sam?" signals subtraction, whereas "How many altogether do Joe and Sam have?" signals addition. Second graders can apply their developing math skills to solving problems related to their jobs in the classroom economy, their everyday life, and board and card games and puzzles that are appropriate for their developmental level.

Reading-Writing

Writing letters and words facilitates learning to read the words. By both reading words orally and spelling them in writing, second graders continue to learn that there is a common underlying word-specific spelling whether the output is through the mouth during oral reading or through the hand during writing. This word-specific spelling contributes to automatic word reading and spelling and thus oral reading fluency and written composition fluency. Also, during independent activities in reading groups, second graders are often asked to write about what they read.

Math-Writing

Second graders' math achievement depends on several math-writing abilities: (a) writing numerals legibly and automatically and (b) conveying numerical quantity by placing numerals in the correct place in a single multiplace number, a written calculation problem arranged in multiple columns and rows, or correct location on a number line.

Math-Reading

Second graders' math achievement depends on several math-reading abilities: (a) reading word problems to identify the problem to be solved, (b) reading the word problems for the key words or phrases that signal the calculation operation required for solving the problem, and (c) identifying the information relevant and irrelevant to solving the problem (see Mayer's translational science in Chapter 2).

Reading-Writing-Math

Increasingly, second graders need to integrate their reading, writing, and math skills to learn and achieve in each of these traditional content domains of the curriculum, such as science and social studies. For example, second graders may read simple texts in science and social studies and then write about what they read, or they may need to apply their math skills to the problem-solving activities in science (e.g., measuring lines or shapes) or social studies (learning about time lines in history). To do so, they apply executive function or self-regulation skills to integrate skills across domains of the curriculum.

Science

Second graders continue to learn science both through hands-on activities and problem solving and use of illustrated written texts and multimedia. Second graders should be given opportunities to express what they learn in science through oral discussion as well as written expression. In addition, they should be encouraged to express themselves in nonverbal formats that may involve the hand but not necessarily language, such as drawings and diagrams, or verbal plus nonverbal formats using words with the drawings or diagrams. They practice data analysis skills and problem-solving skills.

Social Studies

As for science, second graders learn social studies by interacting with the social and physical world and expressing what they learn about people in their own communities, their state, their country, and their world through oral and written language and even art, music, and dance.

English Language Learners

Robert Famiano (Honor Role Model 12), a classroom teacher, pioneered effective ways to teach English language learners, often recent immigrants, in the general education classroom. He also welcomed special education students into his second grade general education classroom. He not only drew on evidence-based reading and writing instruction but also developed innovative ways to keep all students highly engaged in learning. For example, he met with small instructional groups that sat cross-legged in a circle on a rug with him as he led learning activities: (a) training phonological awareness by elongating the pronunciation of English words with emphasis on the continuous vowels rather than segmented consonants within syllables, (b) applying spelling-sound patterns common in primary grade reading material to decoding target written words of the day, and (c) spelling dictated words with common sound-spelling patterns in primary grade children's writing with chalk on individual chalkboards on each child's lap.

Math activities were incorporated throughout the entire school day—for example, counting the number of children lined up for recess or lunch, figuring out change due when lunch fees were collected, and solving addition and subtraction problems for the number of children needed to complete a series of classroom tasks each having different requirements. Throughout the day, this innovative teacher made sure there were frequent teacher–student interactions with each student in his class. He used a variety of assessment tools throughout the year to gather different kinds of evidence to document that each student was learning and knew more at the end than at the beginning of the year.

Assessing Response to Instruction and Branching Diagnosis

The key skills to assess during second grade are (a) automaticity in reading real words on lists and oral reading fluency for text, (b) rate of phonological decoding, (c) vocabulary reading for meaning, (d) sentence-level comprehension, (e) text-level comprehension, (f) automatic alphabet letter writing (lower case printed letters), (g) sustained handwriting over time on copy tasks, (h) spelling pseudowords from dictation, (i) word-specific spelling without handwriting requirements, (j) spelling real words in writing from dictation, (k) sentence combining, (l) compositional fluency (sentence level), (m) compositional fluency (narrative text level), (n) automaticity and legibility of numeral writing 1 to 20, (o) automaticity of addition and subtraction math facts and switching between addition and subtraction, (p) math problem solving, and (q) math self-monitoring. Children who lag behind in any of these target skills should be referred to the problem-solving consultation team to discuss possible supplementary interventions and assessments. Second-grade teachers, with assistance from the interdisciplinary team, should also follow up on any children who were not meeting developmental milestones during first grade so that they could be helped do so during second grade; second-grade teachers should connect with the third-grade teacher regarding any students who have not met target goals by the end of second grade and who will need help with those during third grade.

GRADE 3

Aural Language—Listening

Third-grade target goals are to increase ability to listen to longer stretches of teacher-talk for purposes of learning information (declarative knowledge), to learn steps in new skills (procedural knowledge), to follow directions, and to self-regulate behavior and social interactions. In addition, third graders continue to benefit from listening to high quality children's literature, both narrative and expository, and then discussing what they hear with classmates.

Oral Language—Speaking

Third graders continue to develop their oral language skills in a variety of ways: (a) class discussions; (b) small group discussions during reading group, writers' workshop, or math work groups; (c) assuming the role of teacher in reciprocal teaching; (d) formal presentations to the group related to the science or social studies program that share information and provide explanations; (e) oral reading of play scripts; and (f) word games and searches designed to stimulate vocabulary development, including riddles and jokes.

Reading

Third graders continue to benefit from explicit instruction designed to teach word identification skills for familiar and unfamiliar words, vocabulary meaning, sentence understanding, and text comprehension. As was the case in earlier grades, this instruction, which is designed to facilitate transfer across one level of language to others and create a functional reading system that works in concert with the other functional language systems, should be provided in groups at comparable instructional levels.

At the word level, third graders benefit from learning and applying flexible strategies to word identification: alphabetic principle, word families (rimes in syllables when onset phoneme or blend is deleted), syllable classification and segmentation, and morphological analysis of base words and fixes (prefix at beginning and inflectional suffixes at the end that mark tense, number, and comparison). In addition, they benefit from *anagrams* (reordering scrambled letters) to create a word-specific spelling associated with a specific pronunciation and meaning of a correctly spelled real word.

Third graders benefit from reading comprehension that explicitly teaches across levels of language: (a) vocabulary meaning for words in passages; (b) awareness of how word order, types of words (content words vs. function words), and parts of speech contribute to sentence meaning; and (c) sequential organization across sentences and higher level discourse structures. This explicit instruction can take many forms: (a) teacher-provided questions to guide children's reading of passages to find answers to them; (b) children's answering of teacher questions posed following children's reading of passages; (c) children's summarizing of passages read, including main ideas and supporting details; and (d) reciprocal teaching in which children take turns at being teacher and posing the questions for their classmates to answer.

As do second graders, third graders benefit from wordplay to develop linguistic awareness and engaging in free reading during reading choice time. Students often choose chapter books and read separate chapters in a series of sessions. Magazines and science books with many nonverbal illustrations are also of interest. E-books could be made available through laptops without access to the Internet. Third graders should keep a portfolio in which they record all books and materials they have read.

Writing

Third graders benefit from periodic "tune-ups" in printing lower and upper case letters and also from explicit instruction in lower and upper case letters in cursive, using the same approach as in first and second grade—studying numbered arrow cues for letter formation, writing letters from visual memory, and writing letters for dictated names. Research has shown that they also benefit from the *before and after game*—that is, writing the letter that comes before or after the named letter in the alphabet. They also benefit from systematic spelling instruction that includes the alphabetic principle taught in the spelling direction, coupled with morphology for prefixes and inflectional suffixes (mark number, tense, comparison). They continue to learn that writing is a way to record their own thoughts (e.g., in journal writing or science experiments) and to share their thoughts with others; they benefit from explicit strategies for generating different genres (narrative and informational) and sharing their writing with their classmates as well as teachers. Increasingly, their writing is applied across the curriculum to all content areas.

Math

Two new operations are introduced in third grade: multiplication and division. Third graders, like first graders, benefit from an instructional approach that engages their sensory, motor, and oral language systems in creating an internal number line linked to basic math facts, but in third grade the focus is on basic multiplication facts (multipliers 0–9) and related division facts. Again, children should have a masking tape or paper number line at their desk with numerals written in increasing counting order left to right, or they should have a paper number line with the numerals in counting order. In learning the multiplication math facts, children touch and name numerals as they count forward by increments rather than a single number (e.g., for 4×5 they begin by touching 4 and then move forward by an increment of 4 five times and where they end is the product, 20). In learning the division facts, children start by touching the total amount to be divided (e.g., $20 \div 5$) and then count backwards from 20 by increments (e.g., each of five touches) until they reach 0; they count the number of steps (four) to reach this destination. Each time they count out the multiplication or division facts they write the math facts that represent them. Following the counting forward for multiplication, the child writes the number fact (e.g., $4 \times 5 = 20$). Following the backward counting for division, the child writes the number fact (e.g., $20 \div 5$). Learning multiplication facts will help children with their division facts; many of them will solve $20 \div 5$ by remembering that $5 \times 4 = 20$. Multimodal input–output combinations can be used to automatize the multiplication and division facts: look–say, look–write, hear–say, and hear–write.

Although number facts and operations are taught in some schools along a horizontal axis (e.g., $68 \div 2$) in the early grades, it is easier for students to grasp the concepts of place value and computations if the written calculation is presented in columns in which links to place value and computation operations are made clearer in two-dimensional space. For multiplication, the number to be multiplied may be multi-place, but the multiplier may be a single place number (e.g., 12×8). This operation requires moving through time and space in a more complex way than along the linear number line. First, the operations in multiplication are performed from the top down along a vertical axis in the 1's place, and then from the top down along a diagonal axis between the 10's place and the 1's place. Regrouping must be applied if the quantity in any place exceeds 9.

For division, the operation begins on the left, where the divisor is (e.g., $2\sqrt{68}$), rather than on the right as in addition, subtraction, and multiplication. This number is divided into the number on the left-most place, which is again different from the other operations that begin on the right. Also, division typically requires more changes in attention focus and movement of eyes and hands: left to right for the divisor and then dividend and then to the top to write the quotient and then multiply diagonally by the divisor on left and write the product below and then subtract, and so on until the division is completed in serial steps that repeat this process after bringing down the next number to the right in the dividend to be divided next. Again, practice of this new procedure is important. Third graders should also learn to apply this new knowledge of the multiplication and division operations to math word problems and other kinds of math problem solving. Third graders should review addition and subtraction facts and operations, which are also needed for math problem solving.

Part–whole relationships are critical to learning to tell time, even with digital clocks, and should be taught. Although children first learn that as numbers increase in counting order, they reflect a larger quantity, learning to tell time requires learning an additional concept: Quantity can also depend on the number of parts into which a whole is divided. Thus, although 2 is more than 1, and 4 is more than 2, one half (one of two parts) is more than one fourth (one of four parts), even though the whole number 4 is more than 2. So a quarter of an hour (e.g., 3:00–3:15) is less than one half of an hour (e.g., 3:00–3:30). Third graders also learn to apply their developing quantitative skills to other measurement activities—for example, using rulers to describe the length of objects in their everyday lives and to describe geometric shapes. As in the earlier grades, third graders can learn about math applications through performing class jobs and other activities for which they receive and/or generate economic resources, creating their own self-generated math problems to solve, and playing a variety of games that foster math learning and enjoyment.

Science and Social Studies

See second grade, which is still developmentally appropriate.

Integrated Reading-Writing

Jasmin Niedo, a member of the advisory board, who has been a teacher, reading coach, principal, professional development specialist, and researcher, noted that students benefit from teachers who encourage them to read and think like writers and write and think like readers. Teaching students to become reading-writers and writing-readers requires that they learn to take the perspective of others through assuming the roles of both reader and writers, with a variety of texts that help them find their own voice. They need to learn how to signal in their writing cues to the reader for (a) more is to come, (b) the sequence of the ideas, (c) other organization devices for ideas, and (d) the illustration of ideas through metaphors, similes, and figures of speech. That writing is for an audience becomes more prominent as students engage in writing–reading and reading–writing activities.

Oral Language-Reading-Writing-Math Across the Content Areas of the Curriculum

In all content areas of the curriculum, third graders draw on multiple language skills as well as quantitative skills. They have to process teachers' instructional talk, answer questions orally, and discuss during group activities. Increasingly, third graders have to integrate reading skills (e.g., reading source material) with writing skills (e.g., taking notes) to complete written assignments at school and at home in, for example, social studies and science as well as language arts. When performing science experiments, third graders may be encouraged to record their observations or write about their findings. Math requires reading word problems and writing calculations to solve those problems. Thus, at one level, it may be convenient to subdivide the curriculum into content areas, but at another level, the system level, any of the various sensory, motor, language, cognitive (including quantitative, attention, and executive function), or social and emotional skills may be facilitating or interfering with learning and performance (see Chapter 7).

Assessing Response to Instruction and Branching Diagnosis

The key skills to assess during third grade are (a) automaticity in reading real words, (b) rate of phonological decoding, (c) oral reading of text (accuracy, rate, and fluency), (d) vocabulary reading for meaning, (e) sentence-level comprehension, (f) text-level comprehension, (g) automatic alphabet letter writing (lower case cursive), (h) sustained handwriting over time in manuscript or cursive, (i) word-specific spelling without handwriting requirements, (j) spelling real words in writing from dictation, (k) sentence combining, (l) compositional fluency—sentence level, (m) compositional fluency—narrative text level, (n) automaticity and legibility of numeral writing 1 to 20, (o) automaticity of multiplication and division facts, (p) math problem solving, and (q) math self-monitoring. Children who lag behind in any of these target skills should be referred to the problem-solving consultation team to discuss possible supplementary interventions and assessments, monitor students in third grade who had been flagged as not meeting all target goals in second grade, and communicate with fourth-grade teachers about students who would still need supplementary instruction to meet third-grade target skills.

Linking Assessment and Instruction to Teaching at Students' Instructional Levels in At-Risk Populations in Early Childhood

A team of teachers in a school serving largely English language learners in a large urban school district reached out to a university professor to create a partnership. These teachers had administered a district-approved informal inventory to all first and second graders to create groups on the basis of instructional level that were taught at the same time each day. They emphasized reading comprehension in their instruction but had also incorporated phonological awareness and decoding instruction. They wanted to know whether they were using sufficient evidence-based instruction and how they could evaluate whether the students were making adequate progress.

The university-based team helped them design a screening battery to identify which students were performing below the 25th percentile (in the bottom quartile). Probably because the first and second graders were being taught at their instructional levels, the percentage of children in the bottom quartile was far below the 25% that would be normally expected in the bottom quartile on real word and pseudoword reading, handwriting, and spelling (range 6.7%–10.6%) but not silent reading comprehension (59%). The teachers shared their observations of the child's classroom behavior with the researchers who obtained the test scores. Jointly they decided whether test results were a true reflection of the child's literacy skills and for which children additional diagnostic assessment might be warranted.

The research team then helped the teachers design supplementary instruction at all levels of language (subword, word, and text) for the lowest achieving second graders, at their teacher's request, and differentiated instruction for the others who scored in lowest quartile. By the end of the year, the lowest achieving second graders were reassessed, and individuals showed improvement on age- or grade-normed tests for five to nine of the 10 skills reassessed. Thus, in low-income, linguistically diverse schools, students can learn if given developmentally appropriate, individually tailored instruction.

What made the greatest impression on the researchers partnering with the teachers, however, was the boy who told them that he was poor, but his cousin was really poor. When asked to clarify the difference, he explained that sometimes where he lived there was food in the refrigerator and sometimes there was not, but where his cousin lived there never was food. Teachers in this school district also reported that some children cried at end of the school year because during the summer they never could count on food like they did when they came to school and were fed breakfast and lunch (see Chapter 12).

Teaching Other Skills to Facilitate Academic Learning and Behavior

SELF-REGULATION AND ATTENTION

During early childhood, students need both routines and novelty. These may appear to be contradictory goals, but each is necessary for different reasons. Predictability of classroom routines helps children learn to plan and develop expectations and thus self-regulate their behavior during each school day. Novelty is needed because children habituate easily—that is, they stop attending or responding if the same thing keeps happening over and over and their minds seek change. One way to deal with both these needs is to establish predictable time blocks for language arts (reading and writing), for math, and for content subjects such as science and social studies, but within those time blocks, vary the activities frequently and keep duration reasonably short so that the learners' minds do not habituate. These brief and varying activities can be organized by levels of language or component skills so that the various levels and component skills can function in concert—that is, in synchrony within and across time.

Teachers can also support students in learning supervisory attention skills by providing signals for when children should focus attention and when they should switch attention at transition times during the day; teachers can reward students for sustaining attention and staying on task. Games such as Simon Says can facilitate the supervisory attention needed for self-regulation during early childhood. Children who are overly active may benefit from movement breaks, for example, in a corner of the room where they can put on earphones and dance without disturbing others. Others benefit from structured games during recess that provide opportunities to move for sustained periods of time in purposeful activities with rules to regulate the movement. Not all active children necessarily have hyperactivity, which is a significant difficulty in self-regulating their activity level; they can channel their high energy levels into productive outlets, such as athletics or dance. Some children find it helpful to have something to fidget with (e.g., paper clip, eraser, stress ball), which may help quiet their activity level so they can focus their attention on the task at hand. Childhood is a state of development when activity levels are generally higher than later in development—for example, the middle and senior adult years. Whether a child can learn to self-regulate activity levels in response to targeted interventions can contribute to whether he or she receives a diagnosis of hyperactivity or is simply viewed as a highly active child (see Chapters 7, 8, and 9).

SOCIAL–EMOTIONAL SKILLS

Formal schooling contributes to the socialization of children outside the family. Therefore, an important instructional goal each year is to create positive social communities in K–3 classrooms. Although these social communities exist, on average, for only 9 months (the length of the average human gestation period), they have the potential to have lasting effects on the developing child (as does the intrauterine environment during gestation). One way to build community during early childhood is to assign each child a job that contributes to the classroom—for example, taking the attendance report to the office, lining up the students for recess or lunch or buses at end of day, passing out paper or other supplies, cleaning off white boards, assisting with technology set up, changing bulletin boards, planning activities for rainy day recess, leading Simon Says, and so forth. These jobs can be rotated on a monthly basis so all children have an opportunity to have a job. Other jobs can be created through classroom economies that generate "payment for services" using a classroom token economy. Another way to promote social community is classroom government. At the beginning of the school year, the teacher guides discussion to create classroom rules. When these are violated by anyone, the class government council meets, discusses possible ways to handle the violations, and creates a plan so that rules are followed in the future. Another way to promote positive emotional development is to end each day with a compliment circle. Children gather in a circle and pay compliments to other children for a variety of accomplishments or behaviors during the day. Teachers can also add compliments. The goal is for each child to go home feeling that he or she has succeeded in some way during the day; this might contribute to developing positive self-concepts.

Teachers should also pay attention to social relationships among children in the classroom and promote positive ones. As noted by advisory panel member Jasmin Niedo, one should never underestimate the power of the kindness of teachers themselves. The relationships they develop with colleagues in surrounding classrooms, with parents, and with students can serve as the primary models for how children will interact with others during the school day. What teachers "tell" their students about how to treat others will be far outshadowed by what they "show" them in their own behavior. Other professionals on the interdisciplinary team can assist with issues related to students' relationships outside school with family members (see Honor Role Model 3, Chapter 2) and with the teachers at school. Many students report that the teacher does not like them. Regardless of the reality of these perceptions, they may influence students' learning and behavior in the classroom. One school psychologist successfully transformed the learning and behavior of one such student by acknowledging that he could not change the teacher but he could teach the student behavioral techniques for changing the teacher's attitude and behaviors toward the student. Research, including that of advisory panel member Jennie Warmouth, second-grade teacher and doctoral student, is also finding that animals can promote healthy emotional development in young children.

MOVEMENT

Many kinds of movement activities should be incorporated in the K–3 classroom. These include free and structured play during scheduled recess, movement breaks during class time, and in some schools, despite funding cutbacks, physical education classes. After-school programs in the community are often available for sponsored sports activities and athletic events. Dance can be incorporated in meaningful ways by having children dance to their favorite music shared using a variety of audio media and community dance forms (e.g., hip-hop). Other promising approaches are specific kinds of movement activities designed to develop mindfulness, such as yoga. Some interventions, such as using stability balls, which move slightly as the child readjusts body positions, instead of stationary chairs, help some young children self-regulate their movement and activity levels so that they can attend better and participate more appropriately in classroom instructional activities.

CREATIVE EXPRESSION (ART, MUSIC, DRAMA)

Pretend play emerges in the preschool years and continues to develop during the early school years, facilitating cognitive development through the stimulation of the imagination. Thoughts during early childhood are often most easily expressed through not only language but also many nonverbal modes such as art, music, dance, and play. In schools where budget challenges have eliminated art and music education, creative teachers can incorporate opportunities to promote cognitive development through artistic expression in other ways. Multiple media for art expression (e.g., paints, markers, crayons) should be available to students in the early grades. Many students enjoy illustrating their writing and including their art work in their portfolios. Many teachers display students' artwork on the walls of the school halls or of the classroom. Technology now makes it feasible to play in the classroom many kinds of music to which children enjoy listening or singing, moving, and/or dancing along with the music.

SELF-CONCEPT AND FINDING ONE'S DEPENDABLE SKILLS

Developing children acquire self-concepts about themselves as learners— for example, whether they are good or poor at reading, writing, math, sports, and so forth—and their cultural identity. These self-concepts and cultural identity can influence their response to instruction as much as their other skills in the interdisciplinary framework or the developmental stepping-stones in the academic curriculum. Their self-concept and identity may also play a role in the development of the self that learns to self-regulate learning and behavior. Early childhood educators can have children draw self-portraits using crayons and markers with authentic colors for skin (see Chapter 12); these can be kept in their portfolios and can also be shared with classmates. One reason for keeping portfolios with work samples across the school year is to use them in parent–teacher–child conferences (see Honor Role Model 9, Chapter 3). Portfolios help children begin to acquire a sense of who they are on the basis of their profile of dependable strengths (talents), self-concept, and self-identity. Inviting diverse members of the community who represent the various culture groups into the classroom is an important way to communicate to children that diversity is valued. Also, inviting nontraditional and ethnically diverse forms of music, artwork, and storytelling can facilitate both learning and appreciation for diversity in cultural expression.

Technology

On the one hand, handwriting instruction is still needed in the computer age. Because of the widespread availability of computers, many mistakenly think it is no longer important to teach handwriting at school. However, research has shown that there are benefits from learning to form the letters component stroke by component stroke in serial order beyond just selecting a letter by pressing a key. In fact, there may be advantages for being "bilingual by hand"—in other words, being able to use multiple modalities both with and without technology to produce letters for purposes of written communication. However, now that keyboarding is not the only mode of using computers, more research is needed on which technology tools may be most beneficial during early childhood for children in general and for specific children. For example, tracing on a tablet involves forming a letter without a pencil grip, but writing with a stylus, as by pencil and pen, involves forming a letter with a pencil grip. For young children with disabilities, a variety of new technologies are now available (see http://www.eric.ed.gov/ERICWebPortal/search/detailmini.jsp?_nfpb=true&_&ERICExtSearch_SearchValue_0=EJ918238&ERICExtSearch_SearchType_0=no&accno=EJ918238).

On the other hand, although technology is an integral part of current culture, it is typically not well-integrated into the early childhood curriculum. Children are more likely to use technology tools in their home—for example, to play games or do homework. In addition, just as schools have traditionally provided safety education on paying attention to the color of signals in traffic lights (green = go, yellow = caution, and red = stop), safety issues regarding current technology also need to be taught. Beginning in early childhood, children need to learn, for example, to pay attention to not only what they hear through earphones or text through their cell phones but also to the drivers, vehicles, and other pedestrians when crossing the street.

Thinking Points for Differentiated Instruction

An example of thinking inside the box is to perform the same assessments on all referred children and youth to determine whether they qualify for services under a state approved category for special education services or a reimbursable diagnostic category of a third party health insurer. The assessment results are compared with prescribed tabled procedures and checklists of symptoms, to determine, without best practices professional judgment, whether the student qualifies for special help and/or has a disorder. These eligibility criteria for services or reimbursement are typically not directly linked to specific research-supported instruction linked to what the educational problem is. Best professional practices also requires thinking outside the box—using professional judgments to synthesize multiple sources of assessment data to create, optimal educational programs, which may include differentiated instruction in general education for the student. In addition, best practices include advocating for students (see Chapter 2) and families (see Chapter 15) using legal codes. Best professional practices may also require thinking in the moving box—that is, flexibly juggling the complex and sometimes seemingly contradictory notions of what is required by best practices, institutional policies, ethics, and legal issues (see Chapter 2) to deal with multiple sources of diversity (biological, cultural, linguistic, socioeconomic; see Parts III and IV, this volume), co-occurring conditions, parental concerns, and developmental, medical, and family history.

Readings and Resources[1]

READING, INCLUDING EARLY BILINGUAL READING INSTRUCTION

Adams, M., Foorman, B., Lundberg, I., & Beeler, T. (2012). *Phoneme awareness in young children: A classroom curriculum.* Baltimore, MD: Brookes.

Beck I. L., & McKeown, M. G. (2001). Text talk: Capturing the benefits of reading aloud for young children. *The Reading Teacher, 55*(1), 10–19.

Beck, I. L., McKeown, M. G., & Kucan, L. (2003). Taking delight in words: Using oral language to build young children's vocabularies. *American Educator, 27,* 36–46.

Kim, Y.-S. (2012). The relations among L1 (Spanish) literacy skills, L2 (English) language, L2 text reading fluency, and L2 reading comprehension for Spanish-speaking ELL first grade students. *Learning and Individual Differences, 22,* 690–700. doi:10.1016/j.lindif.2012.06.009

Palinscar, A. M. (1986). The role of dialogue in providing scaffolding instruction. *Educational Psychologist, 21,* 73–98.

Pollard-Durodola, S. D., Cedillo, G., & Denton, C. A. (2004). Linguistic units and instructional strategies that facilitate word recognition for Latino kindergarteners learning to read in Spanish. *Bilingual Research Journal, 28,* 319–354. doi:10.1080/15235882.2004.10162620

Read Naturally. (1997–2008). *Read Naturally masters edition ME.* Saint Paul, MN: Author.

Vygotsky, L., Steinver, V., Cole, M., & Schribner, S. (Eds.). (1980). *Mind in society: Development of higher psychological processes.* Boston, MA: Harvard University Press.

---

[1]Additional research readings and practitioner resources for this chapter can be found at http://www.apadivisions.org/division-16/publications/interdisciplinary-frameworks-supplement/index.aspx

READING-WRITING

Bear, D., Ivernezzi, M., Templeton, S., & Johnston, F. (2000). *Words their way: Word study for phonics, vocabulary, and spelling instruction* (2nd ed.). Upper Saddle River, NJ: Merrill.

Berninger, V., & Abbott, S. (2003). *PAL research-supported reading and writing lessons: Instructional manual and reproducibles.* San Antonio, TX: Pearson.

Fry, E. (1996). *Spelling book. Level 1–6: Words most needed plus phonics.* Westminster, CA: Teacher Created Materials. Retrieved from http://www.teachercreated.com

Slingerland Institute for Literacy. http://www.slingerland.org

Traweek, D., & Berninger, V. (1997). Comparison of beginning literacy programs: Alternative paths to the same learning outcome. *Learning Disability Quarterly, 20,* 160–168.

Zaner-Bloser Handwriting. Provides instruction materials by grade, from prekindergarten to Grade 6. Retrieved from http://www.zanerbloser.com/fresh/handwriting-overview.html

REACHING OUT TO PARENTS

Ford, L., & Amaral, D. (2006). Research on parent involvement: Where we've been, where we need to go. *School Leadership Journal, 1,* 1–20.

MATH

Bryant, B., Bryant, D., Kethley, C., Kim, S., Pool, C., & Seo, Y.-J. (2008). Preventing mathematics difficulties in the primary grades: The critical features of instruction in textbooks as part of the equation. *Learning Disabilities Quarterly, 31,* 21–36.

Geary, D. (1994). *Children's mathematical development: Research and practical applications.* Washington, DC: American Psychological Association.

Greenes, C., Balfanz, R., & Ginsburg, H. (2004). Big math for little kids. *Early Childhood Research Quarterly, 19,* 159–166. doi:10.1016/j.ecresq.2004.01.010

Linking Instruction and Assessment in Middle Childhood

5

This chapter provides a *Developmental Stepping Stones* model for planning and implementing curriculum and instruction and evaluating response to instruction for students during middle childhood. Three critical transitions from the early to middle childhood years or from middle childhood to adolescence are featured: (a) transition from oral reading to silent reading; (b) transition to increasingly complex instruction and assignments at school and home that require self-regulation to integrate reading, writing, and/or aural and oral language across the content areas of the curriculum; and (c) transition to working with multiple teachers and groups of students across the school day. Because in some systems Grades 4, 5, and 6 are located in elementary schools, whereas in others Grades 4 and 5 are in elementary school and Grade 6 is in middle school, the transition to switching among teachers and peer groups is examined from the perspectives of students who have entered or are preparing to enter middle school. Middle childhood students vary greatly

http://dx.doi.org/10.1037/14437-005
Interdisciplinary Frameworks for Schools: Best Professional Practices for Serving the Needs of All Students, by V. W. Berninger

in whether they have mastered the developmental stepping-stones for early childhood and in which ones may still be underdeveloped; Chapter 4 may be used with Chapter 5 to (a) monitor and teach skills not mastered during early childhood, (b) consolidate the foundations created during early childhood, and (c) build on those by expanding the developing child's ability to engage in self-regulated behavior at school and home for academic and other goals. Chapter 6 may be used with Chapter 5 for those students who are advanced beyond the typical developmental milestones in Grades 4 to 6. Thinking points emphasize the role of the interdisciplinary team in bridging early and middle childhood and adolescence.

Developmental Stepping-Stones in Middle Childhood: Grades 4 to 6 Transitions to Silent Reading and Integrated Reading-Writing-Oral Language

Oral reading, which exercises the phonological loop and engages working memory, is developmentally appropriate during early childhood when children are learning to transform written words into spoken words. However, once children master basic oral reading skills for high-frequency words in and out of context, typically during the primary grades, they need to transition to silent reading. Those who still struggle with oral reading should receive instruction and participate in learning activities for both oral and silent reading during middle childhood.

Silent reading draws on and integrates orthographic, phonological, and morphological cues in words during word identification. During middle childhood, readers continue to benefit from instructional activities that support abstracting and integrating orthographic patterns in written words (Manis & Morrison, 1982), phonological patterns in spoken words (Kessler & Treiman, 1997; Treiman, 1985), and morphological patterns that do and do not involve phonological shifts in the base word when suffixes are added (Carlisle, 2000). However, middle childhood readers face two new challenges. First, increasingly, the words encountered in written texts have a different word origin (e.g., French, Latin, Greek) than in the earlier grades, when most words in written books are of Anglo–Saxon origin (old English–German). Words of Anglo–Saxon origin, which tend to have one to two syllables, account for about 90% of the words used in conversation (e.g., *good, mother*). Beginning in fourth grade and continuing thereafter, many of the words in textbooks are of French or Latinate (e.g., *national, education*) and Greek (e.g., *triangle, psychology*) origin; these have different phonological, orthographic, and/or morphological properties and relationships than do Anglo–Saxon words. For example, words of French and Latin origin tend to have three to five syllables and may have different accent patterns than do one- and two-syllable words of Anglo–Saxon origin. Romance language and Greek words, which are used less frequently in conversation, are used frequently in written school texts—that is, the academic register in Grades 4 and above (see Henry, 2010).

Many of the groups showing the largest achievement gaps have narrowed the achievement gap with increased instruction and practice in oral decoding during the early grades, but they lose ground at the transition from third to fourth grade, when the nature of words to be read changes. By providing more instruction in the phonology, orthography, and morphology of words of French, Latin, and Greek origin and their use in the academic register of written texts and guided silent reading, it may be possible to eliminate the achievement gaps for these groups in the upper grades as well.

During middle school, children are increasingly asked to integrate reading and writing. For example, they read a text during reading group and then are asked to write answers to questions about it, write a summary, or write an opinion essay about it. Or they are asked to read a book and write a book report about it. Or they are given assignments to complete at school or at home for content area subjects in science and/or math. They are expected to read source material, write notes from source materials, and then write reports integrating the notes with their own background knowledge and thoughts and organizational structures.

In addition, during middle childhood, students often have to integrate aural language they hear from the teacher during instruction and in making assignments with written note taking, studying for written tests, and completing written assignments in class or at home. They may also need to integrate oral language with writing to explain the nature of a written assignment to parents who may help them with homework. They may also be asked to use oral language to discuss with peers the written material they read or create through writing, and they sometimes engage in cooperative learning projects for oral or written presentations. They are also asked to integrate reading and writing activities with oral instruction specific to content subjects. For example, they read math problems, write down relevant information, and write computations to solve the problem. Or they are asked to read multiple sources in written texts in books, magazines, newspapers, or the Internet, take notes about what they read, and write a report—for example, for social studies or science. They rely on oral language to ask the teacher for help if they do not understand the nature of the written assignment.

Many assignments are not completed in a single session at school or even at home. Thus, a major developmental milestone for middle childhood is learning self-regulation in both time management and integration across modes of language to complete school assignments. To facilitate this transition to increasing demands on students' executive functions for self-regulation, teachers can offer explicit instruction in strategies for self-regulation. In addition, workshop formats for the various subject areas can help middle childhood students learn to self-regulate their learning by integrating cognition and language across modes of interacting with the physical and social environment and academic domains.

Grades 4 to 6: Transition to Switching Among Classes and Teachers Throughout the Day

Frequent changes in teachers and classmates can pose self-regulation challenges for students during middle childhood. Although many children can deal with multiple adults in the same classroom, switching to a different teacher five or six times a day can pose a challenge for many. Team teaching where the same teacher or teaching team stays with the same class for at least two of the content areas of the curriculum or multiple periods of the day is one viable solution. When switching teachers is necessary, students may benefit from explicit discussion of strategies for dealing with multiple teachers—how to make sure they have a clear understanding of what each teacher expects, what each assignment requires and when it is due, and how to ask for clarification or other kind of help in understanding assignments. Some students may also have difficulty with changes in classmates throughout the day. For some students, the problems arise when they move from class to class and see students in hallways who may or may not be in their classes. Strategies for appropriate behavior in walking through halls may also need to be taught. Students with extreme difficulty managing their switching across classes, teachers, and classmates should be referred to the interdisciplinary team for problem-solving consultation.

Developmental Stepping-Stones in the Curriculum for Academic Content Areas

During middle childhood, instruction on reading and writing is often provided within a language arts block, but students may also benefit from instruction in reading and writing strategies used during math, science, and social studies. One way to teach effectively across the curriculum is to use a workshop format that combines intellectually engaging activities, opportunities to interact with classmates as well as the teacher, and teacher-provided explicit instruction and scaffolding (guided support). In addition, during middle childhood, students also benefit from instruction that is aimed at their current developmental and instructional levels. For example, such instruction can be delivered to small groups in a walk-about model during a language arts block and/or to the whole class through team teaching during the math, science, or social studies block. Developmental stepping-stones are not always reached in a single school year. The developmental milestones for middle childhood generally take at least 3 years to consolidate. In the spirit of formative assessment, the interdisciplinary team should support the classroom teachers in monitoring every student's progress toward mastering all the relevant earlier developmental milestones. In addition, the current individually tailored instruction should be designed to support both prior skills not mastered and current, grade-appropriate skills. In keeping with a developmental stepping-stones system model, mastering the earlier skills will support learning the current ones.

LANGUAGE ARTS IN GRADES 4 TO 6

As Exhibit 5.1 shows, systematic reading instruction should continue during middle childhood. As in the earlier grades, both reading and writing instruction should be directed to all levels of language so that students develop functional and integrated reading and writing systems.

At the subword level, students benefit from phonological, orthographic, and morphological awareness activities and explicit instruction in the multiple units for mapping (connecting) written and spoken words in reading and spelling directions: alphabetic principle (correspondences between one-letter and two-letter groups called *graphemes* and sounds called *phonemes*), kinds of syllables (closed, open, vowel teams, diphthongs and digraphs, *r*- and *l*-controlled, and silent terminal *e*; see also Moats, 2000), initial onset and remaining rime units within syllables, and morphology (bases and affixes). These mappings should be taught for words

EXHIBIT 5.1

Middle Childhood Developmental Milestones for the Academic Curriculum

Aural Language

- Developing phonological and morphological awareness of heard words of increasing length and complexity (multisyllabic words of different word origins)
- Understanding word meaning (content-specific vocabulary in instructional talk)
- Attending to, understanding, and following directions (in instructional talk)
- Transition to the academic registrar of teacher talk (learning from decontextualized aural text longer than used in conversational turns)

Oral Language

- Finding, choosing, and using vocabulary words (to express ideas in classroom discussions)
- Constructing syntax units (to express ideas in classroom discussions)
- Using discourse (to express ideas in classroom discussions)

Reading

Subword Mapping of Written Words Onto Spoken Words (words of French, Latin, or Greek word origin) During Oral or Silent Reading:

- Alphabetic principle—correspondences between one- and two-letter spelling units and phonemes (may differ from words of Anglo–Saxon origin)
- Word families—correspondences between written rimes (what remains after onset phoneme[s] of a syllable are omitted) and their pronunciation for words of different word origins
- Morphemes—derivational suffixes that mark grammatical transformations for changing parts of speech (e.g., nouns into adjectives: nation into national), prefixes, and inflectional suffixes marking tense, number, and comparison for words of different word origin
- Syllables—spelling patterns for syllable types and affixed base words

Word Identification (words of French, Latin, or Greek word origin):

- Oral decoding of unfamiliar words—coordinating vertical subword mapping across written and spoken word subunits within horizontal whole word units without any semantic or context clues (accuracy, rate)
- Oral reading of familiar words—same as oral decoding except that semantic cues may be used (accuracy and rate)
- Silent reading of familiar words—accuracy, rate

Silent Reading Comprehension:

- Vocabulary meaning
- Sentences
- Text

Writing

Subword Letter Production:

- Handwriting—manuscript and cursive—legibility, automaticity, rate
- Computer tools—finger or stylus on tablet or screen legibility, automaticity, rate
- Keyboard—touch typing accuracy, rate

(*continued*)

EXHIBIT 5.1 (*Continued*)

Spelling of Words of Different Word Origin (dictated and self-generated):

- Word-specific spelling without handwriting
- Spelling dictated real words
- Spelling during composing

Written Expression:

- Word choice and spelling
- Sentences—constructing, combining text—genre: narrative, expository (informational, compare and contrast, persuasive)
- Integrating reading (note taking) and writing to complete written assignments in class and at home in the short term and long term

Math

Number Concepts:

- Place value
- Rational numbers—fractions (like and unlike denominators, common denominators), decimals, mixed numbers, measurement systems
- Linear number lines—integers (whole numbers only) and mixed numbers (whole numbers and fractions or decimals)
- Circular number lines and telling time

Computations and Calculations:

- Basic number facts—addition, subtraction, multiplication, division (accuracy, rate)
- Four basic operations with whole numbers, fractions and decimals, and mixed numbers—addition, subtraction, multiplication, division

Problem Solving:

- Word problems
- Everyday math

Geometry:

- Length and width for two-dimensional shapes
- Length, width, volume for three-dimensional shapes

Reading-Writing-Math Connections

of French, Latin, and Greek origins and reviewed for words of Anglo–Saxon origin. Two kinds of twice-weekly handwriting "tune-ups" using a pencil or pen reinforce this mapping process: (a) reviewing letter formation in both manuscript and cursive format and lower and upper cases and (b) playing letter-finding games in which the letter before or after a designated letter in the ordered alphabet sequence is written.

At the word level, instruction should focus on the synthesis of the various subword units into a whole word that has stress patterns, which affect spelling and the musical melody (intonation) for oral reading. Students benefit from unscrambling letters to spell a real word (anagrams) and choosing the correct spelling for a particular sentence context so that they learn word-specific spellings that integrate spelling with meaning. General principles for vocabulary instruction in early childhood remain relevant during middle childhood, but the focus should be on the academic register—words used by teachers during oral instruction and encountered in textbooks that are specific to subjects across the curriculum—and accessing word meanings, spelling, and pronunciation in dictionaries. Word work should be supplemented with word play. For example, middle school students enjoy playing "word ball" in which two teams compete against each other in applying what they have learned to decoding, spelling, defining, or applying the word meaning provided by the teacher. As in baseball, each correct answer counts as reaching a base, four bases is a home run (point), and when three strikes (wrong answers) accumulate, the team at bat changes to the other team.

At the text level, instruction should focus on reading comprehension and written composition alone and together. The material read can range from chapter books to basal readers to magazines to newspapers to their classmates' compositions. As in past grade levels, individuals are most likely to make progress along their zone of proximal development if taught at their developmental and instructional levels, but engaging them intellectually in the learning process is also critical. For reading comprehension, the teacher should provide questions to guide silent reading, which are then used to assess comprehension after the text is read during oral question asking and answering. As children become proficient at answering the teacher-provided questions, they should be encouraged to pose their own questions to guide their reading, which they would then answer after reading. In addition, they should be given opportunity to engage in reciprocal teaching in which students take turns in the role of the teacher who questions and guides oral discussions. Students should also write summaries that include the main ideas and supporting details of the texts they read.

As in the earlier grades, free choice reading is important for practicing and consolidating skills and developing pleasure in reading. Book clubs organized by common interests can play an important role here. Each classroom or grade level may have several book clubs, each focused on a different book or interest. However, members of the same book club read and discuss the same book over a period of time. Small reading groups can promote student choice, student-led conversations around themes and insights, note taking, and structured role taking in their discussions (e.g., connector, questioner, literary luminary, illustrator roles that represent the mind-set readers assume as they interact with texts). The Great Books program is an excellent way to introduce students to the great literature of the world. Literature study groups and literature circles also provide opportunities for students to interact with their peers around quality literature. By participating in book clubs and literacy study groups, students learn to read with understanding the perspective of the author of the text and write about what they read with the perspective of the audience in mind.

Three kinds of writing instruction help students in middle childhood move along their zone of proximal development in generating written text. The first is strategies for generating different genres—narrative, informational, and persuasive—and, in some content areas such as science and social studies, comparing and contrasting (see the programmatic research of Graham and Harris and colleagues on strategies for planning, generating, and revising text). The second is taking notes on the source material read. The third is converting notes into reports with content and text organization. These writing skills can be taught and practiced within the format of the Writers' Workshop, in which children assume the roles of author and editor, giving feedback through the author's chair. The Writers' Workshop can be a springboard for publishing class or school newspapers and books, with and without illustrations. In addition, the Writers' Workshop can build connections with other areas of curriculum, including math, science, and social studies, as discussed later in this chapter.

MATH IN GRADES 4 TO 6

During middle childhood, students benefit from "math warm-ups" at the beginning of math lessons for the basic addition, subtraction, multiplication, and division facts using multiple combinations of input–output: look–write, look–say, listen–write, and listen–say. These warm-ups help to put math fact retrieval on automatic pilot, freeing up limited working memory resources for problem solving. Students also benefit from "number line" tune-ups in which they follow directions to add, subtract, multiply, and/or divide numbers and report where they end up on their mental number line and thus enhance the efficiency of their working memory for mental math.

Students in middle childhood also benefit from targeted instruction and practice in one or more of the four basic operations—addition, subtraction, multiplication, and division—for multiplace numbers arranged in columns and sometimes more than two rows. These calculations require not only automatic recall of math facts but also a deep understanding of place value. Regrouping procedures should be reviewed, and procedures for self-checking long calculations should be introduced and practiced (e.g., adding the difference and the number subtracted to compare the sum with the original number, multiplying the divisor by the quotient to compare the product with the original number). Teachers should monitor whether during written calculations, students can negotiate the frequent changes in attentional focus and movement in two-dimensional space (right to left, up and down, down and up, on diagonal, and left to right) and time (sequential steps). Some students understand math concepts but get lost in space or time during calculation. Estimated math skills should be taught to judge whether the calculated outcome of a computation is plausible. By the end of sixth grade, middle school students should have mastered multiplace addition, subtraction, multiplication, and division.

A major developmental stepping-stone during middle childhood is learning the part–whole concept and applying it to understanding fractions. Key to learning the part–whole concept is that numbers are not only cardinal but also rational. *Cardinal* refers to the concept of absolute quantity— one number stands for one quantity, which increases at constant increments across the number line. *Rational* refers to relational numbers—a quantity may depend not on its absolute value but rather on its relationship to another number—for example, how many parts a whole is divided into and how many of those parts are involved, that is, a ratio of number of parts to total number of parts. Although 4 is larger than 2 on the basis of absolute quantity, ¼ is less than ½ because the value of a fraction depends on how many parts the whole has been divided into, that is, on the basis of its relative quantity. Second, fractions (rational numbers) also occur along a number line in between the integers (whole cardinal numbers).

All of the following activities may contribute to understanding and using fractions and mixed numbers (whole numbers plus fractions): (a) manipulating objects with hands to demonstrate part–whole relationships, (b) writing different fractions (e.g., ²⁄₄, ³⁄₆, ⁴⁄₈) that can represent the same quantity (½) or mixed numbers involving whole numbers (integers) and fractions (e.g., ⁷⁄₄, 1⅛, 1¾) alone and between whole numbers on the number line, and (c) verbalizing and discussing concepts such as common denominators in like fractions and different denominators in unlike fractions as well as the lowest common denominator in unlike fractions. Another activity helps avoid confusion between whole numbers and fractions when multiplication and division of fractions and mixed numbers are introduced: For whole numbers, multiplication always results in a answer larger than either of the multiplied numbers, but this is not true for common fractions (e.g., ½ × ¼ = ⅛, which is less than either of the two fractions multiplied together). By the end of sixth grade, students should be able to find common denominators across unlike fractions; perform addition, subtraction, multiplication, and division operations on fractions (with and without common denominators) and mixed numbers; and reduce fractions to their lowest common denominator. These skills are important pre-algebra skills. Students who do not have a solid grasp of fraction concepts (e.g., that fractions are numbers that can be ordered along a number line) and cannot use computational procedures involving fractions will continue to struggle into the high school years, and, thus, may fail to meet the National Math Panel standard to master second-year algebra by high school graduation.

Another developmental milestone is the application of whole numbers (integers), fractions, and mixed numbers with integers and fractions to measure a variety of objects in the real world of space (with rulers, yardsticks, and measuring tapes) and time (seconds, minutes, hours, days, months, and years). Telling time also requires introducing the new concept that the number line is not always a line—it can also be circular, with circles within circles within circles, and so on. That is, a circle of 60 seconds repeats one time in 1 minute, a circle of 60 minutes repeats one time in 1 hour, a circle of 12 hours repeats two times in 1 day, and a circle of 365 days repeats once each year (except every 4 years, in which the circle has 366 days). The underlying concept of the circular arrangement of numbers in repeating cycles facilitates learning the procedural knowledge, even when clocks have read-outs arranged in digital arrays rather than circular clock faces. Fractions are also relevant to learning to tell time (e.g., 2:15, 3:30, 4:45).

To introduce decimals, the teacher might use masking tape or paper number lines as in the earlier grades and count along them as students touch, name, and write mixed numbers with whole numbers and decimals. Of crucial importance is that teachers need to point out that when decimals are introduced on the number line or in writing mixed numbers with decimals, the number line now moves in two directions—from right to left for whole numbers and from left to right from the decimal point marking zero (the absence of quantity) for the decimals (fractions for denominator of 10). As in earlier grades, practice in counting along the number line for decimals only and mixed whole and decimal numbers should be followed by writing the numerals (and decimal point) to symbolize the numbers. Instruction for calculation should be extended to include addition, subtraction, multiplication, and division involving decimals and mixed numbers with decimals.

When students are ready to progress beyond two-dimensional shapes and measurements to shapes and volumes in three-dimensional space, teachers can introduce them to circles and cubes and geodesic domes, all of which have applications to housing, communities in which people live, and the economies that support the work activities of human beings. Geometric understanding is also facilitated by outdoor education, with location points in the three-dimensional world. In the current technology-dominated culture, children spend much time inside in architecture dominated by rectangular solids and miss out on nature's circular skies in the spherical earth.

In sum, if children during middle childhood do not grasp the part–whole concept, like and unlike fractions, mixed numbers with fractions and decimals, and measurement involving fractions, decimals, and mixed numbers, they have not met the developmental milestones necessary for progressing to algebra in middle school. Algebra depends on understanding that the whole on both sides of the equals sign can be divided into parts in multiple ways.

Math workshops can integrate math with other areas of the curriculum. For example, students in middle childhood should be encouraged to apply their new math skills to the classroom economies that generate products and services and economic resources. Teachers can integrate math and social studies in a workshop devoted to the multicultural origins of math, which include ancient Egypt, India, the Middle Eat and indigenous cultures in the American continent. Students can read and write about the fascinating contributions of all these cultures to current arithmetic and mathematics. Math workshops can integrate writing and math by encouraging students to write and solve their own self-generated math problems.

Workshops might have a theme designed to teach students about the world of mathematics and mathematicians—for example, they might learn about Erdös, the mathematician who loved only numbers. Mathematicians are proud of their Erdös number, that is, the number of people they know who also knew Erdös and did math with him. They joke, "Hey Erdös, I got your number!" Students could read the story of Erdös, a Hungarian who spent his adult years traveling around the world to solve math problems collaboratively with other mathematicians. They will learn how higher mathematics is grounded in counting along a number line to find patterns, which can then be used to prove theorems that have advanced both math and math applications in science and engineering. For example, a workshop, "Erdös Mathematicians Constructing, Conversing, and Writing ($E=MC^2W$): A Club for Math Lovers," could link math, history, culture, and writing. Club members could write equations or patterns they discover in the number line (e.g., related to even and odd numbers and prime numbers) and also discover that math can be social and fun.

SCIENCE IN GRADES 4 TO 6

A major developmental stepping-stone in learning science during middle childhood is to draw on multiple ways of knowing to learn the current scientific understanding of the physical world and strategies for finding answers to new questions. For example, students might read texts on scientific topics, with many illustrations and other visual tools on each page, discuss them with the whole group or in small discussion groups, answer questions about the material orally and in writing, and write about what they have learned. Students could conduct hands-on science experiments, make quantitative and other kinds of observations, record the findings, summarize the findings in writing and oral discussions, and formulate hypotheses and methods to test them to extend knowledge. They may also build models out of a variety of materials to illustrate the concepts.

Science units might focus on the external universe—in outer space, the inner space of the human brain, the human body in which the brain is housed, and/or the vast variety of animals and plants and landforms in nature. Teaching listening, speaking, reading, and writing skills in the context of intellectually engaging science units (Scientists' Workshop) and with many hands-on activities that engage ears, mouth, eyes, hands, and minds may also involve students in language learning in a way that language instruction alone does not. Many communities have excellent science museums with opportunities for children to participate in after-school or summer science programs. Zoos and outdoor education programs offer exciting opportunities for science learning outside school.

A "Buckminster Spaceship Earth" workshop could engage students in science problem solving while drawing on math, oral and written language, and social studies. Buckminster Fuller, the inventor of the geodesic dome, applied math and science to solving practical problems to promote social justice causes. Not only did he apply his knowledge of math, science, and engineering to real-world problems on earth but he also envisioned the challenges facing humankind in exploration of outer space, which requires that human beings learn to get along with each other for extended periods of time. One workshop goal is to teach students about geodesic domes to foster geometric understanding of the complexity of three-dimensional shapes. The goal of the workshop is also to find out how space exploration can be designed to deal with both a specific science goal related to outer space and social problems that are likely to arise during the long space voyage. Teachers can learn about Fuller's life's work and mission in his *Operating Manual for Spaceship Earth*. His mission continues through the Buckminster Fuller Institute, which offers a wealth of instructional support materials that can be translated into classroom workshops to promote science, math, and social studies learning.

SOCIAL STUDIES IN GRADES 4 TO 6

Social studies might be taught in workshops that focus on multicultural understanding in students' own communities and beyond their communities to their county and the world. For example, children can share the stories of their family, their community, their culture, and their world using words, art, music, dance, and multimedia tools. Workshops can be conducted on the history and cultures of the many immigrant populations in the United States, as well as the indigenous populations already here. For example, the constitution of the five Iroquois nations served as the foundation for the United States Constitution. History and its multicultural contributions can be taught using multiple media across the curriculum: reading, writing, oral sharing through presentations and discussions, as well as artistic expression through dance, music, and the visual arts. One way to promote understanding of the individual in society is for students to construct masks. These masks can be used to tell the story of the cultural background and history of their ancestors. They can also be used to capture the child's developing personality (sum total of characteristics) that defines his or her sense of self, which also plays an important role in the self-regulation of learning and behavior in present and future development and learning in and out of school. At the same time, the greater good—our collective selves—should be emphasized to ensure that the human species survives.

Jasmin Niedo, a member of the advisory panel, has cautioned that the inclusion of multicultural books or activities alone will not necessarily promote critical reflection that can transform children's understanding of the world and expand their thinking about diversity, unless teachers teach toward those goals by helping children realize our many commonalities (e.g., children around the world develop friendships, nurture relationships with family members, and seek to fulfill their dreams and ambitions).

Assessing Response to Instruction During Middle Childhood

First, the critical skills in reading, writing, and math are assessed initially using group-administered measures. Second, for any student who does not show reasonable response to instruction (at least in the average range on norm-referenced tests, which is maintained or improved across time), branching diagnosis on the basis of individually administered tests is used to identify which earlier skills in the developmental stepping-stone model may be interfering with response to instruction. Such judgments are based not on an arbitrary cut-off in the average or low average range but on the developmental trajectory from the prior year (relative positive or negative change or plateau) and observations of current behaviors in the classroom.

GROUP-ADMINISTERED TESTS OF CRITICAL READING, WRITING, AND MATH SKILLS

For reading, assess silent reading word reading rate, vocabulary word reading for meaning, and sentence-level and passage-level reading comprehension. For writing, assess speed and accuracy of recognizing correct word-specific spellings, accuracy of spelling dictated words in writing and during independent composing, compositional fluency (sentence level and text level), and legibility of handwriting during composing. For math, assess accuracy of basic math facts and computational operations in addition, subtraction, multiplication, and division; math problem solving; and self-monitoring.

BRANCHING DIAGNOSIS

For students who do not meet criteria for positive improvement or maintaining at least an average level for grade level (−⅔ standard deviation or higher) on all measures of silent reading, also assess all the oral reading skills and phonological, orthographic, and morphological awareness skills for mapping spoken and written words in Exhibit 5.1. These students may need additional instruction and practice in oral reading to support their transition to silent reading. For students who do not meet the criteria for handwriting legibility, spelling, or compositional fluency, use branching diagnosis to assess handwriting automaticity and sustaining handwriting over time (see Exhibit 4.2). These children may need additional instruction in automatic handwriting production and in sustaining legible handwriting over time. For students who do not meet these criteria in math computation and problem solving, also assess oral counting (in working memory), writing numerals legibly and automatically, place value, and part–whole relationships. For any student who does not meet the criteria in silent reading, spelling, compositional fluency, or math problem solving, also give the aural and oral language measures at the word, syntax, and text levels, to determine whether weaknesses in aural language or paying attention to aural language may interfere with their response to silent reading, writing, or math problem-solving instruction.

Teaching Other Skills to Facilitate Academic Learning and Behavior

SELF-REGULATION AND ATTENTION

Some self-regulation skills are specific to different content domains of the curriculum, whereas others are relevant to integrating skills across the curriculum (see Chapter 4). Some self-regulation (executive function) skills specific to particular content domains may not transfer (generalize) automatically to all areas of the curriculum. During middle childhood, students benefit from learning specific strategies for reading, writing, and math. For example, programmatic research supports the importance of teaching the following self-regulation processes to guide the translation of thought to written language:

- Generate ideas—think of all the ideas related to the writing topic or task;
- plan ahead—create a plan mentally, orally, or in writing with specific goals and strategies for reaching each goal before writing;
- keep planning—continue to plan while translating ideas into written language;
- review the text in progress—use visual feedback to read what has been written so far and think about what you just wrote and what you wrote earlier; and
- revise to repair the text—make any needed revisions through retranslation at any time during or after composing.

Self-regulation skills may need to be applied in the present or in reference to the future for both academic tasks and behavioral management. Some require short-term management, such as assignments to complete within a class. Others require long-term management, such as homework and assignments due at a later time. Given the complexities of the brain systems and the mind they support, many different kinds of executive systems are needed, and each may be on its own developmental course. On the one hand, regulatory genes, which turn on processes such as myelination in specific areas of the brain at specific times in development, may affect the development and application of self-regulation skills. On the other hand, other support provided by teachers and parents affects development and application of specific kinds of self-regulations skills. Other support contributes to the development of self-regulation beginning in the preschool years and continuing to the adult years, but is especially important during middle childhood in preparing students for academic expectations for learning and behavior during adolescence.

SOCIAL–EMOTIONAL SKILLS

Not only cognitive development but also emotional development (various kinds of affect represented in the limbic system, the emotional brain; see Chapter 7) affects development throughout schooling. However, by middle childhood, most children have developed a sense of their unique characteristics (self-concept) and their ability to learn and achieve goals expected by the adults in their life (self-efficacy). Both self-concept and self-efficacy can affect their social–emotional development and social interactions with others. If children do not have a positive self-concept or sense of self-efficacy, they may lack hope for their future, which can have the adverse effects on their subsequent development.

Teachers can help by introducing hope themes in the curriculum. Where one starts and where one is currently do not have to limit where one will end up. For example, Albert Einstein was not successful in the early grades. Mark Twain was a school dropout. John Muir, a scientist–writer whose life work led to the establishment of the national park system in the United States, was a survivor of an earlier industrial accident. Middle childhood students also can benefit from groups that teach social cognition skills—how to understand how others think about social interactions. Psychologists on the interdisciplinary team can facilitate these or cofacilitate them with teachers in the classroom.

MOVEMENT

During middle childhood, movement continues to be important to development. Developing minds are embodied in moving bodies. Physical education can facilitate the development of gross motor skills and overall health. Sports can facilitate a sense of group spirit based on which groups a student identifies with; sports competitions contribute to the development of this group affiliation. Dance offers a mode of expressing ideas and creativity through movement and is a natural response to many forms of music.

CREATIVE EXPRESSION

Ideas are expressed creatively through many media during middle childhood—for example, visual arts, music, and drama, all of which may have links to language and/or math. For example, musical notation requires reading symbols that have a quantitative basis in whole notes, half notes, quarter notes, and eighth notes, which symbolize temporal duration. Understanding part–whole relationships and fractions also affects musical expression. The notes symbolize the location on a scale of tones from high to low and patterns over time in tone location in vocal space and duration in vocal time. The result of the patterns is the rhythm of recurring and changing patterns, which also have quantitative properties. For some students, music may provide a path to understanding math.

SELF-CONCEPT AND FINDING ONE'S DEPENDABLE SKILLS

Given the multiple sources of diversity in biology and the environment (see Parts III and IV, this volume) and teachers' instructional practices and classrooms, it is not surprising that individual students exhibit unique profiles of relative strengths and weaknesses across development. By middle childhood, these profiles may become reliable indicators of a child's dependable strengths on which schooling and future work outside school might capitalize.

Technology

In the information age, many issues related to the use of technology in instruction and learning are relevant to education during middle childhood. Dealing with these issues appropriately and effectively may depend on many factors, including the educational needs of individual students, a school's resources, and curriculum requirements.

USE IN CLASSROOM VERSUS HOME

Recent research has indicated that during middle (and early) childhood, technology is more likely to be used at home than at school (e.g., for playing games and doing homework). Although during the elementary grades, many schools have a computer lab that the class as a whole may visit once or more a week, rarely are computer tools systematically integrated with curriculum and instruction. The reasons for this are complex and vary across settings. Integration of technology with curriculum and instruction may change in the future.

USE IN SPECIFIC CONTENT AREAS

Research shows that computer games may have a greater effect on motivation than actual learning of skills in content areas of the school curriculum. Many free resources are now available on the Internet for reading and other areas of the curriculum. Web links are used frequently as a source of information for written assignments at school in history, social studies, and science. Middle school students would benefit from systematic instruction in strategies for using the web in school assignments.

ACCOMMODATION WITH AND WITHOUT EXPLICIT INSTRUCTION

Best practices for accommodation include the following. First, the use of computer tools for accommodation should be linked to the nature of the problem. For example, if the child has difficulty with accuracy or rate of reading, then computerized tools are recommended that allow teachers to scan any text material into the computer, which then regulates the rate at which the text is read to the student and highlights each word as it is spoken. If the child has difficulty with legible handwriting, then use of a keyboard that goes with a laptop or desktop may be helpful. However, if the difficulty is with spelling, a spell check, which flags typos, may not be an appropriate accommodation. Unless a child has the necessary ability to recognize the correct spelling from a menu of options, the spell check will not be adequate compensation for the lack of spelling skills. As Charles MacArthur, a member of the advisory panel, pointed out, the goal should be to teach students to use spell checkers intelligently. They need to know that these tools will not find all errors, and they still need to proofread. They also need to know how to select correct spelling once errors are found. Research shows it is possible to teach these skills.

Second, no matter how computers are used for accommodation, during middle childhood, explicit instruction in the skill(s) with which a child has difficulty should continue to be provided. Both reading and writing skills, even if they are behind the typical developmental stepping-stone schedule, can still be remediated during middle childhood in children without developmental disabilities (see also the technology paper by Bryan Bryant posted on the web resources for Chapters 8 and 9).

USE OF TECHNOLOGY IN NOTE TAKING

Most research to date on the use of computer tools for note taking has been done with adolescents or adults. Evidence has shown that there may be many reasons that handwriting appears to be superior to computer-supported writing during note taking. However, computer-supported platforms may be superior to handwriting for transforming notes to text, at least in adolescents and adults. More research on note taking in developing students, beginning in middle childhood, is needed. For children who have difficulty keeping up with the pace of class discussions or lectures, "smart pens" and other audio recording devices may provide assistance. With current smart pen technology, students need only replay the audio-recorded lecture to add notes to what was not written down during the lecture. This technology can remove the stress of missing out on important notes or having to catch up with the speaker.

SAFETY ISSUES

As is the case for early childhood, school safety programs should teach middle school children safety precautions in using cell phones with earphones and texting while crossing at posted intersections or elsewhere. When users are attending to the audio and visual stimuli or manual activity on cell phones, they may have sufficient attention capacity and resources to monitor the changing events in the external environment (e.g., listening or texting and not paying attention to traffic).

ADDICTION TO TECHNOLOGY

Addiction to technology is becoming an increasing societal problem. Addiction may be to texting, social media, or cell phones. Signs of addiction are that the technology user cannot disengage from technology, and that in turn impairs the quality of his or her functioning in life. Psychology is developing specialized treatment for technology addiction, which can emerge as early as middle childhood.

SOCIAL SKILLS ISSUES

Students can benefit from discussion of socially appropriate and inappropriate use of technology. One of the roadblocks to the greater integration of technology into daily instructional programs is the fear that children will use the Internet for bullying or be victims of predators who use it to contact minors. Schools face legal risk if such adverse events occur when students are using a computer with access to the Internet. One way to prevent such events is to use only technology tools with Internet access turned off. Moreover, students need to learn what is and is not appropriate to write to others electronically. Appropriate and inappropriate content, tone, and language should be addressed.

Thinking Points for Differentiated Instruction

As with students in the earlier grades, it is important to identify which developmentally appropriate milestones for academic learning have not been reached in middle school and when schools have not actively listened to parents' concerns and reported developmental and educational history. Comprehensive assessment may be warranted to determine whether a child has a developmental or specific learning disability or other condition that requires instructional modifications beyond those discussed in this chapter or other chapters in Part II. However, the goal of the assessment is not to decide whether a student qualifies for pull-out special education services but rather how best to meet the student's educational needs in the least restrictive environment, which for most middle school students will be in general education.

The teacher and interdisciplinary team face the difficult decision of when individual differences in middle childhood reflect variations in the normal range for children of the same age or when they reflect differences outside the normal range. However, by middle childhood, educational professionals can draw on repeated observations over time by multiple observers using multiple assessment tools to address this issue from the perspective of baseline data. Although developmental disabilities and specific learning disabilities are mutually exclusive (see Chapters 8 and 9), many other conditions may occur within the same child and need to be taken into account in educational planning. Best professional practices consider all available information about sources of biological and environmental diversity and design plans and implement interventions that address all the sources. Some students may have instructional needs that are more related to biological diversity, some more to environmental diversity, and others to both.

Educational professionals should reach out to parents during middle childhood to build ongoing, positive home–school relationships and partnerships for facilitating children's development, learning, and behavior. Some parents may benefit from parent groups at school led by school psychologists or other members of the team that discuss parenting children at home and school during middle childhood. Some parents may benefit from support groups at school that are centered on a given "difference in the family" (e.g., a child with a pervasive developmental disability; see Chapter 8). Other parents seek opportunities to volunteer in classrooms to help not only their child but also other children and the teacher, who has an enormous job differentiating instruction for all students. Again, both home and school variables during middle childhood contribute to resilience later in development. Often, what leads to resilience is relationship building in addition to implementing evidence-based programs for learning and behavior. Each member of the interdisciplinary team should ask themselves whether he or she could be that educational professional who might make a difference in the development of a student and, if so, how?

Interdisciplinary Approaches Can Make A Difference

All too often, speech and language pathologists are not consulted for literacy issues in middle childhood or for issues that involve cultural differences. Jane Coolidge, MA, CCC-SLP (Honor Role Model 13), is a clinical speech–language pathologist whose experience with Native Americans and with early childhood, middle childhood, and adolescence in learning both oral and written language has contributed to her bridging the fields of speech and language, mainstream literacy in education, and neuropsychology with a multicultural, developmental stepping-stones perspective. During 1995–2003 she not only consulted with local schools about specific language impairment and learning disabilities and provided speech and language services in a neuropsychology clinic but she also specialized in emergent literacy in Native American early childhood populations in the Pacific Northwest with the Muckleshoot Tribe in Auburn, Washington, which led to consultant work with the American Indian Head Start Quality Improvement Center at the University of Oklahoma. From 2003 to 2004 she served as the national literacy specialist for the American Indian/Alaskan Native Head Start technical assistance system, and in 2011, working with the National Center for Quality Teaching and Learning, she helped train Tribal Head Start early childhood teachers across the country in emergent literacy, language development, and early childhood practices. She currently resides outside of Augusta, Georgia, where she works with a clinical neuropsychologist in the diagnosis and treatment of children and adolescents with dyslexia.

Coolidge brings developmental and culturally sensitive perspectives to her work on interdisciplinary teams and has been instrumental in helping many children and youth others had given up on. For example, when a school for which she was a consultant had lost hope that a non-reading student in middle school could ever learn to read, she diagnosed an underlying difficulty in articulatory awareness, which she treated in conjunction with phonological awareness and decoding skills. Within 4 months, the student was reading at a fourth-grade level, showing that it is never too late to remediate. Coolidge proposed to the multidisciplinary team a plan to support this student in his continued journey to reach grade level in reading. She recognized that offering individually tailored instruction is the first step, but best professional practices are necessary to support vulnerable students in their future literacy development.

Readings and Resources[1]

READING

Carlisle, J. (1999a). *Beginning reasoning and reading.* Cambridge, MA: Educators Publishing Service.

Carlisle, J. (1999b). *Reasoning and reading: Level one.* Cambridge, MA: Educators Publishing Service.

---

[1]Additional research readings and practitioner resources for this chapter can be found at http://www.apadivisions.org/division-16/publications/interdisciplinary-frameworks-supplement/index.aspx

Carlisle, J. (1999c). *Reasoning and reading: Level two.* Cambridge, MA: Educators Publishing Service.

Carlisle, J. (2000). Awareness of the structure and meaning of morphologically complex words: Impact on reading. *Reading and Writing: An Interdisciplinary Journal, 12,* 169–190.

Denton, C. A., Vaughn, S., Wexler, J., Bryan, D., & Reed, D. (2012). *Effective instruction for middle school students with reading difficulties: The reading teacher's sourcebook.* Baltimore, MD: Brookes.

Henry, M. (2010). *Words: Integrated decoding and spelling instruction based on word origin and word structure* (2nd ed.). Austin, TX: ProEd.

Katzir, T., Kim, Y.-S., Wolf, M., Morris, R., & Lovett, M. (2008). The varieties of pathways to dysfluent reading: Comparing subtypes of children with dyslexia at letter, word and connected-text reading. *Journal of Learning Disabilities, 41,* 47–66. doi.org/10.1177/0022219407311325

Katzir, T., Kim, Y.-S., Wolf, M., O'Brien, B., Kennedy, B., Lovett, M., & Morris, R. (2006). Reading fluency: The whole is more than the parts. *Annals of Dyslexia, 56,* 51–82. doi:10.1007/s11881-006-0003-5

Kessler, B., & Treiman, R. (1997). Syllable structure and the distribution of phonemes in English syllables. *Journal of Memory and Language, 37,* 295–311. doi:10.1006/jmla.1997.2522

Manis, F., & Morrison, F. (1982). Processing of identity and position information in normal and disabled readers. *Journal of Experimental and Child Psychology, 33,* 74–86. doi:10.1016/0022-0965(82)90007-8

Moats, L. C. (2000). *Speech to print: Language essentials for teachers.* Baltimore, MD: Brookes.

Niedo, J., Lee, Y.-L., Breznitz, Z., & Berninger, V. W. (2013, October). Computerized silent reading rate and strategy instruction for fourth graders at risk in silent reading rate. *Learning Disability Quarterly.* doi:10.1177/0731948713507263

Treiman, R. (1985). Onsets and rimes as units of spoken syllables: Evidence from children. *Journal of Experimental Child Psychology, 39,* 161–181. doi:10.1016/0022-0965(85)90034-7

WRITING

Carlisle, J. (1996). *Models for writing: Levels A, B, and C.* Novato, CA: Academic Therapy. See also http://www.highnoonbooks.com/index-hnb.tpl for reproducibles for classroom use.

Dixon, R., & Englemann, S. (2001). *Spelling through morphographs.* DeSoto, TX: SRA/McGraw-Hill.

Fry, E. (2004). *Dr. Fry's Computer Keyboarding for Beginners.* Westminster, CA: Teacher Creative Resources.

Graham, S., Harris, K., & Loynachan, C. (1994). The spelling for writing list. *Journal of Learning Disabilities, 27,* 210–214. doi:10.1177/002221949402700402

Graham, S., MacArthur, C., & Fitzgerald, J. (2007). *Best practices in writing instruction*. New York, NY: Guilford Press.

Harris, K. R., Graham, S., Mason, L., & Friedlander, B. (2008). *Powerful writing strategies for all students*. Baltimore, MD: Brookes.

Masterson, J. J., Apel, K., & Wasowicz, J. (2006). *SPELL-2 spelling performance evaluation for language and literacy* (2nd ed.). Evanston, IL: Learning by Design. Spelling assessment software for Grade 2 through adult; assessment linked to instruction.

Rubel, B. (1995). *Loops and groups*. Tucson, AZ: Therapy Skill Builders.

Ten Thumbs Typing Tutor [Computer software]. Edinburgh, Scotland: Runtime Revolution. http://tenthumbstypingtutor.com

Troia, G. (Ed.) (2008). *Writing instruction and assessment for struggling writers from theory to evidence based practices*. New York, NY: Guilford Press.

TECHNOLOGY

Bryant, D. P., & Bryant, B. R. (2012). *Assistive technology for people with disabilities* (2nd ed.). Upper Saddle River, NJ: Pearson.

MacArthur, C. A. (2008). Using technology to teach composing to struggling writers. In G. Troia (Ed.), *Writing instruction and assessment for struggling writers: From theory to evidence-based practices* (pp. 243–265). New York, NY: Guilford Press.

MacArthur, C. A. (2009). Technology and struggling writers: A review of research. *Teaching and learning writing: Psychological aspects of education— Current trends: British Journal of Educational Psychology Monograph Series II, 6*, 159–174. doi:10.1348/000709909X422954

MATH

Bailey, D. H., Hoard, M. K., Nugent, L., & Geary, D. (2012). Competence with fractions predicts gains in mathematics achievement. *Journal of Experimental Child Psychology, 113*, 447–455. doi:10.1016/j.jecp.2012.06.004

Fink, B., Brookes, H., Neave, N., Manning, J. T., & Geary, D. (2006). Second to fourth digit ratio and numerical competence in children. *Brain and Cognition, 61*, 211–218. doi:10.1016/j.bandc.2006.01.001

Geary, D. (1994). *Children's mathematical development: Research and practical applications*. Washington, DC: American Psychological Association.

Geary, D. C., Berch, D. B., Boykin, A. W., Embretson, S., Reyna, V., & Siegler, R. S. (2011). Learning mathematics: Findings from the National (United States) Mathematics Advisory Panel. In N. Canto (Ed.), *Issues and proposals in mathematics education* (pp. 175–221). Lisbon, Portugal: Gulbenkian.

Geary, D. C., Boykin, A. W., Embretson, S., Reyna, V., Siegler, R., Berch, D. B., & Graban, J. (2008). Report of the task group on learning processes. In National Mathematics Advisory Panel, *Reports of the task groups and subcommittees* (pp. 4-1–4-211). Washington, DC: U.S. Department of Education.

National Mathematics Advisory Panel. (2008). *Foundations for success: Final report of the National Mathematics Advisory Panel.* Washington, DC: U.S. Department of Education.

Siegler, R., Carpenter, T., Fennell, F., Geary, D., Lewis, J., Okamoto, Y., Thompson, L., & Wray, J. (2010). *Developing effective fractions instruction for kindergarten through 8th grade: A practice guide* (NCEE #2010–4039). Washington, DC: National Center for Education Evaluation and Regional Assistance, Institute of Education Sciences, U.S. Department of Education.

SCIENCE

The Buckminster Fuller Institute. http://bfi.org/

Fuller, B. (1969). *Operating manual for spaceship earth.* Carbondale, IL: Southern Illinois University Press.

LITERACY AND NUMERACY

Morris, R., & Mather, N. (Eds.). (2008). *Evidence-based interventions for students with learning and behavioral challenges.* Mahwah, NJ: Erlbaum.

Nunes, T., & Bryant, P. (2006). *Improving literacy instruction through teaching morphemes.* London, England: Routledge.

Nunes, T., & Bryant, P. (2009). *Children's reading and spelling: Beyond the first steps.* Oxford, England: Wiley-Blackwell.

Linking Instruction and Assessment in Adolescence

6

This chapter begins by describing six key issues that emerge during adolescence: (a) moving across instructional blocks with different teachers and classmates during the school day, (b) dealing with increasing diversity among learners who need to find their common and individual developmental paths, (c) the changing expression of genetic vulnerability as curricula change, (d) adapting to changing bodies and changing minds, (e) planning for students' future after high school, and (f) learning about and preparing for the world of work outside school. The chapter continues with the developmental stepping-stones model for planning and implementing curriculum and instruction and evaluating response to instruction (RTI) for students during adolescence. Exhibit 6.1 summarizes developmentally appropriate target skills for adolescents. The target skills for early childhood and middle childhood that students have not mastered are addressed, as are those that are developmentally appropriate for adolescents. Issues related to technology are discussed and thinking points are offered for interdisciplinary teams to use as a springboard for problem

http://dx.doi.org/10.1037/14437-006
Interdisciplinary Frameworks for Schools: Best Professional Practices for Serving the Needs of All Students, by V. W. Berninger

---

EXHIBIT 6.1

Assessment of Reading, Writing, and Math Skills in Adolescents

---

Reading
- Silent reading of familiar words—accuracy and rate of identification
- Silent reading of word meaning—vocabulary
- Silent reading for text comprehension

Writing

Spelling
- Word-specific spelling without handwriting
- Spelling words in writing from dictation
- Spelling during composing

Composing
- Completing written assignments—in class, at home (short-term and long-term)
- McNamara Coh-Metrix and other computerized assessments
- Portfolio of writing assessments (multiple genre)
- High-stakes writing tests
- College board writing tests

Math
- High-stakes writing math tests
- College board math tests

Branching Diagnosis for Adolescents
Continuing from middle childhood. See Chapter 5.

---

solving the issues in their local setting. Because of its relevance to the national focus on science, technology, engineering, and math (STEM subjects; see also Chapter 1), this chapter features the work of the Valdés Institute in increasing math achievement and access to higher education for underrepresented groups. This evidence-based approach, which involves partnerships among middle schools, high schools, and universities, will hopefully inspire educators to adopt innovative approaches to teaching math, the ticket to STEM careers. In addition, a model for comprehensive, interdisciplinary services for adolescents is described.

Multiple Transitions in a School Day

First, in contrast to elementary school students, adolescent students typically receive instruction in five to six 45- to 60-minute daily classes, each taught by a different teacher to a different set of about 25 to 30 classmates.

This switching among teachers and classmates poses great difficulty for students with underdeveloped executive functions for self-regulation (e.g., focusing, switching, and sustaining attention; planning, organizing, self-monitoring, revising, or adapting). Executive functions, which are essential to academic success as well as healthy social, emotional, and behavioral functioning of secondary students, are mediated by the frontal lobes, which are still myelinating during adolescence. Those students with immature executive functions for self-regulation require considerable support from teachers, parents, and even classmates, all of whom may serve as their "external executive functions" until these students acquire developmentally appropriate internal self-regulation. Learning age-appropriate self-regulation, which is the best predictor of functioning within and outside of school throughout development, is a major task of adolescence (for resources in helping adolescents develop self-regulated learning [SLR], see Cleary, 2014). However, for adolescents with appropriately diagnosed attention-deficit/hyperactivity disorder, SLR, although necessary, may not be sufficient alone. A multimodal treatment plan may be necessary to help them manage the attention and language requirements at school and complete homework assignments during adolescence.

Increasing Diversity Among Student Learners

The goal of middle childhood is to consolidate one's resources from early childhood, but the goal of adolescence is to diversify. Although at first glance, consolidation and diversification appear to be conflicting goals, both are recommended in business and are also applicable to education. Rarely is academic learning the result of one-trial learning. Rather, it results from many learning bouts distributed over time, which are consolidated from time to time to provide a springboard for moving forward to support new learning. At the same time, the more students learn, the more they begin to develop their own unique personality and profile of relative strengths (talents) and weaknesses (targets to try to improve but acknowledge) in setting reasonable achievement and career goals.

This increasing diversity among individual students has many sources, both biological and environmental, and becomes even greater across development through nature–nurture interactions (see Part III, this volume). Interestingly, both the mind's eye and the hand work together to translate cognitions into observable behavior (see Chapter 7) and in the process independently record the unique individual signatures of nature–nurture interactions. The patterns in the retina and the fingertips are unique to each individual and can be used to establish the personal identity of an individual.

Consequently, because nature–nurture interactions accumulate across development, the diversity of learners and their learning needs may become even greater in the secondary grades than the elementary grades. The educational challenge in the Common Core Era is to tailor instruction both to common core standards and to each student's unique profile of strengths and weaknesses. Those strengths may be relevant to earning a living after school. The limitations of schools in transforming diversity, which results from nature–nurture interactions, into homogeneity, as implied by the common core standards and high-stakes tests, should be acknowledged so that the standards can be revised to allow for diversity as appropriate.

Although diversity and commonality may at first seem like conflicting goals, both may be important variables in the educational equation. Indeed, unity in diversity is a basic principle on which the United States was founded, and it also exists in consciousness for complex brain systems (see Chapter 7). Although not all typically developing students can be above average, except in the Lake Wobegon of Garrison Keillor's mind, all typically developing students might be able to reach some common goals in literacy, numeracy, and knowledge of past and contemporary world history, all of which are necessary for participating in society as informed citizens in a democracy and as consumers and workers in a global information economy. However, what is optimal for any one individual during or after middle or high school may vary considerably across developing adolescents. The professional judgment of interdisciplinary teams can play an important role in solving the educational equation for helping adolescents find their unique selves for regulating learning and behavior during and after schooling along their career path.

In the long run, diversity may contribute to the future vitality of the economy during the information age. To quote a middle school student who, when asked what he wanted to do when he grows up, responded with insight, "Although my school is preparing me for computer science or aviation industry, it's more likely that what I will do is not yet invented yet—and maybe I will have to help invent that."

Changing Expression of Genetic Vulnerabilities as the Curriculum Changes

The success of translating research into early intervention programs that transform struggling beginning readers into successful ones has led many to conclude that teaching alone can overcome genetic risk factors for reading problems. Teaching, via neural mechanisms that process instructional input and epigenetic mechanisms that may alter behavioral expression of underlying genetic mechanisms (see Chapter 7), may normalize brain functions supporting learning at a particular time in development. However, the genetic vulnerability (variations or abnormalities in genes or gene sequencing established at birth) remains throughout the life span. What may change is how the underlying genetic vulnerability expresses itself when requirements of the curriculum change in nature, amount, and/or complexity in future grades and whether the learning environment and instruction at that time is appropriately tailored to the student.

Thus, RTI—monitoring the academic progress of students—should continue across early childhood, middle childhood, and adolescence. However, using a developmental stepping-stone model followed by individually tailored instruction in general education and progress monitoring for the increasing volume, complexity, and level of expectation of performance on written assignments and tests, will probably result in fewer students dropping out, being recommended for grade retention, being referred for special education, or getting in trouble with the law. More students will probably graduate from high school and pursue postsecondary education relevant to their career goals. Important data to use in evaluating RTI include not just test results but also data for the following factors, all relevant to the cost-effectiveness of multimodal models: dropout rate, legal infractions, referral to special education, promotions, graduation, and access to postsecondary education.

Changing Bodies and Changing Minds

Adolescents are growing in size, need more sleep (though they often go to bed later than when younger), and are entering or have entered puberty. Many adolescents are self-conscious about their changing bodies, both in their own self-perceptions and in the perceptions of peers. Educational professionals can help by providing lessons in nutrition and physical exercise and group counseling sessions on changing bodies.

In many school districts, buses are scheduled to transport middle school and high school students before elementary school students, and thus high school classes may start as early as 7:30 a.m. This scheduling does not mesh with the needs of adolescents for more sleep (see Chapter 7 for the role of circadian rhythms in regulating states of mind, and the role of hippocampus in consolidating learning during sleep). Many adolescents may struggle in school because they are not well-rested and are literally not fully awake. School districts could explore renegotiating union contracts with bus drivers so that high school classes are offered in a time frame synchronized with the sleep requirements of adolescents.

In addition, because of the early dismissal of high schools, typically about 2:30 p.m., many adolescents have no parental supervision for several hours in the afternoon because parents are working. Without supervision or organized after-school activities, adolescents may get into trouble. Some schools have dealt with this issue by involving adolescents in the child care offered in the school for working parents or by placing adolescents in other community service opportunities. Some adolescents are able to find paid work after school. Supervised homework clubs after school are another viable way to ensure that adolescents are engaged in meaningful activities rather than being on the streets, where they are more likely to get in trouble. Sports, drama, and music activities are other viable after-school activities for adolescents, but not all parents can afford the fees that are increasingly charged for these, nor can they provide the transportation to and from these activities. Interdisciplinary teams might seek philanthropic support for extracurricular activities for low-income children. Some teachers also conduct book clubs or literature study groups after school for low-income students.

Although adolescents who have entered puberty are able to reproduce, schools vary greatly as to whether they offer health classes that deal with issues related to reproduction. States vary as to the age at which adolescents have the right to obtain birth control information or discuss, independent of their parents, other health-related issues. School districts may wish to work with interdisciplinary teams to design policy for how educational professionals should work with the students, their parents, and community services in their schools and states regarding these issues.

Not only bodies but also minds are changing during adolescence. Many students still rely on *concrete operational thought*—constructing their minds by hands-on experience with concrete objects. For other students, *formal operational thought* also emerges, that is, the ability to represent and manipulate internal abstract codes and symbols. In many ways adolescence is a state of mind that is influenced by culture, including peer group culture. For example, in some cultures 13-year-old girls enter into arranged marriages in which they are exchanged for a dowry, often one or more cows, and soon after become parents. In mainstream United States culture in the 21st century, adolescence has become a prolonged period of time between childhood and adulthood during which students complete their education and prepare for working and mating in the adult years.

The middle school/junior high and high school grades are the beginning, but not necessarily the end, of this developmental journey. In some cases adolescent girls become mothers, but do not marry, before completing their education or becoming working adults. High schools and community schools have unique opportunities to partner with these girls to provide educational mechanisms for helping them complete their high school degrees and obtain credentials related to marketable employment skills.

Planning for Students' Futures

One task that adolescents face is figuring out what to do after high school, hopefully after graduating rather than dropping out along the way. Thus, the "criterion for the next environment" is used to plan for the transition from high school to the postsecondary years. In some cases parents are able to provide counseling to mentor their children on a career path, especially one that requires postsecondary education at the college level. However, many parents who have not completed high school or college do not have the knowledge or resources to provide this kind of mentoring. Educational professionals can often provide mentoring when parents cannot. Once upon a time schools provided vocational counseling, which included a variety of educational and employment opportunities after high school graduation. Currently, there seems to be an unexamined assumption that everyone has to go to college. Yet college graduates may not have marketable skills in the contemporary work world, which those with technical training but not college degrees often do. However, a large percentage of the population still does not graduate from high school; only some will eventually complete high school equivalencies, and many of these individuals do not have marketable skills.

Policymakers could make a major contribution by examining job needs in the current economy and those projected for the future, sharing these with educational professionals who counsel students on where to find the appropriate training for those jobs, many of which require career training after high school but not a 4-year degree. It is not clear that everyone can earn a living through STEM. Society still needs people to build and repair roads, maintain the electrical sources in and out of homes that fuel many conveniences as well as technology tools, and install and repair indoor plumbing as well as service, sell, and repair automobiles; provide emergency services when there are natural disasters or crime; and provide assistive medical care and paraprofessional services in schools. What is missing is a common core for career-specific paths for preparing for specific jobs in the world of work after school, that is, a road map for the journey to employment in the information era.

An important component of these common core job-specific paths would be helping each student identify her or his dependable strengths during adolescence and providing guidelines for using this knowledge in career planning. In some cases the career path will require college (undergraduate education) and even graduate-level training. In many cases, however, the necessary technical training to qualify for jobs that match one's skill set and strengths and that is needed in the current work-force is available through community colleges, other training institutes, or apprenticeships with experienced members of certain trades, which maintain their own credentialing and continuing education standards.

Educational professionals working with adolescents in Grades 7 through 12 should seek opportunities to learn more about current mar-ket needs and training opportunities. What they learn can be shared to help more students access training programs specialized for the rap-idly expanding job market, which requires skills with rapidly advanc-ing technology tools and services and hires those with postsecondary specialized training that is not always available in 4-year colleges. Some schools share this information with adolescents through annual job fairs or by sponsoring social studies for students investigating the different ways adults earn a living.

In sum, an assumption of the Common Core Standards and the Smarter Balanced Assessments is that all students are college-bound. The focus has shifted from "all children reaching grade-level profi-ciency" to the goal of "college and career readiness" (see http://www.corestandards.org/). A common sense approach to Common Core Standards is needed if schools are to prepare students well for the world of work (see Rothman, 2012).

Preparing for the World of Work Outside School

One of the reasons the business community has advocated for the accountability of teachers is the perception that schools are not prepar-ing students for the world of work. Such preparation, however, requires two-way partnerships between business and schools. Job requirements in the world of work are incredibly varied and depend not only on an organization's business goals but also on its organizational setting and policies for supporting those goals. Schools cannot be expected to pre-pare students for skills specific to a particular business or work setting. So, one way to prepare students more effectively for the world of work is to create partnerships between local businesses and schools, as has been done in Japan, to provide supervised mentoring of high school students to learn what the world of work entails through a cooperative learning (co-op) model. The functions the students perform under supervision in the co-op model earn them modest financial compensation from the business and course credit at school. Participating businesses can make suggestions to schools about curriculum offerings to better prepare students for the co-op experience and thus open a more productive dialogue with schools. Future workers learn to integrate knowledge gained in classrooms with the realities of the work world.

Developmental Stepping-Stones in Adolescence (Grades 7–12)

LANGUAGE ARTS

Adolescents who have not yet mastered oral or silent word reading continue to need instruction that focuses on decoding longer, more complex words than in the earlier grades; highlights how morphology (adding suffixes) may change the phonology of base words; explains how phonology, orthography, and morphology may be interrelated as a function of word origin; and teaches vocabulary words that are specific to content areas of the curriculum. Writing requirements are even more challenging in amount, complexity, and kinds of writing goals. Explicit instruction is needed in strategies for reading materials, taking notes from written sources and lectures, writing different kinds of reports and other assignments, and studying for and taking tests, which also have writing requirements. Individual students in the secondary grades may differ in levels of literacy achievement in specific skills on which they need continued targeted instruction. University professors asked to implement research-based literacy practices in a whole school system found that secondary students varied as to whether they had problems in decoding, reading comprehension (creating mental models from reading text, making inferences, applying strategies for multiple purposes), applying cognitive and metacognitive strategies across specific content areas of the curriculum, and thinking critically. They then designed, implemented, and evaluated RTI for these diverse learning needs in keeping with a developmental stepping-stones framework and found that adolescents could respond to individually tailored instruction.

Adolescents may also continue to have trouble with handwriting, spelling, and/or composing text in different genres. Much of the writing at the secondary level is taught in a language arts block. Sometimes the language arts block is integrated with reading and writing about literature and is designed to educate adolescents about what is considered great writing that has contributed to development of human civilization. Sometimes the writing activities are designed to fulfill a teacher-defined or student-defined rhetorical goal to communicate with an invisible audience (e.g., an author's chair with no one there). That audience may, of course, include some people who do or do not have knowledge of the writing topic, some who have the same or different opinions or perspectives, and some who do or do not care about the topic. Sometimes the task is to generate a specific kind of text structure (or genre). Thus, adolescent writers continue to learn about the many purposes of writing and different ways of using written language to express cognitions and achieve social goals. Regardless of the rhetorical goal, audience or audiences, assigned task and related genre, or content area of the curriculum for which writing is required, the writer's task is to externalize the cognitions in the vast unconscious mind, that is, to translate those cognitions into written language by using the orthographic loop of working memory. The orthographic loop functionally integrates the mind's eye for orthography (letters and word-specific spellings linked to cognitive concepts) and the sequential finger movements of the hand to transform cognitions into different levels of written language (see Chapter 7). Content–domain strategies for doing so can facilitate this process of externalizing cognition so that it can be consciously examined, modified as necessary, and extended through instruction and learning activities in and across domain-specific areas of the curriculum.

An effective way to teach students with specific learning disabilities (see Chapter 9) or other learning differences despite otherwise normal development is to offer one or more special sections of the language arts block in general education. Adolescents tend to perceive pull-out programs to be for students of limited ability. However, in a section in the regular language arts block, adolescents respond well to explicit and structured language instruction in the context of highly cognitively engaging and intellectually challenging reading and writing activities. Instruction offered in a section in the regular program is not perceived to be for less able students, especially when the program is cognitively engaging as well as taught by a teacher with expertise in teaching language by ear, by mouth, by eye, and by hand across levels of language in the explicit and structured ways needed by students with language learning disabilities or differences.

Language arts teachers who adapt reading and writing instruction to the reading and writing requirements of other content areas of instruction in the curriculum and in a block of the regular language arts program should be nominated for or receive recognition as teacher honor role model.

MATH

Arithmetic skills—math facts, computation, and fractions—taught in elementary school are necessary but not sufficient for the secondary school math curriculum. Students who have not mastered the earlier developmental stepping-stones in arithmetic generally do not benefit from simply repeating those procedural skills over and over in pull-out programs or regular sections of math classes. Rather, they benefit from (a) diagnostic assessment to target the number concepts and procedures they still have not mastered and (b) differentiated, intellectually engaging instruction to help them master those skills identified in diagnostic testing. At the same time, they should not be denied access to the new topics introduced in mathematics in middle school and high school. An overview of the developmental stepping-stones in math is presented next; these should be adapted to the particular curriculum a school district uses for specific specializations in math.

Concept of Number

Learning secondary math specializations builds on these earlier developmental stepping-stones: (a) fluency with whole numbers, including understanding place value and composing and decomposing numbers (e.g., $23 = 20 + 3$); (b) automatic recall of addition and related subtraction facts and multiplication and related division facts; (c) relative quantity expressed in fractions, decimals, and mixed numbers and their representation in the number line; use in computational operations; and application to problem solving, for example, in measurement; (d) fluent use of computational procedures to solve math problems that involve math reasoning; and (e) sensitivity to differences in exact versus estimated quantity (later used in evaluating plausibility of solutions). New number concepts introduced in the secondary curriculum include, but are not restricted to, the following: (a) probability (quantity may be probable to a certain degree rather than absolute), (b) exponents that multiply numbers repetitively, (c) roots that generate a number, (d) positive and negative numbers, (e) imaginary numbers that can be applied to solve real problems, (f) numbers that vary along a distribution within a categorical variable, (g) numbers that stay constant (e.g., π),(h) patterns in the number line such as prime numbers that cannot be divided into smaller numbers, and (i) numbers that have meaningful patterns but do not stand for quantity—for example, 1 and 0 code digital patterns rather than quantity in computer programming language.

Indeed, the patterns across numbers in an equation, on the number line, and between or among distributions, which may have linear or nonlinear relationships, are a major focus of instruction and learning. For example, qualitative, categorical variables, each with continuous distributions, can be combined in equations such that (a) the parts and the quantity of each part on each side of the equal sign are different ways of dividing the same whole into different parts (e.g., in algebra) or (b) what appears on the left side of the equal sign can be transformed into one or more qualitative variables, each with continuous distribution, on the right side of the equal sign (e.g., calculus). Patterns of numbers on the number line can be used to prove some geometric theorems. Operations can be performed on distributions for a unidimensional variable or for multidimensional variables (matrix algebra).

Thus, numbers are concepts with multiple meanings. Numerals are symbols for

- absolute quantity in counting order,
- relative quantity in part–whole or rational number relationships,
- exact or estimated quantity,
- probable quantity,
- variable quantity within a category of measurement,
- signals for the number of parts a categorical variable contributes to the whole,
- constant values that can be used to solve many applied problems,
- codes for writing equations in which what is on the left is equivalent to what is on the right but which is patterned differently in whole–part relationships,
- codes for writing equations for transforming what is on the left into a new pattern on the right,
- codes for patterns without quantity that can be used for the language of computation, and
- codes for writing equations for a window into numeric language of the physical universe.

Students pursuing STEM careers should become grounded in algebra, including (a) expression; (b) linear equations and inequalities and their graphs; (c) systems of linear equations; (d) quadratic equations; (e) linear, quadratic, logarithmic, and trigonometric functions; (f) factorization of polynomials; and (g) basic tenets of combinations and probability. Secondary teachers should address the related underlying concept of number in teaching these procedures. They should teach applications of concepts and procedures to real math problems related to academic disciplines, the world of work outside school, and everyday math—finances, employment, savings, investment, and recreation.

Concepts of Space and Time

Developmental stepping-stones in math extend adolescents' understanding of lines from linear (counting), circular (telling time in cycles), or two-dimensional shapes or three-dimensional solids to fractals. *Fractals* are irregular lines, as in coastlines, branches, trees, and dendrites, which describe many geographical structures in the external world of nature and the internal world of the mind. Moreover, the concept of relationships among space, time, and motion is introduced, which is critical to understanding physics and the application of trigonometry to astronomy, and can be applied to animation, which has many applications beyond computer games. The Mobius strip (a narrow strip of paper that is twisted and the ends joined) is a powerful teaching tool to convey the concept of space–time continuums that have no beginning and no end and to convey the nonlinearity of cause–effect relationships. Critical knowledge includes basic geometry, such as an understanding of similar triangles.

Models and Equations

Adolescents should become fluent in fitting simple mathematical models to data, which can have many applications in the world of education and work. Some adolescents may even reach a developmental destination, which allows them not only to solve equations written by others but also write their own. Those who grasp Mandelbrot's equation, which many regard as the most important equation in the early 21st century, might be encouraged to extend the last equation Einstein wrote or write another one that interests them. Prompts to guide their thinking might include the following: (a) Was Einstein correct in thinking that there is no room for chance or randomization in the universe, as the quantum physicists think there is? Or are behavioral scientists and quantum physicists correct that probability is a better model for complex, multidimensional, interacting variables? (b) Was Einstein correct in thinking that there are only nine dimensions in the universe? Did he leave any out in his last equation? (c) Can humans write one equation that explains everything, or do we need many different kinds of equations for different purposes? Those who take courses in programming languages might conceptualize and write models that support computing environments. In this information age, computer programming might be introduced earlier in the curriculum so that adolescents can make informed decisions about career paths in computer science, which is an ever-changing field.

Integrating Math With Other Disciplines

Math is no longer a separate field of study at the college level. It is highly integrated with many other fields, including archeology, anthropology, engineering, biology, neuroscience, genetics, computer science, and the behavioral sciences. Efforts to help adolescents gain access to higher education and to the social as well as biological sciences and engineering should emphasize math instruction.

Applying Math to Everyday Life and the Work World

Secondary school math teachers have an important contribution to make in preparing students for everyday math during and after high school, which is critical to students' current and future participation in the economy. Topics for everyday math for high school students include banking, paying bills, securing loans, making salary deposits (e.g., for jobs after school, on the weekend, or in the summer), saving, and planning one's personal finances. Skill in these areas is dependent on (a) fluency with whole numbers and fractions, (b) an understanding of functions (i.e., the ability to translate a word problem into a solvable algebra problem), and (c) basic geometry and measurement. Advanced courses might cover investments in the stock market, writing business plans for starting a business, and applying math probability to recreational activities such as strategies in card games, casino gambling, and horse racing.

SCIENCE

Curriculum offerings should include traditional subject domains in science—biology, chemistry, and physics—but also the rapidly emerging fields of neuroscience, genetics, and psychology. Curriculum offerings that emphasize interdisciplinary links across these specializations and with math specializations are desirable. All science courses should include a balance between current, established knowledge and problem-solving skills for discovering new knowledge using the scientific method.

SOCIAL STUDIES, HISTORY, ANTHROPOLOGY, AND ARCHAEOLOGY

Secondary school social studies curricula should include United States history, world history, and local history (state and community). The rapidly expanding fields of cultural anthropology and archeology should be covered either alone or in conjunction with world history and the story of human civilizations.

COLLEGE CREDIT FOR HIGH SCHOOL COURSES

Many schools now offer advanced placement courses for high school students. On the one hand, some students are ready for college-level courses, and earning college credit in advance can save tuition costs during the college years. On the other hand, the current climate of high expectations may create anxiety for some students. Moreover, adolescence is a developmental period of self-discovery for many students who may not yet be able to articulate their focus (major) in college studies. Not all adolescents should be pressured to complete college courses before they enter college, even if they have the cognitive ability to do so—social and emotional development and finding oneself are also important in the educational journey.

SERVICE TO COMMUNITY

One way many adolescents find themselves and their life goals is through volunteer work in the community. Increasingly, high schools are organizing, requiring, and giving credit for weekly or monthly community service activities of high school students.

PARENTING

Because some high school students are parents and many high school graduates will at some point become parents, courses and practicum experiences in parenting should also be provided at the high school level. In the United States, more education is available for driving a car than for parenting, both of which are important for the functioning of society. High schools are an excellent venue for disseminating knowledge about early childhood through, for example, child care programs in which high school students provide services under supervision for parents in the community and, in the process, learn about parenting and educating children.

Response to Instruction During Adolescence

Exhibit 6.1 outlines target skills that should be both taught and assessed for RTI during adolescence. Assessment approaches during adolescence draw greatly on group-administered tests by the interdisciplinary team or the school district. For students who are not meeting developmental stepping-stones for adolescence, skills to assess through branching diagnosis, on the basis of the developmental stepping-stones for early and middle childhood, are provided in Chapters 4 and 5 and this book's companion website, which can be used according to the skills not yet mastered.

TEACHING OTHER SKILLS TO FACILITATE ACADEMIC LEARNING AND BEHAVIOR

Self-Regulation and Attention

Middle schools and high schools can contribute to adolescents' development of self-regulation skills. For each content area, students can benefit from instruction in content-specific vocabulary, reading and report-writing strategies, note-taking strategies for report writing and class lectures, study skills, test-taking, and other self-regulation and organization strategies (e.g., for classroom assignments and also homework completion, especially long-term assignments). More attention should be given to cross-curriculum integration of reading, writing, and math skills in middle school and high school. For example, improving math achievement may require more than simply teaching math, because math also requires reading word problems, writing numerals using the place value system during paper and pencil calculations, and writing algebra equations. Adolescents also can benefit from instruction in strategies for (a) sorting out what is relevant and irrelevant information in solving math problems or completing assignments; (b) changing state of minds for learning from different instructors with different styles, goals, and instructional activities; and (c) sustaining attention over time to complete assignments without getting off task, especially when task completion is not possible in a single session.

Social–Emotional Skills

Educational professionals should pay close attention to the social and emotional development of adolescents. On the one hand, adolescents experience changing states of mind in relationship to their parents, switching back and forth between dependence, as earlier in childhood, and desire for independence. On the other hand, they experience changing states of mind in relationships with peers, trying to reconcile a sense of self apart from and in relationship to others of the same age. Some adolescents may exhibit acting-out behaviors (externalizing) and others withdrawing behaviors (internalizing). Often, schools focus on those who act out and disrupt the ongoing activities in the schools and miss those who are loners or who are sad and depressed or even at risk of suicide. Educational professionals should take seriously both kinds of behaviors and provide problem-solving consulting, individual counseling, small group counseling, and referral to community providers as needed. The interdisciplinary team should periodically update their knowledge of the laws related to delivery of health services and mental health services to youth when adolescents report suicidal ideation or engage in threatening behaviors toward others that could result in violence (see Chapter 14).

Movement

Physical education remains an important part of the school curriculum during adolescence both for health reasons during a time of major physical changes in the body and for social reasons. Some adolescents participate in sports as athletes, some as spectators for school spirit, and some in both roles. Movement through social dance can take on an important socialization role during adolescence in some cultures, although currently in the United States many adolescents may be participating more as viewers than participants in dance, as was more common in the past when school dances were held more often. During adolescence some students realize that they want to pursue athletics or dance as a career. Professional athletics and dance typically require special training and coaching outside school, and educational professionals can support this vocational development when they observe talent and interest in a student. At the same time, schools can introduce students to the many positive ways they can incorporate exercise, recreational sports, and dance into their leisure time activities now and in the future.

Creative Expression

Some adolescents exhibit talent and interest in the visual arts, music, and drama. Again, educational professionals should encourage them to pursue career paths in these areas. But these professionals should also explore how all students can incorporate the creative arts into their leisure time activities, both as participants and spectators. Schools that provide educational opportunities in physical movement, dance, visual arts, music, and drama often find that students are then more engaged in the academic curriculum as a result. Such extracurricular activities, whether offered during or after the school day, often help students "find themselves," that is, find the self or personality that underlies the self-regulation of their learning and behavior.

Self-Concept and Finding One's Dependable Skills

One way to help adolescents find their dependable strengths is to acknowledge them privately and publicly. It is also important to help adolescents discover their unique self, their personality that underlies who they are. For example, adolescents may enjoy making or drawing masks that capture the person behind the mask. The mask does not identify the person on the basis of the observable face but rather the person behind the face, the self. Mask-making may also serve as an opportunity for sharing orally with peers the inner self that is still developing. Many oral traditions in different cultures use masks during dance and music to convey the sense of self and characters in the stories of the culture's oral traditions. Mask-making can be integrated into science units on cultural anthropology to teach students about the role of the oral tradition, with storytelling, dance, music, and art (masks) in human history and civilization. In the process, adolescents continue to learn about the individual in society.

Technology

All the issues related to technology in middle childhood discussed in Chapter 8 also apply in adolescence, especially the need to continue to provide instruction in technology use and not just accommodations with technology. Students are likely to use cell phones and text frequently but, because of school policy, may still use laptops more at home for homework assignments than during class. Computer use should be monitored carefully unless access to the Internet is shut off. Adolescents may benefit from ongoing instruction in appropriate and inappropriate ways of using the Internet for finding information and evaluating its authenticity. They should still be taught strategies for learning content through other media. Adolescents may also find handwriting using pens more effective than using keyboards in taking notes during class lectures. They also still benefit from systematic spelling instruction integrated with their writing (see Chapter 5). Because many homework assignments are completed outside of school, issues surface as to whether the work is solely that of the student. Throughout schooling many students get help from their parents for homework, but some parents cannot help their children with homework for many reasons. With the easy access to a variety of kinds of information on the Internet, issues related to plagiarism are harder to monitor. Best professional practice may be to give homework but assess adolescents primarily on activities completed at school when professionals can monitor them.

School safety programs should teach adolescents safety in using cell phones with earphones and in texting while driving as well as crossing at posted intersections or elsewhere. When users are attending to audio and visual stimuli or manual activity, they do not have sufficient attention capacity and resources to monitor the changing events in the external environment (e.g., listening or texting and thus not paying attention to traffic). Adolescents may show addiction to texting, social media, or cell phones. Signs of addiction are that the technology user cannot disengage from technology, which in turn impairs quality of functioning in life. Psychology is developing specialized treatment for technology addiction. Educational professionals might declare technology-free days at school but should be prepared if not all students (or colleagues) can comply.

As in middle childhood, one of the roadblocks to integrating technology into the daily instructional program is the fear that adolescents will use the Internet for bullying or be victims of predators who use it to contact them (see Chapter 5). Students have to learn what is and is not appropriate to write to others electronically. Appropriate and inappropriate content, tone, and language should be addressed. Educators should spend more time teaching etiquette for online engagement—for example, for opinion writing in blogs versus discussion posts versus comments boxes. These lessons can also be integrated into a writing genre study (e.g., "How do we write professional/business letters online?").

Thinking Points for Differentiated Instruction

During adolescence it is important to continue to identify, within the interdisciplinary framework, which developmental stepping-stones have not yet been mastered and which still need instructional attention in the least restrictive environment (a block in the general education program). During adolescence it also becomes important to identify each student's unique profile of relative strengths (and weaknesses) and interests, all of which inform course selection and career planning. Adolescents' learning struggles are not only the result of individual differences in learner and teacher variables but also of social variables: a student's socioeconomic status (SES; the financial and educational level of parents); the school's SES status (the resources and challenges of the school and surrounding community); family variables, including stressors in the home; culture (of students, teachers, and the community within and surrounding a school); and racial diversity. Although student performance on college entrance exams has improved, clear and remarkable discrepancies exist between the educational achievement of White or Asian American students and that of African American or Latino students on college entrance exams and advanced placement exams.

Currently, the achievement gap is largest for Native Americans. Because the African American and Native American populations have endured a long history of educational inequities in the United States and the Latino population is the largest and most rapidly growing ethnic minority in the country, educational innovation is needed to help these groups meet the federal initiative for STEM education to compete in a highly technological world marketplace. Math literacy has thus become an issue of civil rights. The debate often centers on whether traditional or reform curriculum is the better way to approach teaching mathematics, but a complex problem is more likely to be solved by a multidimensional solution.

Cultural issues may be related to race or ethnicity, but not always. On the one hand, students who speak different languages at school and home may face challenges. On the other hand, advantages of bilingualism and immersion in more than one language have also been reported (see Petitto, 2009). None of these environmental sources of diversity rules out biologically based disorders (developmental or learning disabilities or other conditions). Any of these sources of diversity may lower motivation at school due to lack of success resulting in impaired self-concept and sense of self-efficacy and lack of hope (expectation that success is possible). However, some adolescents show remarkable resilience despite their struggles due to environmental and/or biological sources of diversity. Educational professionals can support adolescents in developing such resilience and can make a difference in whether individual students remain in school, receive passing grades, are promoted to the next grade, graduate from high school, or gain access to higher education or employment skills. For each adolescent who is not finding a developmental path to school success, what are the sources of diversity that should be taken into account in educational planning, and how might all the diversity-related needs be most effectively and efficiently met?

Valdés Institute for Raising Math Achievement of Low-Income, Diverse Students

The story of how one immigrant transformed adolescents' school struggles into school success should inspire educational professionals to think that they can make a difference in the educational outcomes of adolescents from diverse backgrounds. The late José Valdés, a Cuban immigrant and teacher in East San José's Andrew Hill High School from 1974 to 1991, created a model summer math institute in 1989 that not only increased the math achievement of his students but also showed that high expectations for students can be "contagious." The institute has been in place for 20 years in San José, and spinoffs have been formed in other areas of California, including Pittsburg, Stockton, Salinas, and Los Angeles.

Sylvia Valdés-Fernández, MEd (Honor Role Model 14), math educator and daughter of the founder of the Valdés Institute, is investigating whether the institute might increase secondary teachers' sense of efficacy, which in turn translates into higher expectations for students, changes in teaching behaviors, and higher levels of achievement. High expectations are theorized to be directly related to *teachers' sense of efficacy*, which is a teacher's belief or conviction that he or she can influence how well students learn and which may be related to student outcomes and achievement, motivation, and a student's sense of self-efficacy. Key components of the institute are its philosophical principles, student recruitment and selection, delivery of instruction and teacher training, high levels of expectation for achievement, parent involvement, location on college campuses, and supplemental activities.

TEACHING PHILOSOPHY

Nine philosophical principles guide the Valdés Institute: (a) All students can learn math; (b) teachers must believe that all students can learn math; (c) teachers must be involved in important educational decisions; (d) a common effort by elementary, middle, and high schools, along with colleges, parents, and community is essential to solving a complex educational problem; (e) sound teaching techniques work with all students, regardless of race, class, or gender; (f) students (especially Latino and African American students) do not need "watered-down" math—all students need to engage in rich and rigorous math to be successful in high-level math; (g) all students should enter high school prepared to succeed in at least Algebra 1; (h) math is a vehicle to teach students how to think—success in math leads to success in other academic areas; and (i) truly heterogeneous classes will be achieved when the number of Latino and African American students taking calculus in high school is proportionate to the general student population. Critical to the Valdés philosophy is the conviction that teachers need to participate in making decisions about what and how to teach their own students. Their involvement in running the institute and making schedules and curricular decisions obliges teachers to collaborate with each other.

RECRUITING PARTICIPANTS AND DETERMINING INSTRUCTIONAL LEVELS

Students in Grades 6 to 8 are recruited from the surrounding area for participation in a summer institute to facilitate their math learning in Grades 7 to 9 and thereafter. Although all students from any ethnic background can apply to be a part of the Valdés Summer Math Institute, a special effort is made to recruit students from underserved populations by targeting underrepresented students representative of the area's population (e.g., Hispanic students in San José); thus, criteria may vary from site to site. Once students have submitted an application, they are given a placement test to determine their individual instructional needs. On the basis of the test score and teacher recommendation, students are assigned to a level: Math 1, Math 2, or Math 3. Those who do well on the arithmetic placement test are asked to return to take the University of California,

Berkeley, algebra readiness test, and according to that score are placed in either Pre-algebra or Algebra 1.

Students are grouped by skill level, not ability, because to cover an entire year's worth of math in 7 weeks, it helps to have students homogeneously grouped at instructional levels. Research has shown that students often get "stuck" in tracks such as remedial math across grades and school careers when grouped by math ability. It is not only possible but also likely for a student to take Math 1 in the summer before Grade 7, return to their home school in the fall and take seventh-grade math, return to take pre-algebra the summer between seventh and eighth grade, and take Algebra 1 during the eighth grade. At that point, that student is not only in the college prep track but is also qualified to be in that track. In San José, on average, 87% of students advanced at least 1 year during the summer. The percentage for Math 1 students was actually higher in that these students are most likely to advance 2 or more years over the summer. Readiness at the end of the summer is determined by a posttest similar to the pretest before summer began. The Valdés standard is that students must earn at least a B to advance to the next level.

Because some students return for numerous summers, some students (many of whom were not "algebra ready" when they began) may pass Algebra 1 or Geometry 1 during the school year and then place into Geometry 2 or Algebra 2 in the summer. In San José, students also often select a class of trigonometry precalculus as well. Most students in these more advanced courses were returning students who began when they were in middle school but who were now in high school.

TEACHING TEAMS

One teacher and two teaching assistants form each of the teaching teams—one teaching team per class. Valdés teachers are interviewed and selected during the fall of the school year prior to summer school. Although in general the institute looks for experienced teachers with positive attitudes toward minority students, some teachers are included who may be skeptical about the possibility of students actually being capable of doing this much work. This inclusion of teachers with mixed perspectives is designed to spread the high expectations of its "best" teachers to the teaching population in general. Wherever possible, teachers with diverse ethnic backgrounds are selected to serve as role models for as many students as possible. Teachers have diverse mathematics teaching backgrounds (e.g., a mix of elementary, middle, and high school teachers) to support individual differences in students at different ages and levels of math development.

THE INSTRUCTIONAL PROGRAM, ORGANIZED BY DEVELOPMENTAL STEPPING-STONES IN MATH

"Backbone" courses are offered in small classes with a student–teacher ratio of about seven to one to create the foundations for math learning: Math 1 (emphasis on whole number operations and introduction to fractions and decimals), Math 2 (emphasis on fractions and decimals with a review of whole numbers), and Math 3 (mastery of whole number operations, fractions, decimals, ratio and percentage, introduction to integers and number theory, relationships, reasoning, and problem solving). These are followed by Introduction to Algebra (number theory, integers, exponents, radicals, problem solving, geometry, graphing solving basic equations and inequalities) and Algebra 1. Enrichment courses are also offered and include Geometry, Algebra 2, and Precalculus.

PROFESSIONAL DEVELOPMENT OF TEACHERS AND PLANNING

Every year the teachers in the institute begin working together in late January, attending monthly 4-hour teacher workshops on Saturdays, for which they are paid. During these workshops, teachers are taught the Valdés philosophy, how the institute works, and how to best use their teaching assistants (TAs). The director solicits input from teachers as to the particulars of the institute, such as schedules, discipline policies, and so forth. The teachers have time to collaborate with each other and make curricular decisions as well as discuss teaching strategies. Teachers also receive in-service training according to their needs and requests— for example, they might want training in complex instruction, how to teach specific units, and how to use particular curricular materials. The teachers choose what type of training they would like, and many teachers lead training sessions themselves. Teachers also compare their experiences and different approaches for reaching and motivating students; some of the most important learning that teachers do is from each other. Because teachers begin working together well before the summer schedule begins, they have time to form a cohesive professional teaching community with teacher empowerment and motivation (and investment in the institute's goals).

In addition to two teachers, every Valdés class has two paid TAs who are college students or high school students in advanced math classes. As the Valdés Institute in San José has now been in operation for 20 years, many of these TAs are former Valdés students with their own set of high expectations for the math ability of participants. They often are underrepresented minorities themselves who serve as role models for students, offer encouragement and enthusiasm, and who are unsympathetic toward complaints about too much work. The TAs, who are also trained in workshops before the summer program begins, grade papers and make copies, but they also become engaged in the teaching process—they go over homework questions, lead discussions, and work one-on-one with students or in small groups. The TAs may contact the parents of any students who may not have completed all their homework or contact parents to praise their children. The TAs also allow for release time for teachers so that the teachers can collaborate through discussion or observation of another institute teacher in action.

REACHING OUT TO PARENTS

The Valdés Institute rejects the myth that parents of underrepresented minorities do not care about their children's education. José Valdés found that because many parents of these students had not themselves experienced success in school and/or had not gone to school in the United States, they did not know what they had to do to help their children. When parents enroll their children in the Valdés Institute, they, along with their children, make a commitment to participate actively in the institute. It is mandatory that parents attend an orientation meeting (conducted in English and Spanish). They are also required to attend two workshops during the summer in which they are given information on how to help their children (such as by giving them space and quiet time to study) and information on high school graduation requirements and college entrance requirements, as well as information on financial aid. Parents also agree to attend a "back to school" night at the midpoint of the summer and a commencement ceremony at the end. The Valdés Institute, aside from offering their children a chance to improve their math skills, offers a safe place for children to be all day during the summer when regular school is not in session, which is a huge benefit for working parents. The institute is free, children are bused to school, and they receive a free lunch. The only requirement is that parents agree to attend all of these required functions, be supportive of their children, make sure they go to class every day and do their homework each night, and attend institute functions.

IMPORTANCE OF HIGH STANDARDS AND EXPECTATIONS

The Valdés Institute holds both students and parents to high standards. Students are not permitted to miss more than 2 days of the summer program or they are dismissed from the institute. Students are required to do their homework. If they show up to school without it completed, parents are immediately phoned. Because they attend class every day and complete all their assignments, students who perhaps had never previously experienced any success in mathematics courses start scoring high on tests and are able to contribute to class discussions. They soon learn that hard work pays off, which can serve as great motivation to continue their newly learned work habits. Soon many children, who may have initially complained about having to be in school during the summer, start coming to school happily, without coercion, and are excited to have the opportunity to learn and succeed. The elevation in self-esteem for these children is visible. Of course, when parents see this change in their children's grades and attitude, they are more than happy to participate in the institute's life.

BENEFITS OF PUBLIC SCHOOL– UNIVERSITY PARTNERSHIPS

The Valdés Institute generally holds classes on college campuses in the area. In San José, five colleges have donated classroom space to the institute throughout the years: Santa Clara University, San José State University, Evergreen Valley College, Mission College, and West Valley College. In the Stockton area, Delta Community College, University of the Pacific, and California State University Stanislaus have all hosted the Valdés Institute. There have also been Valdés Institute classes at Stanford University, Los Medanos Community College in Pittsburg, California, and Hartnell College in Salinas, California. Holding institute classes on college campuses may plant the idea of higher education in the minds of students. For many Valdés students and their parents, attending the Valdés Institute is the first time they have ever set foot on a college campus. The hope is to have these students see college as a place for them, not just for other people, that is, a place where they can feel at home. College professors often volunteer to become the fourth member of the teaching team for a while, sharing information with the students about their departments, projects, students, and possible degree programs and career choices available to college students. Often TAs are students at these colleges and give Valdés students a unique perspective on the campus they are visiting. Other benefits of the college campus venue are being able to use the swimming pool, basketball courts, and playing fields for recess and special activities. Students do not just work at Valdés, they also find time to play. Field trips to science museums or to "physics day" at an amusement park are typically scheduled to expose them to some applications of the math they are studying (or just to take a break).

RESEARCH FOUNDATIONS

The José Valdés Summer Math Institute incorporates many research-supported components (e.g., best-evidence reviews of research show that grouping by skill is more effective than grouping by ability). The institute represents a design experiment in which the goal is not to make causal inference about what works but to draw on many effective instructional and environmental factors to create a desired outcome, consistent with a continuing line of research interest in the effectiveness of summer educational programs. Over the years, considerable empirical evidence was collected to show that the José Valdés Summer Math Institute worked, in that individual student achievement increased in math, the desired outcome. However, this math institute was not conceived through empirical research; rather, it was born from success in practical experience in a real classroom working with real students in achieving high-level math outcomes. Sometimes good solutions to difficult problems stem from experience rather than research. Still, as time has passed, much empirical work has been done to support many of Valdés's ideas, but more research is needed to determine whether the success can be replicated in other settings and to identify why the institute has been successful in increasing math achievement in high school and the number of students who go on to college and even in some cases become mathematicians.

Interdisciplinary Model for Serving Diversity in Adolescents in School Settings

Zenia Lemos Horning, MEd (Honor Role Model 15), worked as a school psychologist in an urban school serving diverse adolescents until she recently accepted an invitation to become director of special education because she was so effective in implementing interdisciplinary team work. Her professional preparation included graduating from a nationally accredited school psychology program with courses and supervised practica at the university and internships in schools, and a research assistantship funded by the National Institutes of Health on early intervention studies for English- and Spanish-speaking, at-risk readers and writers. Initially she worked 2.5 years at elementary schools with a majority of English language learners (ELLs), then 5.5 years at an elementary and middle school with a few ELLs, and eventually 4.5 years at the middle and high school levels with a majority of ELLs. She has learned to be flexible and empathic, and to solve problems at a moment's notice.

Horning has found that the practice of school psychology varies markedly across elementary and secondary school settings. In working with adolescents at the secondary level, she often has had to rely on more than research findings about what works for the mythical average student. Increasingly, as she reaches out to students, teachers, parents, and the community, she has had to find solutions that also take into account the complex challenges facing adolescent students not only in school but also outside school. To begin with, the high school campus is larger than the elementary and middle school campuses. The students are bigger, dress differently, use more crass language, and sometimes engage in behaviors outside school which have implications for their learning or behavioral problems at school. The pace of everything feels faster than in elementary and middle school. The students and teaching staff want more autonomy and less "hand holding" from professionals, including school psychologists. For example, at the elementary school, teachers sought consultation from the psychologist, but at the high school, teachers took the lead on the implementation of interventions and assessing RTI, unless the interventions have not proven successful.

One of the most challenging issues Horning did not encounter when working with younger children is determining whether a student has a learning disability or whether self-reported or school staff–reported drug use alone was the cause of the student's failing grades. How much did drug use affect test results? Published norms for standardization samples do not take drug use into account. It is perplexing that some parents cannot understand why test results might not represent their child's true ability if their child is using large amounts of street drugs regularly. When academic help is requested for a student whose drug use might have had an impact on test scores, Horning has to conduct multiple classroom observations to write a behavioral plan for tracking progress on an observable and measurable behavior; it is not clear how the drug use might affect response to academic instruction or the behavioral support plan provided in the high school. Determining whether a student has a learning disability at the high school level is also more complex because many other factors besides drugs and alcohol may affect school performance, including gangs, suicidal ideation or threats, and intimate relationships. These other factors are educationally relevant regardless of whether it is determined that the student has a learning disability.

Mondays are particularly tough days. For a high school student a lot can happen over the weekend that affects the next week at school: A fight can lead to juvenile hall, attending parties with drugs and/or alcohol can make learning more challenging, a fight with a boyfriend or girlfriend can be distracting, various family issues and conflicts can distract from the focus on learning at school. In a few instances, a student has undergone psychiatric hospitalization and does not return to school. Another significant issue encountered with high school students is the number of students who report feeling unsafe in getting to, being in, or going home from school. To avoid conflicts among students, schedule changes are often made so that certain students are not in the same class with other specific students. Despite repeated parent–student meetings and multiple no-contact contracts in place, certain students are allowed to arrive at school slightly late in strategic student drop-off locations or have professionals escort them from one place in the school to another so they will not come into contact with another particular student. The high school in which Horning works has many rules to help protect the students and create a safe learning environment. For example, none of the students can wear red clothing to school—not even shoelaces—because of the gang-related relevance of this color.

Some assessments have to be completed in juvenile hall, where students are eager to see the psychologist because they are released from their daily activities and allowed into the visiting area for hours. Once students are released from juvenile hall, they typically have a probation officer assigned to them, who helps the student attend classes regularly, stay off drugs (monitored by random drug testing), and stay away from activities that may lead to returning to juvenile hall. A few students have been in and out of juvenile hall three or four times in a school year, but can earn credits in juvenile hall, even though the coursework is not the same as in a comprehensive high school. When they return to the high school campus, these students have to take time to readjust to school demands and distractions. Multiple individual educational plan meetings are held to monitor services they receive.

One significant service the school psychologist provides is working with the school team to connect families and students to community resources. Needs range widely from counseling to medical services to housing to food, but that list is not exhaustive. A student's mother, who had recently separated from her boyfriend and who did not have a job, was applying for the food stamp program, which takes time to qualify for, and approached the school for money for food in the interim. The high school team found a temporary fix: a local organization that gave out bags of food once a week with no questions asked. With budget cuts and fewer in-house resources for the high school to offer, the school team is turning more to finding, through phone calls and Internet searches, community resources to help families of students. Many times, school personnel show parents how to search on their own for community resources.

Some referrals are for students who have recently immigrated to the United States. A few of the students have received an education in their home country, but most have not or have received minimal education. Recently, a 16-year-old boy arrived at the high school after having previously only been in school for kindergarten and first grade. One of the teachers thought he had some oral–motor issues because his Spanish was so poor. The student is now exhibiting significant social–emotional problems and has been refusing to attend school. The special education team is currently assessing the student (in Spanish) to determine whether there are developmental delays. Without a true bilingual education program, providing the appropriate class placement was difficult.

Special education services, which are only provided in English and do not offer primary language support, were not appropriate. The only teacher who speaks Spanish is in a class for newcomers to the United States to help the students transition to school in the United States. There are also specific English, math, and science classes designated as English language development classes taught by teachers who speak English primarily and Spanish as a necessity. Students who know a little more English translate for the students who have not yet acquired English proficiency. Although it is not ideal, school staff members have observed that a sense of community is created out of the students' shared uncertainty and sense of fear, and as more relationships are built, the predominant sense of fear and unease gradually gives way to smiles and laughter. The one negative aspect of the creation of this mini-community within the school is that some of the students do not progress well in English language acquisition because all their friends speak Spanish and there is no perceived need to practice English.

The high school campus also has a program for teen mothers and their children (Cal-Safe) so that they can complete their education. The mothers receive pregnancy education at school and are then allowed to bring their children to the on-campus day care while they attend school. Some students referred for school psychology assessment were pregnant. They were scared about the delivery and the future for them and their babies and asked numerous questions about labor and parenting and expressed a desire to finish their education and go to college. Thus, their special education assessment might not reflect their true ability or achievement because of the mental and physical distraction of the pregnancy; however, the school psychologist has learned that these students want the best for their children, and the students want to complete their own education and go on to college.

Even at this high school, which has a large number of special education assessments, the school psychologist can create interventions for general education students and link general education assessments to these interventions. Recently, the principal asked the school psychologist to find developmentally appropriate, criterion-based reading, writing, and math assessments for the general education population as part of the special education prereferral process. On the one hand, the prereferral process provides more time to sort out whether referred students truly have a learning disability or are failing simply because of drug use, incarceration, failed relationships, pregnancy, gang involvement, or myriad other potential stumbling blocks including developmentally inappropriate instruction that is aimed too low or too high.

Ultimately, setting up a functioning prereferral process will, it is hoped, reduce the number of special education referrals and should therefore decrease the number of assessments while also giving more time for the school psychologist to consult with general education teachers, create and implement general education interventions, and conduct counseling groups—all of which can be beneficial at the secondary level as well as the elementary level. The success will, of course, depend on the collective communication and collaboration among the members of an interdisciplinary team who are mindful of all issues schools face in educating adolescents, especially those from diverse backgrounds but who are willing to apply best practices, ethical principles, law, and institutional practices oriented to advocating for students and their families (see Part I, this volume).

Readings and Resources[1]

DEVELOPMENTAL ISSUES

Allen, J. P., Pianta, R. C., Gregory, A., Mikami, A. Y., & Lun, J. (2011). An interaction-based approach to enhancing secondary school instruction and student achievement. *Science, 333,* 1034–1037. doi:10.1126/science.1207998

Brown, B. B., & Dietz, E. L. (2009). Informal peer groups in middle childhood and adolescence. In K. H. Rubin, W. M. Bukowski, & B. Laursen (Eds.), *Handbook of peer interactions, relationships, and groups* (pp. 371–376). New York, NY: Guilford Press.

Cleary, T. (2014). *Self-regulated learning interventions with at-risk populations: Academic, mental health, and contextual consideration.* Manuscript submitted for publication.

Hafen, C. A., Allen, J. P., Mikami, A. Y., Gregory, A., Hamre, B., & Pianta, R. C. (2012). The pivotal role of adolescent autonomy in secondary school classrooms. *Journal of Youth and Adolescence, 41,* 245–255. doi:10.1007/s10964-011-9739-2

Swain-Bradway, J., & Horner, R. (2010). High school implementation of the behavior education program. In D. Crone, L. Hawken, & R. Horner (Eds.), *Responding to problem behavior in schools: The behavior education program* (2nd ed.). New York, NY: Guilford Press.

---

[1]Additional research readings and practitioner resources for this chapter can be found at http://www.apadivisions.org/division-16/publications/interdisciplinary-frameworks-supplement/index.aspx

TECHNOLOGY

Bryant, D. P., & Bryant, B. R. (2012). *Assistive technology for people with disabilities* (2nd ed.). Upper Saddle River, NJ: Pearson.

LANGUAGE AND LITERACY

Beers, S., & Nagy, W. (2009). Syntactic complexity as a predictor of adolescent writing quality: Which measures? Which genre? *Reading and Writing: An Interdisciplinary Journal, 22,* 185–200. doi:10.1007/s11145-007-9107-5

Cantrell, S., Almasi, J., Carter, J., Rintamaa, M., & Madden, A. (2010). The impact of a strategy-based intervention on the comprehension and strategy use of struggling adolescent readers. *Journal of Educational Psychology, 102,* 257–280. doi:10.1037/a0018212

Christensen, C., & Wauchope, M. (2009). Whole school literacy: Using research to create programs that build universal high levels of literate competence. In S. Rosenfield & V. Berninger (Eds.), *Implementing evidence-based interventions in school settings* (pp. 501–526). New York, NY: Oxford University Press.

Cook, L., & Mayer, R. (1988). Teaching readers about the structure of scientific text. *Journal of Educational Psychology, 80,* 448–456. doi:10.1037//0022-0663.80.4.448

De La Paz, S., & MacArthur, C. A. (2003). Knowing the how and why of history: Expectations for secondary students with and without learning disabilities. *Learning Disability Quarterly, 26,* 142–154.

Graham, S., & Perrin, D. (2007a). A meta-analysis of writing instruction for adolescent students. *Journal of Educational Psychology, 99,* 445–476. doi:10.1037/0022-0663.99.3.445

Graham, S., & Perrin, D. (2007b). What we know, what we still need to know: Teaching adolescents to write. *Scientific Studies in Reading, 11,* 313–336. doi:10.1080/10888430701530664

Kamil, M. L., Borman, G. D., Dole, J., Kral, C. C., Salinger, T., & Torgesen, J. (2008). *Improving adolescent literacy. Effective classroom and intervention practices: A practice guide* (NCEE #2008–4027). Washington, DC: National Center for Education Evaluation and Regional Assistance, Institute of Education Sciences, U.S. Department of Education. Retrieved from http://ies.ed.gov/ncee/wwc

Nagy, W., & Townsend, D. (2012). Words as tools: Learning academic vocabulary as language acquisition. *Reading Research Quarterly, 47*(1), 91–108. doi:10.1002/RRQ.011

Petitto, L. (2009). New discoveries from the bilingual brain and mind across the lifespan and their implications for education. *Journal of Mind, Brain, and Education, 3,* 185–197.

Peverly, S. T., Ramaswamy, V., Brown, C., Sumowski, J., Alidoost, M., & Garner, J. (2007). Skill in lecture note-taking: What predicts? *Journal of Educational Psychology, 99*, 167–180. doi:10.1037/0022-0663.99.1.167

MATH AND SCIENCE

Geary, D. C., Hoard, M. K., Nugent, L., & Bailey, H. D. (2013). Adolescents' functional numeracy is predicted by their school entry number system knowledge. *PLoS ONE, 8*(1), e54651. doi:10.1371/journal.pone.0054651

Hinsley, D., Hayes, J., & Simon, H. (1977). From words to equations: Meaning and representation in algebra word problems. In M. Just & P. Carpenter (Eds.), *Cognitive processes in comprehension* (pp. 89–106). Hillsdale, NJ: Erlbaum.

Hoffman, P. (1998). *The man who loved only numbers: The story of Paul Erdös and the search for mathematical truth*. New York, NY: Hyperion.

Mayer, R. (2005). Should there be a three-strikes rule against pure discovery learning? *American Psychologist, 59*, 14–19. doi:10.1037/0003-066X.59.1.14

National Council of Teachers of Mathematics. (1995). *Standards for school mathematics: Pre-K through 12*. Retrieved from http://www.nctm.org/standards/content.aspx?id=26863

National Mathematics Advisory Panel. (2008). *Foundations for success: The final report of the National Mathematics Advisory Panel*. Washington, DC: U.S. Department of Education.

COMMON CORE OF READINESS FOR WORK

Rothman, R. (2012). A common core of readiness. *Educational Leadership, 69*(7), 10–15.

INTERDISCIPLINARY FRAMEWORKS FOR UNDERSTANDING THE BIOLOGICAL BASES OF DEVELOPMENT AND LEARNING

A Genetics Primer and Brain Primer for Interdisciplinary Frameworks

7

This chapter provides a brief introductory overview of the rapidly expanding research on the biological sources of students' individual and developmental differences. Few teachers, unless they are secondary science teachers, take preservice courses in genetics or neuroscience. Other professionals on an interdisciplinary team may have taken courses in genetics and neuroscience but typically not the educational applications of these fields. Understanding the biological sources of diversity is timely after the Decade of the Brain (1990–1999) and the Human Genome Project (1999–2003). Leroy Hood, who received a Presidential Award for his groundbreaking scientific contributions to the genetics of complex biological systems, had a vision that contributed significantly to the explosion in knowledge about genetics that has served as the foundation for personalized medicine. Genetic analyses and brain imaging are beginning to be used more frequently in assessments of individuals with and without disabilities and disorders. Understanding these biological sources of diversity

http://dx.doi.org/10.1037/14437-007
Interdisciplinary Frameworks for Schools: Best Professional Practices for Serving the Needs of All Students, by V. W. Berninger

may contribute, in part, to developing personalized education in the 21st century for all students.

This chapter is a primer on genetics, covering general background, developmental disorders, specific learning disabilities, and educationally relevant conceptual frameworks for gene–brain relationships. Parents are increasingly sharing genetic testing and brain imaging results with interdisciplinary teams in school settings. The framework outlined in this chapter provides a handy reference for interdisciplinary teams considering the applications of genetic and brain research to understanding nature–nurture interactions in work with school-age children and youth and in making decisions about how to find other relevant information and providing consultation for the cases at hand.

Genetics Primer

MENDELIAN GENETICS

Gregor Mendel was an Austrian monk who contributed to early scientific studies of genetic inheritance. He introduced the concepts of (a) *autosomes* (non–sex-linked chromosomes) and (b) sex-linked chromosomes, and observed that different forms of genes, which he called *alleles*, occur on chromosomes in nature. Humans have two copies of each autosomal gene. A single mutant gene is sufficient to cause a dominant trait, but both alleles must be mutant for a receptive trait to manifest. Mendel postulated four possible outcomes:

- *AA:* homozygous noncarrier, nonaffected;
- *aa:* homozygous mutation for recessive trait, affected;
- *aA* or *Aa:* heterozygous carriers for recessive trait, nonaffected; or
- *aA* or *Aa:* heterozygous for dominant trait, affected.

POST-MENDELIAN GENETICS DEFINITIONS AND MECHANISMS

Since Mendel's pioneering work, research has greatly advanced the understanding of genes and genetic mechanisms. These are defined to help educational professionals understand and communicate with each other and parents regarding the nature of some students' biological variation. Parents are increasingly able to have their child's DNA genotyped, and they are sharing results with schools. Much work remains to validate applications of this information to educational practice, but different kinds of genetic variations have been identified that may affect neural migration, neural regulation, and protein formation and that may account for many different developmental or learning problems: Alleles can be *synonymous* (major population form, benign polymorphisms, or mutant, which may cause a change in transcription, be benign missense, or result in pathogenetic altering phenotypes) or *nonsense* (creating a stop codon or slice site creating or destroying a donor or acceptor site); insertions or deletions of a multiple of three nucleotides, which alters protein; and *frameshift* (interfere with the amino acid sequence leading to the creation of a premature stop codon somewhere). In this chapter, general genetic mechanisms are presented first, followed by those relevant to developmental disabilities (Chapter 8), specific learning disabilities (Chapter 9), and other neurogenetic disorders (Chapter 10).

General Concepts

Chromosomes in humans are arranged in pairs of 23 (22 autosomes and one sex-linked, either XX for females or XY for males). The Y chromosome is one third to one half as long and has a different shape and fewer genes than the X chromosome. Each of an individual's 46 chromosomes (two pairs of 23 chromosomes each) has hundreds of genes, but some have more than others.

Genes are codes that support life. All living organisms have at least 300 genes. The exact number of genes in humans is unknown but is estimated to be 20,000 to 30,000. Single genes in lower organisms code only for single proteins, whereas genes in humans code for multiple proteins, and the combinations result in diversity. Chimpanzees and humans share 99.0% of the same genes, and humans share 99.9% of the same genes with each other. Thus, diversity in higher organisms results not only from single genes but also from the combinations and permutations of multiple genes. This explains why human beings exhibit remarkable diversity despite many common genes.

DNA stands for deoxyribonucleic acid, though it is a protein rather than an acid. Each base of DNA is attached to a sugar and a phosphate to form a nucleotide. Each base is formed from one purine (adenine or guanine) and one pyrimidine (thymine or cytosine). Pairs of bases are thus AT (adenine + thymine) or CG (cytosine + guanine). DNA, which is located in the nucleus of each neuron of the brain, is composed of the base pairs cytosine (C) and guanine (G) or adenine (A) and thymine (T). The resulting doublet coding of nuclear DNA—CG or AT—is arranged in "ladder steps" in the two twisted strands of the double helix, which is about 1.8 meters long until histone, a protein, modifies it to about 0.09 mm so it can fit into the tiny nucleus of the microscopic neuron cell. Note that mature blood cells do not have a nucleus and do not have DNA except in their mitochondria.

Messenger ribonucleic acid (mRNA) transforms DNA through the transcription and translation processes into gene instructions for different functions (e.g., neural migration, neural regulation, protein formation).

Transcription of mRNA begins when DNA unwinds and the two strands of the double helix unzip to expose the code that serves as the template for the formation of mRNA, which has the same nucleotides as in DNA except that uracil (U) substitutes for thymine. Errors or mutations may occur during transcription, but a system of "proofreading enzymes" generally identifies and repairs those errors. If the proofreading process does not repair the errors, the result may be a protein with a mutation that could cause a clinical disorder.

Translation of mRNA begins when, following transcription, a single strand of mRNA detaches from the double-stranded DNA, which zips back together. During translation, mRNA moves out of the nucleus and into the cytoplasm, where it provides instructions for amino acid production and attaches to a ribosome that reads three-letter messages (*codons* or "words") such as CCU, CUA, or UAG (triplet codes for specific amino acids, the building blocks of protein). Once amino acids form protein on the ribosome, they are used in the neuron or released into the bloodstream via the Golgi apparatus (which packages the protein in a form for release). An error in any step of the translation process can cause a structurally abnormal protein, can reduce the amounts of protein, or can result in no protein.

Proteomics is the study of the formation of proteins as DNA is transformed through mRNA transcription (coding) and mRNA translation (generating amino acids, the building blocks of protein).

Mitochondria in neurons take in nutrients and oxygen and break them down into adenosine triphosphate (ATP) for cellular respiration. Mitochondria, which produce energy needed for cellular function through oxidative phosphorylation, possess their own DNA in the form of a double-stranded circular molecule rather than a double helix; however, most genes active in the mitochondria are coded by nuclear DNA.

Mitochondrial DNA (mtDNA), which has 37 genes (16,500 base pairs of DNA building blocks), contains different genes than those in the double helix nuclear DNA. Of the 37 mtDNA genes, 13 make enzymes in oxidative phosphorylation, which uses oxygen and sugar to produce ATP; 22 make transfer RNA; and two make ribosomal RNA molecules, which are chemical cousins of nuclear DNA that help accumulate amino acids into proteins.

Mitochondrial inheritance differs from DNA inheritance in that mitochondria DNA is only passed down from mother to child. Although mtDNA is inherited only from one's mother, the father alone determines the sex of the offspring by contributing a Y or an X chromosome, which is paired with the mother's X chromosome. Both parents contribute to the 22 pairs of chromosomes in the autosome, but mothers alone contribute through transmission of mtDNA. Mutations in mitochondrial genes result in defective energy production. There are over 60 mitochondria disorders or inborn errors of metabolism—for example, mitochondrial seizure disorders, short stature, sensorimotor hearing loss, cataracts, and lactic acidosis.

Gene control of developmental timing involves regulatory genes controlling when other genes turn on (activate) or off (deactivate) specific genes during the life span. Thus, inherited genes may affect the timing of onset of developmental phases throughout the life span as an individual undergoes maturation from infancy to early childhood to middle childhood to adolescence and adulthood. For example, genes may influence when (a) pruning excess neurons or synapses occurs to improve the overall efficiency of brain function or (b) myelination of specific brain regions occurs, thus improving the efficiency of neural conduction and related functions such as language development and executive functions. Individual differences in regulatory genes' timing for turning on the genes controlling myelination could account for the sizable differences in when adolescents develop the executive functions for self-regulated learning and behavior needed for success at school and life.

Single nucleotide polymorphisms (SNPs) are found in DNA. Humans share 99.9% of the same genes; variations in how over three billion base pairs of DNA (AT or CG) are sequenced in their genetic code are one source, but not the only source, of diversity across individuals in the same species.

Stop codons mark the end of a sequence of base pairs (a "sentence").

Mirror image amino acids have been identified in 19 of the 20 naturally occurring amino acids forming proteins in which the same amino acid is arranged in one of two orientations around a central carbon atom. These resulting *L-amino acids* and *D-amino acids*, which are "mirror image" compounds, cannot be superimposed in a looking glass universe of genetics. Rather, they have different functions.

The sizable *normal biological variation* among individuals stems from (a) variation in genes (alleles) and their sequencing in nuclear DNA and circular mtDNA, (b) mirror image amino acids with different functions, and (c) variations in mRNA transcription and mRNA translation processes. Normal variation affects neuronal migration early in gestation, regulation of other genes or neural processes throughout development, or amino acid production related to protein formation and coding.

Developmental Disabilities and Neurogenetic Disorders

Developmental disabilities and neurogenetic disorders may occur at or near conception or later in development and may involve abnormalities in chromosomes or genes.

Meiosis occurs before conception when daughter or germ cells, each containing only 23 chromosomes, are formed from one parent egg cell and one parent sperm cell. The resulting fertilized embryo has 23 pairs of chromosomes. The egg cells come from the mother, who is born with all the eggs she will ever have. The sperm cells come from the father, who produces sperm throughout his life.

Mitosis occurs after conception, when two daughter cells of chromosomal composition identical to the parent cell are formed, each with 46 chromosomes (23 pairs). Although mitosis continues throughout life, it takes longer in adults.

Nondisjunction refers to an abnormality in how the daughter cells are created during meiosis: Only one mature egg is produced, and half the chromosomes go to the polar body that does not become the baby. When this happens, neither usually survives, but if they do, a genetic disorder results.

Translocations occur during mitosis and meiosis when chromosomes break and lose or exchange parts with other chromosomes. A portion of one chromosome is transferred to a completely different chromosome.

Chromosomal abnormalities are frequently found in individuals with developmental disabilities, often because 25% of eggs and 3% to 4% of sperm have extra or missing chromosomes, and an additional 1% of eggs and 5% of sperm cells have structural chromosomal abnormalities. Overall, 10% to 15% of all conceptions have chromosomal abnormalities: more than 50% *trisomies* (one pair has three chromosomes); 20% *monosomies* (one pair has one chromosome); and 15% triploids (69 chromosomes—three sets of 23 pairs). Trisomy 16 is the most common trisomy error and, like most chromosomal abnormalities, results in spontaneous abortions (miscarriages). More than 95% of fetuses with chromosomal abnormalities do not survive during gestation.

Extra chromosomes are found in several syndromes. Down syndrome (Trisomy 21) results from an extra chromosome (90% from nondisjunction during meiosis of egg; 5% from nondisjunction during meiosis from sperm; 5% from translocation or mosaicism). Trisomy 13 and Trisomy 18 result from nondisjunction; these produce more severe cognitive deficits than Down syndrome and often lead to early death.

Missing chromosomes occur in other syndromes. Turner's syndrome results when there are only 45 chromosomes, with only one X. It affects only girls and is the only disorder in which the fetus survives despite an entire chromosome being missing. If a structurally abnormal Y is present, the undifferentiated gonad should be surgically removed. Turner's syndrome occurs in one in 5,000 live births. Affected individuals have short stature, webbed neck, a shield-like chest with wide-spaced nipples, nonfunctional ovaries, heart problems, and visual–spatial impairment. Hormone injections may increase height. An estrogen supplement may cause secondary sexual characteristics to develop, but affected girls remain infertile.

Mosaicism refers to different cells in the same individual having different genetic make-up. From 5% to 10% of all chromosomal abnormalities are thought to involve mosaicisms.

Deletions occur when part, but not all, of a chromosome is lost. *Visible deletions* can be seen in the microscope. *Microdeletions* are identified at the molecular level. Deletions can be diagnosed with fluorescent in situ hybridization, arrays, and next generation sequencing. An example of visible deletion is *cri du chat* (cat-cry) syndrome, in which the short arm of Chromosome 5 is lost. This disorder occurs in one in 50,000 births. Affected individuals have microencephaly, round face with widely spaced eyes, low-set ears, a high-pitched cry, and pervasive developmental disability. Examples of microdeletions (i.e., continuous gene syndrome, deletion of adjacent genes) include the following: Williams syndrome from deletion on the long arm of Chromosome 7, resulting in pervasive developmental disability, unexpected verbal eloquence, cardiac disorders, and distinctive facial appearance, and velocardiofacial syndrome (VCFS) from deletion in the long arm of Chromosome 22, resulting in cleft palate, congenital heart defect, characteristic facial appearance, nonverbal learning problems, and often hearing loss, speech, and language problems.

Genomic imprinting occurs when certain genes with the same DNA sequence are expressed differently at the phenotype level depending on whether they are inherited from the mother or father. For example, one deletion on the long arm of Chromosome 15 will produce Angelman syndrome if the deletion is inherited from the mother or Prader-Willi syndrome if the deletion is inherited from father.

Anticipation refers to phenotype expression that can be more severe in successive generations, as has been observed, for example, in Huntington's chorea.

Mutations are variants of normal genes, that is, abnormal alleles that result from DNA replication errors in the gene itself; these increase with size of gene. For egg and sperm cells, these errors may increase with the age of the parents, especially the father. Errors may occur spontaneously but can also be induced by radiation, toxins, or viruses. Once they are part of one's genetic code, mutations can be passed on from one generation to the next. The most common mutation is *point mutation*, a single base pair substitution. Because of redundancy in human DNA, many mutations have no adverse consequences. However, some mutations do result in handicapping conditions that require educational and other kinds of interventions. Natural selection may remove some mutations but not always.

Some mutations involve a single gene. There are 1,700 disorders that are inherited as *autosomal recessive traits* (both parents contribute an abnormal allele). Examples include Tay–Sachs disease, which results from absence of an enzyme that metabolizes a toxic product of nerve cell metabolism that accumulates and sometimes results in early death, and sickle cell anemia. There are 900 mutations that are X-*linked disorders*, with gene mutations on the X chromosome that primarily affect males. In females, a normal allele on the second X can modulate a mutation in the first X, but males do not have a second X to modulate mutations on the first X. One example is Duchenne muscular dystrophy, which is a mutation in the dystrophin gene on the X chromosome that stabilizes muscle cell membrane and affects all muscles. A second example is ornithine transcarbamylase enzyme disorder, which can cause coma but is treatable with a low protein diet. A third example is fragile X syndrome, which occurs much more frequently in boys than girls. A fourth example is Rett syndrome, which results from a mutated transcription gene on the X chromosome and leads to death in males, though females survive with microcephaly, intellectual disability, and autism-like behavior. Individuals with these disorders may also have significant communication problems.

Some mutations involve a gene sequence. VCFS results from the microdeletion of a number of sequential genes within Chromosome 22q11.2. A *missense mutation* makes changes in a triplet code—substituting a different amino acid in the protein chain. An example of a missense mutation is the inborn error of metabolism in phenylketonuria, which affects an enzyme needed to metabolize the amino acid phenylalanine. A *nonsense mutation* prematurely terminates protein formation at a stop codon at the end of a sequence so that no useful formation is produced, though sometimes the protein still functions when a portion is missing. An example of a nonsense mutation is neurofibromatosis, which occurs when a tumor suppressor is not formed, resulting in multiple benign neurofibroma tumors on the body and in the brain. Although individuals with neurofibromatosis may have attention-deficit/hyperactivity disorder (ADHD) symptoms, the genetic basis for these symptoms is different from that for ADHD alone. A *base frame shift mutation* is a reading frame shifted so that triplets (three base pairs) are misread, as occurs in some cases of Tay-Sachs disease.

Some mutations affect gene regulation. Other mutations do not affect the amino acid sequences but instead influence whether the genes are turned on or off or the rate or efficiency of transcription; that is, they are *regulatory*. An example is Rubinstein–Taybi syndrome, which results in multiple congenital malformations and pervasive developmental disability. In a *triplet repeat expansion mutation*, some nucleotide triplets (codons) are repeated multiple times and turn off a gene. Examples of this mutation are Huntington's disease and fragile X syndrome.

Other mutations involve insertions and deletions of one or more nucleotide bases, that is, a frame shift. An example of an insertion is spinal muscular atrophy in which a survival motor neuron gene is inserted and a polio-like disorder results. An example of a deletion is Duchenne muscular dystrophy.

Specific Learning Disabilities

TWIN STUDIES

The first question genetics studies addressed about learning disabilities in otherwise normally developing students was whether a specific reading disability such as dyslexia was heritable or environmental in origin. A pioneering team of researchers at the University of Colorado headed by Richard Olson conducted studies comparing monozygotic (identical) and dizygotic (fraternal) twins for more than four decades in the United States and other countries and showed that about half the variance is due to genetics and half to the environment. Individuals with genetically based reading disabilities may respond at the behavioral level to appropriate instructional intervention even though their underlying genetic vulnerability may remain. This finding makes sense given what is being learned about epigenetics—that is, that environmental influences and experiences can alter expression of inherited genes.

CHROMOSOME LINKAGE STUDIES

Much genetics research has focused on the chromosomal locus of the genetic abnormalities of specific reading disabilities or selective oral language or speech impairments. As genetics research methods became more sophisticated, earlier chromosome linkage studies have been replaced with studies to identify the location of SNPs on specific chromosomes, that is, gene candidates for the genetic variations in base pairs and their sequencing that may be associated with specific disorders.

GENE CANDIDATE STUDIES

Individuals with a variety of developmental or neurogenetic disorders may have difficulty learning to read. However, recent research has confirmed that the genetic basis of reading problems in individuals with autism and dyslexia is not the same. For specific learning disabilities in individuals with otherwise normal development, more research has focused on dyslexia and selective language or speech impairment than other kinds of specific learning disabilities. The emerging consensus is that the genetic basis of dyslexia is heterogeneous; not all affected individuals at the behavioral level have the same variations in the candidate gene alleles. For dyslexia, a specific learning disability affecting word decoding and spelling, at least nine locations on chromosomes for candidate gene alleles (*DYX1–DYX9*) have been reported, and in some cases preliminary evidence has been reported for their roles (coding proteins, regulatory, neural migration). For example, *DYX1C1* on Chromosome 15 at location *DYX1*, as well as *DCDC2* and *KIAA0319* on Chromosome 6 at location *DYX2*, may alter transcription and protein formation and be involved in neural migration. Three others—*ROB01*, *GRIN2B*, and *CMIP*, located on Chromosomes 3, 12, and 16, respectively—are associated with phonological memory in the general population.

Implications of Genetics for Specific Learning Disabilities

The evidence is strong for a genetic basis of dyslexia. Thus, if a student has persisting word-reading and spelling problems and often a multigenerational history of these difficulties, educational professionals in school settings should not tell parents that dyslexia does not exist and if it did it is a medical problem. Rather, they should explain that although there is a biological basis for dyslexia, twin studies also document environmental influences, and intervention studies have reported effective instructional treatments. However, not all evidence-based instructional practices for teaching word reading and spelling, many of which are based on studies of the general student population, may be appropriate for dyslexia or other specific learning disabilities (e.g., dysgraphia, oral and written language disability, or specific language impairment). Instructional approaches should be used that have been validated in research with students carefully diagnosed with the same kind of specific learning disability as the student at hand. See Appendix A for guidelines on becoming a critical consumer of this research.

Epigenetics

In some cases, the same genotype can be expressed differently depending on environmental influences. *Epigenetics* is derived from the Greek word for *above* (*epi*), which when prefixed to the base word *genetics* refers to mechanisms that operate "above the genes." Such mechanisms may not change the identity or sequencing of the underlying genes, but they may change the behavioral expression of the underlying genetic variables. Rapidly expanding research is identifying chemical markers that control the degree to which a gene is turned on and makes its specific protein. These chemical markers include *methyls* (carbon and hydrogen), *acetyls* (carbon, hydrogen, and oxygen), and *phosphates* (phosphate and oxygen, but hydrogen as well in some states). The epigenetic signatures explain why not all cells behave the same despite having common DNA. The nature of these epigenetic changes can change across the life span depending on environmental influences. The emerging research on epigenetics is promising because it shows that the environment does matter, although this should not be interpreted to mean that all of the genetic disorders can be eliminated solely or completely through environmental interventions.

Sex Differences and Gender Identity

SEX DIFFERENCES

At one level, sex is a source of biological diversity. At conception, the father determines the sex of the offspring by contributing a Y or an X to the 23rd pair of chromosomes. For a fetus with a Y chromosome, regulatory genes control hormonal events early in gestation, a phenomenon known as the *testosterone bath* in genetic males; genetic females, who do not have a Y chromosome, do not have the testosterone bath. Other events during gestation may result in some infants being born with undifferentiated genitalia; in some males, the testicles do not descend in the neonatal period, and pediatricians and physicians with other medical specializations should consult with parents for these biologically based conditions.

At another level, sex differences have also been shown to be related to environmental factors. Researchers continue to seek environmental explanations for why females in general may not excel in math or science in the upper grades or pursue science, technology, engineering, and math careers. Environmental explanations are also being sought for why more males are dropping out of school before high school graduation and why fewer males are graduating from college and in some cases being imprisoned. Although both biological and environmental variables are related to educationally relevant sex-related differences, current research is also emphasizing commonalities that cut across sex differences.

GENDER IDENTITY

Biology determines sex but not *gender*, which refers to one's psychological identity related to sex. Although sex is a binary variable (one of two categories), gender is currently thought to fall along a continuum. Environmental variables may contribute to gender identity because society may treat boys and girls differently and have different expectations for them, which may differ across families and the cultures in which children grow up.

Endophenotypes: Bridging Brain and Genes

Endophenotypes are the behavioral markers related to gene candidates (alleles) and specific brain functions. In pioneering studies, a research team in Germany performed a whole genome search on data collected during brain imaging that assessed timing while children with dyslexia performed an automatic speech-processing task. This team identified a gene candidate on Chromosome 4 that appeared to be associated with neural migration affecting processing of speech sounds, and two gene candidates on Chromosome 12 that appeared to be associated with the mRNA expression of glucose transport of neurons. Thus, the human genome may code in separate chromosomes genetic information for regulating (a) neural migration that affects later speech sound processing and (b) glucose in the blood, which when oxygenated generates the energy supporting functions in specific brain regions. Research on the relationships among genetics, brain, and behavioral tasks holds promise for better understanding how the human brain, which enables individuals to interact with the physical and social environment, develops and learns and in the process may alter brain function through epigenetic mechanisms. Given what is being learned about genetic differences and variations, it may not be possible for all students to reach the same goal posts in the same way at the same speed.

Multilevel Brain Systems Contributing to Biological Diversity

Currently, there is national interest in translation science for brain research—namely, teaching with the brain in mind. Translating research on the brain into instructional practice is a challenge for many reasons. Early knowledge of the brain was based on dissecting the human brain at autopsy, which generated a wealth of information about large (macro) structures of the brain. These were supplemented with microscopic studies of stained layers of brain tissue and animal studies to learn about the small (micro) structures of the brain. Not until the explosion of brain imaging studies, using many different technologies, could brain researchers study the brain at work in living human beings. Researchers use imaging to study the relationships between activated brain regions and specific kinds of target tasks and control tasks. However, structure–function relationships are not simply one brain region or structure to one function. Which regions activate greatly depends on the age and characteristics of the human participants and the task at hand. The same structure or brain region may be involved in more than one function. Just as levels of language are related, though not in a simple one-to-one way, so are multiple levels of complex brain organization, ranging from molecules to neurons to large collections of neurons in macrolevel structures. Each level of brain organization is related to other levels of brain organization, but not in a simple one-to-one way. Adding to the complexity is the fact that genes regulate the wiring and protein coding; consequently, individual differences are often observed in how the brain performs the same task.

Each imaging tool yields different kinds of information about how the brain works, and brain imaging studies are not designed to go directly from brain scan to lesson plan. Although research comparing children with and without specific learning disabilities before and after instruction has shown normalization in specific regions of the brain while specific tasks related to oral and written language are performed, learning in the classroom requires instruction aimed at multiple skills to create functional reading, writing, and math brain systems rather than one or a few skills investigated in any one imaging study. In addition, the recent explosion of brain imaging studies has resulted in brain information overload. To deal with the challenges of translating brain research into educational practice and the current neuroscience information overload, four interdisciplinary conceptual frameworks are offered, which provide one way, but not the only way, to make sense of the cross-disciplinary explosion of knowledge about the brain, which when integrated across studies may be relevant to diagnosing and teaching students with and without specific learning disabilities or developmental disorders. They also provide clues as to why some students struggle and why adults should be empathic about why it is harder for some students to learn and for teachers to teach them.

EXHIBIT 7.1

Conceptual Framework 1: Role of Genes in Multiple Levels of Brain Systems

Level 1: Microlevel Neurogenetics

Structural organization within the nucleus of the cell body of individual neurons:

1. There is *one* double helix in each of 46 chromosomes (23 pairs) in the nucleus of the cell body of each neuron, with nuclear DNA arranged as steps, created from base pairs for *two* base chemical codes (CG or AT), of a ladder formed by the two twisted strands of the double helix. A small amount of DNA is also in mitochondria (mitochondrial DNA or mtDNA).
2. Chemical transformations (of both nuclear DNA and mitochondrial DNA).
   a. During mRNA transcription, uracil, a pyrimidine, combines with a purine to transcribe, that is, create, a *three*-letter word code (CCU, CUA, or UAG).
   b. During mRNA translation, proteins are formed from amino acids.
3. When mRNA moves out of the nucleus into the cytoplasm, it attaches to a ribosome that reads three-letter messages such as CCU, CUA, or UAG for specific amino acids. The resulting amino acids remain in the cytoplasm of cell body or are released via the Golgi apparatus into the bloodstream.
4. The amino acids remaining in the neuronal cell body, which are used to form *four*-layer protein structures, are composed of *five* elements (carbon, oxygen, hydrogen, nitrogen, and sulphur) in the chemical periodic table.
5. The four-level protein structures in the cell body of the neuron may be the computers of mind at the neuronal level (microlevel or nanolevel) in the vast unconscious human mind; the five-chemical elements may be the code used in the neuronal computer programs of mind.

Level 2: Links From Single Neurons to Neural Networks to Cortical Computations

The *six*-level server of mind:

1. Momentary functional synaptic connections form across a synapse (gap) via a digital action potential of the sending neuron's axon, which triggers neurotransmitters that transmit to a receiving neuron (its dendrites, dendrite spines, or in some cases, cell body), causing the next neuron to activate or inhibit.
2. Distributed neural pathways of synapsed neurons activate sequentially and/or simultaneously in time in specific areas of brain, creating patterns of simultaneous and sequential activation across spatial locations of the brain in time.
3. Primary sensory receive and motor areas send in the cerebral cortex.
4. Secondary association areas in cerebral cortex integrate while preserving sensory input or motor output codes.
5. Tertiary association areas in cortex code abstractly independent of sensory or motor codes.
6. The cerebellum coordinates the timing of the cross-space and cross-time neural events.

EXHIBIT 7.1 *(Continued)*

Although the prevailing paradigm is that functional synaptic connections transmit "information," it is likely that they may provide temporary momentary access to the processing in the four-level structures (minicomputers of mind) in specific neuronal cell bodies at specific locations in the multilevel brain organization, as Minsky (1986) envisioned.

Level 3: Bidirectional Links Among Neurons, Networks, and Cortical Computations

Seven neural communication paths along the main brain axes from bottom-up, top-down, right-left, left-right, back-front, front-back, and hind brain (cerebellum) may construct macro-level functional systems that integrate incoming messages from the external world and else-where in the mind within the current mental state, giving rise to brain waves detected during recording of cortical electrical activity:

1. The *brainstem,* an important part of the bottom-up paths, with the reticular activating system, regulates circadian rhythms and sleep–wake cycles and levels of arousal and awareness during wakefulness.
2. The *thalamus* is the way station for all incoming sensory stimuli (except olfactory stimuli) on the path to the primary sensory areas of cortex, and is also the seat of normal brain rhythms, and the *basal ganglia* is involved in switching states of mind; both are important in the bottom-up and top-down paths.
3. The *hippocampus* has connections to many cerebral areas involved in memory while awake and is where consolidation takes place while asleep.
4. The *cingulate* provides self-regulation and executive management for both limbic and frontal systems and their interconnections to support higher order states of mind.
5. The *corpus callosum* coordinates brain regions on the right and left sides of cerebrum to support higher order states of mind.
6. *Cortical back areas* (occipital, temporal, parietal), through connection with *cortical frontal areas,* are involved in the cognitive, metacognitive, language, memory, attention, and executive, and social functions and awareness of higher order states of mind.
7. The *cerebellum* coordinates timing within and across all the multicomponent processes at all levels of functional brain systems underlying the mind.

There may be *eight* branches of microlevel dendrites of individual neurons (the bottom four under genetic control and the top four influenced by environment input). Dendrites receive signals that originate both in the external environment and elsewhere in the internal brain environment. They then contribute to ongoing processing in the neuronal cell body, which in turn may potentially affect functional synaptic connections and access in momentary time.

There are *nine* temporary working memory components that support goal-related tasks drawing on conscious and automatic processing:

1. Three storage and processing units for word forms, accumulating words, and nonverbal images and visual–spatial arrays.
2. Two cross-code output integration loops (phonological [with mouth] and orthographic [with hand] loops):
   a. mind's ear/eye and oral production (mouth, vocal tract and cords, tongue and lips)
   b. mind's ear/eye–hand production (hands, fingers, arms)
3. Four supervisory attention functions: selective/focused, switching, sustaining, monitoring.

There are *10* developmental changes in the brain platform supporting learning and behavior through genetic regulation and interactions with the physical and social environment and the internal mental environment. Genes regulate neural processes and their timing across development: neural migration and wiring of the nervous system, protein coding for the minicomputers of mind, pruning of surplus neurons or synapses not currently used, and myelination.

(continued)

EXHIBIT 7.1 (Continued)

The 10 brain platforms supporting development, learning, and behavior, which change across development as a function of biological–environmental interactions and in the culture of North America in the 21st century include the following:

1. 9-month gestation (early gestation, beginning with conception and followed by neural proliferation, neural migration, and closing of neural tube, and mid and late gestation).
2. Birth and postnatal infancy (1st year)
3. Toddlerhood (2nd year)
4. Early childhood to preschool (3rd–5th years)
5. Early childhood to early school years (6th–8th years)
6. Middle childhood (9th–12th years)
7. Early and middle adolescence (13th–20th years)
8. Later adolescence and transition to early adulthood (21st–35th years)
9. Middle adulthood (36th–54th years)
10. Senior years (55th year–above)

The first conceptual framework (see Exhibit 7.1) outlines the general principle that the complex human brain is organized on many levels, ranging from molecules at the microlevel to connected single neurons in networks at midlevel to large collections of neurons in specific regions of the brain at the macrolevel. The second conceptual framework is that genes play many roles beyond genetic inheritance at conception (see Genetics Primer section). These roles range from (a) neural wiring of the brain that begins after conception and can affect learning throughout development; (b) protein coding, which may contribute to minicomputers of the mind in the cell bodies of each neuron; and (c) regulating neuronal processes throughout development, including pruning (eliminating neurons) or myelinating (forming white sheaths around the axon of a neuron to improve the efficiency of neural functioning). The minicomputers of the mind at the microlevel may explain why the mind housed in the inner universe of a small 3-pound human organ, the brain, can represent and think about the vast external universe, a concept first conceptualized by the poet Emily Dickinson (see Diamond & Hopson, 1999).

The third conceptual framework (see Exhibit 7.2) links each of five kinds of brain systems to the five domains of development (see Chapter 8): (a) sensory and motor systems; (b) four language systems; (c) cognitive and memory systems; (d) social and emotional systems; and (e) self-regulation, attention, and executive function systems. In each of these systems, links with specific brain regions at the macrolevel are highlighted for those who already have training or course work in neuroscience (or may in future) so they can relate this framework to the larger research and clinical literature in neuropsychology.

EXHIBIT 7.2

Conceptual Framework 2: Functional Brain Systems Corresponding to Domains of Development

Sensory, Motor, and Sensory–Motor Systems

Sensory processes:
- touch (skin)—location
- touch (skin)—pressure (amount)
- touch (skin)—temperature
- touch (skin)—texture
- touch (skin)—kinesthesia (sensation of movement)
- auditory (ears)
- vestibular (inner ear)—balance, motion, and position in space
- visual (eyes)
- smell (nose)
- taste (tongue)

Motor processes:
- mouth (lips, tongue, and vocal tract)
- hands and fingers
- face
- limbs
- torso

    Motor–sensory and sensory–motor processes (representative not comprehensive examples that apply only if each sensory or motor process falls within the normal range)

1. Ears receive auditory input and aural feedback from oral productions of mouth and vestibular sense (locating sounds in space)
2. The mouth produces articulatory gestures, engages the vocal tract and tongue during speech, and receives feedback from somatosensory skin sensations during mouth and tongue movements and from air waves in the vocal tract, the vestibular system (location in space), and the ears
3. Eyes receive visual input and feedback from the vestibular system during eye movements
4. Hands produce hand and finger movements, receive feedback from skin sensations for touch—location, touch—pressure, touch—kinesthesia, and touch—texture; from eyes and eye movements; and from the vestibular system (locating hand and finger movements in space)

Four Multilevel Functional Language Systems

1. Language by Ear

Input through the ears from the auditory environment and feedback from the mouth, vocal tract, and vestibular system (locating mouth movements in space)

- Auditory processing: sound waves through the outer, middle, and inner ear (peripheral nervous system) to the thalamus to the primary auditory area in the temporal lobe (BA 41; central nervous system)

(continued)

EXHIBIT 7.2 (*Continued*)

- Sound pattern processing in association areas of the temporal lobe for both music and speech: amplitude, frequency, duration, stress, sequencing, rhythm
- Phonetic processing in association areas of the temporal lobe (speech-specific): perceiving coarticulated speech patterns within and across syllables—segmental consonant sounds and distributed vowel sounds
- Phonemic processing in association areas of the temporal, parietal, and frontal lobes: abstracting phonemes, which are the smallest units of sound that make a difference in meaning and correspond to one- or two-letter spelling units in the alphabetic principle but which are not the same as phonetic speech units by mouth

2. Language by Mouth

Output through the mouth (place and manner of articulation, vocal tract/voice, tongue movements, lip movements) with feedback through the ear, skin in mouth and vocal tract, and vestibular system

- Language production (for words, syntax, and discourse): in conversational turns or academic instructional register (inferior frontal gyrus and dorsal lateral prefrontal cortex and middle frontal gyrus, supplementary, premotor and primary motor frontal regions, and posterior tempo–parietal language regions)
- Speech production: *oral motor planning* (executive functions for speech sounds, sequence, and rhythm in left inferior frontal gyrus and supplementary and premotor areas of frontal lobe); *oral motor control* (premotor and supplementary motor areas of frontal lobe); *oral motor output* from the primary motor area (BA 4) of the cortex of the frontal lobe; to the lower cerebral pathways involving the basal ganglia and eventually the peripheral nervous system related to the mouth (vocal tract/voice, tongue movements, lip movements)
- Related nonverbal production: facial expressions, hand gestures, and torso and limb movements (central nervous system and peripheral nervous system)

3. Language by Eye

Input through the visual sensory sense (eyes) working with the ocular motor control systems (binocular coordination and saccadic eye movements) and with feedback from visible hand acts and the vestibular system for spatial location

- Visual processing: pathways from the retina to the optic nerve to the thalamus to the primary visual area in BA 17 in the occipital lobe
- Visual perception in association areas (nonlinguistic): pathways involving the occipital and parietal lobes and right fusiform gyrus in the temporal lobe (for face recognition)
- Visible language analysis in association area (linguistic) pathways involving occipital, temporal, and parietal lobes, including visual motion, fusiform, and lingual areas and precuneus
- Word form, syntax, and semantic regions in association areas in four cortical lobe pathways involving storage and processing units for written words, spoken words, morphological bases and affixes, and syntax (accumulating words), mapping their interrelationships, text (accumulating syntactic units), and links to semantic and cognitive processors (occipital, temporal, and parietal lobes; supramarginal gyrus; inferior frontal gyrus; dorsolateral prefrontal cortex)

EXHIBIT 7.2 (*Continued*)

4. Language by Hand

Output by hand for hand and finger movements, with feedback from sensory systems for skin—touch (location, pressure, texture, kinesthesia or movement), vision, eye movements, and from the vestibular system for position in space; paths from the frontal premotor, supplementary motor, and primary motor cortex, with links to different levels of language representations and kinds of cognitive representations in the back and front of the cerebral cortex, the middle and lower areas of the cerebrum, and the cerebellum and with links to the peripheral nervous system

Orthographic loop for integrating the mind's eye and output through hand:

- *Graphomotor planning* for coordinating the orthographic loop of working memory linking word spellings and sequential finger movements and text generation (supplementary motor and premotor frontal areas, superior parietal areas, fusiform gyrus)
- *Graphomotor control* for coordinating production processes for letters or written words (premotor and supplementary motor frontal areas and superior parietal areas)
- *Graphomotor output* for executing production processes supported by central nervous system pathways from the primary motor area (BA 4) in the frontal lobe to lower pathways in the basal ganglia to the peripheral nervous system output through nerves and muscles of hand and fingers

Cognitive and Memory Systems

Cognitive Representations

- *Concepts* may draw on any of the kinds of representations that follow and are abstractions that exist independently of language, though they are involved in the language learning of children as they learn to use oral vocabulary, syntax, idioms, and art to express concepts
- *Associations* consist of (a) free associations, (b) paired associations, and (c) spreading activation across networks of associations and across interconnected nodes in human associative memory
- *Categories* are *grouping schemes* based on defining and differentiating features (a) leveled within hierarchies (living organisms, animals, mammals, cats); (b) exhibiting *flexible grouping*—the same case or exemplar can belong to alternate categories, depending on the grouping scheme at hand (e.g., a female might be undergraduate, mother, or wife but does not necessarily belong to each category); (c) consisting of individual exemplars (cases) within categories that vary in how prototypical or representative they are of their categories (e.g., female teacher vs. female plumber)
- *Dimensions* are variables in cognitive groupings that vary along a continuous, quantitative scale; a cognitive grouping may have multiple dimensions
- *Schemata* are noncategorical structures for organizing knowledge
- *Declarative knowledge* is "knowing that," based on representations of facts or other kinds of information, such as "chunks" in adaptive character of thought (ACT) theory
- *Procedural knowledge* is "knowing how," based on representations of how to perform acts, such as in the production rules in ACT theory
- *Episodic events* are life experiences that occur over time, including repeated exposure to stimuli, from which many different kinds of patterns may be abstracted

(*continued*)

EXHIBIT 7.2 (*Continued*)

- *Nonverbal representations* include (a) *imagery* (concrete ties to sensory world; or abstract representations without ties to the sensory world); (b) *visual–spatial representations*—scenes or other visual input that can be viewed, photographed, videotaped, or televised; visual diagrams, tables, graphs, figures, maps (two- and three-dimensional), and models (*n*-dimensional), and geometry; (c) *auditory representations* (nonlanguage including but not restricted to aspects of music); (d) *arts* (visual, graphics, music, dance) with and without associated language; (e) *archetypes* (image forms, such as animated creatures, young and old, good and bad) may be inherited in species-specific ways, but change across development through nature–nurture interactions; (f) *quantitative representations* (concepts such as number line and place value, exact and estimated math, and part–whole relationships)
- *Formal logic* includes *syllogisms* (sequential logic: given A and then B, does C follow?)
- *Personal biographical memory* is personal life experiences recorded in episodic memory and represented in autobiographical memory and accessed in personal unconscious through free-association or flow when writing or talking
- *Family-specific* or *other social group-specific representations* are based on life experiences in social groups in which the individual lives
- *Culture-specific representations* include, for example, time being cyclical for indigenous cultures, whereas time is linear for Western cultures
- *Symbols* stand for something else
- *Statistical regularities* are abstracted from recurring stimuli or events stored in the episodic buffer and are used in pattern recognition, such as three kinds of statistical regularities abstracted for words that make word recognition more predictable: (a) *phonotactic knowledge* of sound identity, detecting change in sounds, and probable sound sequences and positions of sounds in spoken words; (b) *orthotactic knowledge* of letter identity, letter sequences, and letter positions in words; (c) *morphotactic knowledge* of word parts, including base words and affixes appended at beginning and end of words to modify meaning or grammar of spoken and written words
- *Humor* results from play with language or ideas (e.g., jokes, riddles, stand-up comedy)
- *Values* are personal choices about what matters most
- *Beliefs* are strongly held views that may or may not be supported by evidence (including stereotypes)
- *Common sense*
- *Wisdom*
- *Cognitive links to the motor or sensory systems* include (a) movement, including but not restricted to athletics or dance; and (b) tactile (touch) and kinesthetic sensations (sequential touch sensation from movement)
- *Cognitive links to language* may play a role in verbal learning: (a) subword sound, spelling, or morpheme units; (b) vocabulary word meaning, pronunciation, spelling, and morphology, multiple meanings for same word pronunciation (mental dictionary, mental lexicon); (c) propositions, predicates and their arguments; (d) syntax, sequenced word order, content and function words (glue words without meaning that glue other words together), parts of speech, speech acts (intentionality—the goal of talk or writing, statements, questions, exclamations, and commands), phrases, clauses; (e) discourse structures in connected text in oral or written language (subword, word, and syntactic structures interact with discourse structures); (f) idioms not learned as syntax units but rather as culturally specific, arbitrary units that access cognitive representations (e.g., "pull my leg," "make my day")—approximately a third of teachers' utterances contain multiple meaning words or idiomatic expressions, and about 7% of reading materials used in elementary

EXHIBIT 7.2 (*Continued*)

schools contains idioms; and (g) poetry using nonsyntactic, rhythms and music of language, and imagery

■ *Cognitions linked to social–emotional functions* are supported by uni- and bidirectional brain pathways through the limbic system below cortex to lower cortical areas

Cognitive Operations That Operate on Cognitive Representations

General Characteristics of Cognitive Operations

■ May operate on innate inherited representations, representations from life experiences, and/or representations based on nature–nurture interactions
■ May be static and unchanging, changing without form or organization, self-organizing by creating new structures or connections, or reorganizing by changing connections or relationships among existing representations
■ May be created in unconsciousness while asleep or awake, discovered through flow of thoughts into consciousness from unconsciousness or through random exploration (play) with or without conscious attention or goals; or created in consciousness while awake for specific strategic, purposeful goals using controlled strategies
■ May be the result of proximity in space or time for stimulus–stimulus associations, stimulus–response in classical conditioning, or response–reward associations in operant conditioning
■ May be accessed automatically without conscious, controlled strategies

Specific Cognitive Operations

Different kinds of reasoning

■ *Problem solving:* figure out what the problem is, consider all the evidence and perspectives for solving it, adapt problem-solving strategies as needed for context and configurations, and seek language to explain all these steps and observed patterns
■ *Inductive thinking:* abstractions of (a) classes or categories, (b) general principles, (c) rules, (d) patterns, (e) main ideas, (f) supporting details, and (g) schema
■ *Deductive thinking:* applying abstractions or rules to problem solving
■ *Analysis and synthesis:* finding main ideas, details, and patterns and then integrating these into unified representation
■ *Reflection:* metacognitive awareness of thought processes
■ *Controlled processing:* application of strategies
■ *Playing with ideas and language:* finding humor

Thinking during self-regulated bouts

■ Going beyond the information age (quick access to knowledge via rapid search engines) to sustain cognitive operations
■ Flexibly modify an idea according to the context, the opposite of bureaucracy in which rules are applied rigidly without consideration of relevant factors
■ Thinking may require more than logic (sequence of arguments—what follows what) because successful problem solving may not be purely linear, requiring instead consideration of many simultaneous variables and transforming them rather than just applying preexisting knowledge: (a) providing examples to illustrate a point, (b) considering relationships among items in the same or different categories or in different codes in memory (one-to-one correspondence—mapping; non–one-to-one, complex correspondences—multiple and flexible connections), (c) using metaphors (similarities in symbolic form), (d) using analogies (similarities across two examples—a:b :: x:y), (e) making adjustments that take into account qualifications or context

(continued)

EXHIBIT 7.2 (*Continued*)

Memory

Short-term memory:
- Initial coding of incoming sensory information from the external world during brief time intervals at the neuronal level

Working memory:
- Stores and processes information (from short- and/or long-term memory) to achieve goals in temporary memory (fleeting but not necessarily as brief as short-term memory) in macro-structures
- Supports mental travel to the past, present, and future in the mind across inner spaces and timing scales within the brain
- Has the following components (that cannot be fully assessed with a single test): (a) storage and processing units, (b) loops for integrating external and internal codes, (c) supervisory attention (inhibition and focusing attention, switching attention and flexibility, sustaining attention, self-monitoring), (d) episodic buffer (stores and analyzes exposure to stimuli over time)
- Has the following limitations: (a) capacity (space), (b) resources (access to processes used for temporary working memory goals), (c) efficiency (coordination of the components that have to work together in time)
- Supports bringing cognitions from unconsciousness to consciousness
- Supports development of metalinguistic awareness: Initially language is not a fully conscious system, but is used for storing and processing phonological, orthographic, and morphological units in spoken and/or written words; their interrelationships in syntax enables reflection about language and its many aspects
- Supports development of metacognition: Initially, cognition is not a fully conscious system, but is used for reflections on the many aspects of the cognition and its relationships to other functions, and supports the development of metacognitions that support thinking tasks

Long-term memory:
- Longer lasting representations that may vary in accessibility across time and conditions or mental states

Emotional and Social Development
- All brain pathways to the cerebral cortex go through lower limbic system (emotional brain)
- Examples of basic emotional and motivational processes supported by limbic system and limbic–cortical pathways include (a) approach, (b) avoidance (fear), (c) anxiety (worry), (d) conflict, (e) conflict resolution (peace), (f) sadness, (g) happiness, (h) interest and/or engagement, and (i) reward (reinforcement)
- Self as an organizing principle arises from and organizes life experiences: (a) awareness of self begins to develop when infants and toddlers first smile at the reflection of their face in a mirror, and (b) self-regulation of attention, behavior, and learning
- Other—not self: (a) imitation of others, (b) differentiation of self from others necessary for normal social interaction and social development, and (c) understanding perspectives of others that may be different from one's own perspective (theory of minds—not everyone thinks the same)
- Other—other: spirituality; the sense that one is not alone in the universe

Self-Regulation, Attention, and Executive Functions

Low-Level Executive Functions of Supervisory Attention of Working Memory
- focus attention, which requires inhibition to support selective attention
- switch attention, which requires flexibility—release inhibition, switch, and refocus

EXHIBIT 7.2 *(Continued)*

- sustain attention over time
- update (self-monitor working memory contents and processes over time)
- search and find in long-term memory a word or an example for a category

High-Level Executive Functions for On-Line Cognitive Processes in Working Memory

- idea access activates via working memory the vast unconscious thought world
- idea generation creates new cognitions
- goal setting and making plans to reach goals
- translation (transforming one domain into another within and across states of mind)
- reviewing and revising (retranslating)
- imagining, envisioning what does not yet exist
- predicting the future
- playing with ideas (creativity)

Note that for the sensory and motor domain, instead of just five senses (visual, auditory, touch, taste, and olfaction), there are at least 10, including vestibular and five different somatosensory senses, not just one: touch—location, touch—pressure/pain, touch—texture, touch—temperature, and touch—kinesthesia. For the language domain, key functions of the four language systems are provided, each linked to a different sensory or motor system and relevant to assessment and educational planning for school age children and youth. For the cognitive domain, the key functions represent a comprehensive review of all the kinds of cognitive representations and operations studied by cognitive psychologists over the past 5 decades. All of these are relevant to learning and instruction for academic skills and general functioning in the world. Although current psychometric tests do not assess all of these cognitive skills, the variety of cognitive representations and operations included in Exhibit 7.2 can be used in assessment to gain insight into how an individual mind is working and what might be effective educational approaches for that mind. This "process" assessment goes beyond test scores.

For the social–emotional domain, key concepts from the rapidly expanding field of social neuroscience are included, but interdisciplinary team members are encouraged to read this literature on their own. As Mortimer Mishkin demonstrated with primate research, and as many classroom teachers would concur, there is no cognition without emotions and motivation. For the attention, executive function, self-regulation domain, the focus is on mental self-government for the varied functions within the complex human brain. Some of these skills support the supervision of the working memory activities that enable temporary conscious access to the minicomputers in the vast unconscious mind. Working memory, in turn, supports many other executive functions that enable the brain to self-regulate the mind it creates through interactions with the external social and physical world and its internal world. One educational application of this brain-based developmental domain model is that, despite the myth that children with dyslexia need multisensory learning experiences, all children need instruction that integrates sensory and motor systems with each other and with language systems that have multiple levels—subword (smaller than a word), word, multi word (syntax and idioms), and larger discourse units—and team with internal complex cognitive, social–emotional, and attention and executive function systems.

The fourth conceptual framework (see Exhibit 7.3) considers how the complex, multileveled human brain in which myriad activities are occurring at any one moment in time (most outside conscious awareness) and involving ongoing changes in mental states can create and maintain a steady state of mind, that is, a united state of minds. In essence, the brain is an interdisciplinary team that coordinates mul-

---

EXHIBIT 7.3

Conceptual Framework 4: Levels of Awareness Within a United States of Mind

Dimensions of Consciousness
- Sensation
- Perception (detection + recognition, some links to existing knowledge)
- Reflection (*meta-awareness*—thinking about perceptions)
- Goal-directed mental activity (supported by working memory)
- Relational self, other, and other–other
- Integrative mapping and cross-domain translating
- Self-government (united states of mind—unified partial states of mind)

Creating Consciousness From the Vast Unconsciousness
- Representations in the unconsciousness stream in when consciousness is altered (a) during and right after sleep (e.g., writing may proceed more easily in the morning), (b) after setting aside the conscious attempt to gain access (e.g., writing may proceed more easily after a break or setting the writing task aside for a while), or (c) when daydreaming while awake (e.g., getting lost in one's own internal thoughts)
- Spontaneous access during waking state (pops into consciousness): (a) not consciously retrieved (often some best ideas are not consciously retrieved), (b) becomes available through inspiration (an experienced event that calls it forth), (c) involves new content not before consciously available
- Relies on intuition: relies on feelings or sensations not easily articulated rather than logic (e.g., many major mathematical discoveries from sudden insight occur after long periods of "incubation")
- Uses strategic, controlled strategies to search and find or construct. (e.g., the first sound in a word to locate the word on "the tip of your tongue," or schemata for text composing)

tiple codes and processes in space and time. The educational relevance is that some developing learners are better at managing this process than others. They vary in how responsive they are to what is happening in the external environment and (a) they may be lost in their own daydreams rather than paying attention to instruction, (b) experience different levels of awareness or wakefulness at any one moment in time, or (c) vary in whether a unified state of mind is achieved. The bottom line is that, given this complexity, it is a wonder that so many students learn as well as they do.

Readings and Resources[1]

GENETICS PRIMER

Alberts, B. (Ed.). (2010). Epigenetics [Special section]. *Science, 330*, 611–633.

Batshaw, M., Gropman, A., & Lanpher, B. (2013). Genetics and developmental disabilities. In M. Batshaw, N. Roizen, & G. Lotrecchiano (Eds.), *Children with disabilities* (7th ed.). Baltimore, MD: Brookes.

Cassiday, L. (2009, September 14). Mapping the epigenome. *Chemical & Engineering News, 87*(37), 11–16. Retrieved from http://cen.acs.org/articles/87/i37/Mapping-Epigenome.html

Collins, F. (2010). *The language of life: DNA and the revolution in personalized medicine*. New York, NY: HarperCollins.

Kandel, E. R., Schwartz, J., & Jessell, T. (2012). *Principles of neural science* (5th ed.). New York, NY: McGraw-Hill.

Kolb, B., & Whishaw, I. (2009). *Fundamentals of neuropsychology* (6th ed.). New York, NY: Worth.

BRAIN BASES OF CONCEPTUAL FRAMEWORKS

Llinás, R. R., Ribary, U., Jeanmonod, D., Kronberg, E., & Mitra, P. P. (1999). Thalamocortical dysrhythmia: A neurological and neuropsychiatric syndrome characterized by magnetoencephalography. *Proceedings of the National Academy of Sciences of the United States of America, 96*(26), 15222–15227. doi:10.1073/pnas.96.26.15222

Mishkin, M., & Appenzeler, T. (1987). The anatomy of memory. *Scientific American, 256*, 80–89.

---

[1]Additional research readings and practitioner resources for this chapter can be found at http://www.apadivisions.org/division-16/publications/interdisciplinary-frameworks-supplement/index.aspx

NATURE–NURTURE INTERACTIONS

Diamond, M., & Hopson, J. (1999). *Magic trees of mind: How to nurture your child's intelligence, creativity, and healthy emotions from birth through adolescence.* New York, NY: Plume.

Morrison, F., Griffith, E., & Alberts, D. (1997). Nature–nurture in the classroom: Entrance age, school readiness, and learning in children. *Developmental Psychology, 33*, 254–262. doi:10.1037//0012-1649.33.2.254

Olson, R., Byrne, B., & Samuelson, S. (2009). Reconciling strong genetic and strong environmental influences on individual differences and deficits in reading ability. In K. Pugh & P. McCardle (Eds.), *How children learn to read: Current issues and new directions in the integration of cognition, neurobiology, and genetics of reading and dyslexia research and practice* (pp. 215–233). New York, NY: Taylor & Francis.

Olson, R. K., Hulslander, J., Christopher, M., Keenan, J. M., Wadsworth, S. J., Willcutt, E., . . . & DeFries, J. C. (2013). Genetic and environmental influences on writing and their relations to language and reading. *Annals of Dyslexia, 63*, 25–43.

IDIOMS

Warmouth, J. M., & Ayerza, G. J. (2013). *Teacher Trade!* Seattle, WA: CreateSpace.

Diagnosing Pervasive and Specific Developmental Disabilities and Talent

8

This chapter outlines a cross-disciplinary, evidence-based approach to developmental assessment in school-age children and youth based on each of the five domains of development. Children should be assessed when parents report significant developmental concerns in infancy or early childhood and/or the school team is concerned about a child's daily functioning at school. Assessment is also necessary when a student appears to be developmentally advanced. Guidelines are provided for using the developmental profile in Figure 8.1 to (a) diagnose pervasive developmental disabilities (PDDs) and specific developmental disabilities (SDDs) or giftedness and (b) take the five developmental domains into account when planning student interventions and giving parents feedback.

http://dx.doi.org/10.1037/14437-008
Interdisciplinary Frameworks for Schools: Best Professional Practices for Serving the Needs of All Students, by V. W. Berninger

FIGURE 8.1

Name:_____

Date of Birth:_____

Current Age:_____years_____months

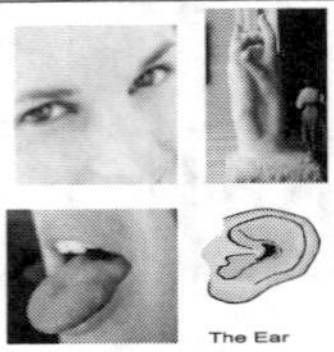 Sensory and motor	 Social and emotional	 Aural and oral language	 Cognitive and memory	 Attention and executive functions
≥145/19	≥145/19	≥145/19	≥145/19	≥145/19
140/18	140/18	140/18	140/18	140/18
135/17	135/17	135/17	135/17	135/17
130/16	130/16	130/16	130/16	130/16
125/15	125/15	125/15	125/15	125/15
120/14	120/14	120/14	120/14	120/14
115/13	115/13	115/13	115/13	115/13
110/12	110/12	110/12	110/12	110/12
105/11	105/11	105/11	105/11	105/11
100/10	100/10	100/10	100/10	100/10
95/9	95/9	95/9	95/9	95/9
90/8	90/8	90/8	90/8	90/8
85/7	85/7	85/7	85/7	85/7
80/6	80/6	80/6	80/6	80/6
75/5	75/5	75/5	75/5	75/5
70/4	70/4	70/4	70/4	70/4
65/3	65/3	65/3	65/3	65/3
60/2	60/2	60/2	60/2	60/2
≤ 55/1	≤ 55/1	≤ 55/1	≤ 55/1	≤ 55/1

Developmental profile. The arrow shows the average level for the population of children of the same age. Mark overall developmental level on the basis of the first assessment in blue ink, the second assessment in black ink, and the third assessment in red ink.

Defining and Assessing the Five Domains of Development

Child development research over many decades has identified five domains of development that correspond to different brain systems (see Chapter 7). Like water molecules, which can be analyzed for the separable hydrogen and oxygen atoms as well as the properties of the molecule when they are combined, these developmental systems may be assessed separately and by how well they work together in the whole child (see Chapter 13). Development in these domains may proceed at different rates within and across children. Describing a student's overall level of development in each of these domains at repeated times can identify students whose overall development falls outside the normal range across the five domains (PDD) or in one or more but not all domains (SDD). For students with PDDs or SDDs, instruction at the student's developmental level(s) is appropriate. Using the diagnostic category of intellectual disability overlooks the important evidence-based principle that not only cognitive development but also other domains of development may be impaired. Because of federal legislation that extended free appropriate public education (FAPE) downward to birth from 3 years, many infants and toddlers may have already been referred for assessment and may have received services before they enter kindergarten at age 5. Thus, an important part of a developmental assessment at kindergarten is to ask for and review any reports with findings from prior developmental assessments a child may have had. The findings can be interpreted in reference to the five developmental domains.

Guidelines for Assessing the Five Domains of Development

SENSORY AND MOTOR

Audition

Hearing should be assessed by an audiologist to determine whether the child may be deaf or have hearing loss and, if so, to what degree. Hearing acuity should be screened using pure-tone audiometry, if appropriate, or by otoacoustic emissions screening if a child is unable to comply behaviorally with pure-tone screening. If the child is found to be deaf or to have hearing loss, the educational team, including the parents, educators, and specialists, should develop an educational plan with recommendations for any communication system that may be needed at school or home, such as amplification (hearing aids), mode of communication (e.g., oral only, signing only, signing with lip reading, or oral and signing—that is, total communication), and possible medical conditions and/or interventions (e.g., fluctuating hearing loss, ear infections, or cochlear implants). These educational decisions should be made with respect for the different philosophies of deaf education, which may be in keeping with or in conflict with the child's clinical and educational profiles, family background, and life circumstances.

Any diagnoses of fluctuating hearing loss and reports of chronic ear infections should be followed by consultation with a physician specializing in ear, nose, and throat, because of the increasing evidence that these may be related to medically treatable infections in the sinuses and tonsils in some children. Early ear infections may also be associated with later delays in speech, language, and educational attainment. Cranial nerve functioning should be assessed by a pediatric neurologist or developmental pediatrician. Any diagnoses of central auditory processing problems should be followed by consultation with a speech–language pathologist (SLP), because central auditory processing can manifest in many ways.

Vision

An ophthalmologist should determine the health of the eye—for example, whether there are any congenital abnormalities such as cataracts (defects that cloud vision) or strabismus (a defect in the binocular coordination of both eyes). In some cases, surgery or other medical procedures (e.g., patching of an eye) may be warranted, and evidence indicates that the earlier in development these procedures are implemented, the better the developmental outcomes. Either an ophthalmologist or an optometrist can assess both far-point and near-point visual acuity and determine whether glasses are needed to improve acuity. Accommodations such as large print or braille should be discussed if acuity cannot be corrected to normal limits with lenses. Large print can also help with problems in binocular coordination.

Tactile Sensory Skills and Gross and Fine Motor Skills

Occupational or physical therapists can identify educationally relevant conditions such as (a) hypersensitivity or hyperreactivity, a condition in which children experience discomfort from typical types of touch, and (b) impaired kinesthesia for sensing sequential movement when skin is touched. Tactile defensiveness can interfere with development of social skills in play with peers. Impaired kinesthesia has been shown to interfere with academic skills such as paper and pencil arithmetic. The assessment should also determine, for both gross motor and fine motor skills, whether the locus of the motor problem is in (a) motor planning of output, (b) motor control and coordination of output, and/or (c) only execution of movement. Identifying the nature of the motor problem is relevant to the educational intervention needed.

Developmental stepping-stones in motor development should also be assessed, both by direct observation of current skills and by history from parents on the basis of interviews, questionnaires, and rating scales. These may not be developing normally in children with PDD across all domains of development or SDD for developmental motor disability. For children in kindergarten through high school, a research-supported, comprehensive assessment tool is the ABC Movement Battery (2nd ed.). The Developmental Neuropsychological Assessment (2nd ed.; NEPSY-II) also has relevant subtests. In some cases a child may have paralysis or weakness of a limb, side of the body, or lower regions of the body or excessive or insufficient muscle tone, and mouths and hands may also be affected. For any of these conditions, consultation is needed from a pediatric neurologist or physiatrist (a physician specializing in rehabilitation medicine), occupational or physical therapist, speech–language specialist, and special educator regarding issues related to feeding, positioning, daily activities, and assistive technology used for learning and communication at home and school.

Differentiating Speech Perception and Production

Heard speech produced by others is perceived by the listener when the speaker's vocal fold vibration sends acoustic signals through air, which are received by the listener's outer ear and processed by the middle and inner ear, then transmitted to the thalamus in the brain, and finally processed in the primary auditory cortex of the temporal lobe. *Produced speech* originates in the frontal lobe, travels down to the basal ganglia, and continues to its final destination in the peripheral nervous system, where it is generated by the vocal fold vibration, supported by the respiratory system, and modulated by the slope of the vocal tract and muscle movements of the mouth, tongue, and lips (see Exhibit 7.2 in Chapter 7). Impaired auditory acuity (hearing) always interferes with speech perception, but sometimes perception of heard speech does not develop normally in children with normal auditory acuity because of their own oral–motor (or oro–motor) problems that result in faulty auditory feedback. If speech is not intelligible to others or if the individual stutters, a referral to a speech–language specialist is necessary for assessment and treatment (see Exhibit 7.2 in Chapter 7).

Speech not intelligible to others may involve immaturities in the oral–motor system for speech production, or it can involve problems with the quality of phonological representations that form the speech sounds of a language. In the latter case, the problem is likely a language development difficulty rather than solely a speech production issue. If an individual stutters, the problem resides in the fixation of the muscles that control the voice box, stopping the airflow necessary for fluent speaking. Some children may have difficulty with both processing and producing speech despite normal auditory acuity. In all cases, treatment plans should be based on evaluations of the affected individual by an interdisciplinary team that includes an SLP and the classroom teacher, who should adapt instruction for these issues.

AURAL AND ORAL LANGUAGE

Aural language refers to the reception of language (initially through the ears), and *oral language* refers to language production (through the mouth). Discussions of aural and oral language assume that the child has sufficient hearing for these language systems to develop. Typically, speech and language specialists assess multiple levels of aural and oral language: word-level meaning, syntax and grammar level, and text level. Language development can be assessed without requiring children to talk. For example, vocabulary understanding can be assessed by asking the child to point to one of four pictures that shows the meaning of the word the examiner pronounces and the child hears. Syntax understanding can be assessed by asking the child to point to one of four pictures that shows the meaning of a sentence the examiner pronounces and the child hears. Text understanding can be assessed by asking the child to first listen to a story and then answer questions about it by pointing to pictures. The assessment goal is to determine whether overall aural language development is not in the normal range as in SDDs or is within the normal range overall despite relative weakness in or one or two levels, as in specific language impairment (SLI). However, language is not only about understanding others' language but also about interactive communication, and production of oral language should also be assessed by asking a child to produce orally examples of words in specified categories, that is, find, retrieve, and produce words (word level), construct an oral sentence from pictured words (syntactic level), and orally retell a heard story (text or discourse level). Two research-supported assessment tools for doing assessment of aural and oral language are the Clinical Evaluation of Language Fundamentals (4th ed.) and the forthcoming Test of Integrated Language and Literacy Skills (see Chapter 9).

Differentiating speech and language is an important assessment goal and should cover speech-sound perception, speech production, and language skills beyond speech-sound perception and production processes alone. For this purpose, a Directory of Speech–Language Pathology Assessment Instruments is posted on the website of the American Speech–Language–Hearing Association (http://www.asha.org/ assessments.aspx). Although tools have been developed to assess non-verbal cognition for students with significant speech difficulties, assessing students' language development can be challenging. Speech–language specialists can perform assessments to address these educationally relevant questions: Are the child's problems specific to speech perception and/or speech production or specific to the language system and not speech perception and/or production, or are they pervasive across speech and language skills? Children with low speech intelligibility due to oral–motor speech difficulties may or may not have normal aural language comprehension or normal oral language expression. Of the children with speech production disorders, about 50% may also have oral expressive language disorders, and about 10% to 40% may also have aural receptive language disorders. Put another way, some children may be able to understand more than they can share in conversation either because their speech is unintelligible to others or they cannot construct the language to express their thoughts. To tease apart whether the source of the problem is speech or language, tasks that assess language comprehension without speech production requirements are given, such as pointing to one of several pictures. Tasks are also given that require speech and language to construct an oral response. Comparing results for language tasks with and without speech requirements indicates whether the problem is language-specific or involves language and speech.

To summarize, all levels of language (word, syntax, and text or discourse) and semantics (vocabulary meaning, sentence meaning, and text meaning) should be assessed to determine whether for an individual child (a) the aural and oral language systems are in general developing normally; (b) the child has an SDD in the language domain only (SDD—language); (c) language is the only one of the five domains of development not in the normal range, as in PDD; or (d) overall language development falls within the lower limits of the normal range, but one or more levels showing weakness or impairment, as in SLI or oral and written language learning disability (see Chapter 9). In most cases, children with SLI have difficulty acquiring syntax and learning to conjugate verbs. During the preschool years, late talking, which may or may not have co-occurring speech difficulties, is one of the best predictors that a student will have difficulty with written language learning during the school years. All levels of aural and oral language should be assessed in determining overall language development and any selective impairment(s) in the aural or oral language systems.

From a brain perspective, a *central auditory processing disorder* diagnosis identifies the bottleneck as not being in the ear, part of the peripheral nervous system, but rather in the central nervous system. However, diagnosing central auditory processing disorder is challenging because speech–sound processing involves multiple brain regions in the central nervous system, and any of these regions may be a bottleneck in speech and aural language processing. Clinically administered behavioral tests of speech and language should be used to determine which aspects of speech and language are problematic for an individual student. Exhibit 7.2 in Chapter 7 shows the journey a sound wave makes from the ear to the thalamus (a way station for all incoming sensory information except smell) and then to the primary auditory sensory area in the temporal lobe and other temporal regions. This journey can be affected by momentary states of arousal, attention, and mind (see Exhibits 7.2 and 7.3 in Chapter 7). All sound signals are received in the primary auditory area, not just those related to speech. Impairments in the primary auditory area can interfere with all auditory processing, not just speech sounds. A central auditory processing deficit will probably affect processing of nonspeech as well as speech sounds.

Other areas of the temporal and other lobes in the cerebral cortex are probably involved in processing incoming aural signals that are language-specific: (a) *phonotactics*—abstracting patterns of statistical regularity in heard words stored in the episodic buffer of working memory related to the identity of specific heard speech sounds within words (e.g., /r/ vs. /l/), position of specific sounds within a syllable or word (e.g., /r/ at the beginning of a word rather than at the end), and sequencing of sounds across the syllable or word (e.g., /el/ or /le/); (b) switching attention among temporally changing syllables that affect auditory discrimination among words; and (c) metalinguistic reflections on the individual sounds at different units of analysis (higher level phonological awareness). One kind of phonological awareness involves *phonemes*, which are abstract categories based on the smallest unit of sound that makes a difference in meaning and that also typically corresponds to a one- or two-letter grapheme in the alphabetic principle used in learning to read and spell words. Phonemic awareness and phoneme–grapheme mapping are supported by the association areas of the word-form region of the temporal lobe and nearby regions in the parietal lobe in the angular gyrus and supramarginal gyrus. Phonological awareness may also involve other units of speech—for example, *rimes* (the part of a syllable remaining after the onset phoneme is deleted). Phonological awareness also involves *accenting* (the relative emphasis of syllables within a polysyllabic word) and the musical melody of oral reading of multiple words.

Speech (oral word production), in contrast, requires packaging sounds in syllables that are coarticulated as continuous vowel sounds and segmental consonants within phonetic units. Speech also requires packaging multiple syllables and their temporal transition(s) within higher level intonation contours, the musical melody of spoken language. Reading researchers used to argue about whether problems in learning to read were related to auditory discrimination problems (phonetic analysis within syllables and syllable transitions) or to phonemic analysis in the alphabetic principle (phonological awareness at a higher level of processing), but converging evidence now shows that there are individual differences in whether children struggle with (a) speech sound processing (phonotactics and switching among phonetic units) and/or production, (b) the more abstract phonemic analysis and phoneme–grapheme mapping, (c) synthesizing phonemes into the speech production units for the decoded words, or (d) a combination of some or all of these.

Much as Holmes and Watson collaborated to solve mysteries, the educational professionals on the interdisciplinary team should collaborate as detectives to solve the puzzle for an individual student of which aspects of the complex, multiple-level, and multimodal (input-output systems) language systems and/or speech systems may be interfering with learning specific skills in reading, writing, math, or other areas of the school curriculum or social functioning in and out of school.

COGNITION

The term *IQ* should not be used because it is no longer based on a quotient. Early in the 20th century, when cognitive tests were first developed to determine whether some students needed to move through the curriculum more quickly or more slowly, quotients were computed that compared chronological ages with age equivalents of test scores. By the middle of the 20th century, a new approach was introduced with standard scores, based on national norming, anchored in the normal distribution with a mean of 100 and a standard deviation of 15, and used to compare test scores across ages of test takers. Related scaled scores with a mean of 10 and standard deviation of 3 were developed for subtests on these test batteries.

Cognition is not a unitary construct. Indeed, the publishers of the most widely used cognitive test, the Wechsler Intelligence Scale for Children (4th ed.), have recommended that the Full Scale score not be used, but rather that the index scores, which have been validated in numerous factor analytic studies, be used instead of the full scale score. More is at stake than multiple intelligences in acknowledging the complexity of cognition. The field of cognitive psychology has identified through decades of research many kinds of cognitive representations and operations (see

Exhibit 7.2 in Chapter 7). No test can possibly assess all of them; all may contribute in different ways to any test used to assess cognition and human activities. Current tests typically differentiate between verbal and nonverbal reasoning, but multiple kinds of cognitions contribute to both, and many cognitive tests draw on both verbal and nonverbal processes—for example, the Woodcock–Johnson III measures of inductive reasoning (concept formation) and deductive reasoning (analysis synthesis).

A sizable research literature has shown that verbal reasoning is one of the best predictors of performance on academic achievement tests and accounts for significant variance. Yet, nonverbal reasoning is also related to achievement in specific areas of the curriculum—for example, math and science. Social cognition, thinking about how others think, can also be assessed with NEPSY-II Theory of Mind subtest. None of the cognitive measures have precise predictive validity prior to age 6, when the brain changes in relation to cognition. Thus, assessment of the cognitive domain should take into account multiple kinds of cognition and age of student.

Memory processes are often assessed along with cognitive processes. Short-term memory, for encoding incoming stimuli into the system that may or may not be consolidated, is of such brief duration that it is difficult to assess clinically. However, when those stimuli are consolidated, often during sleep, they are stored in long-term memory. Many of the measures previously considered short-term memory measures are now viewed as working memory measures of ability to hold incoming information and/or other representations already stored in memory in temporary storage and processing units while goal-related tasks are executed. For example, digit span is now thought to be a measure of working memory—a series of heard digits, of increasing size or span has to be temporarily stored in working memory as aural names and is probably recoded into corresponding visual digits and then processed for serial speech production of names. Further complicating assessment of cognition apart from memory is that many subtests and items used to assess reasoning also assess prior knowledge of the world stored in longer term memory, for which moment-to-moment accessibility can fluctuate.

Moreover, research evidence is accumulating showing that there is not a single measure that captures all working memory ability or functions. Working memory is a complex system, and what is stored and processed in its temporary units depends on (a) the task at hand, (b) the temporal efficiency of the loops that integrate internal codes with external end organs interacting with the external world, and (c) the capability of supervisory attention functions that self-regulate working memory functions. Swanson has found individual differences in students in relative strengths and weaknesses across levels of language stored and processed in working memory for language and visual–spatial codes. Working memory is more likely to improve from instruction tailored to specific academic goals with the components of working memory in mind than from teaching students to take working memory tests.

SOCIAL, EMOTIONAL, AND MOTIVATIONAL FUNCTIONS

Exhibit 7.2 in Chapter 7 provides a representative, not exhaustive, overview of some of the important social skills for developing children and youth. Two evidence-supported measures of social development are the Behavior Assessment System for Children (2nd ed.) and the Social Skills Improvement System. A unique feature of the human brain is that there is no cognition without emotion and motivation. As Mishkin showed in his pioneering demonstration, the human brain has both behavioral and cognitive pathways, and the cognitive pathways to the cortex go through the limbic system, which houses the emotional centers and the behavioral association networks of the brain. On a cautionary note, friendliness should not be confused with age-appropriate social development in students. Some students with PDDs smile a lot and are perceived to have a relative strength in social skills when in fact their social cognition, social skills, and social relationships are below what is age-appropriate. An important assessment issue to consider is not only whether social and emotional development is outside the normal range for development and requires considerable behavioral support but also whether there is evidence of psychopathology, a qualitative difference that requires psychiatric services typically not available in school settings. More research attention has been given to motivational issues in typically developing students, but teaching students with PDDs and SDDs at their developmental levels rather than age levels will engage and motivate them to learn.

ATTENTION AND EXECUTIVE FUNCTIONS

Exhibit 7.2 in Chapter 7 shows the differences between the lower level executive functions (supervisory attention) that self-regulate working memory and the higher level executive functions supported by working memory, which are used in performing cognitive tasks that require planning, organizing, translating, reviewing, revising, imagining, and creating. These higher level functions support self-regulation, which in turn supports learning and behavior. Multiple brain systems on bidirectional bottom–up, right–left, and back–front axes provide the neural mechanisms for self-regulating the internal changing states of mind as the societies of brain do their work so that they function in concert, creating a unified state of minds (see Exhibit 7.3). Bottlenecks anywhere in the complex, multilevel, multi-axis brain system can interfere with regulation of states of mind and thus development and learning.

In some cases a developing child's attention and executive functions are so outside the normal range that a diagnosis of attention-deficit/hyperactivity disorder (ADHD) is warranted. Typically, in such cases the problems were evident in infancy, beginning with extreme difficulty in getting the child at the infant, toddler, and even preschooler stage on a regular sleep–wake cycle. This difficulty may be related to differences in the brain stem's reticular activating system, which regulates circadian rhythms (switching cycles for wakefulness and sleep), general levels of arousal in response to the external environment, and other brain regions involved in the regulation of changing states of mind. Parents also often report unusual difficulty in teaching the child to self-regulate at age-appropriate times for toileting, playing with others without fighting, and sitting still when appropriate. These children may need medication to control brain regulation of states of mind underlying behavior during early childhood and thereafter. However, in other cases weaknesses in self-regulation and attention may not surface until the school years in response to academic tasks and behavioral expectations (see Exhibit 7.2 in Chapter 7 and Chapter 13). The difficult issue for the interdisciplinary team is determining when development in this domain of attention, executive functions, and self-regulation is so outside the normal range as to qualify as an SDD or when it simply represents the low end of normal variation for age along a continuum as a function of environmental requirements.

The Child Behavior Rating Scales and Checklists and Clinical Workbooks, the ADHD Rating Scale–IV, Conners Rating Scales (3rd ed.), Delis–Kaplan Executive Function System, and Behavior Rating Inventory of Executive Function provide evidence-based ways to sort out these issues. The interdisciplinary team should reach out to parents to find out whether a child may be taking medication for ADHD and whether he or she has diagnosed co-occurring conditions; if so, the team may design and implement a plan for monitoring response to medication during the school day. Without a three-way communication system among medical providers, parents, and schools, it may not be possible to determine whether the prescribed medication and dosage are benefiting the child's learning and behavior at school. Response to intervention (RTI) has applications beyond monitoring response to academic instruction; RTI should be applied to monitoring any kind of intervention by any member of the interdisciplinary team—physician, nurse, occupational or physical therapist, SLP, behavioral specialist, or school psychologist or counselor.

*Applying Developmental
Profiles to the Diagnosis and
Treatment of Developmental
Disabilities*

DEVELOPMENTAL PROFILE

Diagnosis benefits from communication and collaboration among professionals from multiple disciplines with expertise acquired through preservice and in-service coursework and supervised training and experiences in each of the developmental domains. Diagnosis should be made in the context of the whole developmental profile across the five domains to assess and identify current levels of functioning for each. However, because development is a dynamic process, best professional practice is to describe the developing child's level of development in each of the five domains in the developmental profile (see Figure 8.1) in an initial assessment. The initial assessment should be repeated at least two more times (for a total of three times, at least 6 months apart, and ideally 1 year apart) before a firm diagnosis is made. All should be entered into the same developmental profile as the parent views and even touches where the scores fall in reference to the line for the most average score in the population (see Figure 8.1). Although professionals differ as to where an arbitrary cutoff should be set for what is within and what is below the normal range (e.g., more than two standard deviations [*SD*] below the population mean or adjusted by 2 × the standard error of measurement at −2 *SD*s to set a confidence band), if patterns of performance across the five domains and three repeated assessments clearly support the conclusion that development is not within the normal range, then a diagnosis should be made. Qualitative behavioral observations across settings typically substantiate the quantitative assessments in cases of developmental disabilities.

In giving feedback to parents on the basis of repeated assessments, professionals should avoid using terms such as *developmental delay*, which may give false hope that the child will catch up and be in the normal range in the future. *Splinter skills* in one or two subtests that fall above most of the other scores and that are still clearly below average should not be overinterpreted as indicating the potential for normal function in the future. Such false hope may postpone the difficult task of facing the reality of developmental disability and dealing with the normal grieving process that follows. For diagnostic purposes, focus on the present and the current developmental profile.

DIAGNOSIS BASED ON DEVELOPMENTAL PROFILE

In contrast to diagnosis based on number of symptoms on a list of possible symptoms, developmental diagnosis looks for a pattern of development across the domains of development. If a student falls below the normal range in all five domains, a PDD should be diagnosed. What has been referred to as *mental retardation* in the past and is labeled *intellectual disability* in the present is more appropriately diagnosed as a PDD that affects development in general—the child falls outside the normal range in all five domains of development not just the cognitive domain. If a student falls below the normal range in one or more, but not all, of the five domains, then an SDD should be diagnosed. An SDD indicates that overall development in one or more, but not all, domains is outside the normal range. Even if the pattern of skill development within the domain is uneven, with a notable weakness in one or more specific skills within the developmental domain and sometimes a relative strength (splinter skill or skills), SDD should be diagnosed if overall level of development is outside the normal range in one or more, but not all developmental domains. Developmental levels within and across domains are relevant to planning instruction and other kinds of interventions.

MULTIPLE DISORDERS IN THE SAME INDIVIDUAL

A student may have one or more co-occurring disorders (see Chapters 10 and 11) that should also be diagnosed and taken into account in the educational program. However, regardless of what other conditions may be present, it is also important to obtain a developmental profile to provide a context for planning, implementing, and evaluating the educational program. For example, some children meet diagnostic criteria for autism. However, some of these children also have PDDs, whereas others have SDDs. Some may have cognitive development within the normal range, but an SDD in the social and emotional, sensory and motor, language, attention and self-regulation skills, and/or sensorimotor domains, though they are not necessarily impaired in all skills in those developmental domains. Such impairments can also co-occur with neurogenetic disorders other than autism. Thus, assessment of developmental domains is the first step in the assessment process, which is followed by assessment of phenotype profiles for specific neurogenetic disorders and, sometimes, genetic tests.

In the case of a child with both PDD and autism, it is not appropriate to expect instructional levels or achievement levels to be at grade level. Failure to take the developmental profile into account along with diagnosis of a neurogenetic disorder (Chapter 10) or medical condition (Chapter 11) and current learning profile (Chapter 9) can lead to unrealistic expectations and inappropriate educational programming for the affected child. For example, a 14-year-old whose development falls overall in the 3- to 4-year range is not ready for reading instruction based on intensive phonological awareness and decoding training used with first or second graders, but he or she may benefit from developmentally appropriate activities for 3- and 4-year-olds for all the domains of development.

In the case of a child with one or more SDD or some specific within-domain impairment (not all skills in a developmental domain fall outside the normal range), instructional levels may be at grade level or even above for some, but not all, areas of the curriculum. In this case it is not appropriate to diagnose specific learning disabilities, even if a cognitive-achievement discrepancy is observed, if the child truly has autism, which is a different disorder than a specific learning disability (SLD) such as dyslexia, which is specific to learning written language (word reading and spelling). One of the defining features of SLDs is that all five domains of development fall within the normal range except learning one or more specific reading, writing, math, and/or oral language skills (see Chapter 9). The appropriate instructional approaches are also very different for dyslexia or other SLDs than for autism. For many reasons, research on evidence-based reading instruction in typically developing students with or without SLDs does not generalize in a simple way to the reading problems of students with PDDs or SDDs. See Appendix A for becoming a critical consumer of educational research, with attention to whom the results should appropriately generalized, that is, applied. Many parents and sometimes professionals are under the false impression that their child with developmental disabilities, even if specific and not pervasive, can only receive appropriate services if diagnosed as having autism, which is only one of the many conditions covered in federal law for FAPE for students with disabilities. Interdisciplinary teams have an important contribution to make in educating parents and other professionals about the variety of biologically based conditions that can interfere with development and learning but which may respond to evidence-based educational programs for the specific disorders with which an individual has been diagnosed.

GIVING FEEDBACK TO PARENTS AND EDUCATORS

Although honest feedback about a PDD is painful for both the parents and the professionals giving it, in the long run honesty can prevent adversarial relationships between parents and schools and better serve students. Some parents even thank professionals for being honest about what they suspected. Professionals can prepare for giving the difficult news by reading the classic book *A Difference in the Family*. They should also practice active listening so that the parents feel heard and the professionals can empathize with what parents are feeling and experiencing about the loss of a normal child. Professionals can also assist in finding support services. The developmental profile in Chapter 8 has 19 levels, which correspond to scaled scores with a mean of 10, SD of 3, and range of 1 to 19, but these scaled scores can be converted into standard scores with mean of 100 and SD of 15. Using the results of the multimodal assessment, the clinician may ask the parent to point to where on the vertical axis in each of the five domains the child is functioning on average, on the basis of test scores, ratings, and professional judgment the interdisciplinary team shares. An arrow points to the most average performance of the population in general. By actively participating in constructing the profile, parents have a visual display of the relative strengths and weaknesses of their child across the five domains of development over time and of which ones fall outside the normal range. The profile can be adapted for age equivalents when appropriate. Some tests have tables of age equivalents, which are more meaningful for developmental assessment when standard or scale scores fall at or below −2 SDs below the mean. Both parents and teachers may find it helpful to learn that for a child who is not developing typically, the developmental functioning falls, for example, in the 3- to 4-year range or 6- to 7-year range, and so on.

These developmental levels are also relevant to knowing which developmental stepping-stones (see Part II, this volume) to target in planning and implementing the educational program. Educational professionals on the interdisciplinary team who are providing the feedback may find it helpful to adapt some of the information in the pattern in a given child's developmental profile in preparing this feedback and to use in educational planning. Above all, educational professionals should focus on the child's current levels of functioning and not make predictions about the future, taking time to listen empathically to parents as they make sense of the feedback provided.

Planning and Implementing Ongoing Intervention

The challenge in planning and implementing an individualized education program for students with PDD is that their developmental and instructional levels may be so below those of other students at their grade level that it may not be possible to provide what they need within a general education program. A self-contained program, with some opportunities to visit mainstream classrooms, may be a more viable option than a daily pull-out program. However, local schools are encouraged to work out viable plans that are appropriate for the students in question. Students with PDD can learn some functional academic skills, but are more likely to do so if taught at their developmental and instructional levels. They do develop and learn, but at their own rate and in their own way. Ongoing progress monitoring is essential in planning the next steps in instruction that are developmentally appropriate for them. That instruction should include skills for daily living as well as academic skills for functional literacy and numeracy.

Decisions about whether mainstreaming in general education, a self-contained special education program, or a combined approach is appropriate should be made on a case-by-case basis for students with SDDs, depending on many factors, including being outside the normal range in some domains. As discussed in Part II of this volume, the academic curriculum for the developmental stepping-stones will need to be adapted to their instructional levels and developmental levels.

It is of great importance that interventions for students with PDD or SDD, with or without other conditions, take into account not only the individualized educational program but also the social–emotional needs of the affected child and the whole family, including siblings. These emotional needs may include grief and/or anger. For parents, the grief of losing a normal child may be revisited at different stages of their child's development. The anger may result in adversarial relationships with schools unless educational professionals reach out, listen, try to understand what is like to have a difference in the family, and show they care. One way schools can help in a constructive way is to help organize parent support groups in the school or community so that parents who are raising a child with a disability can provide support for and get support from each other. Siblings may wonder why their brother or sister is disabled whereas they are not; they are often neglected because the focus is on the child with the disability. They too can benefit from counseling or support groups for siblings of children with a disability. Most important, the affected child may be aware of being different and may benefit from individual or group counseling to deal with these feelings.

Ongoing support for parents is especially important during adolescence and through transition from schooling. Many parents are worried about how to provide appropriate services for their child who is not capable of independent living, especially when parents are no longer able to provide care or financial support for them. Adults with PDDs or SDDs differ in whether they can be trained in specific job skills for employment under supervision and, if so, which job skills. High schools can provide the necessary assessments for vocational planning and independent living that facilitate this transition from schooling, and in the process provide emotional support and practical advice for parents.

Another challenge for schools in the era of evidence-based educational practices is that parents want solutions supported by research to fix the developmental problems their children experience. By building trust between home and school, educational professionals can share with parents examples of how research can lead to solutions so that they do not give up hope. At the same time, educational professionals should acknowledge the frustration parents are likely to experience as they patiently wait. Two examples follow that professionals might share to highlight the contributions and improved developmental outcomes when multiple disciplines, including medical and educational professionals, work collaboratively on research teams.

Forty years ago, children who were deaf were not being identified until age 2 or older, which meant that they missed out on the formative stages of language development and were often taught lipreading without the benefit of signing or total communication. As a result, they had life-long problems in reading comprehension even though they could see the printed page and had received adapted reading instruction. However, after researchers discovered that children who were deaf and born to deaf parents who signed to them from birth did not have these language comprehension problems, most states implemented screening of newborns with auditory evoked potentials (otoacoustic emissions screening) to identify those who are deaf so that signing can be implemented right after birth. The children who are deaf and receive this early intervention can develop normal language comprehension.

Likewise, researchers identified through 40 years of research that one of the causes of PDD was a neurogenetic disorder, phenylketonuria (PKU), resulting from impaired processing of protein. They also showed that through a protein-free diet PKU could be prevented, with children reaching average levels of development if they complied with diet restrictions beginning at birth and maintained throughout development. Now most states screen newborns for PKU, and when it is identified, the special diet is implemented to prevent the PDD associated with intake of protein.

THE OTHER DEVELOPMENTAL DIFFERENCE: HIGHLY CAPABLE CHILDREN

Not all developmental differences are related to disability. In fact, some developing children and youth display talents—strengths considerably above the normal range. When parents and educational professionals observe such children, comprehensive developmental assessment may also be warranted. Talents may occur in many domains—for example, general cognitive areas, language, science and math, leadership, the performing arts (drama, dance, visual arts, music), and athletics. None of these talents can be identified simply on the basis of a single test score, although normed tests may be used as part of comprehensive assessment. Schools vary greatly in how they meet the needs of those students who demonstrate dependable strengths and who are highly capable during the school years. These range from pull-out enrichment classes to acceleration to a higher grade level (for whole day or part of the day) to district-wide self-contained programs to supplementary course work at local community colleges to early entrance to college. Some schools offer enrichment or acceleration or self-contained programs early in schooling. Others offer them during middle school and high school. What is best professional practice for timing and mode of delivery depends greatly on the individual student and the resources of a school. What is important is that talent, which emerges during early childhood, middle childhood, and adolescence across all races, cultures, languages, and socioeconomic levels, should be nurtured and celebrated and not feared or ignored.

Readings and Resources[1]

FAMILY: PARENTS AND SIBLINGS

Featherstone, H. (1981). *A difference in the family: Living with a disabled child.* New York, NY: Penguin Books.

ASSISTIVE TECHNOLOGY

Bryant, D. P., & Bryant, B. R. (2012). *Assistive technology for people with disabilities* (2nd ed.). Upper Saddle River, NJ: Pearson.

INSTRUCTIONAL ISSUES FOR DEVELOPMENTAL DISABILITIES

Horner, R. H., Albin, R. W., Todd, A. W., Newton, J. S., & Sprague, J. R. (2010). Designing and implementing individualized positive behavior support. In M. E. Snell & F. Brown (Eds.), *Instruction of students with severe disabilities* (7th ed., pp. 257–303). Upper Saddle River, NJ: Pearson.

Silliman, E. R. (2004). Inclusion models for children with developmental disabilities. In R. D. Kent (Ed.), *The MIT encyclopedia of communication disorders* (pp. 307–311). Cambridge, MA: MIT Press.

---

[1]Additional research readings and practitioner resources for this chapter can be found at http://www.apadivisions.org/division-16/publications/interdisciplinary-frameworks-supplement/index.aspx

ASSESSMENT INSTRUMENTS

Barkley, R. A., & Murphy, K. R. (2006). *Attention-deficit hyperactivity disorder: A clinical workbook* (3rd ed.). New York, NY: Guilford Press.

Conners, K. (2008). *Conners Rating Scales, third edition (CRS–3)*. San Antonio, TX: Pearson.

DuPaul, G. J., Power, T. J., Anastopoulos, A. D., & Reed, R. (1998). *ADHD Rating Scale–IV: Checklists, norms, and clinical interpretations*. New York, NY: Guilford Press.

Gioia, G. A., Isquith, P. K., Guy, S. C., & Kenworthy, L. (2000). *The Behavior Rating Inventory of Executive Function (BRIEF) professional manual*. Odessa, FL: Psychological Corporation.

Gresham, F., & Elliott, S. (2008). *Social Skills Improvement Systems* (SSIS). San Antonio, TX: Pearson.

Hendersen, S., Sugden, D., & Barnett, A. (2007). *Movement Assessment Battery for Children, second edition (Movement ABC–2)*. London, England: Harcourt Assessment/Pearson.

Delis, D. C., Kaplan, E., & Kramer, J. (2001). *Delis–Kaplan Executive Function System (D–KEFS)*. San Antonio, TX: Pearson.

Korkman, M., Kirk, U., & Kemp, S. (2007). *NEPSY—Second edition (NEPSY–II)*. San Antonio, TX: Pearson.

Mishkin, M., & Appenzeller, T. (1987). The anatomy of memory. *Scientific American, 256*, 80–89.

Nelson, N. W., Helm-Estabrooks, N., Hotz, G., & Plante, E. (2011). *Test of Integrated Language and Literacy Skills (TILLS), standardization version 2*. Baltimore, MD: Paul H. Brookes Publishing Co., Inc.

Reynolds, C., & Kamphaus, R. (2004). *Behavior Assessment System for Children, second edition* (BASC–2). San Antonio, TX: Pearson.

Semel, E., Wiig, E. H., & Secord, W. A. (2003). *Clinical Evaluations of Language Fundamentals, fourth edition: Examiner's manual*. San Antonio, TX: Harcourt Assessment, Inc.

Swanson, H. L. (1992). The generality and modifiability of working memory among skilled and less-skilled readers. *Journal of Educational Psychology, 84*, 473–488.

Swanson, H. L. (1996). *Swanson Cognitive Processing Test*. Austin, TX: Pro-Ed.

Wechsler, D. (2003). *Wechsler Intelligence Scale for Children, fourth edition (WISC–4)*. San Antonio, TX: Pearson.

Woodcock, R. W., McGrew, K., & Mather, N. (2007). *Woodcock-Johnson III Normative Update: Tests of Achievement*. Rolling Meadows, IL: Riverside Publishing Company.

COGNITIVE DISABILITY

Pennington, B. F. (2006). From single to multiple-deficit models of developmental disorders. *Cognition, 10*, 385–413. doi:10.1016/j.cognition.2006.04.008

Pennington, B. F. (2009). How neuropsychology informs our understanding of developmental disorders. *Journal of Child Psychology and Psychiatry Annual Research Review, 50,* 72–78. doi:10.1111/j.1469-7610.2008.01977.x

LANGUAGE DISABILITY

Mody, M., & Silliman, E. R. (2008). *Brain, behavior, and learning in language and reading disorders.* New York, NY: Guilford Press.

Nelson, N. W. (2010). *Language and literacy disorders: Infancy through adolescence.* Boston, MA: Allyn & Bacon.

Washington, J. A. (2008). Language variation in child language disorders. *Handbook of child language disorders.* New York, NY: Oxford University Press.

SENSORIMOTOR DISABILITY

Bazyk, S., & Case-Smith, J. (2010). School-based occupational therapy. In J. Case-Smith & J. O'Brien (Eds.), *Occupational therapy for children* (6th ed., pp. 713–742). St. Louis, MO: Mosby/Elsevier.

Case-Smith, J., & Kuhaneck, H. M. (2008). Play preferences of typically developing children and children with developmental delays between ages 3 and 7 years. *OTJR: Occupation, Participation, and Health, 28,* 19–29. doi:10.3928/15394492-20080101-01

Case-Smith, J., & Miller, H. (1999). Occupational therapy with children with pervasive developmental disorders. *American Journal of Occupational Therapy, 53,* 506–513. doi:10.5014/ajot.53.5.506

SOCIAL–EMOTIONAL DISABILITIES

Hughes, T. L., Crothers, L. M., & Jimerson, S. R. (2008). *Identifying, assessing, and treating conduct disorder at school.* New York, NY: Springer Science.

Li, H., Pearrow, M., & Jimerson, S. R. (2010). *Identifying, assessing, and treating early onset schizophrenia at school.* New York, NY: Springer Science.

Reddy, L., De Thomas, C., Newman, E., & Chun, V. (2009). School-based prevention and intervention programs for children with emotional disturbance: A review of treatment components and methodology. *Psychology in the Schools, 46,* 132–153. doi:10.1002/pits.20359

Thome, J., Drossos, T., & Hunter, S. J. (2013). Neurodevelopmental disorders. In L. A. Reddy, A. Weissman., & J. B. Hale (Eds.), *Neuropsychological assessment and intervention for emotional and behavior disordered youth: An integrated step-by-step evidence-based approach* (pp. 271–298). Washington, DC: American Psychological Association.

Wodrich, D. L. (1998). Review of defiant children: A clinical and research guide to parent training. *Journal of Clinical Child Psychology, 27,* 360–361.

ATTENTION/EXECUTIVE FUNCTION DISABILITY

Mitchell, P. H., Belza, B., Schaad, D. C., Robins, L. S., Gianola, F. J., Odegard, P. S., . . . Ballweg, R. A. (2006). Working across the boundaries of health professions disciplines in education, research and service: The University of Washington experience. *Academic Medicine, 81*, 891–896. doi:10.1097/01.ACM.0000238078.93713.a6

Power, T. J., Hughes, C. L., Helwig, J. R., Nissley-Tsiopinis, J., & Mautone, J. A. (2010). Getting to first base: Promoting engagement in family–school intervention for children with ADHD in urban, primary care practice. *School Mental Health, 2*, 52–61. doi:10.1007/s12310-010-9029-2

Power, T. J., Mautone, J. A., Soffer, S. L., Clarke, A. T., Marshall, S. A., Sharman, J., . . . Jawad, A. F. (2012). A family–school intervention for children with ADHD: Results of randomized clinical trial. *Journal of Consulting and Clinical Psychology, 80*, 611–623.

Springer, C., & Reddy, L. (2010). Measuring parental treatment adherence in a multimodal treatment program for children with ADHD: A preliminary investigation. *Child and Family Behavior Therapy, 32*, 272–290. doi:10.1080/07317107.2010.515522

Willcutt, E. G., Doyle, A. E., Nigg, J. T., Faraone, S. V., & Pennington, B. F. (2005). Validity of the executive function theory of ADHD: A meta-analytic review. *Biological Psychiatry, 57*, 1336–1346. doi:10.1016/j.biopsych.2005.02.006

Wodrich, D. L., Stobo, N., & Trca, M. (1998). Three ways to consider educational performance when determining serious emotional disturbance. *School Psychology Quarterly, 13*, 228–240. doi:10.1037/h0088983

Takeda, T., Stotesbery, K., Power, T., Ambrosini, P.J., Berrettini, W., Hakonarson, H., & Elia, J. (2010). Parental ADHD status and its association with proband ADHD subtype and severity. *The Journal of Pediatrics,157*, 995–1000. doi:10.1016/j.jpeds.2010.05.053

Yoshimasu, K., Barbaresi, W., Colligan, R., Voigt, R., Killian, J., Weaver, A., Katusic, S. (2012). Childhood ADHD is strongly associated with a broad range of psychiatric disorders during adolescence: A population-based birth cohort study. *Journal of Child Psychology and Psychiatry, 53*, 1036–1043. doi:10.1111/j.1469-7610.2012.02567.x

CO-OCCURRING CONDITIONS

McGrath, L. M., Hutaff-Lee, C., Scott, A., Boada, R., Shriberg, L. D., & Pennington, B. F. (2007). Children with comorbid speech sound disorder and specific language impairment are at increased risk for attention-deficit/hyperactivity disorder. *Journal of Abnormal Child Psychology, 36*, 151–163. doi:10.1007/s10802-007-9166-8

GIFTEDNESS

Brody, L. (2004). *Grouping and acceleration practices in gifted education.* Thousand Oaks, CA: Corwin Press and the National Association for Gifted Children.

Brody, L. E. (2009). The Johns Hopkins talent search model for identifying and developing exceptional mathematical and verbal abilities. In L. V. Shavinia (Ed.), *International handbook on giftedness* (pp. 999–1016). Houten, Netherlands: Springer.

Subotnik, R. F., Olszewski-Kubilius, P., & Worrell, F. C. (2012). A proposed direction forward for gifted education based on psychological science. *Gifted Child Quarterly, 56,* 176–188. doi:10.1177/0016986212456079

Worrell, F. C. (2009). Myth 4: A single test score or indicator tells us all we need to know about giftedness. *Gifted Child Quarterly, 53,* 242–244. doi:10.1177/0016986209346828

Diagnosing Specific Learning Disabilities and Twice Exceptionality

9

This chapter discusses the historical difficulties in defining and diagnosing specific learning disabilities (SLDs), reports converging evidence from two federally funded projects, and calls attention to other federally funded research on SLDs. Collectively, this research provides hope that progress is being made toward evidence-based, treatment-relevant definitions and diagnosis. The converging evidence supports taking levels of language and modes of language input and output into account in differentiating three different kinds of oral and written language SLDs from typical language development in instructionally relevant ways. Guidelines are offered for diagnosing the following SLDs on the basis of instructionally relevant learning profiles (specific oral and written language or math skills) and associated phenotype profiles (biological markers of genetic bases): dysgraphia, dyslexia, oral and written language learning disability (OWL LD)—also referred to as specific language impairment (SLI)—dyscalculia, SLDs in nonlanguage areas, and twice exceptionality—that is, students who are gifted but also have SLDs. SLDs should only be

http://dx.doi.org/10.1037/14437-009
Interdisciplinary Frameworks for Schools: Best Professional Practices for Serving the Needs of All Students, by V. W. Berninger

diagnosed in children and youth whose development in each of the five developmental domains (see Chapter 8, Exhibit 8.1) falls at least within the lower limits of the normal range; however, relative weaknesses in a specific oral language or supervisory attention skill or membership in low-income or culturally, racially, and linguistically diverse groups does not rule out a diagnosis of SLD. Evidence-based assessment tools should be used to identify learning and phenotype profiles. Diagnosis cannot be made solely on the basis of response to intervention (RTI); however, RTI should be monitored. Early intervention may prevent SLDs or severe SLDs, but persisting SLDs also respond to intervention in later grades.

Historic Context

As explained in Chapter 1, the federal legislation that provides free and appropriate public education (FAPE) for students with educationally handicapping conditions resulted from the collaborative efforts of parents of children with pervasive developmental disabilities (PDDs) and SLDs. Because professionals were overly focused on the different levels of cognitive functioning of those with PDDs (below normal range) and those with SLDs (in normal range), the resulting federal legislation and state legal code for implementing FAPE placed overemphasis on IQ as an assumed index of overall development. SLD was defined, on the basis of a discrepancy between IQ and achievement, as a category for services. However, neither professionals nor government officials could agree on how large the discrepancy had to be, and no research has validated the use of an arbitrary cognitive achievement discrepancy alone in diagnosing SLD. Whether a child qualified for SLD services often depended on the state of residence and the arbitrary size of discrepancy required in that state to qualify for special education services under the SLD category. Programmatic research by Fletcher, Denton, and Francis in Texas provided evidence that another approach rather than IQ–achievement discrepancy alone was needed.

Nearly four decades later the definition of SLD depends on the state of residence and there still is no consensus. The landmark epidemiological studies at the Mayo Clinic of the various kinds of SLDs, a summary of which is posted on this book's companion website (see the website resources for this chapter), indicated that about one in five school-age children and youth has an SLD and/or attention-deficit/hyperactivity disorder (ADHD). Federally funded research by the Institute of Educational Sciences (IES; Nickola Nelson, principal investigator) and the National Institutes of Health Eunice Kennedy Shriver National Institute of Child Health and Human Development (NICHD; Virginia Berninger, principal investigator) provided converging evidence that both modes of input (eyes and ears) and output (mouth and hands) and levels of language (see Figure 9.1) are related to differential diagnosis of SLDs. At the invitation of Nickola Nelson and Elaine Silliman, both members of the advisory panel for this book, an initial cross-disciplinary conversation was launched among speech and language specialists, psychologists, and educators; this resulted in a special issue of *Topics in Language*

FIGURE 9.1

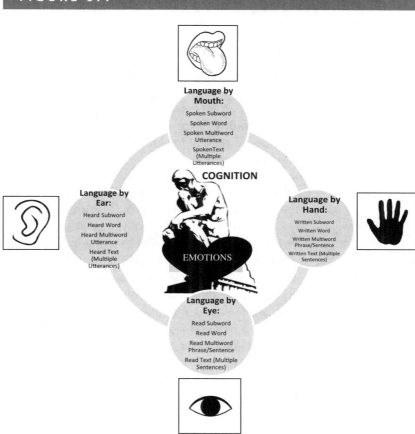

Attention and executive functions self-regulating the sensorimotor, language, cognitive, social–emotional systems. Four-multilevel language systems by ear (listening), mouth (speaking), eye (reading), and hand (writing) interacting with the cognitive and emotional systems, with connections to the peripheral nervous system and autonomic nervous system in the human body. The mouth and hand are larger than ear and eyes because more area of brain is devoted to representing sensory input received via mouth and hand and producing output via mouth and hand than is the case for the ears and eyes.

Disorders on treatment-relevant, differential diagnoses among specific kinds of learning disabilities involving language (see Silliman & Berninger, 2011). The goal of this chapter is to share the resulting model to stimulate more interdisciplinary dialogue and collaboration with public schools on behalf of the 20% of otherwise typically developing students who have puzzling struggles in learning specific oral language, written language, and math skills.

Programmatic Research on Defining and Differentiating Specific Learning Disabilities

The IES-funded research program at Western Michigan University has developed the Test of Integrated Language and Literacy Skills (TILLS standardization version 2.0; Nelson, Helm-Estabrooks, Hotz, & Plante, 2011; in the final stages of development) for differential diagnosis of oral and written language disorders to inform educational intervention in the classroom. Both the assessment and intervention are grounded in the long-standing programmatic research of Nelson and colleagues. The TILLS model assesses two language levels (sound/word and sentence/discourse) by four modalities (listening, speaking, reading, and writing). This language-levels-by-modalities model predicts four diagnostic groupings, each with different implications for intervention, which are being validated: (a) dyslexia (low sound/word level skills, but high sentence/discourse skills; listening comprehension better than reading comprehension), (b) normal language (at least average skills in all components), (c) oral and written language impairment (low skills in all components), and (d) specific comprehension impairment (high sound/word level skills and low sentence/discourse level skills across modalities). See the companion website for more information on the TILLS, including the model, the research on which it is based, and its applications to diagnosis and treatment.

Likewise, the NICHD-funded Multidisciplinary Learning Disabilities Center at the University of Washington began by studying dyslexia, a word-level impairment in decoding and spelling, in a family genetics study and related instructional and brain imaging studies; in the process evidence was found for essentially the same four profiles: (a) impaired reading and spelling at the word level, (b) normal word- and text-level oral and written language skills, (c) impaired reading comprehension and written composition at the text syntax/level, and (d) impaired oral and written language at both the word and text syntax/levels. In addition, evidence was found for impaired written language at the subword level (handwriting). A key collaborator in this research has been Lee Swanson, whose programmatic research on working memory, much of it funded by IES, has helped identify a model of working memory components that support language and math learning.

These results also converge with other NICHD-funded research by Catts, Fey, Tomblin, Scarborough, and Kamhi (on SLIs affecting oral and written language development) and by Olson and Pennington and others at the University of Colorado; research by Wagner and Torgeson and others at Florida State University; Fletcher, Foorman (now at Florida State University), Francis, Vaughan, and others at the University of Texas at Houston and Austin; Perfetti and others at the University of Pittsburgh; Lovett at the University of Toronto; and A. Libermann, I. Libermann, and colleagues at Haskins Laboratory (on word-level reading and spelling disabilities related to impaired phonological skills). Considerable other federally funded research—for example, by Venezky and Ehri at the State University of New York; Carlisle at the University of Michigan; Anderson and Nagy at the Center for Reading; and many others—has shown that orthography and morphology also contribute to word-level reading and spelling in English, a morphophonemic orthography. Other research— for example, by Beck and colleagues at the University of Pittsburgh—has shown the role of vocabulary and comprehension in reading.

In addition, programmatic research by Geary and colleagues at the University of Missouri; Mazzocco and colleagues at John Hopkins University; and Fuchs and colleagues at Vanderbilt University has contributed substantially to diagnostic and instructional procedures for dyscalculia and other specific math learning disabilities. Other research funded by a Javitz grant from the Department of Education to Robinson, Abbot, Berninger, and Busse, provided evidence for math learning in children who were math talented, math disabled, and twice exceptional (math talented and disabled). Many other researchers, including members of the advisory panel and others too numerous to mention, have contributed to knowledge of SLDs. Research advances, such as delivery of educational services, draw on the contributions of interdisciplinary teams. The challenge is to develop coherent frameworks for integrating the numerous research findings to translate them into evidence-based educational practices.

In the section that follows, guidelines are presented for an evidence-based framework for identifying characteristic learning profiles for dysgraphia, dyslexia, OWL LD/SLI, dyscalculia, and other SLDs not involving language in students for whom developmental disabilities can be ruled out. Differential diagnosis of an SLD should always be made in the context of developmental, educational, and medical history and other co-occurring conditions. Although many parents self-diagnose their child as having dyslexia, a reading problem can occur for many reasons, including PDDs, SLDs, specific developmental disabilities (SDDs; see Chapter 8), specific neurogenetic disorders (see Chapter 10), and other brain-related disorders or medical conditions (see Chapter 11). Only if those conditions, pointing to a different causal pathway for the reading problems, can be ruled out, should a diagnosis of dyslexia or other SLD be made. However, all students who struggle with reading should receive developmentally and instructionally appropriate reading instruction geared to their unique profile whether or not they qualify for a diagnosis of dyslexia or another condition.

The key to a treatment-relevant differential diagnosis is to examine the pattern of the symptoms rather than a single symptom out of context. Because there are many causal mechanisms contributing to low reading skill, profiles of phenotype markers shown to be associated with specific neurogenetic disorders should also be examined for patterns. Research provides converging evidence for such phenotype profiles for some SLDs (see Raskind, Peters, Richards, Eckert, & Berninger, 2013; Silliman & Berninger, 2011). The procedures for making these diagnoses based on profiles are described. However, it is important to monitor the progress and RTI over time for students who are diagnosed with SLDs because, although there are biological bases for SLDs, educational treatments are often effective in bringing about improved learning outcomes, and profiles can change, even if they are likely to persist to some degree for some students because the underlying genetic vulnerability remains.

Step 1: Ruling Out Pervasive Developmental Disabilities or Specific Developmental Disabilities

See Silliman and Berninger (2011), Figure 2, for an illustration of this step.

STEP 1(A)

Use Exhibit 8.1 in Chapter 8 of this book to organize the results of assessment of the five domains of development. Record where a child falls overall in each developmental domain, and note whether the child falls on average in the normal range (at −2 standard deviations [SD] or above) in each of the five domains of development: cognitive–memory, language, social–emotional, sensory–motor, and attention–executive function. If the child falls below −2 SDs (70 standard score for a mean of 100 and SD of 15 or comparable scaled score of 4 with a mean of 10 and SD of 3 or −2 z-score with mean of 0 and SD of 1) in each of the five domains, diagnose PDD. If the child falls below −2 SD in one or more but not all of the developmental domains, diagnose an SDD or SDDs. Diagnosis of PDD or SDD or SDDs rules out a diagnosis of SLD. Some clinicians set the cut-off for normal range at −1 1/3 *SD* and above.

STEP 1(B)

Note co-occurring conditions, for example, other neurogenetic disorders (e.g., autism, Down syndrome, spina bifida, fragile X, phenylketonuria, Williams, neurofibromatosis, muscular dystrophy), brain injury (e.g., cerebral palsy, head injury, spinal cord injury, seizure disorder), disease (e.g., sickle cell anemia, Tay–Sachs), or substance abuse syndrome (e.g., fetal alcohol syndrome). Any of these conditions rules out a diagnosis of SLD but not the best practices and ethical responsibility to plan, implement, and evaluate developmentally and instructionally appropriate instruction for the student.

STEP 1(C)

Also note any other relevant factors for treatment planning, such as culture, language, family differences, and educational history. These do not rule out a diagnosis of SLD but may be relevant to treatment planning. Also note any current medical conditions (e.g., diabetes, asthma) that should be taken into account for treatment planning; these rule out SLD only if they are consistent with a different etiology than SLD for the learning problem.

Step 2: Assessing Learning Profiles

See Silliman and Berninger (2011), Table 1, for more information about this step.

STEP 2(A)

Administer normed tests of (a) aural language through the ears (listening comprehension), (b) oral language expression through the mouth (word finding, syntax construction), (c) language by eye (accuracy and rate of oral reading of single real words, pseudowords, and passages, and reading comprehension at sentence and text levels), and (d) language by hand (handwriting—writing the alphabet from memory and copying sentences with all the alphabet letters and paragraphs with multiple sentences, dictated spelling of real and pseudowords, and composing—timed sentence construction from provided words, sentence combining, and timed composing of narrative and expository text).

STEP 2(B)

Use the form in Exhibit 9.1 to construct the aural/oral language profile, the reading profile, the writing profile, and the math profile for the student on the basis of test results and developmental information from parent ratings, questionnaires, and interviews (see Chapters 4, 5, and 6; Exhibits 4.1, 4.2, 4.3, 5.1, and 6.1).

EXHIBIT 9.1

Differential Diagnosis of Specific Learning Disabilities

(Circle the ones that apply and note whether there are co-occurring specific learning disabilities [SLDs], attention-deficit/hyperactivity disorder [ADHD], supervisory attention problems, or twice exceptionality indicators at the end.)

Name_____Examiner_____

Dysgraphia

Developmental Profile

Can pervasive developmental disability (PDD) or specific developmental disability (SDD) with developmental motor disorder be ruled out? Does the student have weakness in somatosensory touch—location, touch—kinesthesia, or vestibular function? If so, refer to the occupational or physical therapist. Or does the student have a neurological syndrome affecting hand function? If so, refer to the pediatric neurologist or developmental pediatrician.

Learning Profile

Is the child impaired (below the 25th percentile or −2/3 standard deviation [SD]) in

- printing lower case letters in alphabetic order from memory in accuracy, automaticity (first 15 seconds), or total time?
- writing lower case letters in cursive in alphabetic order from memory in accuracy or automaticity (first 15 seconds) or total time?
- copying a sentence with all alphabet letters in their best or fastest handwriting?

Phenotype Profile

Is the child impaired (below the 25th percentile or −2/3 SD) in

- receptive and/or expressive orthographic coding for whole word, letter in word, letter group in word?
- finger repetition or finger sequencing?

Has the child been diagnosed with ADHD or weaknesses in switching attention and/or sustaining attention?

Dyslexia

Developmental Profile

Can PDDs or SDDs be ruled out?

EXHIBIT 9.1 (*Continued*)

Learning Profile

Is the child only impaired in accuracy and rate or only in rate (below the population mean and at least 1 *SD* below in Verbal Reasoning Index, which is at least in the average range [at or above −2/3 *SD*], reducing the likelihood of co-occurring neurogenetic disorders) in

- oral reading of single real words or pseudowords on a list?
- accuracy and rate or rate only in oral reading of passages?
- spelling dictated real words or pseudowords?

Phenotype Profile

Is the child impaired (below the 25th percentile or −2/3 *SD*) in

- phonological coding (oral repetition of aural pseudowords) and/or orthographic coding (see dysgraphia)?
- phonological loop (rapid automatic naming [RAN] of letters) and/or orthographic loop (alph 15; first 15 seconds)?

Oral and Written Language Learning Disability

Developmental Profile

Can PDDs or SDDs be ruled out, especially SDD in language?

Learning Profile

Is the child impaired (below the 25th percentile or −2/3 *SD*) in

- listening comprehension or reading comprehension?
- word finding?
- oral and/or written sentence constructing or combining?
- oral and/or written text composing length and/or content and organization?

Phenotype Profile

Is the child impaired (below the 25th percentile or −2/3 *SD*) in morphological and syntactic awareness?

Supervisory Attention in Working Memory (Low Level Executive Functions)

(These tend to be impaired in all SLDs.)

- Focusing attention (inhibition and selective attention) on the Stroop Test
- Switching attention (flexibility) on rapid automatic switching (RAS)
- Sustained attention on RAN or RAS over rows or copying paragraph

ADHD Diagnosis? (Yes/No)

- Inattention
- Hyperactivity
- Impulsive

Twice Exceptional? (Yes/No)

Also co-occurring talent

Dyscalculia

Developmental Profile

Can PDD and SDDs be ruled out?

(*continued*)

EXHIBIT 9.1 (*Continued*)

Learning Profile

Is the child impaired (below the 25th percentile or −2/3 *SD*) in

- counting—one to one correspondence and/or internal number line?
- math facts for addition, subtraction, multiplication, and division?
- math computation operations for addition, subtraction, multiplication, and division?

Phenotype Profile

Is the child impaired (below the 25th percentile or −2/3 *SD*) in

- storing and processing multi-place numbers in working memory?
- phonological loop for naming numerals (RAN) and orthographic loop for writing numerals?

Nonverbal Specific Learning Disabilities

Developmental Profile

Can PDD and SDDs be ruled out?

Learning Profile

Is the child impaired (below the 25th percentile or −2/3 *SD*) in

- visual–spatial problem solving?
- social cognition?

Phenotype Profile

Is the child impaired (below the 25th percentile or −2/3 *SD*) in

- visual–spatial working memory
- pragmatics (integrated language and social functions).

Phenotype Profiles of 3 SLDs

Common Lower Level Executive Function Problems across all 3 SLDs (Supervisory Attention).
Orthographic Loop = Orthographic Coding of Letters and Words and Sequential Finger Movements
Phonological Loop = Phonological Coding of Letters and Words and Sequential Mouth Movements

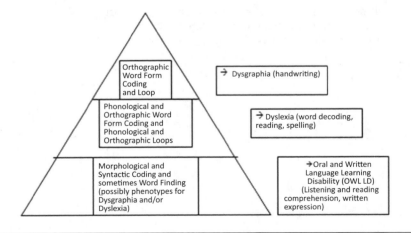

STEP 2(C)

Administer a battery of tests of phenotype markers of SLDs (see Figures 9.2 and 9.3; also see Silliman & Berninger, 2011, Table 1). These are components of working memory that support language or math learning. Phenotypes for language learning (see Figure 9.2) for which behavioral evidence (assessment and intervention), genetic evidence (phenotypes related to genetic mechanisms), and brain evidence exists include the following:

- storage and processing of spoken words (e.g., oral repetition of aural nonwords),
- storage and processing of written words (e.g., writing all letters or a designated single letter or letter group after briefly viewing a written word),
- storage and processing of morphology in spoken and written words (e.g., deciding whether a second word is derived from a first word in pairs that share common suffix spellings that sometimes are and sometimes are not morphemes),
- phonological loop for automatic naming of visual stimuli such as letters (or numerals),
- orthographic loop for automatic writing of letters or numerals, and
- supervisory attention (focusing, switching, sustaining, self-monitoring).

Likewise, working memory components supporting math learning (see Figure 9.3) include storage and processing units for numerals representing the quantitative number concepts and addition, subtraction, multiplication, and division math facts, which when automatized in basal ganglia regions (see Chapter 7) free up working memory resources for math problem solving. Phonological and orthographic loops support naming and writing the numerals, respectively. Supervisory attention for focusing, switching, and sustaining attention and self-monitoring, helps to coordinate naming and writing numerals with basic math concepts, math facts, and computational procedures. Reading and writing skills are also applied to math problem solving.

Step 3: Differential Diagnosis of Specific Learning Disabilities

See Exhibit 9.1 for more information about this step. Supervisory attention (focusing, switching, and sustaining attention) of working memory should be assessed for the phenotype profiles for all SLDs, which share a common impairment in one or more of these low-level executive functions for self-regulation of learning. The specific levels of language that

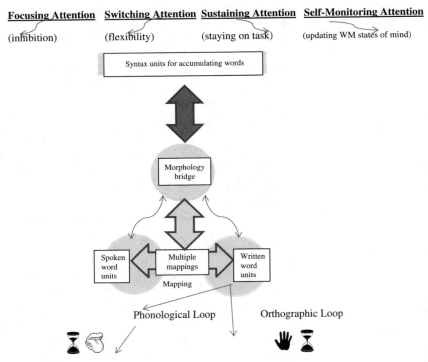

Cognitive Portal

(Window to vast unconscious mind)

Panel of Supervisory Attention

(Low-level executive functions of working memory [WM])

Focusing Attention   **Switching Attention**   **Sustaining Attention**   **Self-Monitoring Attention**

(inhibition)   (flexibility)   (staying on task)   (updating WM states of mind)

Syntax units for accumulating words

Morphology bridge

Spoken word units   Multiple mappings   Written word units

Mapping

Phonological Loop   Orthographic Loop

Time-constrained naming letters or written words   Time-constrained writing letters or written words

Working memory components supporting written language learning.

are impaired in SLDs that affect language learning should be assessed next. Individuals may be impaired in one level of language only (subword letters—dysgraphia) or more than one level of language (word- and subword—dyslexia; or syntax, word, and subword—OWL LD).

DYSGRAPHIA

Dysgraphia, a word of Greek origin, means impaired ability to form letters (graphs). Thus, the subword level of written language by hand is impaired (see Figure 9.1). Issues to consider in completing the devel-

FIGURE 9.3

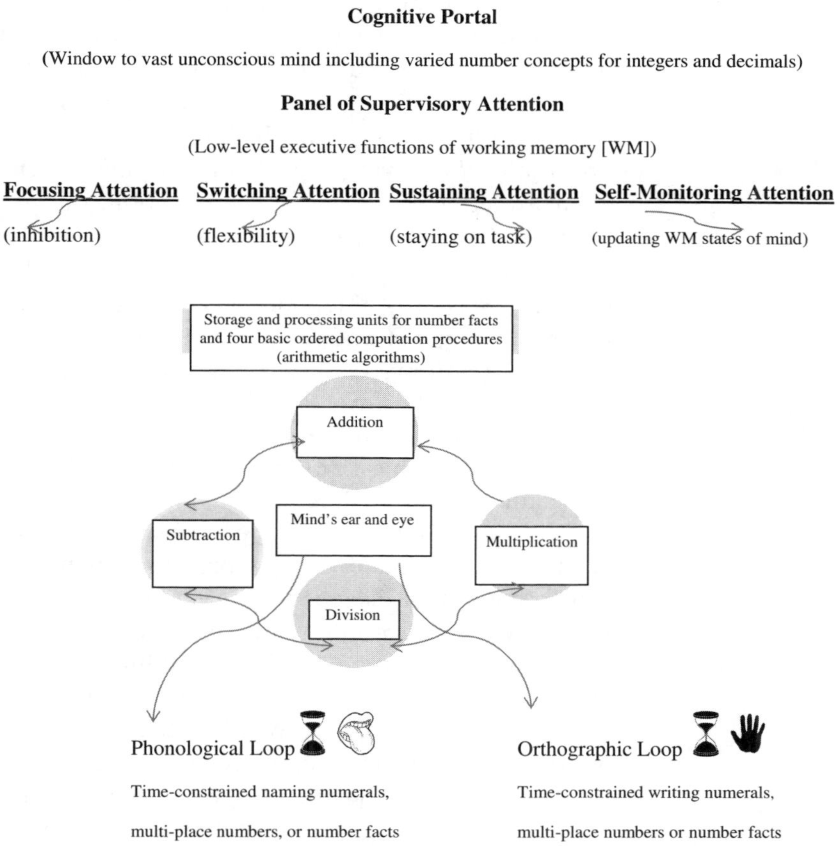

Cognitive Portal

(Window to vast unconscious mind including varied number concepts for integers and decimals)

Panel of Supervisory Attention

(Low-level executive functions of working memory [WM])

Focusing Attention   **Switching Attention**   **Sustaining Attention**   **Self-Monitoring Attention**

(inhibition)   (flexibility)   (staying on task)   (updating WM states of mind)

Working memory architecture supporting arithmetic learning for computation, with units for storage and processing of numerals within place value syntax for whole numbers (integers) and decimals (or fractions), as well as algorithms (steps in basic operations), and time-sensitive loops for automatic fact retrieval.

opmental profile are whether (a) the student falls outside the normal range in the motor domain and thus qualifies for an SDD diagnosis for developmental motor disorder (see Exhibit 8.1), (b) fine motor skills affecting the hand (graphomotor skills) fall outside the normal range, or (c) the student has co-occurring somatosensory impairments (e.g., especially for touch—location, touch—kinesthesia, touch—pressure, or vestibular system; see Chapter 7, Exhibit 7.2). The occupational or physical therapist should be involved in assessment, diagnostic decisions, treatment planning, and delivery for these conditions. If there are co-occurring medical conditions such as carpal tunnel or other syndrome that cause pain while using a writing tool, referral to a pediatric neurologist or developmental pediatrician is warranted. However, neither developmental motor disorder nor graphomotor impairment alone or a medical syndrome impairing use of hands alone is sufficient for diagnosing dysgraphia, which requires an evidence-based learning profile and phenotype profile for dysgraphia, which specifically impairs subword letter processing and production, that is, written language. Teachers should be involved in the assessment and instruction for handwriting for students with dysgraphia. Some children with dysgraphia can draw well, providing additional evidence that it is a disorder specific to written language and not just a motor disorder.

For the learning profile (see Exhibit 9.1), assess legibility and automaticity of writing the lower case letters of the alphabet in order from memory, copying them from a sentence with all the letters of the alphabet from a model, and copying a short paragraph. Typically, these skills are assessed for manuscript (printed) letters, but for students with handwriting problems, it is also useful to assess the same skills for cursive writing and even keyboarding. The handwriting problems often interfere with spelling and composing, but the diagnosis of dysgraphia should not be made if the child is impaired only in word-, sentence-, or text-reading skills.

For the phenotype profile (see Exhibit 9.1), assess receptive and expressive orthographic coding, the ability to view a written word briefly and then spell the whole word or the letter or letter group in the designated word position orally (first to third grade) or in writing (fourth grade and above). Also assess imitative finger tapping tasks: repetitive thumb–index finger tapping, an index of graphomotor execution, and sequential finger tapping (each of four fingers sequentially touching the thumb, an index of graphomotor planning, control, and execution). Together, orthographic coding and sequential finger tapping skills are the *orthographic loop of working memory*—the mind's eye working with the sequential finger movements of hand. Also determine whether the child has ADHD or impaired supervisory attention in switching attention and/or sustaining attention, which may co-occur with dysgraphia. Students with dysgraphia do not differ in cognitive ability from students without dysgraphia and may or may not show discrepancy between their handwriting and verbal reasoning skills.

DYSLEXIA

Dyslexia, a word of Greek origin, means impaired word-level skills. Dyslexia impairs word-level decoding of unfamiliar words and reading of familiar words, but persisting impairment in word-level spelling is also a hallmark characteristic. Students with dyslexia do not have a preschool history of oral language difficulties; in fact, their oral language skills may be a real strength. The problems first surface in kindergarten for naming and writing letters and associating sounds with letters, that is, cross-code integration of spoken words or sounds in them with written letters. The course of these problems should be noted in parent questionnaires.

For the learning profile (see Exhibit 9.1), assess the accuracy and rate of oral reading of real words on a list without context clues and in passages with context clues, accuracy and rate of pseudoword reading (decoding of unfamiliar words), and accuracy of reading comprehension for all grades; in Grade 4 and above also assess silent reading accuracy and rate. Assess spelling, of both dictated real words and dictated pseudowords, and assess the learning profile for dysgraphia, which may or may not co-occur with dyslexia.

For the phenotype profile (see Exhibit 9.1), assess phonological coding (orally repeating heard nonwords) and orthographic coding (identifying a letter or letters in briefly viewed words held in memory), and the phonological loop (rapid automatic naming of letters) and the orthographic loop (rapid automatic writing of letters, alphabet writing—first 15 seconds, Alph 15). Also assess the phenotype profile for dysgraphia, which may or may not co-occur with dyslexia. Students with dyslexia do not differ in cognitive ability from students without dyslexia, but their word decoding, word reading, and word spelling fall below the level expected on the basis of their verbal reasoning on cognitive tests.

SPECIFIC LANGUAGE IMPAIRMENT AND ORAL AND WRITTEN LANGUAGE LEARNING DISABILITY

Problems with oral language learning surface in the preschool years (late talking for single words, combining words, and communicating in syntactic structures) and continue during the school-age years when problems with written language also surface, especially with syntax, morphology, text-level discourse, and sometimes word finding. Listening comprehension, reading comprehension, and written expression of ideas in composing tend to be impaired.

The developmental profile should note whether the overall level of language development does not fall outside the normal range (below −2 *SD*), meaning that the child has SLI or OWL LD rather than SDD in the aural and/or oral language domains. Tests of nonverbal reasoning are often used to assess cognitive development of students with SLI and OWL LD, because measures of verbal reasoning typically require oral answers and do not assess cognitive ability independent of oral expression ability. Thus, children with OWL LD may appear, on the basis of verbal reasoning but not nonverbal reasoning, to have lower cognitive ability than those without OWL LD.

For the learning profile (Exhibit 9.1), assess aural listening comprehension and reading comprehension, oral vocabulary and word finding, sentence combining and composing, and text composing. Also assess the learning profile for dyslexia and dysgraphia, symptoms of which may also co-occur in students with SLI or OWL LD.

For the phenotype profile (Exhibit 9.1), assess morphological and syntactic skills and word finding. Also assess the phenotype profile for dyslexia and dysgraphia, which may or may not co-occur with OWL LD.

DYSCALCULIA

Dyscalculia is a word of Greek origin meaning impaired mental and/or written calculation. For the developmental profile, only diagnose dyscalculia if PDD(s) or SDD(s) can be ruled out. Characteristic learning profiles (see Exhibit 9.1) include impaired counting along the internal number line, math fact retrieval (math facts can be recalled one day but not the next or only slowly), and/or calculation operations for addition, subtraction, multiplication, and division; all of these can interfere with solving math problems. For the phenotype profile, any of the components in the working memory architecture for math learning (see Figure 9.3) may be impaired.

Dyscalculia is not the only disability that can interfere with learning math. Some students have specific problems with the visual–spatial foundations of math, and others do not have a good grasp of quantitative number concepts or have difficulty with the writing math requires. Still others have difficulty with the aural language (ears) or oral language (mouth) needed to learn math-specific vocabulary and to identify the problem to solve in word problems. Regardless of the nature of the math learning problem(s), all students with math difficulties should be assessed to identify and teach the specific math skills interfering with their math acquisition. Some students with dyscalculia have co-occurring dysgraphia, dyslexia, and/or OWL LD, which if present should be diagnosed and treated as well.

NONVERBAL SPECIFIC LEARNING DISABILITY

For many reasons, nonverbal SLD is no longer thought to be a homogeneous diagnostic category. Rather, SLDs may affect visual–spatial processing, reasoning with numbers or number concepts, and/or social cognition. The specific nature of these other SLDs should be described in learning profiles and phenotype profiles for those who do not have developmental profiles with PDD(s) or SDD(s). Sometimes visual–spatial cognition is impaired. The Swanson Test of Cognitive Processing (Swanson,

1996) can be used to assess a variety of visual–spatial cognition abilities, which may be impaired and contribute to the visual–spatial learning disabilities. Sometimes social cognition—that is, thinking about others and understanding their intentions and feelings—is impaired. Part of developing self-regulation skills is also developing a theory about others, which researchers refer to as a *theory of mind.* The Developmental Neuropsychological Assessment (2nd ed.; NEPSY–II) has a subtest that assesses theory of mind. Sometimes the social use of language, referred to as *pragmatics*, which can be assessed with the Test of Pragmatic Language (2nd ed.), is impaired. Both social cognition and social use of language may be impaired in some students with a nonverbal learning disability.

TWICE EXCEPTIONALITY

Some students have SLDs despite also having outstanding cognitive talents. They may have talents in verbal reasoning or other kinds of cognitive skills (advanced levels in their developmental profile; see Table 8.1). Their strong aural and oral language skills may mask written language or math difficulties in their learning profiles (see Exhibit 9.1) that fall in the average range but not at a level commensurate with their cognitive, aural language, and/or oral language skills. However, SLDs may be diagnosed in those who are twice exceptional on the basis of their phenotype profiles (see Figures 9.2 and 9.3), that is, impairments or weaknesses in components of working memory supporting language and/or math learning. In some cases these impairments interfere with the completion of written assignments in a timely fashion or the ability to learn from oral instruction provided by the teacher (e.g., due to a speech sound disorder or inattention, both of which may interfere with processing heard language). Other twice exceptional students may have a specific impairment in word finding that slows their reading or writing fluency and may also interfere with their oral expression of ideas.

EARLY IDENTIFICATION

It is important that any SLDs and associated impaired learning and phenotype skills be identified early in schooling. On the one hand, early identification and intervention may prevent the severity of SLDs later in schooling (though it is always important to continue to monitor RTI throughout schooling). On the other hand, unless the SLDs were identified and documented during the K–12 years, requests for accommodations for extra time for exams or a scribe may be denied during the postsecondary years (community college, undergraduate education, or other kinds of career training).

Instructional Issues

DYSGRAPHIA

Some affected individuals have difficulty with producing letters by selecting them on keyboards. Thus, use of computer keyboards may or may not be an effective accommodation without the explicit instruction to remediate the hallmark phenotype problems in dysgraphia—both orthographic coding and sequential finger movements can affect the use of keyboards as well as other computer and noncomputer tools for writing. Beginning handwriting instruction in the first 2 years is necessary but not sufficient. Students with dysgraphia need ongoing "tune-ups" throughout elementary and middle school as well as instructional activities that support transfer of handwriting or keyboarding to spelling and composition.

DYSLEXIA

Word-reading problems are often easier to remediate than spelling problems. Research shows that this word-level language impairment can cause problems at higher levels of written language at the text level (reading comprehension, through rate of word reading, and written composition, through spelling), but once the word-level problems are treated effectively, reading and writing problems at higher levels of language processing may resolve. Students with dyslexia should receive all components of grade-appropriate instruction in reading and writing that other typically developing students need at their instructional level (see Chapters 4, 5, and 6). In addition, they require specialized instruction in the impaired skills in their learning profile and phenotype profile for word decoding (phonological awareness of sound units in spoken words and orthographic awareness of spelling units in written words), in the transfer of this linguistic awareness to making connections across spoken and written words at different units of analysis (mapping phonemes–graphemes, onset rimes, syllables), and in the transfer of those connections to oral reading of written words and written word spelling. If they also show indicators of dysgraphia, they should also receive the same specialized instruction as outlined for those with dysgraphia.

ORAL AND WRITTEN LANGUAGE LEARNING DISABILITY

Students with OWL LD should receive all components of grade-appropriate instruction in reading and writing that other typically developing students need at their instructional level (see Chapters 4, 5, and 6). In addition, they require specialized instruction in the impaired skills in their learning profile and phenotype profile for morphological and syntactic awareness and transfer of this linguistic awareness to (a) make connections across spoken and written words for inter-relationships among morphological–phonological–orthographic units (mapping), (b) link the word maps with the syntax structures, and (c) transfer those maps to reading comprehension and written composition. Some may also need specialized instruction in word finding or listening comprehension. If they also show indicators of dysgraphia and/or dyslexia, they should also receive the same specialized instruction as outlined for those with dysgraphia or dyslexia.

DYSCALCULIA

Students with dyscalculia should receive all components of grade-appropriate instruction in math that other typically developing students need at their instructional levels (see Chapters 4, 5, and 6). They often benefit from direct, explicit instruction in basic math skills. In addition, they require specialized instruction in the impaired skills in their learning profile and phenotype profile (see Exhibits 9.1 and 9.3) for the four basic math facts, calculation operations, and the concepts of number; place value; part–whole relationships; self-regulation of the math computation process through time, space, and working memory; self-monitoring; and transfer of this procedural and conceptual knowledge to math problem solving. If they show any indicators of dysgraphia, dyslexia, or OWL LD, the math instruction should also be tailored to these individual needs.

NONVERBAL LEARNING DISABILITIES: VISUAL–SPATIAL COGNITION IMPAIRMENT

More research is needed to develop and validate effective interventions for students with visual–spatial deficits that may affect their math learning and that are prevalent in certain neurogenetic disorders. These may require instructional intervention different from that covered for the SLDs in this chapter.

NONVERBAL LEARNING DISABILITIES: SOCIAL COGNITION IMPAIRMENT

Greenberg and Kusché have conducted systematic research on interventions that can be used to develop social cognition skills in the classroom with typically developing students and those with special needs in social cognition. Their PATHS program (Providing Alternative Thinking Strategies) is a program for applying this research on social cognition in classrooms at different grade levels.

TWICE EXCEPTIONALITY

Instruction should be directed to both the talents and the nature of the SLD in twice exceptional students. These students may be confused about why, on the one hand, they learn easily, but on the other hand, struggle with specific kinds of school learning; educational professionals should talk to them frankly about their strengths and weaknesses. It is not advisable to tell them that their gift is the result of their disability. Both talents and disabilities can be inherited independent of each other. A more evidence-based approach provides emotional support, nurtures cognitive strengths, and tailors instruction in a cognitively engaging way to overcome the SLD.

ALTERNATIVES TO SPECIAL EDUCATION IN PROVIDING SERVICES FOR STUDENTS WITH SPECIFIC LEARNING DISABILITIES

Providing differentiated instruction for all students with SLDs in general education is a viable alternative. Federal funding is still needed for interdisciplinary teams, which include intervention assessment leaders in special education, school psychologists, speech and language specialists, and occupational and physical therapists, to support general education classroom teachers in the assessment and instruction required for such differentiated instruction and in reaching out to parents to provide positive supports. Differentiated instruction is not a substitute for necessary diagnostic assessment and RTI monitoring. However, branching diagnosis rather than a standard battery given to all regardless of presenting problems in the classroom is a more cost-effective and outcome-effective approach to assessment (see Chapter 2). This team effort for such an inclusion model can result in a more viable personalized and socialized education than is possible with a pull-out model, in which only a few are targeted for special education services and for which no research evidence exists attesting to its effectiveness.

Neuropsychological Links Between Biological Diversity and Assessment–Intervention

Daniel Miller, a member of the advisory panel for this book, has provided a comprehensive list of resources from the rapidly expanding field of school neuropsychology for linking educational assessment of biological diversity and educational interventions. This list is posted on the companion website for the resources for this chapter.

Parental Feedback

Parents whose families have a multigenerational history of learning disabilities have reported that it is hurtful when schools tell them that dyslexia (or another SLD) does not exist or that it is only a medical disorder (because physicians study its biological bases). Best professional practices are to acknowledge the biological bases but also the need for assessment showing whether a student meets evidence-based, diagnostic criteria for an SLD and identifying instructional needs, rather than focusing on the legal code that qualifies a student for pull-out special education services. Providing evidence-based differentiated instruction for students with SLDs in general education ensures that they receive instruction directed at reaching standards and take the tests that assess whether they do (see Chapters 4, 5, and 6). Pull-out programs cause students to miss part of the instruction designed for the standards and related tests.

Co-Occurring Specific Learning Disabilities, Attention-Deficit/ Hyperactivity Disorder, and Cultural and Linguistic Diversity

MULTIPLE SPECIFIC LEARNING DISABILITIES

Some students have more than one SLD because of multiple impairments in the working memory architecture that supports language and math learning. If so, there are co-occurring SLDs they should be noted in learning and phenotype profiles and in the design of the instructional program, as already discussed.

CO-OCCURRING ATTENTION-DEFICIT/ HYPERACTIVITY DISORDER

There are many unresolved problems in the diagnosis and treatment of educational handicapping conditions related to ADHD. Although earlier research was clear that the most effective treatments for ADHD were stimulant medication plus behavioral intervention, followed by stimula-tion medication only, followed by behavioral intervention only, more recent research results are less clear. Epidemiological studies indicate that there are more children being newly diagnosed with ADHD than there are children with ADHD in the current school population. Possible rea-sons include the following: (a) schools qualifying students for services under the "Other Health Impaired" category for ADHD, on the basis of physician judgment, if students cannot meet legal code criteria for SLD; and (b) medical practices in psychopharmacology, which do not always involve an interdisciplinary team with school representation, are chang-ing and may involve use of multiple medications for multiple disorders without appropriate assessment. For example, the presence of bipolar disorder (depression alternating with hyperactivity), which requires a different kind of medication than ADHD, may be missed or mistreated and may have unfortunate consequences, including suicide.

CULTURAL, LINGUISTIC, AND SOCIOECONOMIC DIVERSITY

According to Jasmin Niedo, a member of the advisory panel for this book, teams need to be particularly aware of how parents of stu-dents in language minority groups view learning disabilities and the parental role and expectations from the school in supporting their child. Understanding cultural perspectives goes a long way in easing tensions.

Readings and Resources[1]

EPIDEMIOLOGY OF LEARNING DISABILITIES AND ATTENTION-DEFICIT/HYPERACTIVITY DISORDER

Barbaresi, W., Katusic, S., Colligan, R., Weaver, A., & Jacobsen, S. (2005). Math learning disorder: Incidence in a population-based birth cohort, 1976–82. *Ambulatory Pediatrics, 5,* 281–289. doi:10.1367/A04-209R.1

Fletcher, J. M., Denton, C. A., & Francis, D. J. (2005). Validity of alterna-tive approaches for the identification of learning disability: Operation-alizing unexpected underachievement. *Journal of Learning Disabilities, 38,* 545–552.

---

[1]Additional research readings and practitioner resources for this chapter can be found at http://www.apadivisions.org/division-16/publications/interdisciplinary-frameworks-supplement/index.aspx

Katusic, S., Colligan, R., Weaver, A., & Barbaresi, W. (2009). The forgotten learning disability: Epidemiology of written-language disorder in a population-based birth cohort (1976–1982). *Pediatrics, 123,* 1306–1313. doi:10.1542/peds.2008-2098

Slavica, K., Colligan, R., Barbaresi, W., Schaid, D., & Jacobsen, S. (2001). Incidence of reading disability in a population-based birth cohort, (1976–1982). *Mayo Clinic Proceedings, 76,* 1081–1092.

RESEARCH ON SPECIFIC LEARNING DISABILITIES

Berch, D. B., & Mazzocco, M. M. M. (Eds.). (2007). *Why is math so hard for some children? The nature and origins of mathematical learning difficulties and disabilities.* Baltimore, MD: Brookes Publishing.

Carlisle, J. (1994). Morphological awareness, spelling, and story writing. Possible relationships for elementary-age children with and without learning disabilities. *Journal of Speech, Language, and Hearing Research, 48,* 1378–1396.

Catts, H., Fey, M., Zhang, M., & Tomblin, B. (2007). Language basis of reading and reading disability: Evidence from a longitudinal investigation. *Scientific Studies of Reading, 3,* 331–361.

Ehri, L. (1980a). The development of orthographic images. In U. Frith (Ed.), *Cognitive processes in spelling* (pp. 311–338). London, England: Academic Press.

Ehri, L. (1980b). The role of orthographic images in learning printed words. In J. F. Kavanaugh & R. Venezky (Eds.), *Orthographic reading and dyslexia* (pp. 307–332). Baltimore, MD: University Park Press.

Fletcher, J. M., Denton, C. A., & Francis, D. J. (2005). Validity of alternative approaches for the identification of learning disability: Operationalizing unexpected underachievement. *Journal of Learning Disabilities, 38,* 545–552.

Fuchs, L. S., Fuchs, D., Compton, D. L., Powell, S. R., Seethaler, P. M., Capizzi, A. M., . . . Fletcher, J. M. (2006). The cognitive correlates of third-grade skill in arithmetic, algorithmic computation, and arithmetic word problems. *Journal of Educational Psychology, 98,* 29–43.

Foorman, B. R. (Ed.). (2003). *Preventing and remediating reading difficulties: Bringing science to scale.* Timonium, MD: York Press.

Geary, D. C. (2004). Mathematics and learning disabilities. *Journal of Learning Disabilities, 37,* 4–15.

Goerss, B. L., Beck, I. L., & McKeown, M. G. (1999). Increasing remedial students' ability to derive word meaning from context. *Reading Psychology, 20,* 151–175.

Katzir, T., Kim, Y.–S., Wolf, M., Morris, R., & Lovett, M. (2008). The varieties of pathways to dysfluent reading: Comparing subtypes of children with dyslexia at letter, word and connected–text reading. *Journal of Learning Disabilities, 41,* 47–66.

Kavanaugh, J., & Venezky, R. (Eds.). (1980). *Orthographic reading and dyslexia.* Baltimore, MD: University Park Press.

Liberman, A. (1999). The reading researcher and the reading teacher need the right theory of speech. *Scientific Studies of Reading, 3,* 95–111.

Liberman, I. Y., Shankweiler, D., & Liberman, A. M. (1989). The alphabetic principle and learning to read. In D. Shankweiler & I. Y. Liberman (Eds.), *Phonology and reading disability: Solving the reading puzzle (IARLD Research Monograph Series).* Ann Arbor: University of Michigan Press.

Lovett, M. (1987). A developmental approach to reading disability: Accuracy and speed criteria of normal and deficient reading skill. *Child Development, 58,* 234–260.

Nagy, W. E., Anderson, R. C., Schommer, M., Scott, J., & Stallman, A. (1989). Morphological families and word recognition. *Reading Research Quarterly, 24,* 262–282.

Olson, R., Wise, B., Connors, F., Rack, J., & Fulker, D. (1989). Specific deficits in component reading and language skills: Genetic and environmental influences. *Journal of Learning Disabilities, 22,* 339–348.

Pennington, B. (2008). *Diagnosing learning disorders. A neuropsychological framework, Second Edition.* New York, NY: Guilford Press.

Perfetti, C. (2007). Reading ability: Lexical quality to comprehension. *Scientific Studies of Reading, 11,* 357–383.

Robinson, N., Abbott, R., Berninger, V., & Busse, J. (1996). Structure of precocious mathematical abilities: Gender similarities and differences. *Journal of Educational Psychology, 88,* 341–352.

Scarborough, H. (2005). Developmental relationships between language and reading: Reconciling a beautiful hypothesis with some ugly facts. In H. W. Catts & A. G. Kamhi (Eds.), *The connections between language and reading disabilities* (pp. 3–24). Mahwah, NJ: Erlbaum.

Swanson, H. L. (1993). Working memory in learning disability subgroups. *Journal of Experimental Child Psychology, 56,* 87–114.

Swanson, H. L., & Siegel, L. (2001). Learning disabilities as a working memory deficit. *Issues in Education: Contributions of Educational Psychology, 7,* 1–48.

Torgesen, J. K. (1995). Learning disabilities: An historical and conceptual overview. In B. Wong (Ed.), *Learning about learning disabilities* (2nd ed., pp. 3–34), San Diego, CA: Academic Press.

Vaughn, S., Wanzek, J., & Denton, C. A. (2006). Teaching elementary students who experience difficulties in learning. In L. Florian (Ed.), *Sage handbook of special education* (pp. 378–389). London, England: Sage.

Vellutino, F., Scanlon, D., & Tanzman, M. (1991). Bridging the gap between cognitive and neuropsychological conceptualizations of reading disabilities. *Learning and Individual Differences, 3,* 181–203.

Wagner, R. K., Francis, D., & Morris, R. D. (2005). Identifying English language learners with learning disabilities: Key challenges and possible approaches. *Learning Disabilities Research & Practice, 20,* 6–15.

CROSS-DISCIPLINARY APPROACHES TO SPECIFIC LEARNING DISABILITIES

Catts, H. W., & Kamhi, A. G. (Eds.). (2005). *The connections between language and reading disabilities.* Mahwah, NJ: Erlbaum.

Silliman, E., & Berninger, V. (2011). Cross-disciplinary dialogue about the nature of oral and written language problems in the context of developmental, academic, and phenotypic profiles. *Topics in Language Disorders, 31,* 6–23. doi:10.1097/TLD.0b013e31820a0b5b

IDENTIFYING AND DIAGNOSING SPECIFIC LEARNING DISABILITIES

Berninger, V., & Richards, T. (2010). Inter-relationships among behavioral markers, genes, brain, and treatment in dyslexia and dysgraphia. *Future Neurology, 5,* 597–617. doi:10.2217/fnl.10.22

Catts, H. W., Adolf, S. M., Hogan, T. P., & Weismer, S. E. (2005). Are specific language impairment and dyslexia distinct disorders? *Journal of Speech, Language, and Hearing Research, 48,* 1378–1396. doi:10.1044/1092-4388(2005/096)

Flanagan, D. P., & Alfonso, V. C. (Eds.). (2011). *Essentials of specific learning disability identification.* Hoboken, NJ: Wiley.

Geary, D. C. (2010). Mathematical disabilities: Reflections on cognitive, neuropsychological, and genetic components. *Learning and Individual Differences, 20,* 130–133. doi:10.1016/j.lindif.2009.10.008

Geary, D. C. (2011). Consequences, characteristics, and causes of poor mathematics achievement and mathematical learning disabilities. *Journal of Developmental and Behavioral Pediatrics, 32,* 250–263. doi:10.1097/DBP.0b013e318209edef

Korkman, M., Kirk, U., & Kemp, S. (2007). *Theory of Mind subtest in NEPSY–II.* San Antonio, TX: Pearson/Psych Corp.

Miller, B., Cutting, L., & McCardle, P. (2013). (Eds.). *Unraveling reading comprehension: Behavioral, neurobiological, and genetic components.* Baltimore, MD: Brookes.

Pennington, B. (2008). *Diagnosing learning disorders: A neuropsychological framework* (2nd ed.). New York, NY: Guilford Press.

Phelps-Terasaki, D., & Phelps-Gunn, T. (2007). *Test of Pragmatic Language, second edition* (TOPL–2). Austin, TX: Pro-Ed.

Raskind, W. H., Peters, B., Richards, T., Eckert, M. M., & Berninger, V. W. (2013). The genetics of reading disabilities: From phenotypes to candidate genes. *Frontiers in Psychology, 3,* 601. doi:10.3389/fpsyg. 2012.00601

Robinson, N., Abbott, R., Berninger, V., & Busse, J. (1996). Structure of precocious mathematical abilities: Gender similarities and differences. *Journal of Educational Psychology, 88,* 341–352.

Scott, C. (2011). Assessment of language and literacy disorders: A process of hypothesis testing for individual differences. *Topics in Language Disorders, 31,* 24–39. doi:10.1097/TLD.0b013e31820a100d

Silliman, E. R. (2010). LLD and individual differences: Can we see between the lines? *Topics in Language Disorders, 30,* 22–27. doi:10.1097/ TLD.0b013e3181d07eac

Swanson, H. L. (1996). *Swanson cognitive processing test.* Austin, TX: Pro-Ed.

Swanson, H. L. (2006). Working memory and reading disabilities: Both phonological and executive processing deficits are important. In T. P. Alloway & S. E. Gathercole (Eds.), *Working memory and neurodevelopmental conditions* (pp. 59–88). Hove, England: Psychology Press.

Swanson, H. L. (2010). *Test of working memory: Experimental edition.* Working Memory Research Center, University of California at Riverside.

Waber, D. P. (2010). *Rethinking learning disabilities: Understanding children who struggle in school.* New York, NY: Guilford Press.

Willcut, E. G., Pennington, B. F., Olson, R. K., Chhabildas, N., & Hulslander, J. (2005). Neuropsychological analyses of comorbidity between reading disability and attention deficit hyperactivity disorder: In search of the common deficit. *Developmental Neuropsychology, 27,* 35–78. doi:10.1207/s15326942dn2701_3

INSTRUCTIONAL TREATMENTS

Berninger, V., & Wolf, B. (2009a). *Helping students with dyslexia and dysgraphia make connections: Differentiated instruction lesson plans in reading and writing.* Baltimore, MD: Brookes. Spiral book with teaching plans from University of Washington Research Program.

Berninger, V., & Wolf, B. (2009b). *Teaching students with dyslexia and dysgraphia: Lessons from teaching and science.* Baltimore, MD: Brookes.

Graham, S., & Harris, K. (2005). *Writing better: Effective strategies for teaching students with learning difficulties.* Baltimore, MD: Brookes.

Greenberg, M. T., & Kusché, C. A. (1993). *Promoting social and emotional development in deaf children: The PATHS Project.* Seattle: University of Washington Press.

Greenberg, M. T., & Kusché, C. A. (1994). *The PATHS curriculum.* Seattle, WA: Developmental Research and Programs.

MacArthur, C. A., & Philippakos, Z. (2010). Instruction in a strategy for compare–contrast writing with students with learning disabilities. *Exceptional Children, 76,* 438–456.

Nelson, N., Bahr, C., & Van Meter, A. (2004). *The writing lab approach to language instruction and intervention*. Baltimore, MD: Brookes.

Silliman, E. R., Ford, C. S., Beasman, J., & Evans, D. (1999). An inclusion model for children with language learning disabilities: Building classroom partnerships. *Topics in Language Disorders, 19*, 1. doi:10.1097/00011363-199905000-00003

TWICE EXCEPTIONALITY

Assouline, S. G., Foley Nicpon, M., & Whiteman, C. (2009). Cognitive and psychosocial characteristics of gifted students with specific learning disabilities. *Gifted Child Quarterly, 54*, 102–115. doi:10.1177/0016986209355974

Berninger, V., & Abbott, R. (2013). Children with dyslexia who are and are not gifted in verbal reasoning. *Gifted Child Quarterly, 57*, 223–233. doi.org/10.1177/0016986213500342

Gilman, B. J., Lovecky, D. V., Kearney, K., Peters, D. B., Wasserman, J. D., Silverman, L. K., . . . Rimm, S. B. (2013). Critical issues in the identification of gifted students with co-existing disabilities: The twice-exceptional. *SAGE Open, 3*. doi:10.1177/2158244013505855

The National Association for Gifted Children. (2013). *Ensuring gifted children with disabilities receive appropriate services: Call for comprehensive assessment*. Retrieved from http://www.nagc.org/index2.aspx?id=10834

CO-OCCURRING CONDITIONS

Tridas, E. Q. (Ed.). (2007). *From ABC to ADHD: What parents should know about dyslexia and attention problems*. Baltimore, MD: International Dyslexia Association.

Tridas, E. Q. (2010). *Diagnosing coexisting conditions in learning problems*. Retrieved from http://files.meetup.com/1080217/Eric%20 Tridas%20Article.pdf

Neurogenetic Disorders 10

T his chapter provides entries, arranged in alphabetic order, for representative disorders with a documented neurogenetic basis, including the more common syndromes and errors of metabolism. However, comprehensive coverage of all neurogenetic disorders would be prohibitive. About 950 autosomal dominant disorders and 65 mitochondrial disorders have been identified, as well as disorders due to inborn errors of metabolism; however, there are many other genetic mechanisms underlying disorders. (See Chapter 7 for definitions of the various kinds of genetic mechanisms that can result in these disorders.) This chapter begins with an overview of the kinds of genetic testing available. Parents are beginning to share results of this genetic testing with educational professionals on the interdisciplinary teams. This trend is likely to increase as personalized medicine becomes more widely available as genetic testing becomes more affordable.

As explained in Chapter 7, genetic mechanisms influence brain functions, hence the term *neurogenetic disorders*. This chapter provides information on specific disorders that

http://dx.doi.org/10.1037/14437-010
Interdisciplinary Frameworks for Schools: Best Professional Practices for Serving the Needs of All Students, by V. W. Berninger

may come to the attention of educational professionals, who can then seek additional information through resources and consultation with other professionals who have relevant expertise for the case at hand. The genetic mechanisms are better understood for some disorders than for others, and genetic bases tend to be heterogeneous for all disorders. Some individuals with genetic disorders have other conditions that should be considered in treatment planning. Rather than focusing on a single symptom, interdisciplinary teams should take into account the total pattern of developmental and medical history and conditions as well as observable symptoms, whose significance can vary according to context.

Genetic Testing

See Chapter 7 for more on genetic testing.

KARYOTYPING

In *karyotyping*, the chromosomes in a single cell in a small blood sample are photographed and arranged in numbered chromosome pairs (1–23). Examples of disorders visible in the karyotype are an added chromosome, an omitted chromosome, translocations (translation of part of a chromosome to another chromosome), or larger deletions or duplications.

FLUORESCENT IN SITU HYBRIDIZATION

Fluorescent in situ hybridization (FISH) detects some of the microdeletions in specific chromosomal regions in a small sample of blood. The method uses sequences (short pieces of DNA), called a *DNA probe*, containing a fluorescent tag, which makes a small region of a chromosome visible under a microscope with fluorescent light. FISH is used in detecting trisomies and variations in X or Y chromosomes. FISH may be performed following the detection of abnormalities in prenatal ultrasound screening.

COMPARATIVE GENOMIC HYBRIDIZATION

Comparative genomic hybridization compares two small samples of blood, one of which is the reference sample. Each sample is labeled with a fluorescent dye. Differences between the fluorescent intensities in DNA are used to identify differences between the genome in each sample. Sometimes single-nucleotide polymorphisms are used to detect small copy number variations in the DNA sequences across the samples.

TESTING METHYLATION PATTERNS IN DNA SAMPLES

Methylation patterns in DNA of blood, urine, or other kinds of samples, which are collected to detect inborn errors of metabolism and certain epigenetic disorders that occur following conception.

DNA SEQUENCING

DNA sequencing is used for detecting small deletions or duplications within a specific gene.

Angelman Syndrome

Angelman syndrome can result from multiple congenital gene defects: deletion of 15q11-q13 on maternally inherited Chromosome 15, paternal inheritance of both copies of Chromosome 15, a point mutation in the maternal copy of the *UBE3A* gene, or an imprinting defect due to deletion or epigenetic effect. The developmental profile is characterized by pervasive developmental disability. The phenotype profile, defined in reference to the developmental profile, is characterized by (a) feeding problems due to difficulties in chewing and mouthing and fascination with water; (b) hand flapping and severe motor problems affecting gait; (c) severe speech impairment; (d) inappropriate happiness, with frequent laughing, smiling, and excitability; and (e) hyperactivity and short attention span. Physical characteristics include microcephaly (small head circumference) and seizures.

Attention-Deficit/Hyperactivity Disorder

Diagnosis of *attention-deficit/hyperactivity disorder* (ADHD) is complex and a source of diagnostic confusion for many reasons, including the seven discussed in this chapter. First, although ADHD appears to be a neurogenetic disorder occurring more often in some families than others, the genetic mechanisms are not fully understood. Second, symptoms of impaired attention, executive functions, and self-regulation of behavior are clinical features of many neurogenetic disorders and thus alone may not uniquely define the ADHD syndrome. For example, occasionally

ADHD has been mistakenly diagnosed when the individual is having a brief absence seizure or simple partial seizure. Third, ADHD appears to have subtypes: inattention only, hyperactivity only, combined inattention and hyperactivity, and possibly a separate impulsivity subtype. Whether these have different genetic bases is unclear.

Fourth, symptoms of ADHD first surface in some individuals during the preschool years, when all children are learning to self-regulate their attention and control their behavioral activity. Symptoms and interventions organized by typical developmental stepping-stones are not currently available for making clinical decisions, but research is beginning to emerge on these issues. Fifth, during the preschool years, it is not clear that standardized, normed measures can capture the essence of atypical self-regulation of attention or behavior. Such measures are now available for age levels during the school-age years, but adult ratings of attention and behavior of a child across more than one setting may better capture some kinds of self-regulation of attention or behavior. However, evidence exists for using some normed measures for specific kinds of attention problems association with specific learning disabilities (SLD), including the Delis–Kaplan Executive Function System inhibition score on the Stroop Color–Word Interference Test and the Rapid Automatic Naming and Rapid Alternating Stimulus Tests (RAN/RAS). Go/no go measures, which assess ability to inhibit behavioral responses, and the Developmental Neuropsychological Assessment (2nd ed.) Tower subtest, which assesses ability to plan, a high-level executive function, can be useful for some diagnostic purposes.

Sixth, problems in some aspects of self-regulation involving supervisory attention or higher order executive functions do not emerge until middle childhood, adolescence, or even the adult years, possibly depending on changes in curriculum or interactions with other disorders such as depression or anxiety. Parent and teacher rating scales are available for these later emerging supervisory attention and higher order executive functions (e.g., Behavior Rating Inventory of Executive Function). Seventh, drugs for management of ADHD are often prescribed without adequate diagnostic assessment to identify whether a student has ADHD (and if so, which subtype) or any relevant co-occurring condition. In addition, information is often lacking on what dosage may have been used in the past, what the response has been to specific kinds of medication (when used alone and with other medications with which it might interact adversely) and dose levels of the medication.

Further research is needed to sort out these definitional issues for ADHD and the co-occurrence of attention and executive function problems with many disorders. One approach might be to link the assessment with what is known about the brain's role in self-regulation of states of mind (see Exhibit 7.3, Chapter 7). ADHD problems in individual students may be related to a variety of difficulties involving (a) circadian rhythms for sleep–wake cycles, (b) levels of awareness during wakefulness, (c) rhythms within steady brain states, (d) switching between brain states, (e) supervisory attention of working memory, and (f) conflict resolution among competing subsystems during self-management of cognitive, language, social–emotional, and behavioral actions. Given the complexity of the ADHD diagnosis, it is not surprising that there is more to learn more about the disorder's causes and evidence-based treatment. However, observation of affected individuals during specific times of day, performing specific tasks, and in different settings may provide clues to interventions that interdisciplinary teams could use to design and evaluate which intervention approaches might help students with ADHD better manage their attention, executive functions, and self-regulation in educational settings and for educational tasks. Clearly, more research is needed to identify effective ways to help affected individuals better manage the brain's complex systems within systems that change over time in a given day and across stages of development.

Autism

An umbrella disorder, *autism* currently covers a variety of conditions that occur in individuals with developmental disabilities (pervasive or specific). Even in those whose cognitive development falls at least in the lower limits of the normal range, specific developmental disabilities may occur in other domains related to sensory and motor, social and emotional, attention and executive, and/or language (especially pragmatic) functions. Angelman syndrome, Rett syndrome, Prader–Willi syndrome, fragile X syndrome, and mitochondrial seizure disorders share symptoms in common with autism but are not autism. Current research implicates genetic mechanisms in autism, both inherited and epigenetic (in the uterine environment). Reported gene candidates are heterogeneous but different from those for dyslexia (Girirajan et al., 2011), consistent with evidence that autism is not an SLD and that it is different from pervasive developmental disorder (PDD; Dager et al., 2013). Clearer differential diagnosis at the behavioral level that differentiates autism from other developmental disabilities (pervasive or specific) and SLDs is likely to improve diagnosis of and treatment for autism. For example, the diagnosis of an SLD should not be made in individuals with autism even if they exhibit an IQ–achievement discrepancy, which alone does not define a learning disability (see Chapter 9). At the very least, it is instructionally relevant (see Part II of this volume) to determine whether an individual who meets criteria for autism also meets criteria for PDD across all five domains or for specific developmental disabilities (see Chapter 8).

Age of onset (from birth or emergent around the second birthday) should be noted. Infants with *early onset autism*, unlike typically developing infants, may seem oblivious to the human face (possibly because they process the features alone, without the configuration of the human face) and may not engage in age-appropriate social imitation. With *later onset autism*, which occurs at about the second birthday when toddlers normally transition from the sensorimotor to preoperational stage of development, affected toddlers show regression (loss of previously acquired functions) and problems in developing self-regulation and theory of mind.

Some reserve diagnosis of *Asperger's syndrome* for cases with a prototypical profile (pattern) of normal or better associated cognitive functioning, with selective deficits in inattention, social cognition (theory of mind or perspective-taking), and fine motor skills. Individuals with this phenotype profile may have very different educational needs than those with specific developmental disabilities resulting in atypical social and communication development. As with ADHD, there is currently considerable confusion about best professional practices in diagnosing autism. The jury is out on whether autism is really a spectrum of related disorders or a collection of separate disorders that share isolated symptoms but have different genetic and brain etiologies. Some professionals are concerned that autism is diagnosed too often because it does not have the negative connotation of intellectual disability or PDD and/or because it qualifies the affected individual for special education or other reimbursable services. Both educational practitioners and research scientists can collaborate to improve differential diagnosis, prevention, and treatment for autism. It should also be noted that autism is not the only disorder that professionals are still trying to define in a way that differentiates it from other disorders and is treatment relevant. Professionals face the same challenging, unresolved issues with defining ADHD, as discussed earlier in this chapter, and SLD (see Chapter 9).

Cri Du Chat Syndrome

Cri du chat (cat-cry) syndrome involves multiple congenital abnormalities and is the result of partial deletion of Chromosome 5p15.2. Deletion of the telomerase reverse transcriptase gene may be involved in the phenotypic expression, which includes the following: pervasive or specific developmental disabilities, small body size, cat-like cry and feeding difficulties in infancy, low set ears, single palmar crease, sleep disturbances, hypotonia, severe hyperactivity, and better receptive than expressive language skills.

Crohn's Disease

Crohn's disease is an inflammatory bowel disease that is the result of a genetic predisposition and environment factors that affect the functioning of the immune system. Point mutations in over 30 genes have been associated with this disorder that has no cure but can be treated through diet.

Down Syndrome

Down syndrome, also known as *Trisomy 21*, results from an extra Chromosome 21, caused by translocation or mosaicism. Phenotype features include pervasive or specific developmental disabilities, characteristic facial features (flat profile with small ears, single palmar crease, short stature, heart disease, eye defects, hearing problems, thyroid problems, and risk of early onset dementia).

Duchenne Muscular Dystrophy

Duchenne muscular dystrophy is a progressive muscular degenerative disorder with onset before age 3 that involves muscle degeneration, muscle wasting, muscle enlargement of calves, and thus loss of prior motor milestones. It results from mutations in the gene on Xp21.1 that encodes dystrophin. By adolescence, affected individuals cannot walk independently. More males are affected than females, for whom the genetic bases of the disorder are different than for males.

Epilepsy

See Seizure Disorders.

Fragile X Syndrome

Fragile X syndrome is one of the *FMR1*-related disorders linked to the X chromosome. The cause is a mutation in the coding sequence on the *FMR1* gene on Xq27-q28, resulting in increased cytosine–guanine–guanine (CGG) trinucleotide repeats. Phenotype profiles for males include specific developmental disabilities, large head, long face, prominent forehead and chin, protruding ears, hyperactivity and other behavioral problems, temper tantrums, hand flapping, hand biting, finger joint hypermobility, joint instability, and large testes. Females with fragile X syndrome are affected to a lesser degree or may be carriers.

Hemophilia

Hemophilia (also spelled *haemophilia*) is a recessive, sex-linked X chromosome disorder that is more likely to occur in males than females and impairs the ability of the body to control blood clotting and thus stop bleeding. The first signs are typically during circumcision, falls when learning to walk, or trips to the dentist when bleeding will not stop. With medical advances, the life span for people with hemophilia has increased from an average of 11 years to 50 to 60 years.

Hydrocephalus

See Neural Tube Deficit I.

Klinefelter's Syndrome

Klinefelter's syndrome is caused by a chromosome nondisjunction resulting in an extra X chromosome (47 instead of 46). Only males are affected. Phenotype profiles include the following traits: tall height, slim build, long limbs, relatively small testes and penis (sometimes breast enlargement), and infertility; individuals may also have intention tremors, scoliosis, reduced muscle strength, vascular problems, and behavior problems.

Landau–Kleffner Syndrome

Landau–Kleffner syndrome involves loss of language skills in association with EEG abnormalities and is also known as *epileptic aphasia*. Affected children lose the ability to distinguish speech sounds, despite normal auditory acuity, and become inattentive.

Leber Hereditary Optic Neuropathy

Leber hereditary optic neuropathy (LHON) involves a bilateral central vision loss and results from point mutations in mitochondrial DNA (mtDNA). Mostly males are affected with LHON, which may co-occur with movement disorder.

Lesch–Nyhan Syndrome

Lesch–Nyhan syndrome involves an inborn error of metabolism of the nucleic acid purine and is caused by a mutation in the *HPRT* gene on Xq26-q27.2, which results in an enzyme defect that elevates uric acid levels in blood and urine. During the first year of life, hypotonia (muscle weakness), spasticity (muscle tenseness), and developmental disability as well as medical problems (e.g., involving heart or kidney) appear. Most concerning to caretakers and most difficult to treat are the involuntary self-injurious behaviors (e.g., biting fingers, arms, and lips) that also appear.

Meningomyelocele

See Neural Tube Deficits, Type III.

Mitochondrial Disorders

Mitochondrial disorders (also see MELAS and MERRF) result from inborn errors of metabolism linked to abnormal function for the energy-producing mitochondria within cells (mtDNA), which may be involved in nuclear DNA processes and affect every organ of the body. Common features include visual problems in the retina or eye muscles, cardiac problems, short stature, hypothyroidism, diabetes, reflux, renal problems, and/or exercise intolerance.

Mitochondrial Encephalomyopathy, Lactic Acidosis, and Stroke-Like Episodes

Mitochondrial encephalomyopathy, lactic acidosis, and stroke-like episodes, also known by its acronym, MELAS, is caused by a mutation in mtDNA encoding transfer RNA, which reduces mitochondrial protein synthesis. The phenotype profile may include migraine headaches, seizures, stroke-like episodes, degenerative diseases of the brain (encephalopathies), or myopathy (muscle disease).

Myoclonic Epilepsy and Ragged Red Filters

Myoclonic epilepsy and ragged red filters, also known as MERRF, are the result of mutations in mtDNA encoding transfer RNA. The phenotype profile may include myoclonic epilepsy, ataxia, spasticity, and myopathy. Muscle biopsy reveals characteristic ragged red muscle fibers.

Neural Tube Deficits

Neural tube deficits are malformations of the spinal cord, brain, and vertebrae, which are principally of three types.

TYPE I

Encephalocele, a malformation of the skull allows a portion of the brain, which is typically malformed, to protrude in a sac, which is usually in the back of the brain but sometimes in the front. Affected children often have co-occurring hydrocephalus (excess cerebrospinal fluid in the four ventricles of brain, which can cause swelling).

TYPE II

Anencephaly, a disorder in which there is no brain development above the brain stem, usually results in spontaneous abortion of the embryo; however, if a live birth occurs, the infant dies early in infancy.

TYPE III

Spina bifida is a disorder in which the meningocele (the membrane sac covering the spinal cord) or the meningomyelocele (a membrane sac plus malformed spinal cord) is exposed. In both cases the severity of symptoms depends on the location of the lesion along the spinal cord.

Neurofibromatosis

Type I neurofibromatosis, von Recklinghausen disease, is a neurological disorder caused by a mutation in the *NF1* gene that codes for neuro-fibromin protein on Chromosome 17q11.2. It has a phenotype profile of multiple café au lait tumors in the body and on the skin, freckling, fibromas (nerve tumors) in the body and on the skin, and Lisch nodules (brown bumps on the iris). Many affected individuals have symptoms of ADHD and verbal or nonverbal learning disabilities and are at risk of benign and malignant tumors throughout the nervous system.

Type II neurofibromatosis, which is caused by a mutation in the tumor-suppressor (*NF2*) gene on Chromosome 22q12.2, differs from Type I in that no Lisch nodules or freckling occurs; however, deafness can occur because of tumors in the auditory nerve.

Phenylketonuria

Phenylketonuria involves an in-born error of metabolism of an amino acid, resulting in phenylalanine hydroxylase enzyme deficiency. It is caused by a mutation in the *PAH* gene on Chromosome 12q24.1. Untreated individuals have PDD, but treated individuals may have cog-nitive functioning in the normal range, although specific or selective disabilities in other developmental domains (e.g., executive functions or movement) may occur.

Prader–Willi Syndrome

Prader–Willi syndrome involves multiple congenital disorders and is caused by a microdeletion on the long arm of Chromosome 15 (15q11-q13), resulting from an imprinting defect. Phenotype profiles are characterized by short stature, abnormally increased appetite and resulting obesity, almond-shaped eyes, small hands and feet, thick saliva, obsessive–compulsive disorder related to eating, and developmental disabilities.

Rett Syndrome

Rett syndrome is a progressive neurological disorder that surfaces at 6 to 9 months and is followed by loss of brain functions and sometimes seizures. It is caused by mutations in the methyl-CpG binding protein 2 (*MeCP2*) transcription gene at Xq28 or in *CDKL5* (Xp22). The phenotype profile includes autism-like behaviors, microcephaly (small head circumferences), and PDD.

Rubinstein–Taybi Syndrome

Rubinstein–Taybi syndrome involves multiple congenital anomalies and is caused by mutations in the CREB building protein gene on Chromosome 16p13.3, as well as mutations of the *EP300* gene (22q13). The phenotype profile includes PDD, small body, broad thumb and toes, small upper jaw, high-arched palate, prominent nose, pouting lower lip, short upper lip, feeding difficulties, hypotonia, and eye, apnea, and heart problems.

Seizure Disorders

Seizures occur when the brain's tolerance for electrical activity is exceeded. They can be provoked by fever, infection, toxic agent, trauma, injury, or overdose of a medication.

FEBRILE SEIZURES

Febrile seizures are provoked by a body temperature elevated beyond 100.4 degrees Fahrenheit.

NEONATAL SEIZURES

Neonatal seizures take different forms, including arm and/or leg tonic–clonic movements, which may resemble bicycling and/or rowing, or spasmodic lip smacking or tongue thrusting; excessive blinking, prolonged eye opening, or staring; or apnea.

EPILEPSY

Epilepsy, which may have a genetic basis, is diagnosed when a seizure occurs at least twice within 24 hours that is unprovoked by infection, toxic agent, trauma, fever, injury, or overdose of a medication.

JACKSONIAN EPILEPSY

Jacksonian epilepsy is diagnosed when seizures, which started in a focal area, spread to another area of the body.

PRIMARY GENERALIZED SEIZURE DISORDERS

Primary generalized seizure disorders include four subtypes:

- *Absence seizures* are brief episodes of momentary impaired consciousness, mediated by the thalamus, usually lasting 30 seconds or less, but not followed by confusion.
- *Myoclonic seizures* are brief contractions of muscles due to cortical discharges.
- *Tonic–clonic seizures* cause loss of consciousness followed by tonic-clonic movements (repetitive jerking of arms or legs).
- *Atonic seizures* cause brief loss of posture.
- *Partial seizures* include three subtypes: (a) *Simple partial seizures* are localized brief events during which consciousness is not lost; (b) *complex partial seizures* are spreading events during which consciousness is lost; (c) *partial seizures with secondary generalization* are spreading events during which consciousness is lost and tonic-clonic motor events follow.

Sex-Linked Disorders

See Fragile X, Hemophilia, Klinefelter's Syndrome, and Turner's Syndrome.

Sickle Cell Disease

Sickle cell disease is an autosomal inherited blood disorder that results in abnormal hemoglobin, hemoglobin S or HbS. It is more frequent in Africans and those of African descent. Although it provides protection against the malaria parasite, it leads to anemia due to excessive breakdown of red blood cells, which become crescent- or sickle-shaped, causing blockage and severe pain in the limbs or organs. Currently, newborns are routinely screened for this disorder, and penicillin is used to prevent bacterial infections and early death. Surviving children may, however, have developmental disabilities.

Spina Bifida

See Neural Tube Deficits.

Spinal Muscular Atrophy

Spinal muscular atrophy (SMA) involves low motor tone and results from the death of motor neurons in the brainstem and spinal cord. It is the most frequent genetic cause of death in infancy and is caused by deletions to the *SMN1* gene. Those with SMA I (Werdnig–Hoffmann disease) have onset before 6 months and never sit or walk. Those with SMA II, with onset between 6 to 18 months, sit but do not walk. Those with SMA III, with onset after 18 months, have gait difficulties and hypotonia.

Tay–Sachs Disease

Tay–Sachs disease, also known as *lysosomal storage disease*, results from an inborn error of metabolism caused by a deficiency of the enzyme hexosaminidase A, resulting from mutations in the *HEXA* gene at Chromosome 15q23-q24. Development is typical for the first several months and then this progressive neurological disorder results in deafness, blindness, and seizures, followed by rapid decline and death by age 5. This disorder occurs in the Ashkenazi Jewish, Cajun, and French Canadian populations.

Tics

Tics are classified as either simple or complex. *Simple* motor tics, which are sudden, brief, repetitive movements that involve a limited number of muscle groups, include eye blinking and other eye movements, facial grimacing, shoulder shrugging, head or shoulder jerking, and simple vocalizations such as repetitive throat-clearing, sniffing, or grunting sounds. *Complex* tics, which are distinct, coordinated patterns of movements involving several muscle groups, include facial grimacing combined with a head twist and a shoulder shrug, and sniffing or touching objects combined with hopping, jumping, bending, or twisting. Simple vocal tics may include throat clearing, sniffing or snorting, grunting, or barking, but more complex vocal tics include words or phrases. Some result in self-harm such as punching oneself in the face. Vocal tics involve *coprolalia* (uttering socially inappropriate words such as swearing) or *echolalia* (repeating the words or phrases of others). Some tics are preceded by a premonitory urge.

Tourette's Syndrome

An example of a tic disorder, *Tourette's syndrome* (TS) is characterized by repetitive, stereotyped, involuntary movements and vocal tics. The diagnosis is made only after verifying that the patient has had both motor and vocal tics for at least 1 year. Current research evidence has pointed to a genetic basis for this disorder, but many genes are probably involved. Onset is between ages 3 and 9 years, but symptoms peak in intensity during the early teens. Males are more affected than females. Coprolalia (use of foul or inappropriate language) is only present in a small number (10%–15%) of individuals with TS. Some affected individuals have an urge to complete a tic in a certain way or a certain number of times to relieve the urge or decrease the sensation. Affected individuals may also have problems with inattention, hyperactivity, impulsivity, anxiety, depression, or obsessive–compulsive symptoms such as intrusive thoughts or worries and repetitive or ritualistic behaviors.

Trisomy 13

Trisomy 13, also known as *Patau's syndrome*, involves multiple congenital anomalies and is caused by a nondisjunction abnormality resulting in an extra Chromosome 13. Of affected infants, half die within the first month after birth. Those who survive have PDD, severe sensory and motor impairments, and other defects involving the heart, kidney, and/or gastrointestinal tract.

Trisomy 18

Trisomy 18, also known as *Edwards syndrome*, involves multiple congenital abnormalities and is caused by nondisjunction resulting in an extra Chromosome 18. Only 10% of those affected survive the first year. Their phenotype profile includes PDD, slow growth, low-set ears, clenched fists, impaired vision and hearing, "rock bottom" feet, feeding problems, and heart impairment.

Trisomy 21

See Down Syndrome.

Turner's Syndrome

Turner's syndrome, which affects only females, is caused by nondisjunction resulting in 45 rather than 46 chromosomes; one X chromosome is missing. Phenotype profiles include short stature, broad chest with widely spaced nipples, short neck with extra skin at bottom, puffy hands and feet, infertility, and nonverbal learning disabilities. Hormone replacement is needed to initiate puberty.

Velocardiofacial Syndrome

Velocardiofacial syndrome is one of several syndromes related to deletions on Chromosome 22q11.2 and point mutations on the *TBX1* gene. The phenotype profile includes characteristic facial features such as a small, open mouth, short eyelid openings, flat nasal bridge and bulbous nasal tip, low set ears, cleft palate abnormalities, feeding difficulties, and expressive language difficulties. Affected individuals may have pervasive or specific developmental disabilities.

Werdnig–Hoffmann Disease

See Spinal Muscular Atrophy.

Williams Syndrome

Williams syndrome involves multiple congenital disorders and is caused by a microdeletion of Chromosome 7q11.23, which contains approximately 28 genes. The phenotype profile includes PDD; "elf-like" face (full lips, cheeks, area around eyes); short stature; star-like iris; hoarse voice; slow trajectory for language skills; personality characterized as friendly, talkative, and extraverted; and heart, kidney, and joint problems.

X-Linked Disorders

See Fragile X Syndrome, Klinefelter's Syndrome, and Turner's Syndrome. They result from *lyonization*, that is, inactivation of one of the X chromosomes.

Multiple Disorders in the Same Individual

For all these neurogenetic disorders, it is important to also obtain developmental profiles. Many affected individuals will have a co-occurring PDD or specific developmental disability (SDD; see Chapter 8) or selective impairments in a domain of development that otherwise is in the normal range. Often an SDD or selective impairment occurs in the domains of language and of attention and executive functions. However, the whole profile should be taken into account in determining whether these are just part of the pattern for the individual's condition or the same as those for SDDs or specific impairments in an otherwise normal developmental domain. Often the diagnostic implications and evidence-based treatment will depend on the context of the total profile in which the developmental disability or selective impairment occurs, which is not necessarily the same as when that disability or impairment occurs in another profile (context) or when it occurs alone without other documented symptoms or neurogenetic bases.

In addition, in many cases, often beginning in infancy, there are also medical issues (see Chapter 14) for which the team should consult with physicians, and feeding difficulties for which the team should consult with occupational or physical and speech and language therapists. Learning profiles should also be assessed to identify developmental stepping-stones and instructional levels for specific reading, writing, math, and visual–spatial skills geared to the developmental levels in each of the five domains. However, diagnoses of SLDs should not be made, with the exception of ADHD, which may co-occur with SLDs. As discussed in Chapter 9, a diagnostic criterion for SLDs is that all the domains of development are in the normal range.

Interdisciplinary Treatment Issues

Treatment issues for these neurogenetic disorders generally require contributions from all members of the interdisciplinary team, whose roles may change across development. Of great importance is reaching out to provide emotional support for parents: to listen to what it is like parenting a child with this kind of developmental difference, what it is like dealing with the loss of a normal child and sometimes the death of a child, and to explain how current research may be relevant to diagnosis and treatment and transition from schooling or loss of parents.

Readings and Resources[1]

GENERAL REFERENCE

Batshaw, M., Roizen, N., & Lotrecchinao, G. (2013). *Children with disabilities* (7th ed.). Baltimore, MD: Brookes.

Delis, D. C., Kaplan, E., & Kramer, J. (2001). *Delis–Kaplan Executive Function System (D–KEFS)*. San Antonio, TX: Pearson.

Gioia, G. A., Isquith, P. K., Guy, S. C., & Kenworthy, L. (2000). *The Behavior Rating Inventory of Executive Function (BRIEF) professional manual*. Odessa, FL: Psychological Corporation.

---

[1]Additional research readings and practitioner resources for this chapter can be found at http://www.apadivisions.org/division-16/publications/interdisciplinary-frameworks-supplement/index.aspx

Golden, C. J., & Freshwater, S. M. (2002). *Stroop Color and Word Test: A manual for clinical and experimental uses.* Chicago, IL: Stoelting.

Korkman, M., Kirk, U., & Kemp, S. (2007). *Theory of Mind subtest in NEPSY–II.* San Antonio, TX: Pearson/Psych Corp.

McKusick-Nathans Institute of Genetic Medicine & The National Center for Biotechnology Information. (2010). *Online Mendelian inheritance in man* (OMIM). Retrieved from http://www.ncbi.nlm.nih.gov/omim/

National Center for Biotechnology Information. (2011). *Human genome resources.* Retrieved from http://www.ncbi.nlm.nih.gov/genome/guide/human

Wodrich, D. L. (2006). Sex chromosome anomalies. In L. Phelps (Ed.), *Chronic health-related disorders in children: Collaborative medical and psychoeducational interventions* (pp. 253–270). Washington, DC: American Psychological Association.

Wodrich, D. L., & Tarbox, J. (2008). The psychoeducational implications of sex chromosome anomalies. *School Psychology Quarterly, 23,* 301–311. doi:10.1037/1045-3830.23.2.301

Wolf, M., & Denckla, M. B. (2005). *Rapid Automatized Naming and Rapid Alternating Stimulus Tests (RAN/RAS): Examiner's manual.* Austin, TX: ProEd.

18Q SEGMENTAL DELETION

Hasi, M., Soileau, B., Sebold, C., Hill, A., Hale, D. E., O'Donnell, L., & Cody, J. D. (2011). The role of the TCF4 gene in the phenotype of individuals with 18q segmental deletions. *Human Genetics, 130,* 777–787. doi:10.1007/s00439-011-1020-y

O'Donnell, L., Soileau, B., Heard, P., Carter, E., Sebold, C., Gelfond, J., . . . Cody, J. D. (2010). Genetic determinants of autism in individuals with deletions of 18q. *Human Genetics, 128,* 155–164. doi:10.1007/s00439-010-0839-y

AUTISM

Carpenter, M., Pennington, B. F., & Rogers, S. J. (2001). Understanding of others' intentions in children with autism. *Journal of Autism and Developmental Disorders, 31,* 589–599.

Case-Smith, J. (2004). Evidence-based practice in autism. In H. Miller-Kulaneck (Ed.), *Autism: A comprehensive occupational therapy approach.* Baltimore, MD: American Occupational Therapy Association.

Corrigan, N. M., Shaw, D. W. W., Estes, A. M., Richards, T. L., Munson, J., Friedman, S. D., . . . Dager, S. R. (2013, September). Atypical developmental patterns of brain chemistry in children with autism spectrum disorder. *JAMA Psychiatry, 70,* 964–974. doi:10.1001/jamapsychiatry.1388

Di Martino, A., Ross, K., Uddin, L. Q., Sklar, A. B., Castellanos, F. X., & Milham, M. P. (2009). Functional brain correlates of social and nonsocial processes in autism spectrum disorders: An activation likelihood estimation meta-analysis. *Biological Psychiatry, 65,* 63–74. doi:10.1016/j.biopsych.2008.09.022

Girirajan, S., Brkanac, Z., Coe, B. P., Baker, C., Vives, L., Vu, T. H., . . . Eichler, E. E. (2011). Relative burden of large CNVs on a range of neurodevelopmental phenotypes. *PLoSGenetics, 7*(11), e1002334. doi:10.1371/journal.pgen.1002334

Griffith, E. M., Pennington, B. F., Wehner, E. A., & Rogers, S. J. (1999). Executive functions in young children with autism. *Child Development, 70,* 817–832. doi:10.1111/1467-8624.00059

Jansiewicz, E. M., Goldberg M. C., Newschaffer C. J., Denckla M. B., Landa R., & Mostofsky, S. H. (2006). Motor signs distinguish children with high functioning autism and Asperger's syndrome from controls. *Journal of Autism and Developmental Disorders, 36,* 613–621. doi:10.1007/s10803-006-0109-y

Lord, C., Luyster, R. J., Gotham, K., & Guthrie, W. (2012). *Autism Diagnostic Observation Schedule, Second edition (ADOS-2) manual (Part II): Toddler module.* Torrance, CA: Western Psychological Services.

Lord, C., Rutter, M., DiLavore, P. C., Risi, S., Gotham, K., & Bishop, S. L. (2012). *Autism Diagnostic Observation Schedule, Second edition (ADOS-2) manual (Part I): Modules 1–4.* Torrance, CA: Western Psychological Services.

Silliman, E. R., Diehl, S. F., Bahr, R. H., Hnath-Chisolm, T., Zenko, C., & Friedman, S. (2003). A new look at performance on theory of mind tasks by adolescents with autism spectrum disorder. *Language, Speech, and Hearing Services in Schools, 34,* 236–252. doi:10.1044/0161-1461(2003/020)

DOWN SYNDROME

Raitano Lee, N., Pennington, B. F., & Keenan, J. M. (2010). Verbal short-term memory deficits in Down syndrome: Phonological, semantic, or both? *Journal of Neurodevelopmental Disorders, 2,* 9–25. doi:10.1007/s11689-009-9029-4

LESCH–NYHAN SYNDROME

Wodrich, D. L., & Long, L. (2010). Lesch–Nyhan syndrome: A sex-linked inborn error of metabolism. In S. Goldstein & C. R. Reynolds (Eds.), *Handbook of neurodevelopmental and genetic disorders in children* (2nd ed., pp. 445–459). New York, NY: Guilford Press.

NEUROFIBROMATOSIS

Kaplan, A. M., Chen, K., Lawson, M. A., Wodrich, D. L., Bonstelle, C. T., & Reiman, E. M. (1997). Positron emission tomography in children with neurofibromatosis-1. *Journal of Child Neurology, 12,* 499–506. doi:10.1177/088307389701200807

SPINA BIFIDA AND HYDROCEPHALUS

Burmeister, R., Hannay, H. J., Copeland, K., Fletcher, J. M., Boudousquie, A., & Dennis, M. (2005). Attention problems and executive functions in children with spina bifida and hydrocephalus. *Child Neuropsychology, 1,* 265–283. doi:10.1080/092970490911324

TOURETTE'S SYNDROME AND TICS

Wodrich, D. L. (1998). Tourette's syndrome and tics: Relevance for school psychologists. *Journal of School Psychology, 36,* 281–294.

TURNER'S SYNDROME

Waber, D. (2008). Neuropsychological aspects of Turner's syndrome. *Developmental Medicine and Child Neurology, 21,* 58–70. doi:10.1111/j.1469-8749.1979.tb01581.x

Brain-Related Disorders and Other Health Conditions

11

The goals of this chapter are to (a) encourage schools to invite medical professionals to participate on the interdisciplinary team as appropriate for the case at hand and (b) provide representative resources and readings for some educationally relevant health conditions occurring in a school-age population. Examples of educationally relevant medical issues include brain and bodily injuries, exposure to toxins, chronic medical conditions, infections, and psychiatric conditions. Parent interviews should cover developmental and medical history, including questions about prescription medicines taken by the mother during pregnancy and by the child throughout development and schooling other than for routine health issues, and questions about adverse reactions to medications. Many times events and conditions that occurred much earlier in development (e.g., premature birth, injuries, chronic health problems) continue to play a role in how parents currently think and feel about their child's educational problems.

A portion of this chapter was contributed by David Wodrich, a member of the book's advisory panel.

http://dx.doi.org/10.1037/14437-011
Interdisciplinary Frameworks for Schools: Best Professional Practices for Serving the Needs of All Students, by V. W. Berninger

In some settings the interdisciplinary team may want to link education plans and implementation to the diagnostic categories of the World Health Organization's *International Classification of Diseases* (10th rev.) or, in cases of psychiatric disorders, to the American Psychiatric Association's *Diagnostic and Statistical Manual of Mental Disorders* (5th ed.). For guidance on which medical specialties may be relevant for a particular developmental or medical condition, the team can consult with two websites:

- The American Congress of Obstetricians and Gynecologists website at http://www.acog.org/
- The American Academy of Pediatrics website at http://www.aap.org/

High-Risk Pregnancies and Premature Births

Advances in research and practice have greatly improved the care mothers receive during pregnancy and in the prenatal and postnatal periods. Ultrasound and amniocentesis have become routine medical practice to identify possible problems during pregnancy. Procedures have been developed to monitor the pre-labor and labor process, intervene when necessary, and care for infants who are born prematurely. As a result, many birth defects that were common in the past are being prevented today, and developmental outcomes for premature infants have improved dramatically—many function in or even above the normal range. However, in some, but not all, cases of premature births, other issues originating early in gestation or neural development prior to the premature birth may pose significant educational challenges during the preschool and school-age years. Newborn screenings are in place for many of the disorders that can affect the health of the developing child; for some of these, evidence-based treatments exist, which may not cure them, but often improve the quality of the developing child's life. In addition, progress has been made in educating women before they become pregnant about what they can do to prevent problems for their future children: not abusing addictive substances, eating a healthy diet, generally maintaining a healthy lifestyle, and adding folic acid to the diet, which has dramatically reduced the number of children born with the neural tube disorder spina bifida.

Toxin-Related Disorders

Developing children have been shown to have adverse reactions to a variety of toxins in the environment, including lead, mercury, arsenic, pesticides, industrial chemicals, and tobacco smoke. Schools can listen to parents who express concerns about these issues and develop parent education programs to make both parents and adolescents aware of these issues as consumers who purchase and use various commercially available products. For example, lead paint is used in many toys and other products, especially those not made in the United States.

Although some children have adverse reactions to vaccinations used to protect them against childhood infectious disease, researchers have found no causal link between these and autism. Also, no clear research evidence shows that food additives cause children's school learning problems.

Developmental Motor Disorders

CEREBRAL PALSY

Cerebral palsy (CP) is a nonprogressive motor disorder that affects movement and posture. It occurs early in development, during gestation, during labor, or after birth. However, prevention of CP has improved due to advances in detecting Rh incompatibility of parents, which was one of the earlier causes of CP, and careful monitoring of the birth process and elevated levels of bilirubin afterward. Either the pyramidal motor system (cortex to spinal cord tract) that controls voluntary movement or the extrapyramidal motor system (e.g., basal ganglia) that controls involuntary movement may be affected. *Dyskinetic CP* results from impairment in the extrapyramidal motor system; symptoms include rigidity of muscles, dystonia (altered muscle tone distorting body positioning), and choreoathetosis (frequent involuntary spasms of the limbs—twitching and flailing). *Dystonic CP* is characterized by the symptoms of dystonia.

MUSCULAR DYSTROPHY

Schools have to deal with issues related to mobility when individuals affected with *muscular dystrophy*, a neurologically progressive disorder that involves loss of motor function, can no longer walk independently. Affected students may begin to show signs of attention or learning difficulties for which they need accommodations and differentiated instruction, and they may also need counseling to deal with depression. They need to work with physicians regarding medical management, including the difficult issue of whether to use life support for breathing when the affected individual is no longer able to breathe without assistance.

Acquired Central Nervous System Injuries

SPINAL CORD INJURY

When the white nerve tissue of the spinal cord, which extends from the base of the brain and downward through the spinal column, is injured along with the spinal column where it is located, the nature of the impairment depends on where in the spinal column and spinal cord the injury is sustained. Functions that are controlled by the spinal nerve below the injured location are usually impaired. The most common causes are traffic accidents and sports injuries. Assistive technology plays an important role in the post-injury rehabilitation process.

TRAUMATIC BRAIN INJURY

Traumatic brain injury (TBI), also known as *head injury*, results from an external force that injures the brain. These injuries occur after a prior period of normal motor development. Symptoms due to the injury vary in severity and duration. All domains of developmental and educational functioning may be impaired both at home and school. Interdisciplinary teams should participate in assessment, treatment, and progress monitoring.

CONCUSSIONS

Closed-head injuries or *concussions* may occur in automobile accidents or sports. When an athlete is knocked to the ground and loses consciousness, he or she should not resume playing the sport until appropriately assessed by an interdisciplinary team to assess the nature and severity of any closed-head injury. Because of current concern about concussions in children and youth who play sports, a primer on concussion, composed by Whitney Griffin, a member of the advisory panel for this volume who specializes in work with student athletes, is posted on the website for the resources for this chapter.

The third international conference on concussion in sport held in Zurich 2008 defined concussion as a direct or indirect force to the head that results in immediate, short-lived neurologic impairment (e.g., amnesia, loss of consciousness, confusion), which may resolve spontaneously, but then is followed by physical, cognitive, and emotional symptoms and sleep disturbance, headache, and dizziness. Although these injuries do not appear to result in structural changes in the brain or in cell death, the brain may be forced to use a less efficient anabolic metabolism. In 1997, the Centers for Disease Control and Prevention reported that, on the basis of data from athletes who lost consciousness, at least 300,000 athletes per year in the United States experience concussions in the context of sports.

Not all concussions cause a loss of consciousness, and players and coaches tend to lack awareness or minimize symptoms of concussions. Failing to self-report concussions is both extremely dangerous and common because of fear of losing playing time. Assessment of sports-related concussion should be based on baseline evaluation before the athletic season begins and then follow-up if a concussion is experienced. Cognitive processes that should be assessed by a neuropsychologist include those most likely affected by concussions: memory, attention, speed of mental processing, and reaction time. An athlete's neurocognitive performance should return to baseline or better, that is, be asymptomatic before returning to play. Two available assessment instruments are the traditional Post-Concussion Symptom Scale and the computerized Immediate Post-Concussion Assessment and Cognitive Testing battery.

Athletes with multiple concussions could have a lingering deficit in memory. One of the most dangerous risks of sustaining a first concussion is *second impact syndrome*, which occurs when an athlete sustains a second head injury before symptoms associated with the first have cleared. Following the second blow, what happens in the next 15 seconds to several minutes sets this syndrome apart from a concussion or even a subdural hematoma. Usually within seconds to minutes of the second impact, the athlete who is conscious, yet stunned, collapses to the ground, and becomes semicomatose, with rapidly dilating pupils, loss of eye movement, and evidence of respiratory failure. Second impact syndrome is a preventable injury if symptoms are recognized and reported and players are sidelined and follow proper protocols. In 2009, the governor of Washington signed the Zackery Lystedt Law, which requires that any youth athlete suspected of sustaining a concussion to be immediately removed from play and then prohibited from returning without written clearance from a licensed health care provider trained in concussion management. In 2006, it fell to the coaches to decide whether Zackery Lystedt was safe to return to play; they decided to send him back in just 15 minutes after he had clearly sustained a concussion. The result was second impact syndrome that left Zackery with irreparable brain damage and confined to a wheelchair for the rest of his life. Even through head injuries cannot be completely removed from sports, brain damage can be minimized if successive concussions are prevented. The question remains: How is it possible to make a dangerous and potentially lethal sport, which is played during the middle school and high school years, safer?

CHRONIC TRAUMATIC ENCEPHALOPATHY

Repeated head trauma may cause a degenerative brain disease, *chronic traumatic encephalopathy* (CTE), which results in tau proteins forming in the brains of football players, causing symptoms of early onset dementia, as well as chronic neuropsychological sequelae, including behavioral and personality changes and clinical depression. Increasingly, professional football players are being diagnosed with CTE.

Chronic Illnesses

Persisting health problems may interfere with a child's ability to function at school or complete homework assignments. These include infections, brain tumors and cancer, epilepsy, sleep disorders, diabetes and inborn errors of metabolism, and other illnesses. In all cases it is imperative that the interdisciplinary team at school work with the child's physicians to develop an educational plan that appropriately addresses educational and psychological needs as well as the medical needs related to the chronic illness.

BRAIN TUMORS AND CANCER

Many children are successfully treated for cancer, but the survivors may develop learning or behavioral problems they did not have before chemotherapy and/or radiation used in treatment. Medical personnel and educators should work closely together as a team to ensure appropriate educational and medical management of students who are cancer survivors.

INFECTIONS

Cytomegalovirus

Cytomegalovirus can cause major malformations in the developing fetus. The infant is likely to have pervasive developmental disability.

Meningitis

Meningitis is an infection that can be bacterial or viral, which attacks the meninges, the membrane that surrounds the brain. When the infection is bacterial, a child should be carefully monitored for adverse reactions to the medication, which may result in hearing problems.

DIABETES AND INBORN ERRORS OF METABOLISM

With parents participating, consultation with medical specialists regarding *diabetes and inborn errors of metabolism* (see also Chapters 7 and 10) is critical for planning and implementing educational programs at school, as well as completing homework outside school. Issues can range from scheduling medication to planning breaks and snacks. Both Type I (failure of the pancreas to produce sufficient insulin) and Type II diabetes (insulin resistance) are fairly common in school-age children; rates of the latter are increasing with the epidemic of childhood obesity. Because the body, including the brain, depends on a stable insulin supply to enable glucose in the blood to be converted to energy, diabetes can cause a host of school problems.

A recent review (Wodrich, Parent, & Hasan, 2011) points to four types of school-related problems in Type I diabetes. First, such students miss more school than healthy classmates—either entire school days when ill or at medical appointments or portions of days during trips to the nurse for disease management. Thus, classroom instruction can be compromised. Second, school achievement, such as in basic reading, mathematics, and writing, is at risk. In part, these risks seem to derive from underlying general neurocognitive or selective neurocognitive (enduring memory or motor) problems. Early diabetes onset and relatively poorly controlled blood glucose seem to heighten the risk. Third, transient problems with attention and work completion sometimes occur even in the absence of persistent neurocognitive and achievement deficits. Stable day-to-day blood glucose seems to help ameliorate attention problems; scrupulous diabetes management consequently may improve the school status of these students. Fourth, personal adjustment and substandard relationships with classmates (and teachers) may occur. School supports and the provision of mental health services, including those addressing family dynamics and diabetes management in the home, seem to help (see Anderson, 2012). In fact, merely sharing a diabetes diagnosis with teachers seems to promote better understanding of classroom problems. Adding information about diabetes sharpens teacher thinking about classroom problems even more (Wodrich, 2005). Thus, effective clinic–school communication appears to matter. Resources for educators and parents include the Juvenile Diabetes Research Foundation (http://jdrf.org/life-with-t1d/) and the University of Arizona's EdMedKids (http://edmedkids.arizona.edu/).

SEIZURE DISORDERS AND EPILEPSY

Seizure disorders (see also Chapter 10) may result from a variety of factors, ranging from fever, infection, toxic agent, trauma, injury, or overdose of a medication to genetic-based epilepsy. For students who have seizure disorders, medical management becomes an important part of the individualized education plan. Isolated seizures occur for many reasons (e.g., toxin ingestion, head trauma, fever); only recurrent seizures, however, are classified as *epilepsy*. In turn, epilepsy can be variously classified to reflect its diverse etiology (e.g., symptomatic when associated with another neurological diagnosis and idiopathic when there is no known etiology) and expression (e.g., simple—with no seizure-associated change in consciousness—and complex—changes in consciousness occur). The International League Against Epilepsy provides a classification system (http://www.ilae.org/Visitors/Centre/ctf/documents/ILAEHandoutV10_000.pdf). In light of its heterogeneity, epilepsy's school consequences are not easily summarized. In general, however, symptomatic epilepsy is associated with much more severe neurocognitive problems (including risk of low IQ) and selective deficits that can limit academic success (Aldenkamp, Weber, Overweg-Plandsoen, Reijs, & van Mil, 2005). However some with epilepsy may have intellectual talents.

Moreover, poorly controlled seizures predict greater social and interpersonal problems because of the potential for classmates to witness a seizure and the stigma likely to result. Seizures severe enough to require multiple antiepileptic drugs (AEDs) for control may predict problems with classroom attention and work completion. AEDs, especially if used in combination with each other or with other drugs, can create inattention or lethargy. As with many pediatric illnesses, epilepsy is associated with a relatively high rate of absenteeism, which itself may create or exaggerate academic, interpersonal, and school engagement difficulty. Many teachers express apprehension about instructing students with epilepsy, and many possess little knowledge about epilepsy and its risk to school success (Wodrich, Jarrar, Buchhalter, Levy, & Gay, 2011). Thus, informing and supporting teachers and providing students with a team (including mental health professionals) to meet their often-complex needs are advisable. Unfortunately, special services, when used in school, appear to seldom accommodate for the exact nature of the student's epilepsy-related problem (Wodrich, Kaplan, & Deering, 2006). Consequently, advocacy for proper school service may be needed. Another resource for educators and parents is the Epilepsy Foundation (http://www.epilepsyfoundation.org/).

CANCER

Pediatric cancer is extremely heterogeneous. It can be associated with the blood (e.g., leukemia), brain or spinal cord (e.g., central nervous system tumors), or other parts of the body (e.g., solid tumors in muscle or bone). Prognosis, and crucially, treatments vary. The latter fact is important because treatment choices can affect outcomes. For example, leukemia is often treated with radiation to the brain and spinal cord. Sometimes, medication is introduced into the cerebrospinal fluid. Although leukemia treatments like this have increased survival rates, they can also affect the brain and its functioning, and effects on cognition and memory may not appear until many years later (hence their common designation as *late effects*). Understanding late cognitive effects, tracking their trajectory in the individual child, and making classroom accommodations thus are often critically important actions. Tumors of the brain, which might require surgical resection and radiation, are understandably associated with a range of neurocognitive problems paralleling the site of the tumor and central nervous system target of treatment.

Besides the obvious neurocognitive effects that may constrain long-term school learning or daily performance, the common consequences of cancer are similar to those of other significant pediatric illnesses. These include peer and personal adjustment problems associated with changed physical appearance; lethargy, depression or discouragement; altered family and peer relations; and frequent school absenteeism. Because the initial diagnostic and treatment procedures associated with cancer are often protracted, a student's eventual return to school can be especially challenging. As a result, school reentry programs are sometimes available to help the affected student, his or her classmates and teacher, and the family (see http://www.chla.org/site/c.ipINKTOAJsG/b.5950017/k.988F/STAR_Services.htm). Of course, a team approach that includes mental health professionals and strong clinic–school communication is vital. Another resource for educators and teachers is the National Cancer Institute (http://www.cancer.gov/cancertopics/types/childhoodcancers).

SLEEP DISORDERS

Sleep disorders are common in children and adolescents. See Dawson (2004) for online resources for parents and educators in managing sleep disorders of school age children and youth.

CYSTIC FIBROSIS

Cystic fibrosis (CF) is an example of a genetic disorder that affects health during the school years but, unlike many of the other medically relevant disorders, does not affect brain structures or functions per se. Rather, CF is a lung disease. Progress is being made on identification of genes involved in this autosomal recessive disorder and its treatment. Although there is no cure, affected individuals now often survive through the middle adult years.

OTHER MEDICAL CONDITIONS

Medical conditions that occur in school age children and youth include, but are not restricted to, hemophilia, sickle cell anemia, Tay–Sachs disease, and neural tube deficits (e.g., spina bifida; see Chapter 10). Celiac disease, for which a gluten-free diet is important (Green & Celler, 2007), occur in school-age children and youths with and without SLDs.

Psychiatric Disorders

Interdisciplinary teams should be alert for signs of possible psychopathology for which diagnostic assessment and relevant treatment beyond positive behavioral support may be needed. Signs that warrant problem-solving consultation and diagnostic assessment as deemed appropriate include students who

- are extremely withdrawn,
- act out frequently and violently,
- have killed or expressed intent to kill an animal,
- have set fires or expressed intent or desire to do so,
- report hearing voices or other indicators of not being in touch with reality,
- exhibit mood swings between being sad and being overly active,
- worry excessively, and/or
- have excessive concentrating difficulties.

It is important to differentiate between the hyperactivity in attention-deficit/hyperactivity disorder (ADHD) and the overly active state of bipolar disorder. Adverse events have followed when children and youth who have bipolar disorder have been placed on medication for ADHD. Both have different neurogenetic bases and require different kinds of medication. It is also important to determine whether ADHD may be a symptom of an underlying specific language impairment (SLI) that is causing the attention difficulties or whether inattention may be causing language-processing problems independent of an SLI. This differentiation has treatment implications. Also note that excessive worrying and concentration difficulties co-occur with many psychiatric disorders and alone do not constitute a differential diagnosis; treatment plans should deal with these symptoms as well as the other diagnosed psychiatric conditions.

Substance Abuse
(Alcohol and Other Drugs)

DURING PREGNANCY

Fetal alcohol spectrum disorder (FASD) refers to fetal alcohol syndrome (FAS), partial fetal alcohol syndrome (partial FAS), alcohol-related birth defects, and alcohol-related neurodevelopmental disorder, conditions in which the mother's drinking has adverse effects on her child's development (see the website for the Consensus Statement on Recognizing Alcohol-Related Neurodevelopmental Disorder [ARND] in Primary Health Care of Children, a conference organized by the Interagency Coordinating Committee on Fetal Alcohol Spectrum Disorders).

Alcohol is not the only substance that a mother may have abused. Other abused substances may include both illegal substances and ones manufactured from common household chemicals. Many mothers who abuse alcohol also abuse other substances. The child may experience adverse effects not only from the effects of the substances on the nervous system but also from the lack of parenting; parents who are abusing substances often neglect their children.

STUDENT DRUG ABUSE DURING DEVELOPMENT

Because of many legal issues for schools, it is difficult to deal up front with student use and abuse of substances during middle childhood and adolescence. Such use and abuse is very real in contemporary society and can interfere with learning and behavior, especially during adolescence (see Honor Role Model 15, Chapter 6).

Multiple Disorders in
the Same Individual

Medical conditions co-occur with many developmental disabilities and neurogenetic disorders. Some, such as CF, may co-occur with specific learning disabilities (SLDs). Some, such as substance abuse (not related to FASD resulting from parental alcohol abuse during pregnancy), may emerge during adolescence (and sometimes earlier) in a student previously diagnosed with ADHD or with an SLD.

Interdisciplinary Treatment Issues

As with the other disorders covered in Part III of this book, those involving health and medical management issues require participation from all the disciplines on the interdisciplinary team. The team should discuss educational issues for any student with chronic health conditions, not just those who qualify under the category of Health Impairment for Special Education Services. The evolving and expanding practice of assessing response to intervention should incorporate gathering evidence about how a student responds to medical management in general and to medication in particular for the relevant health or medical conditions for the case at hand.

Readings and Resources[1]

COLLABORATIONS BETWEEN HEALTH PROVIDERS AND EDUCATORS

Cunningham, M. M., & Wodrich, D. L. (2006). The effect of sharing health information on teachers' production of classroom accommodations. *Psychology in the Schools, 43*, 553–564. doi:10.1002/pits.20166

Phelps, L., Brown, R. T., & Power, T. J. (2002). *Pediatric psychopharmacology: Combining medical and psychosocial interventions.* Washington, DC: American Psychological Association.

Power, T. J., & Blom-Hoffman, J. (2004). The school as a venue for managing and preventing health problems: Opportunities and challenges. In R. T. Brown (Ed.), *Handbook of pediatric psychology in school settings* (pp. 237–248). Mahwah, NJ: Erlbaum.

Power, T. J., & Bradley-Klug, K. (2013). *Pediatric school psychology: Conceptualization, applications, and strategies for leadership development.* New York, NY: Routledge.

Wodrich, D. L., & DuPaul, G. J. (2007). A survey of pediatricians regarding the other health impairment category. *Communique, 36*, 27–30.

Wodrich, D. L., & Kaplan, A. M. (2005). Indications for seeking a medical consultation. *Journal of Applied School Psychology, 22*, 1–28. doi:10.1300/J370v22n01_01

---

[1]Additional research readings and practitioner resources for this chapter can be found at http://www.apadivisions.org/division-16/publications/interdisciplinary-frameworks-supplement/index.aspx

Wodrich, D. L., & Spencer, M. L. S. (2007). The other health impairment category and health-based classroom accommodations: School psychologists' perceptions and practices. *Journal of Applied School Psychology, 24,* 109–125. doi:10.1300/J370v24n01_06

BRAIN TUMORS

Long, L., Wodrich, D. L., Levy, R., Etzl, M. Jr., & Gieseking, A. (2010). Students with brain tumors: Their post-treatment perceptions of teachers, peers, and academics and retrospective views on school during treatment. *Journal of Child Health Care, 14,* 111–125. doi:10.1177/1367493509355531

CANCER

Waber, D. P., & Pomeroy, S. L. (2008). Introduction: Survivors of childhood cancer: The new face of developmental disabilities. *Developmental Disabilities Research Reviews, 14,* 183–184. doi:10.1002/ddrr.28

DIABETES

Wodrich, D. L. (2005). Disclosing information about epilepsy and type I diabetes mellitus: The effect on teachers' understanding of classroom behavior. *School Psychology Quarterly, 20,* 288–303. doi:10.1521/scpq.2005.20.3.288

Wodrich, D. L., Parent, K. B., & Hasan, K. (2011). Type 1 diabetes mellitus and school: A review. *Pediatric Diabetes, 12,* 63–70. doi:10.1111/j.1399-5448.2010.00654.x

EPILEPSY

Aldenkamp, A. P., Weber, B., Overweg-Plandsoen, W. C. G., Reijs, R., & van Mil, S. (2005). Educational underachievement in children with epilepsy: A model to predict the effects of epilepsy on educational achievement. *Journal of Child Neurology, 20,* 175–180.

Anderson, B. J. (2012). Behavioral research in pediatric diabetes: Putting the evidence to work for advocacy and education. *Pediatric Diabetes, 13,* 77–80. doi:10.1111/j.1399-5448.2011.00778.x

Wodrich, D. L. (2005). Disclosing information about epilepsy and type I diabetes mellitus: The effect on teachers' understanding of classroom behavior. *School Psychology Quarterly, 20,* 288–303.

Wodrich, D. L., & Cunningham, M. M. (2008). School-based tertiary and targeted interventions: The examples of epilepsy and type 1 diabetes mellitus. *Psychology in the Schools, 45,* 52–62. doi:10.1002/pits.20278

Wodrich, D. L., Jarrar, R., Buchhalter, J., Levy, R., & Gay, C. (2011). Knowledge about epilepsy and confidence in instructing students with epilepsy: Teachers' responses to a new scale. *Epilepsy and Behavior, 20,* 360–365. doi:10.1016/j.yebeh.2010.12.002

Wodrich, D. L., Kaplan, A., & Deering, W. (2006). Children with epilepsy in schools: Special service usage and assessment practices. *Psychology in the Schools, 43,* 169–181. doi:10.1002/pits.20123

HEAD INJURY

Lovell, M. R., Iverson, G. L., Collins, M. W., Podell, K., Johnston, K. M., Pardini, D., . . . Maroon, J. C. (2006). Measurement of symptoms following sports-related concussion: Reliability and normative data for the post-concussion scale. *Applied Neuropsychology, 13,* 166–174.

Stuss, D. T. (2011). Traumatic brain injury: Relation to executive dysfunction and the frontal lobes. *Current Opinion in Neurology, 24,* 584–589. doi:10.1097/WCO.0b013e32834c7eb9

HIV/AIDS

Wodrich, D. L., Swerdlik, M. E., Chenneville, T., & Landau, S. (1999). HIV/AIDS among children and adolescents: Implications for the changing role of school psychologists. *School Psychology Review, 28,* 228–240.

INFLAMMATORY BOWEL DISEASE

Green, P. K., & Celler, C. (2007). Celiac disease. *New England Journal of Medicine, 357,* 1731–1743.

Mrakotsky, C., Bousvaros, A., Chriki, L., Kenney, E., Forbes, P., Szigethy, E., . . . Grand, R. (2005). Impact of acute steroid treatment on memory, executive function, and mood in pediatric inflammatory bowel disease. *Journal of Pediatric Gastroenterology and Nutrition, 41,* 540–541. doi:10.1097/01.mpg.0000182010.77322.de

LEAD POISONING

Agency for Toxic Substances Disease Registry. (2013). *Lead poisoning.* Retrieved from http://www.nlm.nih.gov/medlineplus/?leadpoisoning.html

National Institute of Environmental Health Sciences. http://www.niehs.nih.gov/

PAIN MANAGEMENT

Engel, J. M., & Kartin, D. (2004). Pain in youth: A primer for current practice. *Critical Reviews in Physical and Rehabilitation Medicine, 16,* 53–76. doi:10.1615/CritRevPhysRehabilMed.v16.i1.40

Engel, J. M., Kartin, D., Carter, G. T., Jensen, M. P., & Jaffe, K. M. (2009). Pain in youths with neuromuscular diseases. *American Journal of Hospice and Palliative Care*, 26, 405–412. doi:10.1177/1049909109346165

SLEEP DISORDERS IN CHILDREN

Dawson, P. (2004). *Sleep and sleep disorders in children and adolescents: Information for parents and educators.* Retrieved from http://www.nasponline.org/resources/health_wellness/sleepdisorders_ho.aspx

SPINAL CORD INJURY

National Institute of Neurological Disorders and Stroke. (2013). *Spinal cord injury: Hope through research* (NIH Publication No. 03–160). Retrieved from http://www.ninds.nih.gov/disorders/sci/detail_sci.htm

STROKE

Lubetsky-Vilnai, A., & Kartin, D. (2010). The effect of balance training on balance performance in individuals post-stroke: A systematic review. *Journal of Neurological Physical Therapy*, 34, 127–37. doi:10.1097/NPT.0b013e3181ef764d

SUBSTANCE-RELATED DISORDERS

Curran, M., Fuertes, J., Alfonso, V. V., & Hennessy, J. J. (2010). The association of sensation seeking and impulsivity to driving while under the influence of alcohol. *Journal of Addictions and Offender Counseling*, 30, 84–98. doi:10.1002/j.2161-1874.2010.tb00059.x

Jirikowic, T., Kartin, D., & Olson, H. C. (2008). Children with fetal alcohol spectrum disorders: A descriptive profile of adaptive function. *Canadian Journal of Occupational Therapy*, 75, 238–248. doi:10.1177/000841740807500411

Jirikowic, T., Olson, H. C., & Kartin, D. (2008). Sensory processing, school performance and adaptive behavior of young children with fetal alcohol spectrum disorders. *Physical & Occupational Therapy in Pediatrics*, 28, 117–136. doi:10.1080/01942630802031800

TOXINS INCLUDING PESTICIDES AND LEAD EXPOSURE

American Academy of Pediatrics Council of Environmental Health. (2012). Policy statement: Pesticide exposure in children. *Pediatrics*, 130, e1757–e1763. doi:10.1542/peds.2012-2757

TRAUMATIZED CHILDREN

Cole, S. F., O'Brien, J. G., Gadd, M. G., Ristuccia, J., Wallace, D. L., & Gregory, M. (2009). *Helping traumatized children learn: Supportive school environments for children*. Retrieved from http://www.massadvocates.org/documents/HTCL_9-09.pdf

INTERDISCIPLINARY FRAMEWORKS FOR UNDERSTANDING ENVIRONMENTAL BASES OF DEVELOPMENT AND LEARNING

IV

Racial, Cultural, Family, Linguistic, and Socioeconomic Diversity and the Story of Rose

12

T his chapter calls attention to the diversity among children and youth of comparable ages that stems from environmental variables. This diversity may pose challenges but also enrich the human experience. These include environmental variables, but are not restricted to, parents and extended family, home or other living arrangement, stressors and resources within the family, resources and challenges in the communities where students live outside school, languages and dialects spoken at home and school, and socioeconomic variables such as parental levels of education, family income level, and racial and cultural backgrounds.

A portion of this chapter was contributed by Thomas Power, a member of the book's advisory panel.

http://dx.doi.org/10.1037/14437-012
Interdisciplinary Frameworks for Schools: Best Professional Practices for Serving the Needs of All Students, by V. W. Berninger

Families

LIVING ARRANGEMENTS

School-age children and youth vary greatly in where they live outside school. Some live in houses, some in apartments, some in cars or tents, and some in the streets. In some schools serving a large proportion of homeless students, the interdisciplinary team focuses on issues of safety outside school and linking parents to community resources for shelter, food, and health care.

FAMILY MEMBERS

Who lives in the home can also vary greatly. Some children and youth live with two parents, who may be of different sexes or the same sex. Parents may be biological parents, stepparents, or foster-care parents, or they may have adopted the child. Other children and youth live with one parent, either a mother or father, and in many urban contexts this is the predominant family structure for students. For some children, parents have never been divorced, but for others one or both parents may have been divorced, and children may have to deal with issues related to a blended family, shared custody and visitation with a parent in different homes, or custody disputes and lack of access to one of the parents. Some live in homes where parents are manufacturing or trading drugs, whereas others may be dealing with a parent who is incarcerated. Sometimes a child or youth is parenting one or more other children in the family because a parent is unable to do so. Siblings may still live at home or may have left home and visit at times. In some cases, other adults who are not parents live with the family. These may be extended family members or unrelated adults. Extended family members, such as aunts or uncles and grandparents, may not live with the family, but still play an important role in the child's development and identity. Asking students and parents about who their family is, who lives with them, and listening to what they share may be the key to understanding how relationships outside school can affect learning and behavior in school (see Honor Role Model 3, Chapter 2).

PARENTAL LEVELS OF EDUCATION AND INCOME

Parents vary greatly in their levels of education. In contemporary society many still do not graduate from high school. Some have technical or vocational training with or without a high school diploma. Some have attended undergraduate programs, and some have graduated from them. Some have received graduate education. Research has clearly shown that parents' (especially mothers') level of education affects the language learning environment and other aspects of a child's learning before the transition to schooling in kindergarten or first grade. Income levels are related to levels of education but not always. Some parents are unemployed or underemployed or are in careers that do not pay as well as some that require less formal education. Still, level of parental income can affect whether children and youth have adequate food, living environments, and health services outside school or whether parents can provide their children with supplementary educational services or enrichment activities outside school. Income levels can vary greatly within a local school if it serves students from single-family dwellings and apartments, which may have populations that are transient due to inability to pay rent.

FAMILY ISSUES

Regardless of parent level of education or income, many families have stressors that can affect children's performance at school. In addition to issues related to parental employment and insufficient money or the lack of a place to live, other stressors might include illness of a parent, sibling, or other family member—for example, a grandparent being cared for in the home by a parent—or the death or impending death of a family member. In some cases, the stressors are related to interpersonal relationships, including fighting among family members, violence, or physical or sexual abuse or separation, divorce, or remarriage of parents. In other cases, parents who were not parented well themselves may lack the necessary parenting skills, or parents may have mental health or other problems that interfere with their being available to their children, who are neglected. Fortunately, in some cases, children and youth who have significant learning or behavioral problems live in families with social supports and resources to help them.

COMMUNITY RESOURCES

Some, but not all, communities have many resources that are available to school-age children and youth and their families, ranging from libraries with computer stations to sports teams to music, drama, or dance groups to community centers with swimming pools and summer camp programs to medical and mental health services.

Racial Diversity

DIFFERENCES BETWEEN RACE AND CULTURE

One's *race*, which is based on family origin and typically has characteristic skin color and facial features, is not the same as culture. Moreover, racial features are not the same as racial identity, which is psychological, not physical. *Culture* is the shared social traditions and experiences in which one grows up. People with similar racial features may come from quite varied cultural traditions. People who share culture may come from quite varied racial traditions (e.g., Hispanics who may be European, African, and/or indigenous in racial origin). Census data are based on racial categories and do not reflect the cultural diversity of those who share only the color of their skin or speak the same language. For example, the culture of African Americans who have been in the United States for generations is very different from the culture of the growing number of African Africans who have voluntarily immigrated to the United States from a variety of African countries, each with their own cultural traditions, or from the culture of Africans who moved from the Caribbean. Likewise, Hispanic culture may be very different for those who immigrate from Cuba, Puerto Rico, or other countries in the Caribbean or from Mexico, Central America, or South America; these individuals also vary greatly in racial origin and identity. Even within the country of origin of immigrant populations, cultural identity may vary greatly.

DIFFERENCES BETWEEN RACE AND ETHNICITY

The concepts of race and ethnicity are also not identical. *Ethnicity* refers to a social categorization of human beings belonging to a group whose members identify with each other on the basis of a real or presumed common genealogy or ancestry. *Race* refers to a set of physical characteristics resulting from genetic ancestry that distinguishes a group of people from others. Thus, ethnicity refers to psychological identity, and race refers to physical characteristics. To learn more about this important distinction, see http://www.diffen.com/difference/Ethnicity_vs_Race.

AN INCREASING BIRACIAL AND MULTIRACIAL POPULATION

The fastest-growing racial group in the United States is biracial. Intermarriage among racial groups has always existed in the United States, and its frequency is increasing. It is also increasingly being acknowledged. Educators should not make assumptions about a student's racial background only on the basis of facial features or skin color, but rather should ask students and parents to self-identify their racial (and cultural) background or backgrounds.

SKIN COLORS ACROSS RACES

Skin color does not fall neatly into pure colors of black, brown, or white. Rather, skin color falls along a continuum of hues and does not always correspond to categories based on ethnicity or culture. Crayons and colored markers are now commercially available for the full array of skin tones that exist in the real world. Students can use them to portray more realistically the skin color of the people they draw or their own racial identity.

WHITE MYTH

Historian Nell Irvin Painter, Professor Emeritus, Princeton University, explained in *The History of White People* that the concept of *white* is a myth invented after World War II. Many European groups who immigrated to North America to escape persecution in Europe had very different cultural backgrounds and languages and struggled to learn to get along in the new world—with each other and with mainstream society in the United States. A well-documented example is the fervent discrimination against Irish Americans in the 21st century. In the post-war era when the immigrants from many other parts of the world became more visible and numerous, the Europeans who had been here for one or more generations began to be perceived as "white," when in fact their skin colors also varied considerably, as did their cultural traditions.

Cultural Diversity

INVOLUNTARY VERSUS VOLUNTARY IMMIGRANTS

In her address as president of the American Educational Research Association and in a subsequent article, Gloria Ladson-Billings educated American educators about the unpaid educational debt to two groups in the United States who were involuntary immigrants: Native Americans and African Americans. Not only did Europeans take away the land from the indigenous peoples already living in the North American continent but they also took children away from their parents and their language and culture. Willard Bill, of the Muckleshoot Indian tribe, has written about the boarding school experience. On the one hand, some living elders who were forced to attend schools at long distances from their home and who were punished for speaking their native languages have reported the psychological consequences of these experiences, which may still affect their children and grandchildren. On the other hand, it is a tribute to the spirit of Native American peoples that they survived these injustices. The tribes were also forced to "immigrate" to reservations within the larger country the newcomers established. Many Native Americans have left the reservations, but not their tribal affiliation, and now live in urban areas. The educational achievement gap is largest for both Native Americans living on reservations and urban Indians who no longer live on reservations.

In contrast, early African Americans were brought involuntarily to the United States as slaves. In many cases during the slavery era, men were removed involuntarily from their families, and women remained to raise the children, giving rise to matriarchal families. Even after they were freed from slavery in the mid-19th century, whether they remained in the South or migrated to other areas of the country, the legacy of removing fathers from the family affected relationships between mothers and fathers in parenting. This legacy may account, in part, for the contemporary crisis in the number of African American males being raised without a close or ongoing relationship with a father, dropping out of school, getting in trouble with the law, and being imprisoned (see Chapter 1 and the efforts of the Los Angeles Unified School District to deal constructively with this remaining educational debt for African American students).

The lesson for educators is to be mindful of the cultural differences among all students and to realize that the history of how they have been treated by the mainstream culture still affects the contemporary generation of students belonging to some groups. Even among those who have been voluntary immigrants seeking economic opportunity, injustices have occurred that may still affect their children for generations to come. One example is of the Japanese living in the United States during World War II who were forced to leave their homes and were sent to internment camps. School-age children of Japanese descent may still have grandparents who remember and discuss these events with their children and children's children.

GENERATIONAL DIFFERENCES AND EXTENDED FAMILIES

Immigrants to the United States go through stages of acculturation to the mainstream culture. This acculturation process may occur over several generations. Educational professionals should take into account whether a student is a first-generation immigrant (who lived in another culture before coming to the United States), a second-generation immigrant (whose parent or parents immigrated from another country), or a third-generation immigrant (one or more grandparents immigrated). Many immigrants form their own communities in order to preserve cultural identities and support one another in the new country. Asking about these cultural roots, and listening carefully to the answers, can go a long way in establishing positive home–school relationships.

In many cultures, the extended family across multiple generations plays a greater role in parenting than may be typical for many families in the mainstream culture in the United States. For one thing, newly arrived immigrants may live in closer proximity to the extended family, either in the same home or in the nearby neighborhood. For another, often a grandparent or aunt or cousin may be a major caretaker or key player in the family dynamics. In contrast, because of where they are employed, many adults in the mainstream culture raise their children in a different part of the country than where they were raised or where their families live. Even with technology to keep in touch, not living in close proximity may change the way children and youth interact with other members of the extended family. Understanding the dynamics of the extended family is critical to effective counseling for mental health issues in many cultural groups.

EDUCATIONAL LEVELS AND LANGUAGE ISSUES

Educational professionals should not make assumptions about the parental level of education or home language. Rather, they should ask and listen to what they discover when they ask about parental educational background and language or languages spoken in the home. Just because a child has immigrated to the United States and English may not be the first language of a parent, it does not follow that English is not spoken in the home and is not the child's first language. Among immigrants, some parents have completed little formal education before coming to the United States, though others have completed considerable education. The same range of educational accomplishments is found within immigrant groups as it is in the general population. However, just because a parent reports that English is spoken in the home, it does not mean that the child is exposed to mainstream English. The child may be learning English from a parent who is also learning English. Just because a child is bilingual, it does not follow that English is the child's second language. Even for students whose families are not recent immigrants, it is relevant to find out whether mainstream English or another dialect of English is spoken in the home. Regardless of dialect spoken, some children may have difficulty in making the bridge between the forms of English spoken at home and at school.

In the case of Native Americans, effects of previous oral language traditions still used in some homes may have effects on the use of English in academic learning, because differences exist in the use of grammar, expression, prosody, phonology, and comfort with oral versus written expression. In addition, Native Americans hold ideas and belief systems that are not easily expressible in the English used in academic learning.

RELIGIOUS ISSUES

Within and across cultures there is considerable diversity in religions and spiritual traditions, which vary in their historical origins, belief systems, and practices. Although religion has historically been a source of conflict among peoples, it can also be a source of support for individuals and families. For some families who cannot afford private services for their children experiencing stressors in or out of school, religious groups with which they may be affiliated may be able to provide those support services. Alternatively, some religious groups provide support services in the community for those who cannot afford to pay for them or can only afford reduced fees. In some school contexts, it may be possible for students to share about their religions to develop tolerance and understanding.

OTHER CULTURAL GROUPS LIVING IN THE UNITED STATES

Educational professionals should continue to learn about the various cultural groups represented in the student populations where they work. To facilitate the process, see Readings and Resources at the end of this chapter.

MATCH BETWEEN LANGUAGE AT HOME AND SCHOOL

Not only do students bring different language backgrounds to their learning at school but also the language or languages spoken at home may be different from the language spoken at school—either by the teacher or by the other students.

MISMATCH BETWEEN LANGUAGE OR DIALECT AT HOME AND SCHOOL

Research results have been mixed on whether students benefit from instruction at school that matches the language heard and/or spoken in the home, instruction only in mainstream English, or a mix of the two. These mixed results may reflect the numerous other variables that interact with language at home and language at school, including parental level of education and income and nature of home literacy experiences. If a child is struggling at school because of home–school language differences, pull-out special education services may not be the most appropriate way to deal with the underlying language learning issues.

Some students speak the same language at home as at school, but they speak different versions, or dialects, of it. Some students are easily able to switch between the dialects, that is, they are good at cross-code switching and are able to learn at school. Other students have considerable difficulty in cross-code switching and benefit from instructional activities to help them learn to deal with the dialect differences within English. These differences may involve sound, syntax, and vocabulary usage and can affect their ability to learn to decode and spell written words, understand what they read, and express their ideas in writing. Not only are there many dialect variations among African Americans speaking English but also within English spoken in the United States as well as in the United Kingdom (England, Scotland, Northern Ireland, and Wales), Canada, and Australia. The reason English-speaking peoples can read each other's writing is because of the approximately comparable orthography, not the speech or idioms (see Warmouth & Ayerza, 2013).

BILINGUALISM—ADVANTAGE OR DISADVANTAGE?

Research has shown that for individuals without developmental or learning disabilities, advantages may be associated with being bilingual. However, those with developmental or learning disabilities may struggle with learning a second language because of those disabilities. In some cases a student will have to deal with both learning a second language at school and a specific language disability.

OPTIMAL TIMES FOR LEARNING A SECOND LANGUAGE AT SCHOOL

Historically, in the United States "foreign languages" were taught beginning in middle school or high school grades. However, research has shown that it is easier to learn a second language earlier in development, beginning in the early grades. Some school systems have therefore developed bilingual immersion programs in elementary schools. There may also be advantages to learning multiple languages during the preschool years before elementary school, especially through the use of technology in the home that supports communication with extended family members who speak languages other than English; however, more research is needed on this issue.

Educational Applications of Environmental Sources of Diversity

Interdisciplinary teams of educational professionals should actively listen when parents share any environmental sources of diversity and not dismiss any as not being important to school learning and behavior.

Educational professionals may have to seek consultation from other professionals, depending on the diversity issues raised. Often, just being aware of any challenge(s) outside school or the mismatch between home and school environment allows educational professionals to convey that they care and want to be supportive of the child at school. That kind of compassion goes a long way in building home–school relationships.

Across cultural and language groups, there are some parents who do not know how to foster literacy in the home. Schools can organize parent groups at school to teach parents how to read storybooks and discuss them with their children. If parents do not speak English fluently, it is better that the parents read to children in the language in which they are fluent rather than not reading at all. Parents with limited literacy skills may be encouraged to engage their child in conversation about the pictures in books and other reading material. In addition, parents should be encouraged to provide paper and writing tools so that children can engage in "invented writing" in which young children learn that they can use letters to spell speech sounds to express ideas and draw pictures to go along with their writing. Some children may benefit from instruction that emphasizes the commonalities across the language heard or spoken at home and the language heard or spoken at school.

Throughout schooling, all students should have opportunities to share their stories about who they are (self-identity), who their family is (psychological relationships in and out of the home as they grow up), and what their culture is (cultural identify or identities). Stories can be shared orally, in writing, and using media (audio and/or visual with or without technology support). Such sharing educates the students about the others in their classes and also educates their teachers. For example, some teachers have children draw their self-portrait and a family portrait using the crayons or markers that more realistically represent skin colors of human beings.

Masks have played a role in all cultures. Some teachers have children use skin color crayons or markers and a variety of other materials to create masks that reflect students' inner selves, their personalities. In the United States, masks are also used in pretending to be someone else, as at Halloween.

Multimedia can also be used to share one's story or autobiography and the story or stories of one's culture or cultures. This sharing can be healing as students, especially those whose families are still dealing with cultural traumas from history of unfair treatment, become aware of the contributions of their people to world history.

Some schools and teachers are developing curricula and lessons to teach the value of diversity as well as unity in diversity in the United States and an increasingly global world. An excellent source of material for this educational goal is *The Better World Handbook: Small Changes That Make a Big Difference* (Jones, 2007).

As pointed out by Julie Washington, a member of the advisory board, the primary challenge educators face is the fundamental differences among students (and teachers) from different racial and cultural backgrounds. There is an expectation in mainstream culture that students will come to school and "assimilate" with little difficulty. There is little respect for understanding of the magnitude of the transition that many students must make to accommodate to the culture of the school environment. These differences include language, adult–child interactive expectations, ways of interpreting the same events, behavioral differences, and just different ways of being. There is little appreciation of how important it is with all the different cultures now in our schools to be sure that students and teachers have shared understandings and expectations about schools and each child's place in them.

The following quotations illustrate the long-standing struggle to deal with diversity (from http://www.betterworld.net/quotes/diversity-quotes.htm):

- "United we stand, divided we fall."—Aesop, storyteller
- "In world history, those who have helped to build the same culture are not necessarily of one race, and those of the same race have not all participated in one culture. . . . The peoples of the earth are one family."—Ruth Fulton Benedict, anthropologist
- "It is time for parents to teach young people early on that in diversity there is beauty and there is strength."—Maya Angelou, poet laureate
- "Although we are in different boats you in your boat and we in our canoe we share the same river of life."—Chief Oren Lyons, Onandaga Nation
- "We may have all come on different ships, but we're in the same boat now."—Martin Luther King Jr., civil rights leader
- "We live now in a global village and we are in one single family. It's our responsibility to bring friendship and love from all different places around the world and to live together in peace." —Jackie Chan, Chinese actor and UNICEF goodwill ambassador
- "All humanity is one undivided and indivisible family, and each one of us is responsible for the misdeeds of all the others. I cannot detach myself from the wickedest soul. . . . It is easy enough to be friendly to one's friends. But to befriend the one who regards himself as your enemy is the quintessence of true religion. The other is mere business."—Mohandas K. Gandhi, spiritual and political leader
- "We are not going to be able to operate our spaceship earth successfully nor for much longer unless we see it as a whole spaceship and our fate as common. It has to be everybody or nobody." —R. Buckminster Fuller, architect and scientist

The Story of Rose: Interdisciplinary Teams Reaching Out to the Community

This chapter ends with an example, provided by advisory panel member Thomas Power, of how interdisciplinary teams in schools working with the community can make a difference. The story of Rose, in particular, shows that it takes a team of professionals and paraprofessionals working with students, their families, and the community.

The impact of poverty on the development of children cannot be overstated. Poverty places children at risk of ongoing periods of stress and episodes of trauma. The repeated experience of stress and trauma has debilitating effects on children's neurodevelopmental maturation, which may manifest in impairments academically and socially. Although schools, primary care practices, and community agencies may have a buffering effect, these systems often are highly stressed and underresourced, which places limits on what they have to offer children and youth.

In this context, it is remarkable what has been achieved in so many schools, health systems, and community agencies situated in high poverty neighborhoods. A defining element of these successful systems is that they understand that their most valuable resources are the individuals who work in or are associated with their agencies. Leaders in these systems find a way to support providers in establishing and maintaining strong attachments to children and their families. Of course, providers in these systems include the professional staff (e.g., teachers, counselors, primary care pediatric providers, nurses), but they also include faith leaders and paraprofessionals (e.g., classroom aides, playground aides, community volunteers).

Paraprofessionals are a resource that is generally underappreciated and underutilized in schools. These individuals, who are typically residents of the neighborhoods surrounding the schools, are experts in the culture of enrolled students and their families. In addition, they generally are passionate about the development of the children in their communities. Like all individuals who provide services to children, they have limitations. The limitations of paraprofessionals may include a lack of training with regard to providing evidence-based academic and behavioral programming for children and insufficient preparation to work effectively with professional staff.

There are countless examples of university–community partnerships that have been formed to address the training needs of community professionals and paraprofessionals. These partnerships have the benefit of building the capacity of community providers, and they provide the vehicle through which university-based professionals can make a difference in real world settings. Through these partnership models, paraprofessionals have served vital roles in improving children's academic skills, reducing violence on school playgrounds, and promoting healthy eating and exercise habits at school and home.

The success of programs that place community partners in key roles typically requires a leader among the paraprofessionals. An example in our work was Rose, a paraprofessional and mother of a child attending an inner city school in a large metropolitan area. Rose was a natural leader with good organizational skills and the ability to form strong relationships with the diverse population of folks living in the community. Also, Rose was adept at relating to professionals; she understood formal systems (e.g., schools and health clinics) and how to operate effectively through them. The success of our university–community partnership was due in large measure to the commitment and leadership ability of Rose, who built relationships between them. The program was based in an elementary school and designed to build the reading skills of kindergarten and first grade students. Rose served as the organizer among the community providers as well as the cultural guide for the university-based consultants. Through the partnership, the paraprofessionals were able to implement an evidence-based reading program so that the program was acceptable to the students and their families. Not surprisingly, the students were highly engaged in the program and most of them achieved favorable outcomes.

Examples of interdisciplinary teams promoting success of students living in poverty should be submitted to the American Psychological Association (APA) Division 16 for consideration for a Rose Award. Given the impact of poverty on educational success, names of professionals or paraprofessionals who show by example how students living in poverty can also succeed in schools should be submitted for consideration for the Rose Award and to be added to the Honor Role Model List for school teams inspired by the Rose in this chapter. Schools serving large numbers of students living in poverty that develop school-wide models for helping these students succeed academically and behaviorally are encouraged to submit the model to APA Division 16 for sharing with other schools.

Conclusion

Perhaps the most important high-stakes test is whether individual students can learn to manage their diverse societies of mind so they can live in diverse societies within their schools, community, country, and world in the unity that emerges from peaceful resolution of inevitable conflicts (see Figure 12.1; Table 8, Fulgham, 2004; McLean, McLean, & McLean, 2003).

FIGURE 12.1

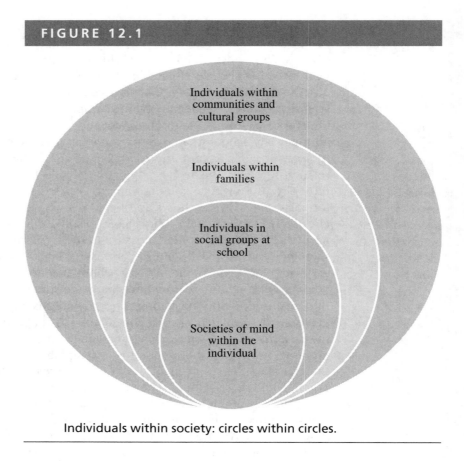

Individuals within communities and cultural groups

Individuals within families

Individuals in social groups at school

Societies of mind within the individual

Individuals within society: circles within circles.

EDUCATING STUDENTS LIVING IN POVERTY

For more information on how interdisciplinary teams can serve students living in poverty, see Heckman (2006), a Nobel Laureate economist whose work is being widely cited in government with respect to the federal early learning initiatives. Heckman has done a lot of work on the cost–benefit analysis of early childhood programming. The Executive Summary and corresponding Research Brief funded by the Council of Chief State School Officers (Halle et al., 2009) also provides valuable information for what can be done during early childhood to deal with poverty issues. Duncan and Murnane (2011) provide evidence for the relationship between poverty and failure to meet standards in high-stakes tests during the school year; they also provide insight into addressing these issues that have a major impact on individuals' lives during and after the formal education years.

Readings and Resources[1]

Duncan, G., & Murnane, R. (Eds.). (2011). *Whither opportunity? Rising inequality, schools, and children's life chances.* New York, NY: Russell Sage Foundation.

Halle, T., Forry, N., Hair, E., Perper, K., Wandner, L., Wessel, J., & Vick, J. (2009). *Disparities in early learning and development: Lessons from the early childhood longitudinal study—Birth cohort (ECLS-B). Executive summary.* Washington, DC: Child Trends.

Heckman, J. (2006). Skill formation and the economics of investing in disadvantaged children. *Science, 312,* 1900–1902. doi:10.1126/science.1128898

SOCIALIZING INDIVIDUALS IN SOCIETIES

Fulgham, R. (2004). *All I really need to know I learned in kindergarten.* New York, NY: Ballantine Books.

McLean, D., McLean, J., & McLean, W. (2003). *You've got to share: Songs for children* [CD]. Camden, ME: Don McLean. Music. Songs about each developmental domain (see Chapter 8, Table 8.1).

MULTICULTURAL EDUCATION

Banks, J. (2012). *Encyclopedia of diversity in education.* Thousand Oaks, CA: Sage.

Banks, J., & Banks, C. (Eds.). (2011). *Handbook of research on multicultural education.* Flagstaff: Northern Arizona University.

Erwin, J. O., & Worrell, F. C. (2012). Assessment practices and the underrepresentation of minority students in gifted and talented education. *Journal of Psychoeducational Assessment, 30,* 74–87. doi:10.1177/0734282911428197

Gay, G. (2010). *Culturally responsive teaching: Theory, research, & practice* (2nd ed.). New York, NY: Teachers College Press.

Jones, E. (2007). *The better world handbook: Small changes that make a big difference.* Vancouver, Canada: New Society.

Jones, J. (2009). *The psychology of multiculturalism in the schools: A primer for practice, training, and research.* Bethesda, MD: National Association of School Psychologists.

---

[1]Additional research readings and practitioner resources for this chapter can be found at http://www.apadivisions.org/division-16/publications/interdisciplinary-frameworks-supplement/index.aspx

Skiba, R. J., Horner, R. H., Chung, C. G., Rauch, M. K., May, S. L., & Tobin, T. (2011). Race is not neutral: A national investigation of African American and Latino disproportionality in school discipline. *School Psychology Review, 40,* 85–107.

U.S. Department of Health and Human Services. (2001). *Mental health: Culture, race, and ethnicity—A supplement to mental health: A report of the surgeon general.* Rockville, MD: U.S. Department of Health and Human Services, Substance Abuse and Mental Health Services Administration, Center for Mental Health Services.

Warmouth, J. M., & Ayerza, G. J. (2013). *Teacher Trade!* Seattle, WA: CreateSpace.

Worrell, F. C., Mendoza-Denton, R., Telesford, J., Simmons, C., & Martin, J. F. (2011). Cross Racial Identity Scale (CRIS) scores: Stability and relationships with psychological adjustment. *Journal of Personality Assessment, 93,* 637–648. doi:10.1080/00223891.2011.608762

Worrell, F. C., & Watson, S. (2008). A confirmatory factor analysis of Cross Racial Identity Scale (CRIS) scores: Testing the expanded nigrescence model. *Educational and Psychological Measurement, 68,* 1041–1058. doi:10.1177/0013164408318771

AFRICAN AMERICANS, AFRICAN AFRICANS, AND CARIBBEAN AFRICANS

Shaw-Taylor, Y., & Tuch, S. (2007). *The other African Americans: Contemporary African and Caribbean immigrants in the United States.* New York, NY: Rowman & Littlefield.

Worrell, F. C. (2005). Cultural variation within American families of African descent. In C. Frisby & C. Reynolds (Eds.), *The comprehensive handbook of multicultural school psychology* (pp. 137–172). Hoboken, NJ: Wiley.

Worrell, F. C. (2013). Gifted African Americans. In C. M. Callahan & H. Hertberg-Davis (Eds.), *Fundamentals of gifted education: Considering multiple perspectives* (pp. 388–400). New York, NY: Routledge.

ASIAN AMERICANS

Azuma, E. (2005). *Between two empires: Race, history and transnationalism in Japanese America.* New York, NY: Oxford University Press.

Brown, B. B., & Nguyen, J. (2010). Making meanings, meaning identity: Hmong adolescent perceptions and use of social and cultural identity symbols. *Journal of Research on Adolescence, 20,* 849–868. doi:10.1111/j.1532-7795.2010.00666.x

Kim, I. J. (Ed.). (2004). *Korean-Americans: Past, present & future.* Elizabeth, NJ: Hollym.

Lee, J., & Zhou, M. (Eds.). (2004). *Asian American youth: Culture, identity, and ethnicity.* New York, NY: Routledge.

Sue, S., Nakamura, C. Y., Chung, R., & Yee-Bradbury, C. (1994). Mental health research on Asian Americans. *Journal of Community Psychology, 22,* 181–187.

Terrazas, A., & Devani, B. (2008). *Chinese immigrants in the United States.* Retrieved from http://www.migrationinformation.org/USfocus/display.cfm?id=685

HISPANICS

Amparano, J. (2003). *America's Hispanics: Their rich history, culture, and traditions.* Chanhassen, MN: Child's World.

Noble, J., & LaCasa, J. (1991). *The Hispanic way: Aspects of behavior, attitudes, and customs of the Spanish-speaking world.* Chicago, IL: Passport Books.

Rivera, B. M., & Ford, L. (1998). Parental perceptions of child development among low-income Mexican American families. *Journal of Child and Family Studies, 7,* 469–491.

Rodriguez, S. (1995). *Hispanics in the United States: An insight into group characteristics.* Washington, DC: Department of Health and Human Services.

INDIA AND THE MIDDLE EAST

Bates, D., & Rassam, A. (2001). *Peoples and cultures of the Middle East* (2nd ed.). New York, NY: Prentice Hall.

Helwig, A., & Helwig, U. (1990). *An immigrant success story: East Indians in America.* Philadelphia: University of Pennsylvania Press.

Leonard, K. (1997). *The South Asian Americans.* Westport, CT: Greenwood Press.

NATIVE AMERICANS

Bill, W. E. (1990). *From boarding schools to self-determination.* Olympia, WA: Office of the Superintendent of Public Instruction.

Keoke, E., & Porterfield, K. (2003). *American Indian contributions to the world: 15,000 years of inventions and innovations.* New York, NY: Checkmark Books.

Ladson-Billings, G. (2006). From the achievement gap to educational debt: Understanding achievement in U.S. schools. *Educational Researcher, 35,* 3–12. doi:10.3102/0013189X035007003

McCardle, P., & Berninger, V. (Eds.). (2015). *Narrowing the achievement gap for Native American students: Paying the educational debt.* New York, NY: Routledge.

Phillips, C. (2010). *Aztec & Maya: The complete illustrated history*. New York, NY: Metro Books.

Romero-Little, M. E., Ortiz, S. J., & McCarty, T. L. (Eds). (2011). *Indigenous languages across generations—Strengthening families and communities*. Tempe: Arizona State University Center for Indian Education.

PACIFIC ISLANDERS

Harris, P., & Jones, N. (2005). *We the people: Pacific Islanders in the United States* (Census 2000 special reports). Washington, DC: U.S. Census Bureau.

Lott, J. T. (2006). *Common destiny: Filipino American generations*. Lanham, MD: Rowman & Littlefield.

U.S. Department of Health and Human Services. (2001). Mental health care for Asian Americans and Pacific Islanders. In U. S. Department of Health and Human Services (Ed.), *Mental health: Culture, race, and ethnicity—A supplement to mental health: A report of the surgeon general*. Rockville, MD: Author.

WHITE EUROPEANS

Painter, N. I. (2010). *The history of white people*. New York, NY: Norton.

BIRACIAL CHILDREN AND YOUTH

Palacios, E. D., & Trivedi, P. A. (2009). Increasing cultural literacy. In J. Jones (Ed.), *The psychology of multiculturalism in schools: A primer for practice, training and research*. Bethesda, MD: National Association of School Psychologists Press.

Trivedi, P. (2009). *Situating children's multiracial identities in sociocultural worlds: A mixed methods approach* (Unpublished doctoral dissertation). University of Washington, Seattle.

Trivedi, P. A. (2009, February). *Multiracial identities in middle childhood*. Paper presented at the meeting of the National Association of School Psychologists, Boston, MA.

Trivedi, P. A. (2011, February). *Situating multiracial identities in school settings*. Paper presented at the meeting of the National Association of School Psychologists, San Francisco, CA.

LINGUISTIC DIVERSITY

Brice Heath, S. (2012). *Words at work and play: Three decades in family and community life*. Cambridge, England: Cambridge University Press.

Washington, J., & Thomas-Tate, S. (2009). How research informs cultural–linguistic differences in the classroom: The bi-dialectal African American child. In S. Rosenfield & V. Berninger (Eds.), *Implement-

ing evidence-based academic interventions in school settings (pp. 147–163). New York, NY: Oxford University Press.

CULTURAL AND LINGUISTIC DIVERSITY AND DEVELOPMENTAL DIFFERENCES

Jegatheesan, B. (2011). Multilingualism and autism: Perspectives of South Asian Muslim immigrant parents on raising a child with a communicative disorder in multilingual contexts. *Bilingual Research Journal, 34*, 185–200. doi:10.1080/15235882.2011.597824

HOMELESSNESS

Trivedi, P. A., Linas, K., Jacobstein, D., Thomas, M. J., Kupferman, E., Perez, T., & Lewis, C. (2010). *A transdisciplinary approach to early childhood mental health consultation focused on children and families experiencing homelessness.* Nashville, TN: National Health Care for the Homeless Council.

MULTICULTURAL DIFFERENCES IN ACADEMIC LEARNING

Delgado, B. M., & Ford, L. (1998). Parental perceptions of child development among low-income Mexican American families. *Journal of Child and Family Studies, 7*, 469–481.

Han, Z. H., & Peverly, S. T. (2007). Input processing: A study of learners with multilingual backgrounds. *International Journal of Multiculturalism, 4*, 17–37.

Kearns, T., Linney, J. A., & Ford, L. (2005). African American student representation in special education programs. *Journal of Negro Education, 74*, 297–310.

Peverly, S. T. (2005). Moving past cultural homogeneity: Suggestions for comparisons of students' educational outcomes in the U.S. and China. *Psychology in the Schools, 42*, 241–249.

Zhou, Z., Peverly, S. T., & Xin, T. (2006). Knowing and teaching fractions: A cross-cultural study of American and Chinese mathematics teachers. *Contemporary Educational Psychology, 31*, 438–457.

INTERDISCIPLINARY FRAMEWORKS FOR UNDERSTANDING LEGAL, ETHICAL, AND INSTITUTIONAL ISSUES

V

Perspectives of a Neuropsychologist Working in an Interdisciplinary Setting With Students With Learning Disabilities and Their Parents and Teachers

13

For nearly three decades, I have had the privilege of working on an interdisciplinary evaluation team, the Learning Disabilities Program at Boston Children's Hospital. I cannot imagine performing a diagnostic evaluation without the collaboration and input of my colleagues, nor can they imagine doing their work without my input as a neuropsychologist. With the contribution of speech and language pathologists, our group long ago recognized the essential role of oral language in literacy and practiced accordingly. Indeed, we have always treated oral and written language competence in an integrated fashion in our evaluation process. As a neuropsychologist, I am cognizant of the importance of a child's general cognitive profile, which plays itself out in all aspects of academic as well as social cognition and emotional functioning.

The theoretical orientation of our team is both developmental and neuropsychological, focused on the whole child,

This chapter was contributed by Deborah Waber, a member of the book's advisory panel.

http://dx.doi.org/10.1037/14437-013
Interdisciplinary Frameworks for Schools: Best Professional Practices for Serving the Needs of All Students, by V. W. Berninger

with academic skills being one component of that understanding. In our model, academic skills are not an isolated appendage of cognition, as they are often treated; rather, they are an organic manifestation of the developing cognitive system. Academic performance thus provides one window into the cognitive system. By the same token, understanding the cognitive system provides insight into the sources of academic struggle. Academic struggles are often the source of psychological and emotional distress that further impedes academic progress as children become discouraged and disengaged. Within this theoretical framework, the child's cognitive, social, and emotional development is understood as an evolving system that is constructed in interaction with the context, most especially the school context. In this regard, our approach derives directly from the great developmental psychological theorists of the last century, Piaget (constructivist) and Vygotsky (contextual).

This broad theoretical framework has powerful implications when translated into clinical practice. Although the brain by its nature imposes certain structural constraints that cause behaviors to cohere in relatively predictable ways, it is above all essential to understand each child and his or her context as an evolving system. Group data derived from research studies can inform our understanding, but in the end, each child is a unique product of multiple interacting internal and external factors. A branching approach holds the promise of being able to accommodate this individuality. Just as we are moving toward an era of personalized medicine, we must implement strategies for personalized education if we are to "leave no child behind."

Within this developmental systemic framework, however, researchers and practitioners will have to appreciate the strengths and weaknesses of individual children who may not fit neatly into diagnostic packages that educators are expected to implement uniformly for all. Children with trouble reading often exhibit multiple cognitive inefficiencies that contribute to the reading problem, and they may experience problems with elements of the different components even when few of the individual elements rise to an "impaired" level on a specific diagnostic test. More frequently than not, there are other cognitive features of a child's profile that affect reading and oral language that need to be acknowledged as well. Finally, the environment is crucial. A child who appears discrepant in one school or school system may be less challenged in another, and vice versa. We found, for example, that a sample of children who had been given individualized education plans for specific learning disability in a suburban school system had mean scores on achievement testing that were exactly at the population mean, but their nonreferred peers had a mean score that was above the mean (Waber et al., 2003).

In fact, there may be too many moving parts to integrate into any single diagnostic system. But that complexity and confusion is a natural reflection of the underlying phenomenology: Generalities and broad theories of course have utility, but in the end, we will find that each child has a distinct story to tell us, and we must be prepared to listen to that story and not be overly constrained by prior theoretically guided expectations.

It would be a mistake to define our mission as professionals strictly in terms of outcomes in specific academic subject areas, important though they may be. Our task should be more broadly developmental. For example, oral language certainly affects reading, but it also has wide ranging impacts beyond reading comprehension. Teachers often perceive children with oral language problems as having a deficit in attention (and they often rate them high on inattention on an observational scale), when in fact the child becomes overloaded with language in a classroom and then disengages because he or she cannot sustain comprehension. A child with oral language deficits may be unable to monitor a math lesson accurately or use language as a tool for problem solving, impairing mathematics achievement over and above the impact of constituent subprocesses such as working memory. With development, moreover, oral language problems can interfere with social functioning with peers because children cannot keep up with the rapid and more nuanced language of adolescence. Thus, a child with early oral language problems, but for whom social skills were a strength in the early years, may predictably withdraw over time as oral language becomes a more central component of social interaction. In addition to these effects, the psychological impact of these undetected or misinterpreted problems may undermine the child's engagement and willingness to participate in academic activities, particularly those that are remedial and effortful. My own barometer for a positive outcome is not necessarily a normalized skill but rather a happy and productive young person.

Equally important is that each child has a unique profile of competencies that need to be orchestrated efficiently, especially as curricular demands escalate and become more complex and/or abstract. Recent developments in neuroimaging have highlighted the importance of efficient functional connectivity in the developing brain. We routinely see children who can diligently master many of the discrete skills needed for successful academic functioning but who struggle to integrate and orchestrate them in service of more complex tasks (e.g., reading, understanding, and commenting on an expository text). As the academic demands escalate as the child progresses in grade levels, some children inexplicably falter because they cannot integrate their skills to achieve the escalating academic demands. Thus, a child may possess all the requisite building blocks in terms of phonology, semantics, syntax, and morphology and achieve average scores on an IQ test, yet fail at the higher level tasks of inferential understanding or concept formation. These "integration" problems (for want of a better word) may be misinterpreted as higher order executive function deficits. Nevertheless, they are treatable: Once their incomplete understanding and confusion are addressed, they can often be remarkably well regulated and systematic.

This leads to another essential component of a developmental model, the context. A learning disability is not contained within the child; it arises because of the lack of compatibility between the child's complement of skills broadly conceived and the demands of the world within which the child functions. Elsewhere, I have defined a *learning disability* as "a social construction that serves to correct for the inherent incompatibility between normally occurring biologically heterogeneity and socially determined expectations" (Waber, 2010, p. 43). Thus, the goal of intervention should not be to repair deficits in the child but to address the incompatibility between the child and the world, focusing on both sides of the equation.

Finally, and along these lines, a word about teachers and the significance of a teacher's worldview—that is, whether it is developmentally oriented versus academic skill–oriented. Clinically, when parents recount an academic history for their child, I am frequently impressed with how teacher-dependent school functioning can be. Parents readily identify good and bad years and invariably attribute the variation to the attitude, worldview, and acumen of the teacher. It is clear that some teachers, who are more child oriented, intuitively understand their students' individual needs ("She really *got* my child"). While promoting academic skill development, these teachers invariably strive to make the child feel successful and comfortable with demands, parenthetically enhancing the efficacy of any intervention. Even a child who has significant cognitive impediments to learning can have a rewarding and successful year when the teacher is willing and able to understand and value him or her in terms of who he or she is and adapt accordingly. Other teachers are more rigorously oriented to academic outcomes, focusing on production and standards, and at times, sadly, blaming the child for not paying attention or not working hard enough when the child is in fact flailing. Imagine having to show up every day at a place where you feel incompetent and your efforts are not valued by the most important person in the room, the teacher. The emotional fallout from such a situation can be devastating, not to mention counterproductive in terms of academic progress. Added to the "branching" strategy, therefore, I would urge schools to explicitly value the developmental, whole child approach for struggling learners over an approach that more narrowly focuses on skills and curriculum, to identify teachers who are skilled at working with the whole child in an empathetic fashion, and to invest those teachers with authority to mentor teachers with struggling learners in their classrooms.

In the process I have also noted changes in the field of learning disabilities over the years. Theory, research, and practice in learning disability (LD) have been characterized over the decades by increasing fractionation of the developing child as an organism into a collection of cognitive molecules. Whereas in the early years the focus was on the learning-disabled child, during the 1990s the field shifted its focus to specific academic skills and even further to cognitive components of those skills, which were understood to be relatively independent of the psychological and developmental context (including IQ), with a search for essential endophenotypes (behavioral markers of gene and brain). LD came to be viewed not in terms of a developing child but of a discrete set of modules in need of repair (hence *learning disability* was replaced by reading disability, phonologic disability, writing disability, executive function disorder, and so on and so on). Like the surgeon who drapes the patient's body and focuses only on the area where the incision is to be made, the field has too often draped the child and focused on a specific skill or piece of a skill, assuming the rest to be irrelevant (which it can be with an N of 200, but not with an N of 1). This led to a rather mechanistic approach to intervention, with evidence-based practices focused on fixing the broken module or modules with the promise that such intervention would remove the impediment and allow the more complex skill, typically reading, to flourish unimpeded.

This approach indeed led to measurable successes, particularly for beginning readers, and there is a good argument to be made that on an epidemiologic basis, focusing teachers on the relevant cognitive processes has been more effective than more heterogeneous and often unproven approaches. Yet these successes have proven over time to have limitations. Some children fail to respond to these evidence-based interventions and continue to struggle even at basic single word decoding. More typically, children do make gains in phonologic awareness and single word decoding and recognition but do not then go on to become competent readers. With development, problems surface in other areas, in "whack-a-mole" fashion. Rate and comprehension have become the new frontiers, not to mention writing (and math). Moreover, it turns out that, more often than not, children with reading problems demonstrate difficulties involving various other cognitive domains, which can interfere with their ability to manage the curriculum in many subjects, as well as social skills.

Within that historic context, there is much to cheer about regarding the progress being made. First is the interdisciplinary mind-set, which acknowledges the complexity of the profiles presented by individual children who struggle in school and thus the need for multiple kinds of expertise among a team of collaborating professionals to accurately address them. Hopefully, the interdisciplinary training and service model, which began in medical centers in the 1970s, will spread to university training programs and school settings. Often, a reading problem is but the tip of the iceberg, the sentinel symptom that provides the ticket to special attention in the school setting because of the privileged place occupied by reading in academics. But children who have trouble learning to read frequently encounter difficulty with oral language and learning more generally. The language problem may or may not have been evident earlier in life, but it surfaces (or resurfaces) with demands for managing more complex and precise academic language. This should not be surprising, because common territories of the brain are engaged by both oral and written language. Nevertheless, the underappreciated role of oral language goes a long way toward explaining why the single word, phonologic approach has not succeeded in normalizing literacy in all children or why problems emerge in children who had been relatively successful readers or well-remediated readers in the early grades.

Second, the branching approach to diagnosis, based on the premise that all children have different learning profiles whether they merit a diagnosis or not, is an eminently sensible, albeit radical, approach in the context of the current diagnostic muddle. It acknowledges the unspoken reality that after nearly half a century of experts struggling to settle on a diagnostic definition, deciding who does or does not "have" an LD is a far more subjective process than we would like to admit. Clear criteria are elusive and vary between jurisdictions within a few miles of each other or even from school to school within the same jurisdiction (and sometimes from child to child within the same school). If there existed a clear-cut set of phenomena that could define who does or does not have this disability, it surely would already have been discovered, given the immense effort that has been invested to that end. Resources devoted to deciding whether someone does or does not qualify would likely be far better spent on actually trying to understand individual children's needs and improving that child's school functioning, with the presumption that all children merit a "free and appropriate education." Instead, we continue to engage in a process that is overly bureaucratic, contentious, and too often ad hoc with no discernible guidelines that parents can understand as to who does or does not qualify for limited resources (often conceding our expertise to that of test companies).

Third, evidence is converging across research groups for an inattention factor that uniquely predicts reading and writing, independent of subtype. In our research over a decade ago (Singer-Harris, Forbes, Weiler, Bellinger, & Waber, 2001; Waber et al., 2003), when we matched children from a referred sample with community controls on a standard psychoeducational measure of achievement, the referred children were differentiated by their performance on a series of nonverbal "low-level" information processing measures and on a teacher observational measure of inattention, even though their achievement scores on psychoeducational tests were indistinguishable and no child met criteria for attention-deficit/hyperactivity disorder. These information processing tasks were extremely basic, with outcomes measured largely in terms of subtle differences in response time, pointing to a bottom-up, processing efficiency difference rather than a top-down executive function dynamic. The findings reinforce the notion that some children may not respond to instruction because they have subtle difficulty in paying attention to instruction for a variety of reasons, rather than attention-deficit/hyperactivity disorder.

Ultimately, LD, whatever it may be, is a developmental phenomenon; an academic skill deficit may be the sentinel problem that brings the child to attention, but that deficit importantly arises in a developmental context. In over three decades of clinical work on an interdisciplinary medical center team, I have come to understand several core developmental principles that routinely guide my work with students referred for LDs: (a) the importance of a whole child approach in which multiple functional domains must be appreciated in systemic interaction; (b) the evolution of the LD phenomena over time, using past history diagnostically and predicting future risks; and (c) the essential role of context broadly conceived in understanding the child's development and functioning. Although normalization of all academic skills may or may not be a realistic goal for every student, an educational experience that will support students in their efforts to become productive, confident, and independent young adults can and should be both realistic and achievable for all in formulating an intervention strategy.

Readings and Resources[1]

Singer-Harris, N., Forbes, P., Weiler, M., Bellinger, D., & Waber, D. P. (2001). Children with adequate academic achievement scores referred for evaluation of school difficulties: Information processing deficiencies. *Developmental Neuropsychology, 20*, 593–603. doi:10.1207/875656401753549816

Waber, D. P. (2010). *Rethinking learning disabilities: Understanding children who struggle in school.* New York, NY: Guilford Press.

Waber, D. P., Weiler, M., Forbes, P., Bernstein, J., Bellinger, D., & Rappaport, L. (2003). Neurobehavioral factors associated with referral for learning problems in a community sample: Evidence for an adaptational model for learning disorders. *Journal of Learning Disabilities, 36*, 467–483. doi:10.1177/00222194030360050801

---

[1]Additional research readings and practitioner resources for this chapter can be found at http://www.apadivisions.org/division-16/publications/interdisciplinary-frameworks-supplement/index.aspx

Opportunities for Educators to Advocate for Students

14

T his chapter reviews the broad legal framework within which educators practice, and it describes the way school-related laws support advocacy for students on both a system and an individual level. The content of this chapter is heavily based on Sharan Brown's research and subsequent online course developed for the College of Education at the University of Washington and the Washington Educational Association over the last 10 years. In her view, professional educators have a duty, from a variety of sources of law, to advocate for their students. That is, not only parents but also educational professionals have a responsibility to advocate for students. As a preliminary matter, what is educational advocacy?

This chapter was contributed by Sharan Brown, a member of the book's advisory panel.

http://dx.doi.org/10.1037/14437-014
Interdisciplinary Frameworks for Schools: Best Professional Practices for Serving the Needs of All Students, by V. W. Berninger

Defining Educational Advocacy

Advocacy is not typically thought of as the responsibility of educators. Even special educators, who clearly have the duty—in collaboration with parents—to ensure that the rights of students with disabilities are protected under the Individuals With Disabilities Education Improvement Act of 2004 (IDEIA) and the Rehabilitation Act of 1973 (Section 504), are not typically considered advocates for their students. Advocacy is more often used to describe the actions of parents, lawyers, and others outside the professional educational system; indeed, the term is often tainted with the "adversarial" brush associated with legal action. Taking a more neutral perspective, there are several common characteristics of advocacy in the context of a school environment. First, *educational advocacy* involves intervention when "needed services are not accessible; are not available; are not appropriate; are not effectively provided; or when the voice of a child is not being heard" (Herbert & Mould, 1992). An effective problem-solving strategy to correct problems in the delivery of services is speaking on behalf of or in partnership with someone, such as a child or parent, to procure needed services (Stoecklin, 1994). Advocacy has also been described as information, advice, and representation provided to individuals and their families to help them acquire appropriate services (Bonney & Moore, 1992). Keeping the definition of advocacy and the duty to advocate in mind, deciding when and how to intervene in a variety of situations in which best practice implementation is at risk becomes easier.

The American Legal System and Sources of Law

Staying current on the body of school law is an enormous task. Educational professionals can best prepare themselves for a practice that is guided by legal, professional, and ethical considerations by understanding the primary underpinnings of the American legal system and sources of law. The current federal law or codes of professional practice may change over time, but the basics of our legal system are unlikely to change substantially. Understanding these basics provides the information educational professionals need to advocate for individual students and/or with public service systems (e.g., education, health, child welfare) in effective ways.

The diverse sources of the law complicate educators' ability to address school-related laws. Not only does the United States have federal and state laws that directly affect the delivery of educational services but we also have four independent sources of that law. All educational professionals work with these laws on a daily basis but may not be aware of the relationships among them. Although the United States Constitution gives authority for the education of American children to state governments, the federal government has also been involved from the beginning of our national history. Therefore, in addition to extensive state law that guides the school systems in each state, the federal government has increasingly provided financial support to state educational agencies that is contingent on the provision of specific services and even outcomes. In both the federal and state systems, there are four sources of law: constitutional, legislative, administrative, and judicial. In addition, there are numerous professional guidelines that are relevant to practice but do not rise to the level of law. Nonetheless, they are important in understanding the scope of the duty to advocate and are discussed later in this chapter.

Professional educators—both as individual citizens and as professionals—have the ability to influence all sources of law, but it is the professional role that is the focus of this chapter, and it begins with constitutional law. This source of law is, for the most part, the purview of the highest court in either the state or federal system. The nine justices sitting on the U.S. Supreme Court ultimately interpret the meaning of the Constitution and/or the constitutionality of any federal laws passed by Congress. Educational professionals' ability to influence U.S. Supreme Court decisions is, in most cases, quite tangential. Nonetheless, the justices receive their "knowledge" of the issues before them from the legal briefs written by the attorneys representing both sides in the litigation. The attorneys, in part, receive their information from professionals in the area of dispute. As many educators are aware, their knowledge and experience in educational matters—research and practice—are often requested by attorneys who seek to understand not only how other courts have interpreted law relevant to their case but also how the content experts understand the issues and what the best practice knowledge base demands.

Attorneys are most interested in getting assistance from the experts, especially those who are willing to go on the record and/or testify. Although it is not a role that many educators are comfortable with, educating the legal system can be a valuable way that professionals can advocate for individual students in a particular case. On a more neutral level, professional associations—for example, the National Association of School Psychologists—can and often do write amicus curiae, or friends of the court, documents that are submitted to the court for consideration. The amica curiae are provided in addition to the briefs submitted by each side of the controversy and can be extremely influential to the justices as they weigh the issues before them.

On another level, expert testimony (or even behind-the-scenes educational efforts within the process) can also influence legislators who may not be familiar with the effect legislation has or will have on individual students and their families, as well as on the educational system itself. Legislation that mandates certain duties or limits actions or liberties of individuals or governments is typically adopted as the result of lobbying efforts, although there are examples where the impetus is the direct result of the personal interest of an individual legislator. Professional groups as well as individuals can and do testify or comment on proposed legislation (state and federal). In addition, the extensive regulations (or rules) that are promulgated by state or federal agencies, interpreting the broad statutory language, are also heavily influenced by citizen input following publication of proposed regulations. Individual educators or professional associations are both provided the opportunity to comment in person during open meetings or to submit written commentary. Examples of the federal legislation and regulations that have been heavily influenced by the comments from professional organizations include IDEIA and the No Child Left Behind Act of 2001, among others. Similar examples can be identified at the state level.

The role of the courts in the American legal system often includes interpreting a state or federal law or regulation in the context of a factual debate, as well as determining the constitutionality of the legislation. Many of the legal debates in American school law involve statutory interpretation and application of the statute or regulation to factual situations. However, courts may also be using common law (case law) to determine liability in school related cases. Without going into extensive detail, the general duty under common law as it applies to education is an important consideration, and it is described briefly below.

Using Law to Advocate at an Individual Student Level

There are numerous opportunities for professional educators to intervene on behalf of an individual student; these are supported by either the common law duty of an educator to a student or by specific legislatively mandated duties. Many of society's expectations of an educator that were originally based in common law have now also become codified in statutory law, but in certain situations, the reasonable person standard will apply.

COMMON LAW DUTY

Educational professionals have a general duty to anticipate foreseeable problems during the performance of their job and to act as a "reasonable" professional would to prevent dangerous situations and to respond to any incidents that arise. This duty arises from *tort law*, which provides civil, not criminal, redress to those who have been harmed by the unreasonable acts of another. Tort law is considered *common law*, meaning that it has developed primarily through court decisions, not through legislation or statutory law. Although there are several types of torts, negligence is the most relevant to this discussion and is the only tort outlined here.

The basic question a court will ask in determining whether a particular educator has been negligent in any situation is whether a "reasonably prudent educator" with the skills and training relevant to the type of educational professional involved would have acted in a similar manner. A similar question would be relevant to an educational professional who is not a classroom teacher specifically, but a licensed psychologist or nurse, for example; that is, how would a "reasonably prudent psychologist" have acted? Regardless of the licensure, to prove negligence, four elements must be satisfied in a negligence cause of action, as follows:

1. the individual, such as an educator, has a duty to protect the individual harmed—for example, a student;
2. the duty is breached by the failure to exercise the appropriate standard of care;
3. the negligent conduct is the proximate cause of the injury; and
4. an actual injury has occurred.

The first task is to define the duty owed by an educator to a student. If there is no duty owed, then there can be no liability for any resulting harm. Similarly, if there is no harm (the fourth element), there is no liability. After thousands of court cases, the legal system has made it clear that there are some basic expectations or duties that society places on educators. As a general rule, educators owe their students the following:

- proper instruction (when involving an activity that may be dangerous);
- adequate supervision;
- safe equipment, facilities, and grounds; and
- warning students of known dangers.

The second element requires a clarification of the appropriate standard of care. This depends on the specific credentials of the educator. For example, a special education teacher is held to a different standard of care than a teacher without that extra training in certain instances. Similarly, the standard of care differs if the educator is teaching third grade than if he or she is teaching 10th grade—society expects more supervision of third graders than 10th graders, as a general rule. Accidents happen everywhere, including schools. Nonetheless, society holds educators to a standard of care toward their students that is more rigorous than the care owed by the general public. Because children are required to be in school under state law, for those in public schools, the state has assumed responsibility to ensure not only that they receive an education but also that it takes appropriate steps to keep them safe while in school.

Although negligence law has not been used successfully to prove that a teacher has failed in his or her duty to adequately teach a student (this is known as *educational malpractice*), there are many cases where a court has found liability because a teacher failed to adequately instruct a student on, for example, the hazards in a welding or chemistry class when serious injury resulted. And unfortunately, there are numerous cases where an educator has been found liable for injuries to a student caused by another student because of what the court determined to be inadequate supervision. One of the primary considerations when injury occurs is whether the event was foreseeable. So, for example, if the welding activity can easily injure a student, the courts would expect explicit instruction on safety and the close supervision of the child. If there was no safety instruction given or inadequate supervision, and injury resulted, the educator would likely be considered negligent.

In the case of a student harming another student, the courts might ask whether the educator responsible for supervision knew or should have known that the two students had a history of altercation. If so, the educator would be expected to pay close attention and be more attentive than usual. If that history was withheld from the teacher by, for example, a psychologist or other educational staff, thereby placing the teacher in a dangerous situation, the other educator could be liable for failure to provide vital information that would potentially have kept the teacher safe. The ethical and/or legal constraints on sharing information about a particular student with educational staff must be balanced with the duty to provide information that will benefit the student's educational experience and keep others safe. Sometimes privacy concerns trump the possible benefits in sharing information, but this is usually a decision that must be made on an individual student basis. In these situations, the state laws on access to health care, counseling, drug and alcohol treatment, and so forth, must be considered.

The standard of care is measured by what a reasonable person would do. The *reasonable person* is a fictional individual who is modeled on the basis of the expected skills and abilities a professional would have gained from his or her professional training and experience (along with any additional skills that individual possesses). Therefore, a credentialed teacher is considered to have the "normal" skills of all licensed teachers.

If the teacher has a special education endorsement, he or she is considered to have the skills of a special educator. If the teacher also has had many years of experience, that fact can be added to the reasonable person model to determine the standard of care in the case.

The final two elements must also be proved in any negligence case before liability is found. Specifically, the educator's conduct must have been the proximate cause of the injury, and there must in fact be an injury. The proximate cause standard is a measure of the relationship between the action—or inaction—of the educator and the injury. An educator may be negligent in some way, but that negligence may not be part of the chain of events that resulted in the injury. Sometimes there will be an intervening event that is, in fact, the cause of the injury and not the result of any negligence by the educator. In this case, there is no liability for the injury that results.

As stated previously, American courts have been unwilling to support educational malpractice complaints under common law, and it is unlikely that this will change in the near future. Nonetheless, educators are expected to keep their students generally safe from harm when there is reasonable cause to believe harm is likely. Professionals in the school setting are held to a higher standard than the "normal" citizen and are expected to act accordingly. In addition, the federal government is expanding the statutory duties of educators under specific legislation that mandates positive student outcomes. Tied to these duties are numerous rights of students and their parents ensuring that their rights are protected. The following section outlines some of these laws.

FEDERAL STATUTORY DUTIES FOR THE INDIVIDUALS WITH DISABILITIES EDUCATION IMPROVEMENT ACT

It is not uncommon for special education professionals to confront barriers to the provision of services required to ensure that their students receive a free and appropriate public education (FAPE) under IDEIA. These barriers include such things as parental resistance to an initial evaluation, the services provided and documented on the individualized education program (IEP), and/or the educational placement. The barriers can also include insufficient resources available in the school or district and/or disagreement on services from other professional staff, including administrators. When these or other barriers exist, a special educator is forced to make decisions on how to resolve the conflicts. Educators can be put in the uncomfortable position of choosing between what they believe is their professional responsibility and best practice toward a student and agreeing to a contrary decision by either parents and/or other educational staff. What is the duty of an educational professional when he or she faces resistance from others in the decision-making process?

It is important to remember that the professionals and the parents involved in this decision are all advocates for the student. All perspectives are legitimate and must be considered part of the team collaborative process. Ideally, the team should come to some consensus on the best course of action to take. Psychologists have a significant role to play throughout the special education process, from the initial referral for evaluation to determine eligibility for services through the designing and implementation of an IEP. In some cases, their initial evaluation will provide the information needed by the parents and teachers to determine that the child is eligible for services under IDEIA. For other students, the findings will not support sufficient barriers to educational success but will help teachers initiate response to intervention strategies to provide supports and documentation to help the child develop his or her skills in the areas of concern. Regardless of whether an IEP team is ultimately created to support a student eligible for special education services, the psychologist has a responsibility to provide the necessary information needed by educators and parents to develop interventions that will help ensure educational success. IDEIA intends that no one person on the evaluation or IEP team has more power in the decision-making process than another. However, the professionals involved in the IEP process all have the duty under IDEIA to contribute their best professional assessment of what services or supports the child needs to ensure his or her right to FAPE. The professionals and parents may not agree as to a course of action, even after a genuine and respectful debate. Therefore, to ensure that a child's rights to special education and related services are not delayed unduly by internal team debates, the ultimate decision lies with the administrator under federal law.

IDEIA provides for a complaint process that gives parents a clear, if not always easy or quick, avenue to raise their concerns through a variety of administrative complaint procedures when they disagree with the IEP team. Although each state's dispute resolution process differs somewhat, IDEIA mandates some options, including mediation and due process hearings. In addition, the federal courts will hear an IDEIA complaint after the due process hearing has been tried. Other members of the IEP team—such as educators—who disagree with the final decision of the IEP team should make their concerns known in a written *memo to file* documenting their professional rationale for disagreeing with the course of action as articulated on the IEP.

CHILD ABUSE PREVENTION AND TREATMENT ACT

Throughout the world, parents (biological or legally recognized as parents) are considered the primary care providers for their children. The assumption is that all parents will appropriately exercise authority over their children and act in their best interests. Although the range of what is appropriate differs according to time and place, communities do set limits on the power of parents over their children. When a child is not adequately cared for, for whatever reason, society will intervene to protect the child.

Children are vulnerable at any age, with few resources available to them when their health or safety is at risk. The federal government passed the Child Abuse Prevention and Treatment Act (CAPTA) in 1974 in recognition of the problem. The law sets minimum standards regarding the reporting of abuse and neglect to quality for funding under the law. As a result, all states in America have passed mandatory reporting laws requiring certain individuals who come into contact with children to report to Child Protective Services (CPS) and/or law enforcement when there is a reasonable suspicion of abuse or neglect. Because all states also have compulsory education laws that mandate children between certain ages spend a significant amount of time in school settings, educational professionals have consistent contact with most children and are included as a mandatory reporter in all states.

There is no question that the incidence of abuse and neglect among children in this country is high, as documented by numerous national reports published during the past decade, including a 2010 report to Congress (National Incidence Study of Child Abuse and Neglect, 2010). The National Incidence Study of Child Abuse and Neglect reported that more than 1.25 million children experienced maltreatment during the 2005–2009 study year (one in every 58 children in the United States). Almost one half of the neglected children experienced "educational neglect" (47%), more than one third were "physically neglected" (38%), and one fourth were "emotionally neglected" (25%). With the exception of the number of children emotionally neglected, the good news is that the other types of abuse and neglect measured in the national study have declined since the first national study and report to Congress.

Although there is a great deal of information that is well worth reviewing in this report, a few facts are highlighted here. In the findings, important sources of identification of abused and neglected children were hospitals (11%), police and sheriff departments (12%), and the general public (6%). However, educators were most likely to recognize and report children to CPS (52% of the study children), although the researchers made the assumption that not all maltreated children are reported to or investigated by CPS. According to the authors, professionals at schools may not report suspected maltreatment due to the following reasons: (a) definitional ambiguities as to what types of cases they should report to CPS and (b) attitudes and assumptions: for example, educators feel they can provide better help than CPS, fear they may lose the trust of the family, or are apprehensive about becoming involved in an official investigation. Even when educators report the suspected abuse or neglect, investigations may not occur because a child's case does not meet the agency's criteria, is outside the agency's jurisdiction, or the reporter did not provide sufficient information to meet the threshold for investigation (see the National Incidence Study of Child Abuse and Neglect; Sedlak et al., 2010).

As stated earlier, all states in this country mandate that certain individuals report suspected abuse and neglect to a state-level child protective agency, but each state has different reporting responsibilities and procedures. These differences notwithstanding, Washington state law can be used to illustrate the duty of educators. The first paragraph of the Washington mandatory reporting law, Revised Code of Washington (RCW) 26.44, states that when any "professional school personnel" has reasonable cause to believe that a child has suffered abuse or neglect, he or she shall report such incident, or cause a report to be made, to the proper law enforcement agency or to the department (CPS or the Department of Social and Health Services). The law is straightforward: Any educator with a reasonable suspicion of abuse or neglect must report it at the first opportunity, but in no case longer than 48 hours after there is reasonable cause to believe that the child has experienced abuse or neglect. It is important to remember that RCW 26.44.080 makes it a gross misdemeanor if an educator "knowingly fails to make, or fails to cause to be made . . . [a report of suspected abuse or neglect]" (from http://apps.leg.wa.gov/rcw/default.aspx?cite=26.44.080). The statute is available from the Washington State Legislature website (http://apps.leg.wa.gov/rcw/default.aspx?cite=26.44.030). In addition to possible civil or criminal charges, the failure to report can be an act of unprofessional conduct under the Washington State Code of Professional Conduct for Educators.

It is not always an easy decision for professionals in the educational setting to make a CPS call. However, when one is unsure, it is better to make concerns known rather than risk continued harm to the child. Remember, the duty is to report suspected abuse and neglect, not to prove it. Although educators have to be respectful of the choices parents make regarding their children, the rights of the child to be safe (free from abuse and neglect) trump the parental rights. Educators who report to CPS that they suspect abuse and/or neglect may not be supported in that evaluation by CPS, and there may be unpleasant personal consequences from irate parents. Nonetheless, educators do not face legal consequences for good faith reporting; they do face liability when they fail to report.

The first and most critical way educators can support—that is, advocate for—an abused or neglected child is to recognize and respond to the suspected maltreatment by reporting as required by law. Initially, when an educator is following up on a concern of possible abuse or neglect—that is, asking about injuries and/or behaviors—he or she can help the child by being supportive (including taking any report by children seriously) and gentle in any discussion of events, as outlined in the earlier link. However, a mandatory reporter should not assume the role of "investigator" to prove abuse or neglect; that is the role of the state agencies.

It is also important that educators remember that their legal duty is to either report directly to CPS or ensure that a report is made. Best practice is the individual who is suspicious of the maltreatment directly reporting it to CPS. Nonetheless, educators may well need to share their concerns with other appropriate professionals in their school, such as the school nurse, social worker, or psychologist. However, if the district policy is that an administrator is to be told of the "suspicion" and will report on behalf of the educator, the ultimate responsibility remains with the educator to be sure that the report is made. Raising a concern of abuse or neglect is a serious matter to all involved, and children and their parents have certain rights to confidentiality. Educators should talk and share information only with those professionals who need to know.

Once the report has been made, and the responsibility is in the hands of CPS and/or law enforcement to investigate as appropriate and intervene to ensure the safety of the child, what can educators do to support the child? Traditionally, the responsibilities for ongoing support lie outside the educational setting; more recently, there has been recognition that educators can play an important role in the comprehensive plan to ensure the child is safe. This may mean that for certain children, particularly those who receive special education and/or bilingual support, the state social service professionals become part of the multidisciplinary team designing appropriate services.

TITLE IX OF THE EDUCATION AMENDMENTS OF 1972

Sexual harassment in the schools is widespread, occurs across grade levels, race, and socioeconomic backgrounds, and has been linked to adverse outcomes comparable with those associated with bullying. It is also illegal. Title IX of the Education Amendments of 1972 prohibits discrimination on the basis of sex, including sexual harassment, in education programs and activities. Sexual harassment can occur between students and between school employees and can involve nonemployee third parties, such as a guest speaker. Further, the harassment can take many forms, including physical, verbal, and nonverbal behaviors.

This chapter covers only peer-to-peer harassment; it does not address employee-to-employee or employee-to-student harassment.

Girls still report experiencing more sexual harassment than boys, but the rate at which boys report such experiences may be increasing. Sexual minorities (lesbian, gay, bisexual, or transgendered [LGBT] youth) report experiencing the highest levels of sexual harassment. Girls and LGBT youth also report more negative psychological effects from sexual harassment than do heterosexual boys; these include anxiety, embarrassment, self-consciousness, depressive symptoms, and thoughts of suicide (Duffy, Wareham, & Walsh, 2004; Espelage, Aragan, Birkett, & Koenig, 2008). Students with educational disabilities may also be more likely to experience harassment and to harass as well, due to difficulties using appropriate social skills and lack of insight regarding how their behavior may affect interpersonal relationships (Young, Heath, Ashbaker, & Smith, 2008).

Addressing sexual harassment in the schools can prove challenging given the broad federal guidelines encompassing a wide range of behaviors. Recent years have brought increased attention to the topic of sexual harassment in schools, and some schools have responded by instituting strict zero tolerance policies. Some such policies have resulted in extreme cases of young children being removed from school following charges of sexual harassment (Schulte, 2008). Zero tolerance policies of this sort arguably leave little room for education and prevention efforts.

Schools must respond in a timely and meaningful way to reported incidents of sexual harassment and must also take steps to prevent harassment and provide remediation when it occurs. This is true whether the victim requests informal action or files a formal complaint. If a school fails to take swift and appropriate action, it may face legal consequences and ultimate liability. Appropriate action while investigating a complaint may include taking interim measures to keep the victim and alleged harasser(s) separated. If a victim requests confidentiality, the school should honor this request in such a way that still allows for investigating and responding to the complaint. The federal department of the Office for Civil Rights (OCR) has advised that when deciding how to honor confidentiality requests, the school should also consider the seriousness of the conduct, the age of the students involved, and whether there have been other complaints about the accused individual. OCR recognizes the importance of using judgment and common sense in deciding how best to respond to a suspected instance of sexual harassment. Nonetheless, sexual harassment must be addressed to ensure that students are not denied their rights to education under Title IX.

It is important to know and refer to your school or district's procedures for reporting and investigating sexual harassment complaints. Sexual harassment is not always easy to detect; students do not always make complaints. Although the law may not hold schools or individual educators liable for student harm, being educated on the issue and educating others—both educators and students—can be a powerful intervention.

CHILDREN WHO HAVE EXPERIENCED TRAUMA

The goal of educators is to help students learn, but students who are experiencing trauma, regardless of the source, will not be at their best academically. There has been some excellent work done recently on creating "trauma-sensitive schools" to support the role of educators in helping traumatized children learn. Many professionals have a good background in the effect of trauma on children's ability to learn and in the guidelines and practice recommendations for designing interventions for students dealing with issues of abuse. Those who do not have this background would find the research in this area, such as that described below, valuable for all students.

Helping Traumatized Children Learn (Cole et al., 2009) provides an excellent introduction to the effect of trauma on a student and describes in some detail the approaches to creating trauma-sensitive school environments and communities that support traumatized children and thereby moderate the effects of trauma. This manual helps educators understand the effect of trauma on a child's brain and the subsequent impact on the child's ability to learn. The common results of traumatic experiences on a child—hopelessness, self-blame, and a lack of control, for example—may all be exhibited in the classroom and should be considered as possible evidence of symptoms of trauma. In addition, the authors stress the importance of appreciating the complexity of the problems by understanding the biological changes that can occur when children experience trauma. Chapter 2 of *Helping Traumatized Children Learn* describes the authors' approach to helping make schools environments that are trauma sensitive. Although it does not place all the responsibility with educators by any means, this report reinforces the idea that without school involvement in implementing interventions that mitigate the effects of trauma, student success is unlikely. In particular, schools can do the following:

- partner with families as appropriate and strengthen traumatized children's relationships with adults in and out of school,
- help children to modulate and self-regulate their emotions and behaviors, and
- enable children to develop their academic potential.

Helping Traumatized Children Learn provides concrete suggestions on how a school might create such a supportive environment, recognizing that not all of these suggestions will be appropriate for every school. The specific teaching strategies that should be included in staff training include

- helping students regulate emotions to master social and academic skills,
- maintaining high academic standards,
- helping children feel safe,
- managing behaviors and setting limits,
- reducing bullying and harassment,
- helping children have a sense of agency,
- building on strengths,
- understanding the connection between behavior and emotions, and
- avoiding labels.

In addition to educating staff on how to design and offer a supportive environment for all students who have experienced trauma, it is important to note the unique vulnerabilities of students who are considering suicide. The American legal system has been reluctant to find another person liable for the suicide of an individual—child or adult. There have been cases brought against individual educators or administrators and the state educational agency for the suicidal death of a student, but to date, no court has found liability. The courts are certainly not suggesting that educators should ignore the signs that a student is thinking of suicide—whether it is something in writing, something spoken out loud, or simply changes in behavior that raise warning flags. At a minimum, society as a whole has an ethical duty to protect children, and educators have the professional duty to intervene when children are suicidal. What intervention is appropriate will depend on the role of the educator involved, the policy and procedures of the particular school regarding suicidal students, and the particular indicators that are of concern. Because courts have recognized that families have a cause of action, meaning that a claim against the school for the death of a student can be litigated, the possibility of liability, which will depend on the facts of the case, remains.

What can educators do when they suspect, or know, that a child is struggling with mental health issues, whether suicidal ideation or something else? Although there are never enough resources available, and many mental health disorders are complicated and require a multidisciplinary approach to intervention, there are things that educational staff can do. The following suggestions were developed with input from the 3 Rivers Wraparound Program, the Washington State Office of the

Superintendent of Public Instruction, Washington State Department of Health, and Massachusetts Advocates for Children.

The first step that educators can take to assist in improving the mental health of students is to educate themselves about the issues. There is no debate about the importance of healthy emotional development for children to maximize the likelihood that they will be successful in school and the adult world. Educators can do a great deal simply by being attentive to the emotional aspect of a child's development and being sensitive to the signs that a child is in trouble; early intervention can prevent or ameliorate serious mental health problems in the future. For students who receive special education services, it is critically important that IEP teams remember that the eligible student has a right to all services and supports that will ensure that he or she achieves FAPE. A child who has a learning disability, for example, may also be dealing with mental health challenges that are negatively affecting his or her educational achievement. If this is the case, services should be provided to address those issues in addition to the learning disability. One eligibility category is necessary for a student to receive services under IDEIA, but many students have barriers to education in numerous areas, and all these should be addressed.

Professional Standards of Practice, Codes of Conduct, Ethical Considerations

In addition to the common law duty of educators to keep students safe at school and the duties as described earlier in the relevant federal law examples, each state has created statutory and/or regulatory duties that are specific to education professionals. To ensure that educators exhibit certain standards of behavior and conduct, states have established credentialing requirements, monitor teacher preparatory programs, issue teaching certificates following a review of qualifications, and require continuing education of all certificated educators. When educators fail to adhere to the expected standards of practice, serious consequences may result, affecting their ability to work in schools. There are a number of professions represented in education—for example, psychology, social work, occupational therapy, physical therapy, speech/language therapy, nursing, and teaching. Each has state-regulated licenses governing their practice. Therefore, every state is unique in its laws and regulations, but all will define the parameters of practice. A failure to adhere to the practice code can result in disciplinary action, including removal of one's certificate to practice.

The Washington State Code of Professional Practice illustrates this point. It is "unprofessional conduct" when an educator "flagrantly disregards or clearly abandons generally recognized professional standards in the course of any of the following professional practices: assessment, treatment, instruction, or supervision of students" (Acts of Unprofessional Conduct, 2006). In a nutshell, this regulation means that if a licensed teacher knows that a student has been improperly assessed or is not receiving appropriate services, ignoring the situation could be an act of unprofessional conduct. Although identifying a failure to adhere to professional standards resulting in an act of unprofessional conduct is not always straightforward, it is clear that professionals can legitimately disagree on appropriate treatment, instruction, or methods of supervision. Disagreeing with colleagues or making a professional decision that turns out to be wrong is not necessarily an act of unprofessional conduct. Rather, the practice code is concerned with those situations where a professional educator knows that an action he or she is taking or not taking is clearly a denial of what is expected by the profession, including what is legally required.

As well as the obligations under state practice codes, it is also important for educators to be familiar with the practice standards set forth by professional organizations, whether or not they are individually members, because they are generally considered best practice. Although standards adopted by professional organizations do not carry the same legal weight as legislatively enacted laws, regulations, or other administrative rulings and court decisions, they do set behavioral expectations.

Systems-Level Advocacy Opportunities

In addition to advocacy for a particular child, educational professionals can be effective advocates at a systems or policy level. Systems-level advocacy efforts can include working directly with state or federal legislators or agencies to implement best practice standards state- or district-wide. In addition, they can include advocating within the school environment by implementing school best practice programs. Although individual students benefit, the strategy is designed to change systems of service. Two examples of mental health wraparound services are given next.

There is some disagreement among researchers about the number of children with mental health problems in this country. Part of the difficulty in getting accurate numbers is that studies do not consistently use the same psychological criteria. However, it is generally accepted that approximately 20% have "at least mild kinds of functional lim-itations," according to a review in *School Psychology Review* (Espelage et al., 2008), while the Centers for Disease Control and Prevention esti-mates that it is approximately 3.2 of every 100,000 children ages 9 to 18. Almost all these children would benefit from treatment, but most require short-term interventions and some will "heal" with time. Only a small minority requires intensive and protracted services. Mild disorders can become chronic and prevent healthy development, including educa-tional development. Yet it is estimated by the United States Department of Health and Human Services that only approximately 50% of these children will get the treatment they need. Although the research contin-ues to document the value of evidence-based practices to ensure positive outcomes for children, such services are rarely provided.

Many reports have identified certain groups of children as being at higher risk of mental health disorders than other children. In a March 2006 needs assessment completed by the Washington State Department of Health, a prevalence of 20% or more of mental illness diagnoses in a population group was required to consider the group at risk. The groups that meet that criterion included

- children in foster care;
- children and youth with special health care needs;
- children in the juvenile justice system; and
- children of parents with mental illness.

In addition, on the basis of national reports and the lack of Washington state–specific data, the report identified additional vulnerable groups (Center for Health and Health Care in Schools, 2012):

- gay, lesbian, bisexual, transgender, questioning, and intersexed youth;
- children of incarcerated parents;
- homeless children;
- American Indian/Native American children; and
- refugee and immigrant children.

Numerous federal government studies have made recommenda-tions for improving the delivery of mental health services in the United States, including services for children. In addition to the more obvious issues of adequate access to health care, one of the common threads throughout these studies is the recommendation that partnerships should be promoted between community mental health providers and schools. Many argue that schools are the logical venue to deliver most mental health services for children. The rationale—and one commonly touted for a host of other interventions—is that most children are in public education settings, and for substantial parts of their day. Educators have intense interactions with students, often on a daily basis, and these experiences can be valuable in identifying children in trouble. Whether students are identified as needing special education services under IDEIA or accommodations under Section 504 of the Rehabilitation Act, professionals who advocate to improve access to mental health services for children through professional organizations as well as at an individual student level have an opportunity to address the gap in services that currently exists.

Practice Considerations

When an educator faces barriers to best practice implementation, he or she will address and hopefully resolve them with information and experience from a variety of sources. Legislatively enacted laws at both the state and federal level, regulations adopted by state or federal agencies, and court and hearing officer opinions all guide practice to the extent that the professionals are aware of these laws. In addition, professional organizations typically pass ethical codes or standards of conduct that describe the practice expectations of the members. Of course, the individual professional also relies on practical knowledge as well as personal ethical standards.

Given the limitations in the law and professional guidelines, how does an educator advocate for the child? How does he or she ethically accept decisions made on behalf of the child that are contrary to his or her professional judgment? In answer, consideration must be given to short-term action as well as long-term systems change efforts. First, when there is dissension among staff and/or with parents, it is likely that the child will not be immune from the conflict. Therefore, in the short term, the best interests of the child require that the conflict be resolved as amicably and rapidly as possible. Discussion with all relevant parties is the most appropriate first step, and the hope is that there will be resolution. If the conflict is among professionals, they must focus on the interests of the child and come to some agreement among themselves as to the appropriate recommendations. This may require assistance from professional associations, such as unions or internal dispute resolution services offered by the lead agency, to mediate the conflict. The reluctance of a professional to advocate for a child when it means taking a stand against colleagues is, undoubtedly, based on the real fear of job retaliation, or at the very least tense working relationships. In addition, some professionals may not be clear on where their responsibility lies—is it with the child, other professionals, or the state agency?

When the conflict is between professional recommendations and family choices, efforts to educate and inform the parents as to the reasoning behind the recommendations may be all that is necessary. Helpful approaches are to keep the disagreements as objective as possible and maintain respect for a variety of perspectives. When negotiation is not satisfactory, mediation is a potential option for resolving the dispute in a satisfactory manner.

Although the legal and administrative guidance on dispute resolution between professionals and families is not always clear, there is no question that educators have the duty to measure their decisions against their professional standards. At times, this may mean taking an unpopular position. As an advocate for children, the educator must focus on the child in the context of his of his or her family and how he or she can receive appropriate services. This may mean that a professional disagrees with another educational professional in concert with a family. It may mean the opposite, and a professional might find him- or herself advocating for a child's rights contrary to parental wishes

Readings and Resources[1]

FEDERAL LAWS FOR PHYSICAL AND DEVELOPMENTAL DISABILITIES, VOCATIONAL EDUCATION, SPECIAL HEALTH NEEDS

Acts of Unprofessional Conduct, W.A.C. § 181-87-060 (2006).

Americans With Disabilities Act of 1990, 42 U.S.C.A. §12101 *et seq.* (1993).

Brown, S. (1990, June/July). The Carl D. Perkins vocational education act of 1984: A review of the 1989 reauthorization. *FOCUS*, 1–5.

Brown, S. E. (1999*). Legal issues in serving students with special health care needs in the school setting.* Seattle: Washington Education Association and College of Education.

Brown, S. E. (2008, March). *Washington state debates the future of residential habilitation centers for people with developmental disabilities.* Seattle: University of Washington, Evans School of Public Affairs. Retrieved from http://hallway.evans.washington.edu/cases/washington-state-debates-future-residential-habilitation-centers-people-developmental-disabili

---

[1]Additional research readings and practitioner resources for this chapter can be found at http://www.apadivisions.org/division-16/publications/interdisciplinary-frameworks-supplement/index.aspx

Individuals With Disabilities Education Improvement Act, 20 U.S.C. § 1400 (2004).

No Child Left Behind (NCLB) Act of 2001, Pub. L. No. 107–110, § 115, Stat. 1425 (2002).

Rehabilitation Act of 1973, Pub. L. No. 93–112, 87 Stat. 355.

Valluzzi, J. L, Brown, S. E., & Dailey, B. (1997, October). Protecting the rights of children with special health care needs through the development of individual emergency response plans. *Infants and Young Children, 10,* 66–80. doi:10.1097/00001163-199710000-00010

NATIONAL STUDY OF CHILD ABUSE AND NEGLECT

Sedlak, A. J., Mettenburg, J., Basena, M., Petta, I., McPherson, K., Greene, A., & Li, S. (2010). *Fourth National Incidence Study of Child Abuse and Neglect (NIS–4): Report to Congress.* Washington, DC: U.S. Department of Health and Human Services, Administration for Children and Families. Retrieved from http://www.acf.hhs.gov/programs/oprc/resource/fourth-national-incidence-study-of-child-abuse-and-neglect-nis-4-report-to

EDUCATIONAL IMPLICATIONS AND APPLICATIONS OF SPECIAL EDUCATION LAW

Brown, P. A., & Brown, S. E. (2007). Accessible information technology in education: Addressing the "Separate but Equal" treatment of disabled individuals. In S. Danforth & S. Gabel (Eds.), *Vital questions facing disability studies in education* (pp. 253–270). New York, NY: Lang.

Brown, S. E. (2003, July/August). Advocacy for young children under IDEA: What does it mean for early childhood educators? *Infants and Young Children, 16,* 227–237. doi:10.1097/00001163-200307000-00005

Brown, S. E., & Cannon, K. (1993, January 28). Educational malpractice actions: A remedy for what ails our schools? *West Education Law Reporter, 78,* 643–657.

Brown, S. E., & Johnson, K. L. (1993, February–March). The impact of recent federal legislation on special education practice: developing linkages with outside agencies. Part I. *FOCUS,* 1–7.

Brown, S. E., & Johnson, K. L. (1993, April–May). The impact of recent federal legislation on special education practice: Developing linkages with outside agencies. Part II. *FOCUS,* 1–7.

Brown, S. E., & Johnson, K. L. (1994, June). Recent federal legislation and the role of vocational rehabilitation in the transition from school to community. *Rehabilitation Education, 8,* 67–78.

Brown, S. E., & Norse, S. (1993, November). *What every educator needs to know about Section 504: A Guide to Compliance.* Salem, OR: Oregon Department of Education.

Julnes, R. E., & Brown, S. E. (1992). *Leading cases in special education law: Vols. I–III. School Law Division.* Seattle: University of Washington.

Julnes, R. E., & Brown, S. E. (1993, July 15). Assistive technology and special education programs: Legal mandates and practice implications. *West Education Law Reporter, 82,* 737–748.

LAW AND CHILDREN'S RIGHTS

Bonney, L. G. & Moore, S. (1992). Advocacy: Noun, verb, adjective or profanity. *Impact, 5(2),* 7.

Brown, S. E. (2014). *Medical and legal collaborations in advocating for the right to health for children in developing countries.* Manuscript in preparation.

Brown, S. E., & Guralnick, M. J. (2012, October–December). International human rights to early intervention for infants and young children with disabilities: Tools for global advocacy. *Infants and Young Children, 25,* 270–85. doi:10.1097/IYC.0b013e318268fa49

Center for Health and Health Care in Schools. (2012). *Children's mental health needs, disparities, and school-based services: A fact sheet.* Retrieved from http://www.healthinschools.org/News-Room/Fact-Sheets/MentalHealth.aspx

Herbert, M. D., & Mould, J. W. (1992). The advocacy role in public child welfare. *Child Welfare, 70,* 114–130.

HELPING TRAUMATIZED CHILDREN

Cole, S. F., O'Brien, J. G., Gadd, M. G., Ristuccia, J., Wallace, D. L., & Gregory, M. (2009). *Helping traumatized children learn: Supportive school environments for children traumatized by family violence.* Boston: Massachusetts Advocates for Children.

Duffy, J., Wareham, S., & Walsh, M. (2004). Psychological consequences for high school students of having been sexually harassed. *Sex Roles, 50,* 811–821. doi:10.1023/B:SERS.0000029099.38912.28

Espelage, D. L., Aragon, S. R., Birkett, M., & Koenig, B. W. (2008). Homophobic teasing, psychological outcomes, and sexual orientation among high school students: What influence do mom and schools have? *School Psychology Review, 37,* 202–216.

Schulte, B. (April 3, 2008). For little children, grown-up labels as sexual harassers. *The Washington Post.* Retrieved from http://www.washingtonpost.com/wp-dyn/content/story/2008/04/02/ST2008040203589.html

Stoecklin, V. L. (1994) Advocating for young children with disabilities. *Quarterly Resource, 8,* 1–35.

Young, E. L., Heath, M. A., Ashbaker, B. Y., & Smith, B. (2008). Sexual harassment among students with educational disabilities. *Remedial and Special Education, 29,* 208–221. doi:10.1177/0741932507311635

Child Custody Litigation and School Personnel Fostering Positive School–Family Relationships

15

In this chapter, we cover legal issues related to high-conflict tactics, family law litigation, comprehensive family evaluation, custody litigation, school personnel, high-conflict parents, individualized education plans, independent education evaluation, and parental separation.

School personnel often come into contact with family law litigation that requires deft advocacy of the concerns that are raised by children and by parents who are in confliction with each other. The number of divorces has increased since the early 1960s, with approximately half of all marriages ending in divorce and an estimated 1.4 million divorces in the United States in 2001 (National Center for Health Statistics, 2001). The divorce rates reached a high around 1980 and then began to decrease slightly, finally leveling off between 1996 and 2009 (United States Census Bureau, 2011). Recent statistics reveal that approximately 3.6 out of

This chapter was contributed by G. Andrew H. Benjamin, a member of this book's advisory panel, and Kristen Bishop.

http://dx.doi.org/10.1037/14437-015
Interdisciplinary Frameworks for Schools: Best Professional Practices for Serving the Needs of All Students, by V. W. Berninger

1,000 people divorce annually (Centers for Disease Control and Prevention, 2013). However, current trends show a decrease in marriage and increase in cohabitation (Copen, Daniels, Vespa, & Mosher, 2012; United States Census Bureau, 2011). The National Survey of Family Growth revealed that 48% of women cohabited before marriage, and approximately 27% of these unions ended before marriage (Copen, Daniels, & Mosher, 2013). Furthermore, 19% of women in the 2006–2010 survey, up from 15% in 1995, became pregnant within the first year of cohabitation (Copen et al., 2013).

Custody litigation for most people involves feelings of failure, anger, betrayal, loss, and grief for the relationship they had envisioned. The consequences of the emotional and financial stress on family law litigants can be severe (Heatherington, Cox, & Cox, 1985). The worst harm resulting from high-conflict family law cases is the negative effect they have on children. In fact, in a meta-analysis of 35 articles from the 1990s about divorce and children's well-being, researchers found that children fared worse than in the previous decade in terms of psychological adjustment, social adjustment, self-concept, conduct, school achievement, father–child relations, and mother–child relations (Reifman, Villa, Amans, Rethinam, & Telesca, 2001). A substantial number of children involved in parental separations are placed at significant risk of emotional and behavioral disturbances due to the ongoing exposure to parental conflict. Such conflict can result in a lack of social support, financial insecurity, and disruptive changes in routines, schools, and residences.

Factors such as the age of the child at the time of parental separation, the child's gender, and the level of parental conflict may mediate the impact on the child. Research has shown that the age of the child at the time of parental separation can lead to different negative consequences, with children in elementary school experiencing increased rates of internalizing and externalizing symptoms, whereas older children's grades are directly affected (Lansford et al., 2006).

Children's disruptive behaviors can be a significant problem in the school environment. Higher rates of conduct disorder and oppositional defiant disorder were found among boys with attention-deficit/hyperactivity disorder (ADHD) experiencing parental separation than among those who were not experiencing parental separation, thereby suggesting that this population displays more disruptive behaviors (Heckel, Clarke, Barry, McCarthy, & Selikowitz, 2009). School personnel can provide substantial insight into children's academic performance and their behaviors in the school environment. Indeed, as mandatory reporters, what school personnel learned from their charges must result in reports about parental misconduct.

School personnel are confronted with the demands of separating parents, who are engaged in high-conflict tactics that often emerge during the worst of family law litigation. The issues in such cases are not resolved through negotiation or mediation but are litigated and often involve allegations about the health, safety, and welfare of the children. Parental separations involving higher levels of litigation have been shown to lead to increased conflict, dysfunction, and reduced child coping and adjustment, including declining academic performance and aggression (Bing, Nelson, & Wesolowski, 2009). Bainbridge (2001) identified several types of cases that resulted in family law litigation to support or change the residential placement of the children and/or the type of parental decision making (joint or separate) on the basis of (a) the use of school quality evidence, (b) evidence of parental fitness or misconduct related to decision making regarding schooling issues, (c) relocation to higher quality school systems, and (d) the lack of appropriate schooling opportunities for children with learning disabilities.

Disagreements between parents about child rearing, schooling, discipline, parental access, and visitation arrangements may interfere with maintaining positive parent–child attachments. Adolescents, especially those who experienced parental separation when they were young, may express decreased attachment to parents and perceive them as more overprotective and less caring (Woodward, Fergusson, & Belsky, 2000). Children may also be subjected to physical or sexual abuse, domestic violence, or the emotional and physical impairment of a parent after a divorce. Longitudinal studies have found that the negative impact of divorce conflict can persist into the adolescent and young adult years (Kelly, 2002; Kelly & Emery, 2003; Lansford, 2009; Long, Slater, Forehand, & Fauber, 1988). The legal, financial, and emotional impact of ongoing conflict between parents increases the risk of trauma to the children, who are frequently drawn into the middle of disputes even when parents have the best intentions of protecting them.

Parental adjustment problems can lead to poor outcomes because of grief, impaired conflict resolution skills exacerbated by mental illness or addiction problems, and economic hardship because of financial decline in the residential household of the child (Sbarra & Emery, 2005). Not surprisingly, parents with serious adjustment problems typically use some of the following high-conflict tactics (Benjamin & Gollan, 2003) against the other parent and child:

- threatening to mistreat or harm the child or other parent;
- physically or emotionally mistreating or harming the child or other parent;
- sexually mistreating or harming the child or other parent;
- trying to control the other parent through finances (e.g., withholding child support);
- trying to control or scare the child or the other parent through damaging property;

- invading the privacy or monitoring the whereabouts of the other parent;
- threatening or actually physically harming him- or herself in front of the child or the other parent;
- creating or using conflict in a way that creates distress for the child;
- withholding contact or access to the child;
- refusing to comply with the court order regarding adult or child issues;
- refusing to coparent with the other parent (e.g., will not talk with the other parent about parenting issues); and/or
- making negative comments about the other parent that makes the child confused, upset, or sad.

Those who litigate custody cases are distinguishable from those who separate more amicably because the former are much more likely to engage in such abusive use of conflict tactics. In addition, poor outcomes for the children are typically exacerbated when either party is "out-lawyered." Out-lawyering occurs when someone is not represented (the party is a *pro se* litigant) or the party has selected an ineffective lawyer who fails to respond appropriately to high-conflict tactics. The antipathy of the other party and the abusive use of conflict tactics will fail to be checked if one or both parties lack competent legal representation. This increases the negative impact of parental separations on the children, which in turn leads to increased involvement by school personnel.

Often the sequelae of parental conflict lead to child adjustment issues in school settings. The chapter reviews how such families and their lawyers attempt to enlist the assistance of school personnel and how school personnel can best serve the children during their involvement in the legal matters that encroach on the school environment.

Comprehensive Family Evaluation and School Personnel

Increasingly, the legal system has turned to alternative dispute resolution approaches, such as mediation and parenting coordination, to settle disputes involving children. These approaches are aimed at relieving the high emotional and financial costs of litigation for families and the burden of increased litigation for the courts. However, parties who are engaged in abusive use of conflict tactics do not mediate well or engage in other forms of therapeutic structuring such as parenting coordination (Brewster, Beck, Anderson, & Benjamin, 2011).

Comprehensive family evaluations can provide findings about the myriad allegations raised by the parties in acrimonious custody litigation. The conclusions are based on multiple sources of data, including information from school personnel, and often assist the various parties in finding resolution through settlement. Research has indicated that such evaluations may serve as a significant bargaining chip because the courts are likely to accept an expert's recommendations (Halon, 1991). In addition, an evaluation may function to mitigate risk factors associated with the negative results of an ongoing conflict by providing a process to be heard in a fair, objective manner. If the matter must be resolved before a judge, these corroborated findings provide rich psychological evidence that enables the judge to apply the best interests standard in a more informed manner.

High-conflict custody litigation can lead to a number of hotly contested allegations, and a typical battleground involves schooling issues. Most evaluations of child custody litigants include collateral information from school records and interviewing school personnel to determine school adjustment and quality. In addition, disrupting the healthy relationships of a child in the supportive setting of the existing school is considered carefully by custody evaluators when school placement becomes an issue between parents (DeClue, 2002). Changes to a child's school environment should only be recommended following the use of methodologically sound evaluation practices.

Yet, many custody evaluators fail to engage in methodologically sound practices (Emery, Otto, & O'Donohue, 2005). As a result of procedural errors widespread among custody evaluators, faulty clinical judgments are common because of the following factors (Garb, 1989, 2005): (a) the lack of consistent definitions regarding the characteristics of the subjects under observation, (b) the differing context in which subjects were observed, (c) the differing perspectives of the individual assessors, and (d) inherent errors in the various measurement tools used by evaluators. Clinical judgment is fallible and, by itself, does not suffice to constitute a reliable approach for conducting a comprehensive family evaluation. Further, reliance on protocols for measuring just parental capacity will collude with the adversarial process of the parties. Instead, a comprehensive family evaluation should result in a fair, respectful analysis of each concern raised by both parties, including concerns that involve schooling.

To address these common methodological errors, key components for reaching accurate results during a comprehensive family evaluation were delineated by qualitative research that was designed and implemented while supervising lawyers (guardian ad litem) and psychologists

(Benjamin, Gollan, & Ally, 2007). The evaluation protocol was refined through studies of videotaped interactions with parties and subsequent discussion with evaluation teams, supervising experts, and family court lawyers and judges, involving more than 900 separate court-ordered or self-referred parenting evaluations for families. Modifications to the protocol occurred whenever interactions of the evaluation process appeared to produce feelings of abandonment or surprise, expressions about the lack of fairness of the evaluation process, or where clinical judgment errors occurred. As a result of the adjustments made during the last 23 years of work, concrete and standardized procedures were developed for producing a comprehensive family evaluation in high-conflict family law cases (Benjamin & Gollan, 2003). The efficacy of those evaluations has been shown by the high rate of case settlement and by the fact that no ethics complaint has ever been filed, a rare phenomenon.

The results of the research led to the following recommendations for how to conduct comprehensive family evaluations, including how to interact with collateral reporters such as school personnel:

1. Specific referral questions should be delineated by the lawyers before the evaluation commences so that the lawyers and parties (each parent) focus on understanding party allegations in order to minimize the emotional and financial costs associated with mismanaged evaluations. Competent counselors at law should set the stage for fair evaluations to be conducted.

2. Unless one evaluator is able to conduct a broad-based, multiple-measure evaluation of both parties, the biased reporting of just one party may affect the reliability and validity of widely used psychometric tests, interview data, parent–child observational evidence, and collateral evidence (Weissman, 1991). With both parties participating fully during the process, bias is limited in order to arrive at objective conclusions that are confirmed by multiple measures.

3. Except for the structured meetings of the evaluation process, the parties and their attorneys must only use written correspondence to communicate with the evaluator. This approach reduces the likelihood of poor communication. Further, written records from these communications rarely cause confusion or a sense of being treated unfairly. It also creates a written record that lends itself to corroborating the findings of the evaluation.

4. Both parties receive a standardized agreement and disclosure statement about the evaluation process. Making the evaluation process transparent by describing each step of the process in advance eases the transition of the parties into the process. This step minimizes parties being surprised by any part of the process. The evaluation should not begin until a court order

directs both parties into the evaluation process, and the structure of the evaluation has been clarified sufficiently for both attorneys and the parties. Each phase of the evaluation does not end until both parties have engaged in a parallel process so that the data from each phase are assimilated similarly. The greater the evaluator's effort to behave objectively and with fairness, the more likely it is that the results of the evaluation will lead to a settlement rather than to a trial.

5. In advance of the clinical interviews of each party, data are collected about the concerns of the parties, each parent's routine with the children, and demographic and psychosocial history. This generates a standardized collection of data to use to assess the range of allegations from the beginning of the process. These data are reviewed again during the clinical interview of each party for clarity and consistency. By delineating the allegations at the beginning of the evaluation and by providing repeated opportunities to clarify each allegation, the language of the parties can be used to create an ideographic narrative that represents the characteristics of the parties operationally. Parties are more likely to feel heard if their voices are quoted accurately. Using a standardized questionnaire to collect these data promotes a comprehensive preview process that identifies details that will prompt additional investigation throughout the remainder of the evaluation process.

6. Structured interviews and standardized psychological testing of the parties should occur so that errors of clinical judgment are less likely to occur (Emery et al., 2005). Data from the interviews help to ascertain contributing factors associated with functional aspects of parental capacity and behaviors, the relative stability of both households, and the developmental and attachment needs of each child. The evaluator should be expected to build the evaluation report on the day of the interview so that the narrative details and nuances of the party's behavior can be accurately recorded to further minimize clinical judgment errors. Such errors are more likely to occur with overreliance on memory, confirmatory or hindsight bias, and overreliance on unique data (Garb, 1989, 2005). Subsequently sending each party a copy of their own psychosocial section and allegation section about the other party to make additions provides a further check for accuracy of the interview data. This part of the process increases transparency and models treating the parties fairly. The final report incorporates any additions the parties have made.

7. Observations of parent–child interactions should be conducted in a standardized manner in the clinical office to reduce error

variance from viewing the child(ren)–parent interactions in different settings. A structured process that is conducted similarly on two separate occasions permits comparisons of parenting strengths and deficits, attachment and bonding with the child, and parental judgment. After the observation, if the parent being evaluated suggests that the parent–child observation was compromised by any factor, the evaluator clarifies how the observation was compromised, and in light of those facts, conducts separate, second observations. This also serves the interest of fairness.

8. By the end of the parent–child observation phase of the evaluation, data from hypotheses generated to that point are formed into preliminary findings about the psychological evidence. The evidence is organized under the legal factors used by the judges of the jurisdiction to determine the best interest of the children. The discussion section focuses on the consistency of the data across multiple collection points. It notes discrepancies and limitations of the data (e.g., problems with the reliability or validity of the psychometric testing, which is used sparingly and only for hypothesis generation because of the validity and reliability limitations of psychological test data for this population). Allegations that remain uncorroborated are considered with great care during the initial review of the legal documentation that has amassed before the evaluation and that includes past professional evaluation or treatment notes of the parties or their children.

9. Writing the preliminary report before reading any of the collateral documentation or talking with collateral reporters lessens the likelihood that the evaluator's credibility will be impugned. None of that evidence is reviewed or incorporated into the report until the evaluator has written the preliminary report. Basing impressions on the direct interactions with the parties and the children powerfully negates any inference that the collateral evidence unduly influenced the evaluator and affected the independence of the evaluation. It also provides an opportunity to anticipate collateral evidence that may lead to the rejection of hypotheses. When the collateral evidence fails to corroborate the hypotheses, an inquiry must occur as to why disparate evidence exists. The report addresses disparate evidence directly. Any discrepancies may be the result of limitations in the manner of collecting the data (e.g., the credibility of the collateral reporter because of his or her limited objectives or experience) or in the interpretation of the data (e.g., evaluator bias).

By the time that collateral documentation is reviewed, the parties have provided declarations or affidavits of first-hand nonprofessional witnesses who witnessed specific instances of poor parenting or harmful adult activity. Each jurisdiction has a declaration or affidavit form that subjects the person to the laws of perjury if facts alleged in the form lack veracity. Such a process helps prevent nonprofessionals from changing the stories as the evaluation process unfolds and prevents the parties from exerting pressure for support.

Professional collateral reporters, such as school personnel, who report their firsthand observations through this process, provide rich details about what they have observed. For instance, acting on legally sufficient releases, sometimes a parent with legal authority will prevent a stepparent or a recent significant other from attending parent meetings. Or conflict emerges when a parent with temporary visitation volunteers to participate in school-sanctioned activities, the hours of which are not noted with the court order. In both examples, the parental interaction with the school personnel, often in front of their child, reveals important evidence about judgment, insight, and affect regulation. Teachers usually make excellent collaterals. They also are less likely to change their reports about the observations at cross-examination.

On the day each collateral interview is completed, the evaluator forwards a written summary of the interview for review. In many cases, issues about schooling are addressed by the evaluation, and school personnel should insist that any of the evidence they have provided be reviewed before the evidence is incorporated into the evaluation report. Such insistence will lead many evaluators who do not follow this aspect of the protocol to include school personnel review of any summary of statements or school data that are used by the evaluator in the final evaluation report. Such a review deters a party from complaining later that the evaluator misrepresented or failed to insert a detail that allegedly might have affected the outcome of the evaluation. Not only does this approach help to ensure that both parties will believe that they were fairly and thoroughly evaluated but it also produces a contemporaneous record of the collateral reporter's satisfaction with the evaluator's treatment.

10. At separate closing interviews with the parties, the evaluator describes each fact that led to the support of a finding about a particular allegation. If a party disagrees with the finding, the evaluator gently challenges any of the inconsistencies or discrepancies

that arise during the party's explanations. This type of Socratic questioning is commonly used in empirically supported psychotherapy (e.g., cognitive behavior therapy), and similar procedures are effective in eliciting information in this therapeutic jurisprudential setting (American Psychological Association, 2006). This step of the evaluation process appears to lessen the anger of the parties and may be integral in diminishing their desire to litigate. It provides them an in vivo opportunity to challenge the evaluator and the evaluator's findings. After this step, the parties usually believe that they have had a full and fair opportunity to dispute any evidence that emerged from the evaluation process.

Finally, throughout the evaluation and until the completion of the final report, the evaluator remains skeptical about the hypotheses that are generated during the evaluation process so that evaluator bias is tested. The report includes (a) allegations that lack independent corroborating evidence, (b) hypotheses that have failed to be corroborated by at least two independent measures, and (c) statements made earlier by the parties about who would provide first-hand contemporaneous evidence concerning an alleged incident that are not substantiated by the declarations from the nonprofessionals, later collateral documentation, or interviews.

Instead of using diagnostic labels, the evaluator delineates adult behaviors or parenting behaviors that might affect current and future parenting competency. Such descriptive examples of behavior help the lawyers understand the complexities of the case. If the data corroborate allegations about impaired parenting skills, the report provides recommendations for protecting a child from harmful parental involvement. Given the findings of the evaluation, the final evaluation report should include recommendations about primary residential placement of the children, access schedule, allocation of the decision-making authority, future dispute-resolution processes for resolving later disagreements, and psychotherapy or skill-building approaches that the parents and children should pursue. High-conflict cases often will require follow-up with therapy for victimization, substance abuse and other addictions, domestic violence, and parenting skills training.

As soon as the final report is completed, the evaluator meets with both lawyers in the case. In the meeting, the methodology of the evaluation is described, all concerns that were evaluated are addressed, and the lawyers' questions are answered. The final report is given out at that point so that the lawyers can continue the process of arriving at an equitable settlement in light of the findings from the psychological evidence.

Special Education Services, School Personnel, and High-Conflict Parents

In school systems there is a large population of children whose parents request special education services for their children. A 2011 report by the National Center of Education Statistics revealed that in the 2008–2009 school year 6.5 million children, representing 13% of the public school population, received special education services (Aud et al., 2011). These services were provided for children deemed eligible under the Individuals With Disabilities Education Improvement Act (IDEIA, 2004) or Section 504 of the Rehabilitation Act (1973).

A recent large-scale study revealed a 13.1% prevalence rate for *Diagnostic and Statistical Manual of Mental Disorders* (4th ed.) diagnoses among children ages 8 through 15 (Merikangas et al., 2010). Rising prevalence rates and diminution of funding for services present a challenge for families and professionals alike. The rapidly increasing need for educational services leaves many parents looking for strategies for how best to advocate for their child to receive timely and appropriate services (such an advocacy resource is available for parents if they obtain the TeamChild, 2008, Education Advocacy Manual). And yet, high-conflict family law litigants may not advocate effectively for their children and, in fact, engage in behaviors that affect their children and school personnel during the evaluation and service provisions.

To determine eligibility for special education services, an evaluation of the child is required. The initial evaluations are conducted for the purpose of determining whether the child has a disability and to ascertain her or his educational needs. The content of these evaluations is governed by Section 504 or IDEIA and state requirements. Beyond determining eligibility, one of the goals of the school district's evaluation is to gain information about a child's academic functioning for later use in the creation of an individualized education plan (IEP). It is the IEP that ultimately guides the special education services a child receives. The IEP team consists of individuals such as the parents, mainstream teacher, special education teacher, school psychologist, principal, the child when appropriate, and "other individuals who have knowledge or special expertise regarding the child, including related services personnel as appropriate" (IDEIA, 2004, p. 64). In constructing the IEP, this team considers "(i) the strengths of the child, (ii) the concerns of the parents for enhancing the education of their child, (iii) the results of the initial evaluation or most recent evaluation of the child, and (iv) the academic, developmental, and functional needs of the child" (IDEIA, 2004, p. 65–66).

Different rights and services are delivered under Section 504 as opposed to IDEIA. Whereas Section 504 provides broader protections for any individual with a disability and access to accommodations, IDEIA outlines specific eligibility criteria and special education services. A child with a disability can be afforded protection under Section 504 and receive services governed by IDEIA. However, it is possible for a child to receive protection and accommodations under Section 504, even if not eligible for special education services under IDEIA (Breiger, Bishop, & Benjamin, 2014).

Personal information that is revealed about a family may complicate the assessment process. For example, if a child is receiving an evaluation because he or she is struggling in school with inattention, incomplete schoolwork, and impulse control problems, the evaluator may be conducting the assessment with a hypothesis of ADHD in mind. However, if the evaluation evidence suggests that extensive conflict in the home has recently occurred and the parents are discussing separation, this may shed a different light on the child's behavior. If the child has a diagnosis that is contributing to his academic challenges, he or she may qualify for special education services, but not if the situational stress of the child responding to his or her family conflict is responsible for the symptoms. School personnel often have trouble conveying such results to parents whose child is struggling in this manner. Although the foremost objective of school personnel involved in such cases is to maintain objectivity for both parents throughout all interactions by engaging in respectful, concrete communication, one or both parents in such a high-conflict family may challenge the school's decision if the child is denied eligibility for special education services.

Parents can request an independent educational evaluation (IEE) at the district's expense by a qualified person who is not an employee of the district (IDEIA, 34 CFR § 300.502 (a)(3)(i)). The parents can request an IEE if concerns arise about the school's decision or the results of the district's evaluation, and such a request may be necessary for the district to fully involve the parents in the planning and implementation of services (Schrank, Miller, Caterino, & Desrochers, 2006). Although districts typically have a list of the evaluators that can perform IEEs (IDEIA, 34 CFR § 300.502 (a)(2)), evaluations can be done by someone who is not on the district's list (IDEIA, 34 CFR § 300.502 (a)(3)(i)). Unless the school district objects to the IEE by asking for a due process hearing that must occur under the law without unnecessary delay, the school district must pay for an independent evaluation (IDEIA, 34 CFR § 300.502 (b)(2)). At the due process hearing, if the hearing officer determines that the district's evaluation is appropriate, the family still has a right to an independent evaluation at the parents' expense (IDEIA, 34 CFR § 300.502 (b)(3)). Parents are entitled to one IEE at public expense each time the district conducts an evaluation with which the parents disagree (IDEIA, 34 CFR § 300.502 (b)(5)).

School Personnel Response to Domestic Violence Judicial Restrictions on a Parent

Cases in which a restraining order has been issued or a parent has been restricted to only supervised visitation also require the attention of school personnel. If a parent informs the school that a restraining order has been issued or that the other parent can see the child only under supervised conditions, the school should obtain a copy of the court order for its administration's records and the records of the child's teacher. Also, a picture of the restrained parent should be requested. For all cases of restricting contact and access to a student or a student's records, school personnel should not publish in the school directory any address or phone numbers of the protected parent and child.

Most often, the order restrains the parent from contact and access to the child specifically, and the school setting in general. Judges tend not to list the school by name or address. Nevertheless, the parent restrained under the order may come to the school. Police should be notified immediately and given a copy of the restraining order or the order restricting the parent to only "supervised visitation" so that the offending parent will not be left at large, and the offense will be prosecuted. The offending parent will be processed by the courts. This approach keeps the focus on the judicial process rather than on any interactions with school personnel.

Other cases restrict decision-making authority and the release of school records to another parent. Once a parent provides a court order identifying such restrictions, school personnel should not release any records to the restricted parent. Copies of the order should be placed in the student's record and be provided to the teacher. School personnel may need to enforce the court order in a manner that does not trigger the wrath of the restricted parent. Showing the order that is on file and talking about school personnel needing to obey the law often defuses any escalation.

Conclusion

In recent decades, children have faced parental separations quite frequently. Nearly half of all first marriages end in divorce. Furthermore, new statistics have shown a trend toward cohabitation and increasing pregnancy rates among unmarried couples. These trends have led to an unprecedented number of children having to experience a parental separation and the potential negative emotional, behavioral, and academic consequences.

Professionals conducting comprehensive family evaluations are in a position to help mitigate these consequences through methodologically sound evaluation practices that are built on the use of thorough, transparent, and parallel process. These practices reduce evaluator bias and clinical judgment errors when providing evaluation results and recommendations. This is a crucial element given that the courts place significant weight on these comprehensive family evaluations in determining what is in the best interest of the child.

An important component of these evaluations is the collateral interviews conducted with pivotal people who can provide insight into the child's functioning. School personnel working with the child on a daily basis are invaluable resources when learning about the child's behavior, academic functioning, any special education services provided, and interactions with teachers and peers.

Although school personnel are often interviewed and contribute to evaluation findings, they also receive evaluation results. These results may present challenges, such as restricting a parent's access to the child or records, and may place the school personnel in a position to uphold the court order. School personnel are crucial in the lives of the children they educate, and as such they are key players in helping to maintain children's academic and school functioning.

Readings and Resources[1]

American Psychological Association. (Producer). (2006). *Child custody* [DVD]. Washington, DC: Producer. Available from http://www.apa.org/pubs/videos/4310753.aspx. Closing interviews in high conflict family law evaluations with G. A. H. Benjamin.

Aud, S., Hussar, W., Kena, G., Bianco, K., Frohlich, L., Kemp, J., & Tahan, K. (2011). *The condition of education 2011* (NCES 2011-033). Washington, DC: U.S. Department of Education, National Center for Education Statistics.

Bainbridge, W. L. (2001). Effectively using school evaluation in a child custody case. *American School Board Journal*. Retrieved from http://schoolmatch.com/articles/ASBOCT01.htm

Benjamin, G. A. H., & Gollan, J. (2003). *Family evaluation in custody litigation: Reducing risks of ethical and malpractice infractions*. Washington, DC: American Psychological Association.

[1]Additional research readings and practitioner resources for this chapter can be found at http://www.apadivisions.org/division-16/publications/interdisciplinary-frameworks-supplement/index.aspx

Benjamin, G. A. H., Gollan, J., & Ally, G. A. (2007). Family evaluation in custody litigation: Reducing risks of ethical infractions and malpractice. *Journal of Forensic Psychology Practice, 7,* 101–111. doi:10.1300/J158v07n03_07

Bing, N. M., Nelson, W. M., & Wesolowski, K. L. (2009). Comparing the effects of amount of conflict on children's adjustment following parental divorce. *Journal of Divorce and Remarriage, 50,* 159–171. doi:10.1080/10502550902717699

Breiger, D., Bishop, K., & Benjamin, G. A. H. (2014). *Educational evaluations of children with special needs: Clinical and forensic considerations.* Washington, DC: American Psychological Association.

Brewster, K. O., Beck, C. J. A., Anderson, E. R., & Benjamin, G. A. H. (2011). Evaluating parenting coordination programs: Encouraging results from pilot testing a research methodology. *Journal of Child Custody, 8,* 247–267. doi:10.1080/15379418.2011.620926

Centers for Disease Control and Prevention. (2013). *National marriage and divorce rate trends. Provisional number of divorces and annulments and rate: United States, 2000–2011.* Retrieved from Centers for Disease Control and Prevention website: http://www.cdc.gov/nchs/nvss/marriage_divorce_tables.htm

Copen, C. E., Daniels, K., & Mosher, W. D. (2013). First premarital cohabitation in the United States: 2006–2010 national survey of family growth. *National Health Statistics Reports, 64,* 1–16.

Copen, C. E., Daniels, K., Vespa, J., & Mosher, W. D. (2012). First marriages in the United States: Data from the 2006–2010 national survey of family growth. *National Health Statistics Reports, 49,* 1–22.

DeClue, G. (2002). The best interests of the village children. *Journal of Psychiatry & Law, 30,* 355–390.

Emery, R. E., Otto, R. K., & O'Donohue, W. T. (2005). A critical assessment of child custody evaluations: Limited science and a flawed system. *Psychological Science in the Public Interest, 6,* 1–29. doi:10.1111/j.1529-1006.2005.00020.x

Garb, H. N. (1989). Clinical judgment, clinical training, and professional experience. *Psychological Bulletin, 105,* 387–396. doi:10.1037/0033-2909.105.3.387

Garb, H. N. (2005). Clinical judgment and decision making. *Annual Review of Clinical Psychology, 1,* 67–89. doi:10.1146/annurev.clinpsy.1.102803.143810

Halon, A. (1991). The comprehensive child custody evaluation. *American Journal of Forensic Psychology, 8*(3), 19–46.

Heckel, D. L., Clarke, A. R., Barry, R. J., McCarthy, R., & Selikowitz, M. (2009). The relationship between divorce and children with AD/HD of difference subtypes and comorbidity: Results from a clinically referred sample. *Journal of Divorce and Remarriage, 50,* 427–443. doi:10.1080/10502550902766324

Hetherington, M. E., Cox, M., & Cox, R. (1985). Long-term effects of divorce and remarriage on the adjustment of children. *Journal of the American Academy of Child Psychiatry, 24*, 518–530. doi:10.1016/S0002-7138(09)60052-2

Individuals With Disabilities Education Act, 20 U.S.C. § 1400 (2004).

Kelly, J. B. (2002). Psychological and legal interventions for parents and children in custody and access disputes: Current research and practice. *Virginia Journal of Social Policy & the Law, 10*, 129–163.

Kelly, J. B., & Emery, R. E. (2003). Children's adjustment following divorce: Risk and resilience perspectives. *Family Relations, 52*, 352–336. doi:10.1111/j.1741-3729.2003.00352.x

Lansford, J. E. (2009). Parental divorce and children's adjustment. *Perspectives on Psychological Science, 4*, 140–152.

Lansford, J. E., Malone, P. S., Castellino, D. R., Dodge, K. A., Pettit, G. S., & Bates, J. E. (2006). Trajectories of internalizing, externalizing, and grades for children who have and have not experienced their parents' divorce or separation. *Journal of Family Psychology, 20*, 292–301. doi:10.1037/0893-3200.20.2.292

Long, N., Slater, E., Forehand, R., & Fauber, R. (1988). Continued high or reduced inter-parental conflict following divorce: Relation to young adolescent adjustment. *Journal of Consulting and Clinical Psychology, 56*, 467–469.

Merikangas, K. R., He, J. P., Brody, D., Fisher, P. W., Bourdon, K., & Koretz, D. S. (2010). Prevalence and treatment of mental disorders among U.S. children in the 2001–2004 NHANES. *Pediatrics, 125*, 75–81. doi:10.1542/peds.2008-2598

Rehabilitation Act of 1973, Pub. L. No. 93–112, 87 Stat. 355.

Reifman, A., Villa, L. C., Amans, J. A., Rethinam, V., & Telesca, T. Y. (2001). Children of divorce in the 1990s: A meta-analysis. *Journal of Divorce & Remarriage, 36*, 27–36. doi:10.1300/J087v36n01_02

Sbarra, D., & Emery, R. (2005). Co-parenting, conflict, non-acceptance, and depression among divorced adults: Results from a 12-year follow-up study of child custody mediation using multiple imputation. *American Journal of Orthopsychiatry, 75*, 63–75. doi:10.1037/0002-9432.75.1.63

Schrank, F. A., Miller, J. A., Caterino, L. C., & Desrochers, J. (2006). American academy of school psychology survey on the independent educational evaluation for a specific learning disability: Results and discussion. *Psychology in the Schools, 43*, 771–780. doi:10.1002/pits.20187

TeamChild. (2008). *Make a difference in a child's life: A manual for helping children and youth get what they need in school.* Seattle, WA: Author. Retrieved from http://www.teamchild.org/index.php/education/manual/

United States Census Bureau. (2011, May). *Number, timing, and duration of marriages and divorces: 2009.* Retrieved from http://www.census.gov/prod/2011pubs/p70-125.pdf

Weissman, H. N. (1991). Child custody evaluations: Fair and unfair practices. *Behavioral Science and the Law, 9*, 469–476. doi:10.1002/bsl.2370090409

Woodward, L., Fergusson, D. M., & Belsky, J. (2000). Timing of parental separation and attachment to parents in adolescence: Results of a prospective study from birth to age 16. *Journal of Marriage and the Family, 62*, 162–174. doi:10.1111/j.1741-3737.2000.00162.x

PROFESSIONAL STANDARDS FOR CHILD CUSTODY EVALUATIONS, ETHICS, AND ETHICS AND THE LAW

American Psychological Association. (2010). *Ethical principles of psychologists and code of conduct (2002. Amended June 1, 2010)*. Washington, DC: Author. Retrieved from http://www.apa.org/ethics/code/principles.pdf.

Jacob, S., Decker, D., & Hartshorne, T. (2010). *Ethics and law for school psychologists* (6th ed.). Hoboken, NJ: Wiley.

Liang, T., Davis, A., Arnold, T. H., & Benjamin, A. (2012). *Ethics for psychologists: A casebook approach*. Thousand Oaks, CA: Sage.

Michaels, M. H. (2006). Ethical considerations in writing psychological assessment reports. *Journal of Clinical Psychology, 62*, 47–58. doi:10.1002/jclp.20199

Becoming a Critical Consumer of Interdisciplinary Research for Translating Research Into Practice

I n an era emphasizing evidence-based educational practice, educational professionals need to become critical consumers of interdisciplinary research. The following are guidelines for practitioners for becoming critical consumers of educationally relevant research.

Kinds of Validity

INTERNAL VALIDITY

Internal validity is whether the conclusions about research questions are warranted on the basis of the research design and methods used. To begin with, a critical consumer of research should carefully read an article to find out (a) what the question was, (b) what the methods and research design were, and (c) whether the methods and research design permitted the conclusions drawn about the question asked. For example, if the design used descriptive or correlational methods, were any conclusions drawn about causal relationships? If so, internal validity is lacking because conclusions about causality cannot be drawn from descriptive or correlational studies.

Currently, many research groups conducting meta-analyses of research make claims about what multiple research studies have found about a variety of educational issues. Although some of the meta-analyses are carefully conducted and provide valuable overviews of research evidence on specific issues, other meta-analyses are based on comparisons of studies that did not address the same research question(s) or did not use comparable research designs or study participants who were comparable in developmental level or other characteristics. Consumers of research should be cautious in accepting the conclusions of meta-analyses without reading the research articles on which they were based to determine whether comparable questions were addressed or whether there were important differences in research methods, research design, or research participants.

One alternative to meta-analyses is evidence-based reviews of programmatic lines of research in which a series of studies addresses questions that arise from and extend prior studies. Research findings for the same research question with comparable methods and populations (ages and characteristics) are synthesized to summarize which research findings are reliable and provide converging evidence across studies. Those findings should be organized in an educationally relevant conceptual framework for translating the research into practice. For example, rarely are desired learning outcomes achieved by teaching only a single skill in isolation or using only one method or approach. Educational practice should be informed by evidence-based conceptual frameworks that organize knowledge from research addressing multiple but related and/or contrasting questions coherently.

EXTERNAL VALIDITY

External validity is whether the results of a study can be generalized beyond the sample studied. For example, if kindergarteners or first graders were studied, the results cannot be generalized to upper elementary students in Grades 4 and above. Policy may sometimes be based on research evidence without paying attention to the age or other characteristics of the participants in the research. That is why an important question to ask for any instructional research findings is, what works for whom? To answer this question, whether using group or single-subject designs, scientist–practitioners have to take into account characteristics of participants in translating research into practice. The setting in which a research study was conducted is also relevant to generalizing findings.

Kinds of Research Designs

DESCRIPTIVE

Descriptive research designs provide valuable information about normal variation or characteristics of a well-defined group. Both tests and other kinds of assessment tools (e.g., scales with quantitative ratings, oral or written protocols or interviews that are coded according to a conceptual scheme with qualitative categories, and behavioral ratings and observations) are appropriate for addressing research questions and drawing conclusions relevant to describing results. An example of scientific contributions of descriptive research is Darwin's descriptions of normal variation in nature (biological diversity).

Linguists have learned a lot about the different levels of language from descriptive research. However, descriptive measures alone, although necessary for some research questions, do not support conclusions about causality. Darwin's descriptive studies provided evidence for the concept of normal variation but not for the biochemical mechanisms underlying human genetics, such as messenger RNA transcription and translation (see Chapter 7). Descriptive methods are also useful for defining the characteristics of participants in a research study, which are relevant to external validity. Descriptive methods are also sometimes used in longitudinal studies to identify how one or more variables of interest may change across development within the same individuals.

CORRELATIONAL

Correlational research designs provide useful information about the functional relationship(s) among two or more variables. *Bivariate correlations*, show the change in one variable when a second variable changes (across time or across individuals). *Multivariate correlations*, represent how each variable changes as a function of variation (across time or individuals) of multiple other variables. Although correlational designs do not permit conclusions about causality, they have made scientific contributions. For example, observations of correlations between the contents of spilled test tubes and death of bacteria led to the programmatic research yielding antibiotics that revolutionized medical treatment for infectious diseases. Numerous studies have validated the use of educational and psychological tests on the basis of correlations between tests hypothesized to measure the same or different constructs, or between tests predicted to be diagnostic of outcomes and tests of those educational outcomes. Also, statistical techniques have been developed to evaluate alternative conceptual models underlying the correlations among multiple variables and/or among multiple factors, each based on multiple measures to improve the reliability of measurement. Sometimes correlational and statistical modeling methods are used in longitudinal designs to show how the relationships between or among variables change over time.

EXPERIMENTAL

In *experimental research designs*, variables are manipulated in systematic ways so that conclusions can be drawn between the manipulated (independent) variable and outcome (dependent) variable. In group designs, participants are randomly assigned to the manipulated conditions so that systematic bias is unlikely operating that could lead to false conclusions about the effects of what was manipulated and is thought to have caused the observed outcome. In some designs, different groups of participants receive different manipulations, and thus conclusions about cause and effect pertain to the groups in the design, not to individuals within each group. In other designs the same participant receives all the manipulations, and thus conclusions about cause and effect pertain to the different manipulations each participant receives. In some designs multiple independent variables are systematically manipulated and/or multiple outcome variables are assessed. Interactions between them can be evaluated that place qualifications on the cause and effect relationships. For example, the effect may only be observed in primary grade children, but not adolescents.

SINGLE-SUBJECT

Single-subject research designs can be used to infer cause and effect relationships over time within the same individual: The treatment is introduced in several sessions to get a baseline, withdrawn to see the effect on the baseline without it, and then reintroduced to see the effect of using it again. Two treatments can be compared in the same individual by alternating Treatment 1 and Treatment 2 and observing the effect of each. Experimental designs and single-subject designs can be useful in programmatic lines of systematic research to yield educationally relevant knowledge of how students with defined characteristics learn and effective instructional practices for teaching them or improving their behavior or mental health.

DESIGN EXPERIMENT

Because effective learning and instruction in the classroom may be complex, depending on how multiple variables are packaged together to bring about the desired educational outcome, the relevant question may not be what causes what but rather what variables have to be in place to achieve the effect. *Design experiments* address that question: How can a teacher integrate multiple variables to cause a desired, well-specified learning outcome?

Evaluating Research Studies

Educational professionals should read research articles with a critical mindset to find the answers to five sets of questions related to the purpose, design, method, interpretation of results, and application of the research results.

PURPOSE

What is the purpose of this research? Why is it being conducted, and how does it relate to prior research? What specific question or questions are being asked in the study?

DESIGN

What kind of research design is being used—descriptive, correlational, experimental, or mixed? Is the research design appropriate for the research questions addressed?

METHOD

What are the methods, and are they appropriate for the questions asked and the design used?

RESULTS

What are the findings? Is the interpretation of the findings justified based on the research design and methods?

APPLICATION OF RESULTS

To whom can the results be generalized? How do the findings advance knowledge? Why are the findings important? How might they be translated in educational practice in assessment or instruction? Or are the findings more appropriately used to advance knowledge in basic science?

Honor Role Model List Representing Exemplary Practices by Members of Different Professions on Interdisciplinary Teams in Schools

1. Ted Alper
2. Alnita Dunn
3. Jim Van Velzer
4. Tina L. Cheng
5. Barry Solomon
6. Devin McLane
7. Greg Baker
8. Sharon Missiasen
9. Julie Ryan
10. Jeanne Patton
11. Jennifer Katahira
12. Robert Famiano
13. Jane Coolidge
14. Sylvia Valdés-Fernández
15. Zenia Lemos Horning

To be continued—Please honor the Honor Role Models where you work and send nominations to APA Division 16.

Index

A

ABC Movement Battery, 2nd ed., 201
Absence seizures, 261
Academic Pediatric Association, 29
Accountability
    with interdisciplinary teams and teamwork,
        39–41
    and preservice professional development,
        12–13
    of teachers, 144
Acculturation, 294–295
Acetyls (chemical markers), 181
Acquired central nervous system injuries,
    274–276
Adding and addition skills (mathematics), 71,
    73, 74, 82, 88–89, 93–95, 97, 110, 117,
    120–121, 125, 134–135
ADHD. *See* Attention–deficit/hyperactivity
    disorder
ADHD Rating Scale–IV, 208
Administrators, educational, 7, 11, 325
Adolescent instruction and assessment, 137–168
    behavioral and learning skills in, 151–153
    case examples of, 156–166
    in college-credit courses, 150
    and community service, 151
    differentiated instruction, 155–156
    and diversity of student body, 139–140,
        162–166
    and genetic vulnerabilities, 140–141
    in language arts, 145–146

    in math, 138, 146–150
    for multiple transitions during school day,
        138–139
    in parenting practices, 151
    and preparing students for careers, 143–145
    and puberty, 141–143
    in science, 150
    in social studies and humanities, 150
    target skills for, 137–138, 151–153
    technology in, 154–155
Advocacy, educational. *See* Educational advocacy
AEDs (antiepileptic drugs), 278
Aesop, 299
African Americans, 155, 292
After-school activities, 142
Alcohol abuse, 281. *See also* Substance use
Alice's Adventures in Wonderland (Lewis Caroll), 58
Alleles, 172, 173, 175, 177, 180
Alper, Ted, 20–21, 46, 365
American Academy of Pediatrics, 272
American Congress of Obstetricians and
    Gynecologists, 272
American Educational Research Association, 293
American Indian Head Start Quality Improve-
    ment Center, 132
American Psychiatric Association, 5, 272
American Psychological Association, vii
American Psychological Association Division
    16 (School Psychology), viii, 6, 301
American Speech–Language–Hearing
    Association, 203

Amicus curiae, 321–322
Anagrams, 99, 118
Anencephaly, 259
Angelman syndrome, 251, 253
Angelou, Maya, 299
Anthropology, 150
Anticipation (phenotype expression), 177
Antiepileptic drugs (AEDs), 278
Archaeology, 150
Arithmetic, 8. *See also* Mathematics
Art activities
    in adolescent instruction, 153
    in early childhood instruction, 106–107
    in middle childhood instruction, 127
Asperger's syndrome, 254
Assessment(s), 51–66
    adolescent. *See* Adolescent instruction and
        assessment
    for children with disabilities, 3–4
    communicating results of, 63–64
    in descriptive research designs, 361
    early childhood. *See* Early childhood instruction
        and assessment
    educational decision-making based on, 52–53
    and evidence-based instruction, 64
    examples of effective use of, 65–66
    guidelines for curriculum-based, 60–61
    individual student evaluation with, 56–60
    links between intervention and, 62
    middle childhood. *See* Middle childhood
        instruction and assessment
    multimodal, 19–21
    of response to instruction, 4
    and response-to-intervention measures, 61–62
    school/curriculum evaluation with, 53–56
    teacher-designed classroom, 59
    testing vs., 52
    using multiple tools for, 4
Associations (cognitive representations), 189
Atonic seizures, 261
At-risk populations, 59, 103–104
Attention and executive functioning development.
        See also Self-regulation
    in adolescence, 151–152
    attention–deficit/hyperactivity disorder, 241–242
    biological bases, 171–196
    with brain disorders and health conditions,
        271–286
    with developmental disabilities, 177–220
    in early childhood, 104–105
    in middle childhood, 125–126
    with neurogenetic disorders, 249–270
    with specific learning disabilities, 221–248
Audiology, 18–19, 62, 199–200
Audio-recorded lectures, 129
Auditory impairment, 199–201, 214
Auditory processing, 187, 199–200. *See also* Aural
        language skills

Aural language skills
    Relationship to other academic skills, 4, 77–79,
        113–114, 125, 236
    Teaching and assessing in early childhood,
        70–71, 75–76, 83–84, 91, 98
    Teaching and assessing in middle childhood,
        113–114, 116
    Teaching and assessing students with develop-
        mental disabilities in, 202–205
    Teaching and assessing students with specific
        learning disabilities in, 226–229
    Understanding the biological bases, 171–196
Autism, 26, 178, 180, 210, 211, 227, 267,
        253–254
Autobiographical memory, 190
Automaticity (memory access), 60, 86–89, 97, 102,
        116, 125, 228, 234–236, 279
Autonomy, professional. *See* Professional autonomy
Autosomal recessive traits, 178
Autosomes, 172–173
Awareness, 22, 66, 73, 79, 82–83, 85, 91, 97, 99,
        103, 109, 115–116, 125, 131–132, 133, 185,
        191–192, 194–195, 204–205, 211–211, 229,
        238–239, 243, 253, 275, 315

B
Bacterial infections, 276
Bainbridge, W. L., 343
Baker, Greg, 32–33, 365
Base frame shift mutation, 178
Beck, Isabelle, 78, 80
Behavioral interventions
    in comprehensive K–12 models, 42
    in community–school partnerships, 29–31
    Team-Initiated Problem Solving (TIPS) program, 39
    three-tier model of, 23–29
    STRIVE/STP, 47
Behavioral observations, 209
Behavioral skills, 75–83, 104–107, 151–153
Behavior Assessment System for Children, 207
Behavior Rating Inventory of Executive Function,
        208
Belief systems, 190
Bellingham Public Schools, WA, 32–33
Benedict, Ruth Fulton, 299
Best professional practices
    in assessment, 49–168
    for early childhood curriculum and instruction, 75
    and educational advocacy, 333–334
    instruction and assessment–instruction links,
        49–168
    for interdisciplinary teams and teamwork, 18–21
    general principles of, 1–48
    for school districts, 55
The Better World Handbook (Ellis Jones), 298
Bilingualism, 156, 297
Bill, Willard, 293
Biological diversity, 240–241, 361

Bipolar disorder, 280
Bivariate correlations (research), 361
Boston Children's Hospital, 5, 311–317
Bountiful language interactions, 80
Brain, 182–195. *See also* Brain-related disorders;
    Neurogenetic disorders
    Brain primer, 183–196, 249–270
    Bridging brain and genetics, 182–184
Brain cancer, 276
Brain-related disorders, 271–282
Brain tumors, 276, 279
Branching diagnosis
    use in problem solving consultation, 20–22,
        240
    use in response to instruction (RTI), 90, 97, 102,
        124–125, 138, 151
Brown, Sharon, 319
Bryant, Brian, 6n1

C
Cancer, 276, 278–279
CAPTA (Child Abuse Prevention and Treatment
    Act), 326–329
Cardinal numbers, 82, 120
Career preparation, 12, 143–145, 213–214
Carnegie Foundation for the Advancement of
    Teaching, 12
Carroll, Lewis, 58
Cash, Johnny, 28
Centers for Disease Control and Prevention, 275,
    335
Central auditory processing deficits, 200, 204
Central nervous system injuries, 274–276
Cerebral palsy (CP), 273
CF (cystic fibrosis), 279–280
Chan, Jackie, 299
Cheng, Tina L., 29, 31, 365
Child Abuse Prevention and Treatment Act
    (CAPTA), 326–329
Child Behavior Rating Scales and Checklists and
    Clinical Workbooks, 208
Child Protective Services, 327–329
Chromosomal abnormalities, 176
Chromosome linkage studies, 179
Chromosomes, 172, 173, 175–176. *See also* Genetics
Chronic illness, 276–280
Chronic traumatic encephalopathy (CTE), 276
Classroom teachers. *See* Teachers
Class switching, 114, 139–140
Clinical Evaluation of Language Fundamentals
    (CELF), 202
Coach House after-school program, viii
Cogiphobia, 21
Cognition and memory systems
    assessment for identification of developmental
        and specific learning disabilities, 197–248
    multiple kinds of representations and operations,
        188–196

College-credit courses, 150
College education, 10, 143, 144
College entrance exams, 155
Colligan, Robert, 6n1
Common core standards
    developmental stepping-stones for helping
        adolescents achieve, 137–168
    developmental stepping-stones for helping early
        childhood students achieve, 69–110
    developmental stepping-stones for helping middle
        childhood students achieve, 111–116
    for academic subjects, 45
    for arts, 45
Common law duty, 323–325
Communication sciences, 18. *See also* Speech–
    language pathology specialists
Community resources, 291
Community service, 142, 151
Comparative genomic hybridization, 250
Complex tics, 263
Composing and compositions, 20, 66, 194, 228–229,
    234–236
    in adolescence, 138, 145, 147
    in early childhood, 72, 81, 86–87
    in middle childhood, 117, 125–126, 134
Comprehensive family evaluation, 344–350
Computer games, 128
Computerized testing, 56–57
Computer tools. *See* Technology
Concepts (cognitive representations), 189
Concrete operational thought, 142
Concussions, 274–275
Conduct disorder, 342
Conners Rating Scales, 208
Consciousness, 194–195
Co-occurring disorders, 210–211
Coolidge, Jane, 131–132, 365
Co-op career preparation programs, 12, 144–145
Coprolalia, 263
Correlation research designs, 361–362
Cortical back areas, 185
Counseling, vocational, 143
Counting skills, 88
CP (cerebral palsy), 273
Creative expression
    in adolescent instruction, 153
    in early childhood instruction, 106–107
    in middle childhood instruction, 127
Cri du chat syndrome, 177, 254–255
Crohn's disease, 255
Cross-content areas of the curriculum
    in adolescence, 149–15
    in early childhood, 89–90, 95–96, 101–102
    in middle childhood, 122–124
Cross-disciplinary assessment. *See* Multimodal
    assessment
CTE (chronic traumatic encephalopathy),
    276

Cultural considerations. *See also* Diversity
Cultural issues and achievement gaps, 155–186
Cultural issues in diagnosing specific learning
disabilities, 241–242
Cultural diversity, 293–297
Cultural identity, 107
Curriculum-based assessment, 60–61
Curriculum evaluation, 53–56
Custody issues, 290, 341–345
Cyberbullying, 130
Cystic fibrosis (CF), 279–280
Cytomegalovirus, 276

D
D-amino acids, 175
Dance activities, 106, 152–153
Darwin, Charles, 361
Deafness, 200, 214
Decade of the Brain, 171
Decision-making, educational, 52–53
Declarative knowledge, 84, 189
Deletions, chromosome, 177, 250
Delis–Kaplan Executive Function System, 208, 252
Denton, C. A., 222
Deoxyribonucleic acid (DNA), 173–175, 251
Dependable skills
in adolescence, 153
in early childhood, 107
in middle childhood, 127–128
Descriptive research designs, 361
Development, domains of
Five developmental domains—defining and
assessing, 199–208
Use of the five developmental domains in
diagnosing and treating pervasive and
specific developmental disabilities, 209–219
Use of five developmental domains in defining
specific learning disabilities, 221–223
Developmental delay, problems with using this
expression, 209
Developmental disabilities, 5, 197–215
Cautions in using the term developmental delay,
164, 209
Assessing each of five developmental domains to
create developmental profile, 199–208
Defining pervasive and specific developmental
disabilities based on developmental
profiles, 209–219
Planning and implementing interventions for,
212–214
Feedback for parents/educators, 211–212
Developmental talents in highly capable,
214–215
Developmentally talented children, 214–215
Developmental motor disorders, 233–234, 273
Developmental Neuropsychological Assessment,
201, 237, 252
Developmental profiles
Angelman syndrome, 251

for assessing developmental disabilities, 197–198,
209–212
for differentiated instruction, 57–60
for ruling out specific learning disabilities,
226–227
specific language impairment, 235
Developmental stepping-stones
in adolescence, 137–168
in early childhood, 69–110
in middle childhood, 111–116
Diabetes, 277
Diagnosis. *See also* Branching diagnosis and
Differential diagnosis
Brain-based disorders and health conditions,
271–286
Highly capable, 214–215
Neurogenetic disorders, 249–270
Pervasive or specific developmental disabilities,
209–219
Specific learning disabilities including twice
exceptional, 221–248
Diagnostic and Statistical Manual of Mental Disorders
(DSM–5), 5, 272, 351
Dickinson, Emily, 186
A Difference in the Family (Helen Featherstone), 211
Differential diagnosis and treatment of specific
learning disabilities, 63–64, 180, 221–237
of dysgraphia, 232–234
of dyslexia, 234–235
of oral and written language learning disability
(OWL LD), 235–236
of dyscalculia, 236
of nonverbal specific learning disabilities,
236–237
of twice exceptional, 237
Differentiated instruction, 11, 20–29, 40, 54, 58–60,
64, 66, 103, 108–109, 130–131, 147, 155–156,
240–241, 247, 273
Digit span tasks, 206
Discourse level (reading), 78
Diversity, racial, linguistic, cultural, family, and
socioeconomic, 289–302
and adolescent instruction, 139–140, 155–156,
162–166
biological, 240–241, 361
case example of effective approach, 300–301
challenges with, vii
Division skills (mathematics), 100–101, 119
Divorce, 290, 341–344
DNA (deoxyribonucleic acid), 173–175, 251
DNA probe, 250
DNA sequencing, 251
Domain-specific skills, 4
Domestic violence judicial restrictions, 353
Down syndrome (Trisomy 21), 176, 255
Drama activities
in adolescent instruction, 153
after-school, 142

in early childhood instruction, 106–107
in middle childhood instruction, 127
Drug use. *See* Substance use
DSM–5. See Diagnostic and Statistical Manual of Mental Disorders
Duchenne muscular dystrophy, 178, 179, 255
Dunn, Alnita, 21–22, 365
Duplications, chromosome, 250
Dylan, Bob, 44
Dyscalculia. *See* differential diagnosis and treatment of specific learning disabilities
Dysgraphia. *See* differential diagnosis and treatment of specific learning disabilities
Dyskinetic cerebral palsy, 273
Dyslexia. *See* differential diagnosis and treatment of specific learning disabilities
Dystonic cerebral palsy, 273

E
Early childhood instruction and assessment, 69–109
with at-risk populations, 103–104
behavioral and learning skills in, 75–83, 104–107
developmental stepping-stones for, 69–74
differentiated instruction, 108–109
with first-grade students, 83–90
with kindergarten students, 75–83
with second-grade students, 91–98
technology in, 107–108
with third-grade students, 98–102
Early onset autism, 254
Echolalia, 263
EdMedKids, 277
Educational advocacy, viii, 319–337
within American legal system, 108, 320–322
and Child Abuse Prevention and Treatment Act, 326–329
for children exposed to trauma, 331–333
and common law duty, 323–325
definitions of, 320
and IDEIA, 320, 322, 325–326, 336
potential sources of conflict in, 336–337
professional standards for, 333–334
systems-level, 334–336
and Title IX, 329–331
Educational challenges, 8–13
Educational decision-making, 52–53
Educational malpractice, 324, 325
Educational testing. *See* Testing
Education Amendments of 1972, 329–331
Educators. *See* Teachers
Edwards syndrome (Trisomy 18), 176, 264
Einstein, Albert, 127, 149
Eligibility categories (disabilities), 11
ELLs. *See* English language learners
Emotional development. *See* Social and emotional development
Encephalocele, 258–259
Endophenotypic research, 182, 315

Engineering. *See* STEM
English language learners (ELLs), 162, 165, 295
Environmental sources of diversity. *See* Diversity
in epigenetics, 181
of toxin-related disorders, 272–273
in twin studies, 179
Epidemiological studies, data on frequency of occurrence of specific learning disabilities and ADHD, 218, 242
Epigenetics, 179, 181
Epilepsy, 261, 277–278. *See also* Seizure disorders
Epilepsy Foundation, 278
Episodic memory, 189
Ethnicity, 292
Evidence-based assessment and instruction, 17–68. *See also* Assessment(s); Instruction
and classroom teachers, 5
cost-effective and time-effective, 64
gathering evidence for, 39
in history of American education, 10–11
role of developmental milestones in, 4
Evidence-based research reviews, 360
Executive functioning development. *See* Attention and executive functioning development
Experimental research designs, 362
Expert testimony (educational advocacy), 322
Extended families, 294–295
External validity (research), 360

F
Famiano, Robert, 97, 365
Family issues, 290–291. *See also* Parents; School–family relationships
FAPE. *See* Free and appropriate public education
FASD (fetal alcohol spectrum disorder), 281
Febrile seizures, 260
Federal special education codes, 11
Fetal alcohol spectrum disorder (FASD), 281
Fine motor skills, 200–201, 254
Finland, 12
First-grade students, 83–90
FISH (fluorescent in situ hybridization), 250
Fixsen, Dean, 38
Fletcher, J. M., 222
Flexner, Abraham, 12
Fluency (brain processing), 61
Fluorescent in situ hybridization (FISH), 250
FMR1-related disorders, 256
Food additives, 273
Formal logic, 190
Formal operational thought, 142
Formative assessment, 57
Fractals, 148
Fractions (mathematics skill), 120–121, 127
Fragile X syndrome
and autism, 253
genetic basis of, 178, 179
overview, 256

Francis, D. J., 222
Free and appropriate public education (FAPE), 10–11
  barriers to ensuring, 325
  and best professional practices, 19
  creation of legislation for, 222
  mental health services as part of, 333
  starting from birth age, 199
Frequency of occurrence of specific learning disabilities and ADHD, 218, 242
Fry, Edward, 85
Fuller, Buckminster, 123
Funding, for interdisciplinary teamwork, 41–42, 240

G
Games
  computer, 128
  letter-finding, 117
  looking, 79, 83, 85
  and self-regulation, 104
  sound, 79, 83, 85
  word, 98
Gandhi, Mohandas K., 299
Geisel, Theodor Seuss, 12
Gender, of educators, 9, 10
Gender identity, 182
Gene candidate studies, 180
General education, 213
Genetics, 171–182
  and brain research, 182–186
  and descriptive research methods, 361
  of developmental disabilities, 176–179
  endophenotypic research in, 182
  epi-, 179, 181
  and gender identity, 182
  general concepts, 173–175
  learning-disability study approaches, 179–180
  Mendelian, 172
  neuro-, 184. *See also* Brain; Neurogenetic disorders
  of neurogenetic disorders, 176–179
  post-Mendelian, 172–173
  regulatory genes, 126, 173, 178–179, 181, 183
  research on dyslexia, 179, 180, 224
  sex differences in, 181–182
  vulnerabilities of adolescents, 140–141
Genetic testing, 250–251
Genomic imprinting, 177
Geometry, 121
Giftedness
  guidelines for diagnosis of, 197, 198
  identification of, 214–215
  team screening for, 59
  in twice exceptionality. *See* Twice exceptionality
Go/no go measures, 252
Graphemes, 85
Graphomotor control, 189
Graphomotor output, 189
Graphomotor planning, 189

Great Books program, 118–119
Greenberg, M. T., 239
Griffin, Whitney, 6n1
Gross motor skills, 200–201
Guthrie, Woody, 43

H
Haemophilia, 256
Hands, language use with, 189, 223
Handwriting, 8, 20, 71, 72, 74, 80, 86–89, 90, 92–93, 97, 102–103, 107, 110, 117, 125, 129, 138, 145, 154, 225, 227, 234, 238.
Harassment, sexual, 329–331
Harriet Lane Clinic, 29–31
Head injury, 274
Head Start, 132
Health Impairment for Special Education Services, 282
Health Leads, 31
Heard speech, 201
Hearing problems, 199–201, 223
Helping Traumatized Children (Susan Cole), 331–332
Hemophilia, 256
Highly capable children. *See* Giftedness
High-risk pregnancies, 272
High school graduation rates, 10, 143
High-stakes testing, 12, 67
History coursework, 123–124, 150
The History of White People (Nell Irvin Painter), 293
Homeless students, 290
Homeschooled children, 23
Homework clubs, 23, 142
Hood, Leroy, 171
Hooray for Diffendoofer Day (Dr. Seuss), 12
Horning, Zenia Lemos, 162–164, 365
Human Genome Project, 171
Humanities, 150
Humor, 91, 190
Huntington's chorea, 177
Huntington's disease, 179
Hydrocephalus. *See* Neural tube deficits
Hyperactivity, 104–105, 280. *See also* Attention-deficit/hyperactivity disorder
Hyperreactivity (tactile sense), 200
Hypersensitivity (tactile sense), 200

I
ICD–10 (International Statistical Classification of Diseases and Related Health Problems), 5, 272
IDEIA. *See* Individuals With Disabilities Education Improvement Act
Identity development, 107
IEE (independent educational evaluation), 351
IEPs. *See* Individualized education plans
Immediate Post-Concussion Assessment and Cognitive Testing battery, 275
Immigration, 123, 164, 292–294
Inborn errors of metabolism, 277
Incarceration, 28–29, 290

Independent educational evaluation (IEE), 351
Independent living, 213
Individualized education plans (IEPs)
    educational goals in, 4
    function of, 351
    and IDEIA, 325
    mental health services as part of, 333
    for students with PDDs, 212–213
Individual student evaluation, 56–60
Individuals With Disabilities Education Improve-
    ment Act (IDEIA)
    educational advocacy with, 320, 322, 325–326,
        336
    and families, 351–352. *See also* Special education
        services
    recent reauthorization of, 34
Industrial age, 8–9
Inflectional suffixes, 92
Injuries
    classroom, 324
    spinal cord, 274
    traumatic brain, 274
Institute of Educational Sciences, 222, 224
Instruction. *See* Developmental stepping-stones;
        Differentiated instruction
    adolescent. *See* Adolescent instruction and
        assessment
    defined, 37
    developmentally appropriate, 4
    differentiated. *See* Differentiated instruction
    early childhood. *See* Early childhood instruction
        and assessment
    examples of, 37
    linking developmental profiles to, 57
    linking learning profiles to, 58
    middle childhood. *See* Middle childhood instruc-
        tion and assessment
    response to. *See* Response to instruction
Intelligence quotient, reframing the concept, 205, 222
Intelligence testing, 205
Interdisciplinary frameworks, 1–48
Interdisciplinary research, 35–39, 363. *See also* Inter-
        disciplinary research designs
    evaluating research articles, 363–364
    implementing into practice, 5, 35–39
Interdisciplinary research designs, 359–363
    correlation, 361–362
    descriptive, 361
    and desired learning outcomes, 363
    experimental, 362
    external validity of, 360
    internal validity of, 359–360
    single-subject, 362
Interdisciplinary teams and teamwork, 3–8, 17–44
    accountability in, 39–41
    alternative funding approaches for, 41–42, 240
    best practices for, 18–21
    disciplines represented in, 18

implementation of K–12 models, 42–44
importance of, 3–4
local, 7
medical professionals, role of, 18, 29–31
and research, 35–39
resources on, 45–47
role models for, 20–31
school psychologists, role of, 21–23
and systems-level change, 31–35
and three-tier model of behavioral interventions,
    23–29
Internal validity (research designs), 359–360
International League Against Epilepsy, 278
*International Statistical Classification of Diseases and
        Related Health Problems (ICD–10)*, 5, 272
Internet
    cyberbullying on, 130
    and middle childhood instruction, 128
    plagiarism using information from, 154
Intervention(s). *See* Behavioral interventions;
        Developmental stepping-stones; Differentiated
        instruction

J
Jacksonian epilepsy, 261
Jacobson, Lenore, 43–44
Job fairs, 144
Johns Hopkins Medical School, 29–31
Jones, Ellis, 298
José Valdés Summer Math Institute, 161–162
Juvenile Diabetes Research Foundation, 277

K
K–12 models, 42–44
Karyotyping, 250
Katahira, Jennifer, 81, 365
Katusic, Slavica, 6n1
Kindergarten students, 75–83
Kinesthesia, 200–201
King, Martin Luther, Jr., 299
Klinefelter's syndrome, 256
Knowledge. *See also* Cognitive and memory systems
    algebraic, 148
    declarative, 84, 189
    procedural, 84, 189
    specialized, 7
Kusché, C. A., 239

L
Ladson-Billings, Gloria, 293
L-amino acids, 175
Landau–Kleffner syndrome, 257
Language, *See* Developmental stepping-stones
    cultural considerations with, 242, 295–297. *See
        also* English language learners
    multi-leveled nature of, 62
    and neurogenetic disorders, 265
Language arts, 115–119, 145–146

Language production, 188
Later onset autism, 254
Latinos, 155, 292
LAUSD (Los Angeles Unified School District), 21–22, 28–29
Lawyers, 321–322
Learning disabilities
    and autism, 253–254
    genetic bases of, 179–180
    in history of American education, 10–11
    as incompatibility between child and world, 314
    perspectives of a developmental neuropsychologist, 311–317
    prevalence of, 11–12
    recent changes in research and practice, 314–317
    specific. See Specific learning disabilities (SLDs)
Learning Disabilities Program (Boston Children's Hospital) case study, 311–317
Learning outcomes, 363
Learning profiles
    and developmental profiles, 210
    for differentiated instruction, 58–60
    dyscalculia, 230, 236
    dysgraphia, 228, 234
    dyslexia, 229, 235
    in learning disability diagnosis, 227–233
    neurogenetic disorders, 266
    nonverbal specific learning disabilities, 230
    oral and written language learning disability, 229, 236
    specific language impairment, 236
Learning skills, developmentally appropriate
    in adolescent instruction and assessment, 151–153
    in early childhood instruction and assessment, 75–83, 104–107
    in middle childhood instruction and assessment, 125–128
Leber hereditary optic neuropathy (LHON), 257
Legal issues
    with divorce and custody, 342–343
    with educational advocacy, 108, 320–322
    and interdisciplinary teams, 18
Lesch–Nyhan syndrome, 257
Letter-finding games, 117
Leukemia, 279
LGBT youth, 330
LHON (Leber hereditary optic neuropathy), 257
Limbic system, 126
Listening skills. See Aural language skills
Literacy
    at home, 296, 298
    and oral language skills, 311, 313, 316
    and speech–language pathology specialists, 131–132
Local interdisciplinary teams, 7
Long-term memory, 192
Looking games, 79, 83, 85
Los Angeles Unified School District (LAUSD), 21–22, 28–29

Lovitt, Thomas, viii
Lyonization, 265
Lyons, Oren, 299
Lysosomal storage disease (Tay–Sachs disease), 178, 262
Lystedt, Zackery, 275

M
MacArthur, Charles, 129
Mainstreaming, 213
Malpractice, educational, 324, 325
Mapping (language skill), 77, 78, 115, 117
Mask-making activity, 153, 298
Maternal substance abuse, 281
Mathematical models, 149
Mathematics. See also STEM
    for adolescents in Valdés Institute, 158, 159
    in adolescent instruction and assessment, 138, 146–150
    in arithmetic calculation. See Dyscalculia
    in early childhood development, 71, 73, 74
    evidence-based conceptual model for learning, 37–38
    in first grade assessment and instruction, 88–90
    in kindergarten, 82
    in middle childhood instruction and assessment, 117, 119–122, 124–125
    in second grade assessment and instruction, 93–96
    in third grade assessment and instruction, 100–102
Mayer, Richard, 36, 37
Mayo Clinic, 11–12, 222
McKeown, Margaret, 78, 80
McLane, Devin, 32, 365
Medical conditions, 271–286. See also Brain-related disorders; Neurogenetic disorders
    disabilities co-occurring with, 210, 227, 281
    neurogenetic disorders co-occurring with, 266, 281
    and student evaluation, 57
Medical professionals, 18, 19, 29–31
Medication
    antiepileptic drugs, 278
    for treating ADHD, 208, 242, 252
Meiosis, 176
MELAS, 258
MELAS (mitochondrial encephalomyopathy, lactic acidosis, and stroke-like episodes), 258
Memory. See also Cognition and memory systems
    autobiographical, 190
    episodic, 189
    long-term, 192
    short-term, 192, 206
    working. See Working memory
Mendel, Gregor, 172
Mendelian genetics, 172
Meningitis, 276
Meningomyelocele. See Neural tube deficits
Mental health services, 152, 277, 332–333

Mental illness prevalence, 334–335
Mental retardation, 210
MERRF (myoclonic epilepsy and ragged red filters), 258
Messenger ribonucleic acid. *See* mRNA
Meta-analyses, 360
Metabolism, inborn errors of, 277
Methylation patterns in DNA, 251
Methyls (chemical markers), 181
Microdeletions (genetics), 177, 178
Middle childhood instruction and assessment, 111–132
   and academic/learning behaviors, 125–128
   differentiated instruction, 130–131
   and integrated reading-writing-oral language, 112–114
   in language arts, 115–119
   in math, 119–122
   response to instruction, 124–125
   in science, 122–123
   and silent reading, 112–114
   in social studies, 123–124
   speech/language pathologists' role in, 131–132
   technology in, 128–130
   and transition to switching classes/teachers, 114
Miller, Daniel, 240
Mind
   orchestra as, 69–70
   theory of, 206, 237
Minsky, M., 185
Mirror image amino acids, 175
Mishkin, Mortimer, 193, 207
Missiasen, Sharon, 33, 365
Mitochondria (genetics), 174
Mitochondrial disorders, 253, 257–258
Mitochondrial DNA (mtDNA), 174, 257–258
Mitochondrial encephalomyopathy, lactic acidosis, and stroke-like episodes (MELAS), 258
Mitochondrial inheritance, 174–175
Mitosis, 176
Mobius strip, 149
Monosomies, 176
Morphology (language development), 92, 115, 225, 231
Mosaicism (genetics), 177
Motivation, 207
Motor development. *See* Sensory development
   brain systems linked to, 186–187
   developmental disabilities affecting, 199–202
   integrating language systems with, 189, 194
   as interdisciplinary framework, 4
   linking assessment with, 58
   specialists for, 18, 19
Motor disorders, 18, 233–234, 273
Movement activities
   in adolescent instruction, 152–153

   in early childhood instruction, 106
   in middle childhood instruction, 127
mRNA (messenger ribonucleic acid), 174, 175, 183
MtDNA (mitochondrial DNA), 174, 257–258
Mukilteo School District, WA. *See* McLane, Devin
Muir, John, 127
Multidisciplinary Learning Disabilities Center, 224
Multimodal assessment
   best practices in, 20–21
   as component of interdisciplinary teamwork, 19–20
Multiplication skills (mathematics), 100, 119
Multivariate correlations (research), 361
Muscular dystrophy, 273
Music activities
   in adolescent instruction, 153
   after-school, 142
   in early childhood instruction, 106–107
   in middle childhood instruction, 127
Mutations, genetic, 177–178
Myoclonic epilepsy and ragged red filters (MERRF), 258
Myoclonic seizures, 258, 261

N
National Association of School Psychologists, 26, 321
National Cancer Institute, 279
National Center of Education Statistics, 351
National Implementation Research Network, 38
National Incidence Study of Child Abuse and Neglect, 327
National Institute of Child Health and Human Development (NICHD), 222, 224, 225
National Institutes of Health, 222
National norming (testing), 52
National Panel on Single-Subject Design, 61
National standards, 54
National Survey of Family Growth, 352
National testing, 12. *See also* High-stakes testing
Native Americans, 131–132, 155, 293–295
Negligence (tort law), 323–325
Nelson, Nickola, 6n1, 223
Neonatal seizures, 261
NEPSY–II Theory of Mind subtest, 206
Neural tube deficits, 258–259, 272
Neurofibromatosis, 178, 259
Neurogenetic disorders, 249–266
   Angelman syndrome, 251, 253
   attention–deficit/hyperactivity disorder, 251–253
   autism, 210, 211, 253–254
   co-occurrence of PDDs and, 210
   cri du chat syndrome, 177, 254–255
   Crohn's disease, 255
   Down syndrome, 176, 255
   Duchenne muscular dystrophy, 178, 179, 255
   fragile X syndrome, 178, 179, 253, 256

Neurogenic disorders *continued*
genetics of, 176–179
genetic testing for, 250–251
hemophilia, 256
interdisciplinary treatment issues with, 266
Klinefelter's syndrome, 256
Landau–Kleffner syndrome, 257
Leber hereditary optic neuropathy, 257
Lesch–Nyhan syndrome, 257
MELAS, 258
mitochondrial disorders, 253, 257–258
multiple occurrences of, 265–266
myoclonic epilepsy and ragged red filters, 258
neural tube deficits, 258–259, 272
neurofibromatosis, 259
phenylketonuria, 259
Prader–Willi syndrome, 253, 260
Rett syndrome, 178, 253, 260
Rubinstein–Taybi syndrome, 260
seizure disorders, 253, 258, 260–261, 277–278
sickle cell disease, 262
and specific learning disorders, 227
spinal muscular atrophy, 262
and student evaluation, 57
Tay–Sachs disease, 178, 262
tics, 263
Tourette's syndrome, 263
treatment issues with, 266
Trisomy 13 (Patau's syndrome), 176, 263–264
Trisomy 18 (Edwards syndrome), 176, 264
Turner's syndrome, 176–177, 264
types of testing available for, 250–251
velocardiofacial syndrome, 264
Williams syndrome, 177, 265
Neurologists, 201
Neuropsychology, 240–241. *See also* Brain
Neuroscience. *See* Brain
NICHD. *See* National Institute of Child Health and Human Development
Niedo, Jasmin, 101–102, 124, 242
No Child Left Behind Act, 322
No-fault approach (K–12 models), 43
Nondisjunction (meiosis abnormality), 176
Nonsense mutations, 178
Nonverbal learning disabilities, 230, 236–237, 239
Nonverbal representations, 190
Normal biological variation, 175
Norming (testing), 52, 62
Northshore School District, WA, 34–35
Note-taking technology, 129
Number concepts, 82, 120, 147–148

O

Occupational and physical therapists (OT/PTs)
and developmental disabilities, 200–201
and differential diagnosis of dysgraphia, 233–234
on interdisciplinary teams, 18, 41

OCR (Office for Civil Rights), 330
Office for Civil Rights (OCR), 330
Olson, Richard, 179
Olympic View Middle School (Mukilteo, WA), 32
Operating Manual for Spaceship Earth (Buckminster Fuller), 123
Ophthalmologists, 200
Oppositional defiant disorder, 342
Optometrists, 200
Oral and written language learning disability (OWL LD), 229, 235–236, 238–239. *See* Differential diagnosis and treatment of specific learning disabilities
Oral language skills
brain systems linked to, 188
developmental disabilities affecting, 202–205
in dyslexia, 235
in early childhood development, 70–73
of first-grade students, 84–85, 89–90
in kindergarteners, 76–77, 80, 81
and literacy, 311, 313, 316
in middle childhood instruction and assessment, 112–114
of middle childhood students, 116
of second-grade students, 91
of third-grade students, 98
Oral reading skills, 86
"Orchestra of mind," 69–70
Ordinal numbers, 82
Ornithine transcarbamylase enzyme disorder, 178
Orthographic awareness, 85, 115, 146, 225
Orthographic loop, 231, 234
Orthotactic patterns, 85
OT/PTs. *See* Occupational and physical therapists

P

Painter, Nell Irvin, 293
Paraprofessionals. *See also* Special educators
cultural insights of, 300–301
expertise of, 300
teacher support from, 11
Parent rooms, 23
Parents
as active members of interdisciplinary teams, 20, 23
active participation of, 160
adversarial relationships with schools, 11
of children with neurogenetic disorders, 266
communicating assessment results with, 63–64
and concerns about toxins, 273
and developmental disabilities, 211–212
feedback with learning disability diagnosis, 241
income and education levels of, 290–291
information obtained from, 59, 63
role in adolescent instruction and assessment, 151
roles of, 8
Parent support groups, 23, 213

Parent–teacher conferences
  benefits of, 23
  sharing portfolios in, 65, 107
Partial seizures, 261
Participants, research, 360–361
Part–whole relations (mathematics skill), 120–121,
    127
Patau's syndrome (Trisomy 13), 176, 263–264
PATHS (Providing Alternative Thinking Strategies)
    program, 239
Patton, Jeanne, 65–66, 365
PDDs. *See* Pervasive developmental disabilities
Peer relationships, 105–106
Peripheral nervous system, 188
Personalized education, 172
Pervasive developmental disabilities (PDDs)
  aural and oral language impairment with, 203
  and autism, 253–254
  cognitive functioning with, 222
  co-occurrence of multiple, 210–211
  diagnosis of, 210
  differential diagnosis of, 59
  and domains of development, 197–199
  genetic basis of, 177, 179
  guidelines for diagnosis of, 197, 198
  interventions for students with, 212–214
  motor impairment with, 201
  neurogenetic disorders co-occurring with, 265
  ruling out, in learning disability diagnosis, 226–227
Phenotype profiles, 210, 228–231
  Angelman syndrome, 251
  dyscalculia, 230, 236
  dysgraphia, 228, 234, 235
  dyslexia, 229, 235
  nonverbal specific learning disabilities, 230
  oral and written language learning disability
      (OWL LD), 229, 236
  specific language impairment, 229, 236
Phenylketonuria, 178, 259
Phonemes, 85, 188, 204–205
Phonemic processing, 188, 204–205
Phonetic processing, 188
Phonics, 85
Phonological awareness, 85, 115, 204, 315
Phonotactic patterns, 85, 204
Phosphates (chemical markers), 181
Physiatrists, 201
Physical activities. *See* Movement activities
Physical therapists. *See* Occupational and physical
      therapists
Piaget, Jean, 312
Plagiarism, 154
Play scripts, 91
Point mutation, 177–178
Politics, 7
Portfolios, student, 59, 65, 107
Positive Behavioral Interventions and Support
    program, 39

Posner, Michael, 69
Post-Concussion Symptom Scale, 275
Post-Mendelian genetics, 172–173
Poverty, 300–301
Prader–Willi syndrome, 253, 260
Pragmatics (language), 85
Premature birth, 272
Preservice professional development, 12–13, 18
Prevention programs, 59
Primary generalized seizure disorders, 261
Principals, 12
Privacy, of students, 324
Probe measures, 59, 61
Problem-solving consultation, 20, 22–23, 41
Procedural knowledge, 84, 189
Processing speeds, 60–61
Produced speech. *See* Speech production
Professional autonomy, 7, 12–13, 40
Professional development
  in-service, 18
  preservice. *See* Preservice professional
      development
  self-guided, 42–43
  at Valdés Institute, 159–160
Project Heal, 30
Protein coding, 186
Proteomics, 174
Provided Thinking Points, 70
Proximal development, zones of, 86
Psychiatric conditions, 280
Psychologists
  assessments by, 52
  on interdisciplinary teams, 18
  role in special education process, 326
  school, 21–26, 41
Psychometric testing, 54–55. *See also* Assessment(s)
Puberty, 141–143. *See also* Adolescent instruction
      and assessment
Public school–university partnerships, 161
Publisher-designed assessments, 59
Pull-out special education services, 11–12
Pygmalion in the Classroom study, 44

R
Racial diversity, 291–293
Rapid Alternating Stimulus Test, 252
Raskind, Wendy H., viii
Rate (assessment unit), 60
Rating scales, teacher and parent, 59
Rational numbers, 120
RCW (Revised Code of Washington), 328
Reading problems
  developmental approaches to, 313, 315–316
  genetic basis of, 179, 180
  in dyslexia. *See* Dyslexia
  in OWL LD, 225–226, 229–231.
  three-tier models for dealing with, 11
  with deafness, 214

Reading skills
in 19th-century classrooms, 8
of adolescents, 138, 140–141
attention as predictive of, 316–317
in early childhood development, 70–71, 72, 73
of first-grade students, 77–79, 89–90
of kindergartners, 77–79
in middle childhood instruction and assessment, 112–114, 116, 118–119, 124–125
of second-grade students, 91–92, 95, 96
of third-grade students, 98–99, 101–102
Reasoning skills, 191
Recessive traits, 178
Reciprocal teaching, 85, 98, 99, 118
Regulatory genes, 126, 178–179, 181, 183
Rehabilitation Act, 320, 351
Reliability (testing), 52
Religion, 296
Research, on interdisciplinary frameworks. *See* Interdisciplinary research
Residential treatment centers, 10–11
Response to instruction
during adolescence, 137, 151–153
assessment of, 4
examples of, 59
in first grade, 90
and genetic vulnerabilities, 141
in kindergarten, 82–83
in middle childhood, 124–125
and response-to-intervention. *See* Response-to-intervention
in second grade, 98–99
in third grade, 102
Response-to-intervention
and assessment, 61–62
for children with ADHD, 208
examples of, 59
with learning disabilities, 222
in Los Angeles Unified School District, 22
Restraining orders, 353
Rett syndrome, 178, 253, 260
Revised Code of Washington (RCW), 328
Rose Award, viii, 301
Rosenthal, Robert, 43–44
Rubinstein–Taybi syndrome, 179, 260
Ryan, Julie, 65, 365

S
Safety
as legal responsibility of educator, 323–324
with technology, 129, 154
Safety Lanes, 31
Scaffolding, 78
School evaluation, 53–56
School–family relationships, viii, 341–354. *See also* Parents
achieving goals for instruction in, 64
and adolescent instruction, 155

and comprehensive family evaluation, 344–350
and divorce/custody issues, 341–345
and domestic violence judicial restrictions, 353
and special education services, 351–352
in three-tier model of behavioral interventions, 23–28
School–parent–community partnerships, 27–28
School psychologists
on interdisciplinary teams, 21–23, 41
role in behavioral interventions, 23–26
Science
in adolescent instruction and assessment, 150
evidence-based conceptual model for, 37
in first grade instruction and assessment, 90
in middle childhood instruction and assessment, 122–123
in second and third grade instruction and assessment, 96–97, 101
translational, 29, 41, 183
Science, technology, engineering, and math. *See* STEM
SDDs. *See* Specific developmental disabilities
Secondary schools, 8
Second-grade students, 91–98
Second impact syndrome (concussions), 275
Seeger, Pete, 32
Seizure disorders, 252, 253, 258, 260–261, 277–278
Self-concept
in adolescence, 153
cultural considerations with, 156
in early childhood, 107
in middle childhood, 126–128
Self-efficacy
cultural considerations with, 156
in middle childhood, 126–127
Self-guided professional development, 42–43
Self-regulated learning (SLR), 139
Self-regulation
and ADHD, 252–253
in adolescence, 139, 151–152
brain systems linked to, 186, 191–193
and developmental disabilities, 207–208
in early childhood, 104–105
in middle childhood, 125–126
Sensory development. *See also* motor development
brain systems linked to, 186–187
developmental disabilities affecting, 199–202
integrating language systems with, 189, 194
as interdisciplinary framework, 4
linking assessment with, 58
specialists for, 18, 19
Sex differences, 181–182
Sex education, 142
Sex-linked disorders. *See* X-linked disorders
Sexual harassment, 329–331
Short-term memory, 192, 206
Sickle cell disease, 262
Silent reading, 112–114, 116

Silliman, Elaine, 223
Simple motor tics, 263
Single nucleotide polymorphisms (SNPs), 175, 179
Single-subject research designs, 362
SLDs. *See* Specific learning disabilities
Sleep, 141–142, 253
Sleep disorders, 279
SLI. *See* Specific language impairment
SLPs. *See* Speech–language pathology specialists
SLR (self-regulated learning), 139
SMA (spinal muscular atrophy), 262
Smarter Balanced Assessments, 144
"Smart pens," 129
SNPs (single nucleotide polymorphisms), 175, 179
Social and emotional development
    in adolescence, 152
    brain systems linked to, 186, 192, 193
    in comprehensive K–12 models, 42
    developmental disabilities affecting, 207
    disciplines relevant to, 19
    in early childhood instruction, 105–106
    as interdisciplinary framework, 4
    linking assessment with, 58
    in middle childhood instruction, 126–127
    and technology use, 130
Social cognition, 206, 237, 239, 254
Social Skills Improvement System, 207
Social studies
    in adolescent instruction and assessment, 150
    in first grade instruction and assessment, 90
    in middle childhood instruction and assessment, 123–124
    in second/third grade assessment and instruction, 96–97, 101
Socioeconomic status, 155, 242
Solomon, Barry, 29, 31, 365
Somatosensory senses, 193
Sound games, 79, 83, 85
Sound pattern processing, 188
Space, concepts of, 148–149
Speaking skills. *See* Oral language
Special education services
    alternatives to, 240
    boundaries between general education and, 11
    bridging gap between general education and, 21–22
    eligibility for, 63, 108, 326, 351–352
    Health Impairment qualification for, 282
    and school–family relationships, 351–352
    in three-tier models, 11–12
Special educators. *See also* Paraprofessionals
    and developmental disabilities, 201
    on interdisciplinary teams, 41
    and standard of care, 323
Specialized knowledge, 7
Specific developmental disabilities (SDDs)
    aural and oral language impairment with, 202, 203

co-occurrence of multiple, 210–211
    diagnosis of, 210
    differential diagnosis of, 59
    and domains of development, 197–199
    guidelines for diagnosis of, 197, 198
    interventions for students with, 213
    motor impairment with, 201
    neurogenetic disorders co-occurring with, 265
    ruling out, in learning disability diagnosis, 226–227
Specific language impairment (SLI). *See also* Oral and written language learning disability (OWL LD).
    and ADHD, 280
    determination of, 202, 203
    differential diagnosis of, 235–236
    evidence-based diagnosis of, 63
Specific learning disabilities (SLDs), 221–242
    assessing learning profiles for diagnosis of, 227–233
    attention problems associated with, 252
    and communicating with parents, 63
    of co-occurring ADHD, 241–242
    cultural and socioeconomic considerations with, 242
    differential diagnosis, 59
    dyscalculia, 229–230, 236, 239
    dysgraphia, 228, 232–234, 238
    dyslexia, 228–229, 234–235, 238
    early identification of, 237
    historic context, 222–224
    instructional interventions following, 238–240
    medical conditions co-occurring with, 281
    with multiple specific learning disabilities, 241
    nonverbal, 230, 236–237, 239
    oral/written language learning disability, 229, 235–236, 238–239
    parental feedback with diagnoses of, 241
    prevalence of, 222
    research on defining and differentiating, 224–226
    and ruling out developmental disabilities, 226–227
    specific language impairment, 235–236
    and twice exceptionality, 237, 240
Speech–language pathology specialists (SLPs)
    assessments by, 52
    and central auditory processing, 200
    and developmental disabilities, 201, 203
    on interdisciplinary teams, 18, 19, 41
    and middle childhood instruction and assessment, 131–132
    and speech production problems, 84
Speech perception, 201–202
Speech production, 188, 201–202, 205
Spelling skills
    in adolescence, 145
    and dyslexia, 234–235
    in early childhood development, 71, 72
    in first grade, 85, 87
    in second grade, 92, 93, 95

Spina bifida, 259, 272
Spinal cord injuries, 274
Spinal muscular atrophy (SMA), 262
Splinter skills, 209
Sports, 142, 274–275
Standard of care, 323–325
State-local school partnerships, 34–35
State special education codes, 11
State standards, 57
Statistical modeling, 362
Statutory law, 322, 325–326
STEM (science, technology, engineering, and math)
    achievement gaps in, 155
    algebraic knowledge needed for careers in, 148
    interdisciplinary research on, 37–39
STEAM, 39
Stop codons, 175
STP (Successful Transition Program), 28–29
STRIVE (Successful Transition and Re-Integration Into a Viable Education), 28–29
Stroop Color–Word Interference Test, 252
Student advocacy. See Educational advocacy
Stuttering, 202
Substance use
    by mothers during pregnancy, 281
    by students, 163, 281
Substance use syndrome, 227
Subtraction skills (mathematics), 82, 88–89, 119
Subword level (reading), 77, 115, 117, 225
Successful Transition and Re-Integration Into a Viable Education (STRIVE), 28–29
Successful Transition Program (STP), 28–29
Suicidal ideation, 152
Summative assessment, 57
Supervisory attention, 231, 252, 253
Supplementary instruction, 11
Swanson, Lee, 225
Swanson Test of Cognitive Processing, 236–237
Syntax, 77–78, 188
Systems-level change
    with educational advocacy, 334–336
    and interdisciplinary teams, 31–35
    role models for, 31–35

T
Tactile sensory skills, 200–201
Talent. See Giftedness
TAs (teaching assistants), 159–161
Tay–Sachs disease, 178, 262
TBI (traumatic brain injury), 274
Teacher-designed classroom assessments, 59
Teachers
    accountability of, 5, 39–40
    blame put on, 43
    cooperation among, 12
    and developmental disabilities, 211–212
    in early 20th century, 9
    history of training programs for, 8

roles of, 7
sense of efficacy felt by, 156–157
special education. See Special educators
and standard of care, 323–325
worldviews of, 314
Teaching assistants (TAs), 159–161
Team differential diagnosis, 59
Team-Initiated Problem Solving (TIPS) program, 39
Team monitoring, 60
Teams and teamwork, interdisciplinary. See Interdisciplinary teams and teamwork
Team screening, 59
Technology. See also STEM
    in adolescent instruction and assessment, 154–155
    in early childhood instruction and assessment, 107–108
    evidence-based conceptual model for learning, 37
    in middle childhood instruction and assessment, 128–130
Teen mothers, 142–143, 165
Teresa, Mother, 43
Testing
    assessments vs., 52. See also Assessment(s)
    computerized, 56–57
    educational decision-making based on, 52–53
    validity in, 52, 55, 362
Test of Integrated Language and Literacy Skills (TILLS), 202, 224
Testosterone bath, 181
Theory of mind, 206, 237
Third-grade students, 98–102
Three-tier models, 11–12, 23–29
Tics, 263
Tier 1 interventions, 22, 26–27, 42
Tier 2 interventions, 22, 42
Tier 3 interventions, 28–29
TILLS (Test of Integrated Language and Literacy Skills), 202, 224
Time
    concepts of, 148–149
    learning how to tell, 101
TIPS (Team-Initiated Problem Solving) program, 39
Title IX (Education Amendments of 1972), 329–331
Tonic–clonic seizures, 261
Topics in Language Disorders, 223, 224
Tort law, 323
Tourette's syndrome (TS), 263
Toxin-related brain disorders, 272–273
Transitions,
    critical transitions beyond early grades, 56, 111
    in words, 205
    multiple transitions during school day, 138–139
    re-entry to school, 28
    transitions oral to silent reading, 112
Transcription skills (writing), 86, 92
Translational science, 29, 41, 183

Translation skills (writing), 86, 92
Translocations (genetics), 176, 250
Trauma, 331–333, 343
Traumatic brain injury (TBI), 274
Triplet repeat expansion mutations, 179
Trisomies, 176, 250. *See also specific disorders*
Trisomy 13 (Patau's syndrome), 176, 263–264
Trisomy 18 (Edwards syndrome), 176, 264
Trisomy 21 (Down syndrome), 176, 255
Trust, 12
TS (Tourette's syndrome), 263
Tumors, 276. *See also* Cancer
Turner's syndrome, 176–177, 264
Twain, Mark, 127
Twice exceptionality, 229, 237, 240
Twin studies, 179

U
Unconsciousness, 194
University-affiliated programs (UAPs), 5
University partnerships, 161

V
Vaccinations, 273, 300–301
Valdés, José, 156, 160
Valdés-Fernández, Sylvia, 156, 365
Valdés Institute, 138, 156–162
Validity
    of research designs, 359–360
    in testing, 52, 55, 362
Van Velzer, Jim, 23–26, 44, 365
Velocardiofacial syndrome (VCFS), 177, 178, 264
Vestibular system, 187–189, 193
Viral infections, 276
Visible deletions (genetics), 177
Visual processing and perception, 188, 200, 223
Visual–spatial cognition impairment, 239
Vocabulary, 79–80, 188
    in early childhood instruction, 80, 99
    in middle childhood instruction, 118
Vocational counseling, 143
Von Recklinghausen disease, 178
Vygotsky, Lev, 312

W
Washington, Julie, 299

Washington State Code of Professional Conduct for Educators, 328, 334
Washington State Department of Health, 335
Wechsler Intelligence Scale for Children, 205
Werdnig–Hoffman disease (spinal muscular atrophy), 265
Whiteness, as race, 293
Williams syndrome, 177, 265
Woodcock–Johnson III measures, 206
Word games, 98
Word level of language, 77
Working memory
    and ADHD, 253
    and genetics, 192–194
    individual differences in, 206–207
    in language and math learning, 225
    in specific learning disabilities, 229, 231, 234
World Health Organization, 5, 272
Writers' Workshop program, 119
Writing skills, learning and instruction
    in 19th-century classrooms, 8
    of adolescents, 138, 145–146
    attention as predictive of, 316–317
    in early childhood development, 71, 72, 74
    of first-grade students, 77–79, 86–90
    in kindergarten, 80
    of middle childhood students, 112–114, 116–117, 119, 124–125
    of second-grade students, 92–93, 95, 96
    of third-grade students, 99–102
Written language learning disability, 63, 224. *See also* Oral and written language learning disability
Written language skills, 311

X
X-linked disorders
    fragile X syndrome, 178, 179, 253, 256
    genetic basis of, 178
    hemophilia, 256
    Klinefelter's syndrome, 256
    Turner's syndrome, 176–177, 264

Z
Zackery Lystedt Law, 275
Zones of proximal development, 86

About the Author

Virginia Wise Berninger, PhD, is a professor of learning sciences and human development at the University of Washington, Seattle. She brings an interdisciplinary background to writing the interdisciplinary frameworks, which includes being a general education teacher (5 years in urban and suburban schools), special education teacher (3 years in a rural school), reading specialist (1 year in an urban school), experimental psychologist (cognitive psychology and psycholinguistics), clinical psychologist on interdisciplinary teams (predoctoral and postdoctoral clinical training at Boston Children's Hospital and licensed psychologist in Washington), school consultant (33 years in Boston and Seattle), research psychologist (Harvard Medical School, Tufts–New England Medical Center, University of Washington), trainer of school psychologists (1989–2006), and trainer of educators in K–12 and academics (2007–present). Her research experience includes serving as a principal investigator on research funded by the National Institute of Child Health and Human Development on normal and disabled reading, writing, and oral language development (1989–2008), as well as principle investigator and director of the University of Washington Interdisciplinary Research Center (genetics, assessments, brain imaging, and instruction; 1995–2006, 2011–present).